THE MEN OF COMPANY K

THE MEN OF COMPANY K

THE AUTOBIOGRAPHY OF A
WORLD WAR II RIFLE COMPANY

Harold P. Leinbaugh and John D. Campbell

WILLIAM MORROW AND COMPANY, INC.
New York

Library of Congress Catalog Card Number: 85-71977

ISBN: 0-688-04421-2

Printed in the United States of America

First Edition

1 2 3 4 5 6 7 8 9 10

BOOK DESIGN BY RICHARD ORIOLO

In Memory of

Junior G. Alpern
R. J. Bell
George W. Bond, Jr.
John A. Bowe, Jr.
Frederick I. Butler
Bert G. Christensen
James Clark
Olen Copeland
John T. Corkill
Leroy Goats
John Gima
Lewis B. Goins
Lorenz E. Graf
William D. Hadley
Kermit K. Hagy
Frank Hair
Robert D. Henderson
Thomas J. Hogan

Clarence A. Jarvis
Raymond V. Klebofski
Ervin Koehler
John F. Lavele
Bill A. McMillan
John S. Moore, Jr.
Joseph J. Sobczynski
Richard S. Stagg
Oliver H. Tandy
James A. Teague
William T. Termin, Jr.
Emmett L. Tomlinson
Pete Visconte
Walter G. Warner, Jr.
Lyle A. Williams
Bruno Ytuarte, Jr.
Paul Zupen
Edward R. Zurga

The young dead soldiers do not speak.
Nevertheless, they are heard in the still houses. . . .
We were young, they say. We have died. Remember us.

ARCHIBALD MacLEISH

ACKNOWLEDGMENTS

Foremost among those who contributed to the making of this book are the men of K Company and their wives and families. Their generosity, candor, and patience in sharing their experiences cannot adequately be acknowledged. Some men's recollections have entered more into our narrative than others, but we would not want to suggest that those whose experiences have been recounted only briefly or omitted in any way contributed less to our company's wartime efforts. We collected enough material for four books and there wasn't room to include all the accounts we picked up from men in the company.

Relatives of K Company men killed in action or who died since the war provided much needed information. They include Bob Bowe, John Bowe's brother; Mrs. William Corkill, John Corkill's sister-in-law; Betty Wood, Franklin Brewer's sister, a brother-in-law, Arthur Lange, and his niece Rosmary Olson.

Others from the 333rd Infantry providing information not available from company sources included Albert Blanton and Bill Wooten from Third Battalion headquarters, and Sam Grizzard and Richard Roush from our regiment's medical detachment. John J. O'Grady, an officer from Ninth Army's historical section who followed our company's first attack from a vantage point in our battalion headquarters, provided us with copies of his reports on that operation.

Stanley Christopherson, former commander of the British army's Sherwood Rangers Yeomanry, and David Render and David Alderson, along with other veterans of their famed tank regiment, provided essential information on their actions during the battles around Geilenkirchen.

Gerhard Tebbe, commander of tanks in the 116th Panzer Division Kampfgruppe, which we met unexpectedly on Christmas Eve 1944, spent many hours with us discussing events in the Ardennes and sent us pertinent maps and German after-action reports.

Hannah Zeidlick at the U.S. Army Center of Military History and staff members of the Federal Records Center and National Archives assisted in locating after-action reports and other documents relating to the 84th Division, and provided data from postwar interviews with German commanders. K. T. Johnson shared his supply of vintage Army manuals. Ted Draper's splendid history of the 84th Division—one of the outstanding World War II unit histories—served as a key source of information on Railsplitter operations. Letters saved by Nelle Campbell and Marion Leinbaugh and by other wives and mothers helped document aspects of the smaller, more personal picture of our war.

Maps and charts were prepared by Billy C. Mossman and Harry Brunhoefer. Monica Bowen, Claire Horowitz, Elizabeth Howell, Clarice Radabaugh, and Linda Snyder assisted in interview transcription and other chores.

Warm thanks and appreciation go to our editor, Bruce Lee, and his assistant, Elizabeth Terhune. At the outset Bruce furnished critical guidelines for our efforts and provided needed encouragement throughout our project. Others who supplied valuable comments based on critical reading of draft material include Donald Campbell, Ellen Pskowski, Eleanor Schlaretzki, Caren Carney, Allan Lefkowitz, Norma Hettinga, and Marge, Tom, Tim, Terry, Ted, and Cooley Leinbaugh.

We owe a particular debt to Melvin Kohn and Carmi Schooler, Campbell's former colleagues at the National Institute of Mental Health, who proffered critical help and encouragement in the book's early days and also gave useful suggestions based on careful reading of the manuscript.

Andrew Scott and Bill MacKaye offered a closely reasoned series of suggestions that helped direct our initial efforts. Ben Smethurst raised valuable questions and carefully proofread our manuscript. Gary Allison, Bernie Holmbraker, and particularly the late Julian Morrison made helpful suggestions and gave encouragement.

Charles MacDonald, preeminent American military historian with an encyclopedic knowledge of the war in Europe, provided encouragement and valued criticism at every stage of our venture. His counsel was invaluable.

Finally we want to single out Stephen Goodwin, novelist, professor, critic, editor, and friend. Steve, more than anyone beyond the K Company family, contributed significantly to the completion of this book. As an "outsider" he helped us take a more objective look at the company and keep the story in focus. And when writing problems became especially vexing, his critical judgment, constructive suggestions, and patient persuasion assisted immeasurably in reaching reasonable solutions. His experience as a writer was beneficial in many ways, perhaps most of all in convincing us that the vast quantity of materials we had collected could be boiled down and brought together within the covers of a book.

CONTENTS

INTRODUCTION

It was Christmas Eve, 1944—near midnight. K Company moved out on a Belgian road winding toward Verdenne. On ahead we would pick up Sherman tanks and attack the village. The guide led us up the hill, into a woods, and straight to the tanks. But the tanks weren't ours, they were German. By accident K Company had discovered a task force of Wehrmacht armor and infantry and prevented it from breaking through American lines.

Histories of the fighting in the Ardennes mention that encounter because of its tactical significance. Our chance discovery of the German task force marked a small turning point in the Battle of the Bulge. It is now a source of pride to think that our actions mattered in the big picture, but on that winter night forty years ago we weren't thinking of strategy or tactics. We were GIs doing a job, but we were also a small band of young men, anxious, uncertain, and afraid.

The date, the surprise, the light of German tracers on a forest road—that's what we remember. The events themselves, the personal reactions, the small, private, vivid details are what give meaning to the battle for those who were there. The story of Company K is the sum of such details. We were too close to the war to have any other perspective. Like other infantrymen who went into combat, we weren't trying to make history. We were trying to carry out orders and, above all, to survive.

We were K Company, of the 333rd Infantry Regiment, 84th Division. We spent over a hundred days on the line during the most costly phase of combat, so we had a crack at nearly every type of action that the war in

Europe had to offer. We attacked pillboxes, defended small towns, fought German armor and German paratroops, played a minor role in a river crossing, and took part in the final, swift pursuit of a defeated German army.

We have our own "history" now, a litany of dates and places: Geilenkirchen. The château. Lindern. Christmas Eve. February 28. Our "archives" are the memories of those who were there. These places, these dates, evoke our shared experience. It doesn't matter, not to us, that our battles were mostly obscure—they were ours.

Other companies have their histories, their dates and places to remember. We know K Company didn't win the war single-handedly. And other companies' experiences were similar to ours. We were just one of twenty-seven rifle companies in the 84th Division, one of more than twelve hundred such companies whose men were the infantry's cutting edge in Europe. K Company was a part of it, though, and we learned the cost of combat that is typical of rifle companies.

We began with about two hundred men. By the end of the war twice that number had seen action with the company, and our battle casualties had reached two hundred. The company's strength varied widely. After our initial bloody action in the Siegfried Line, the three rifle platoons and the weapons platoon rarely came close to their full complement. A handful of the old originals made it all the way through, but by the end of the fighting, replacements filled a major portion of the roster. Still, despite the wear and tear, from the Siegfried Line to the Elbe River the company developed and maintained a core identity. And this book tells the company's story.

The two of us who assembled this account look back to those combat days and even beyond. We'd been friends in college in the early 1940s. Leinbaugh was a platoon leader with the company when its fighting began. On the third day, the captain was severely wounded. Leinbaugh became the company commander and was one of the few who made it all the way through. Campbell came up on Thanksgiving Day, 1944, the company's fourth day of action, as the company's first replacement officer. He left two months later, one of many K Company casualties in the Ardennes. So we have different memories and perspectives of the company.

Over the years we have shared these memories, and in our own conversations and talks with others we have concluded that we had only part of the company story. As one old noncom commented after he and two others had gone back to tramp the battlefields, all three had been there, but they'd seen three different wars. Several years ago, Campbell suggested to Leinbaugh that they could fill out the picture of K Company's war and fit the pieces together by drawing on the recollections of others. Would he be interested? He was. So we crossed and recrossed the country to talk with old comrades, to look at one company's war as it was remembered by its citizen soldiers.

Here is a war seen through the eyes of those who were there. It is a story of combat, but not just of combat. It's about what life was like for the men on the line—men coming to terms with themselves and others in trying circumstances. Our account also concerns the way time, men, and events combined to mold the character of a company. There is more to combat than fighting. So boredom and leisure, letter writing, holidays and holiday packages, and handling the simple routines linked to food, clothing, and shelter—these, too, enter the picture.

K Company's war goes beyond the battlefield. Many of the men spent a sizable fraction of their combat career away from the front. Replacements came up. Casualties went back, mostly wounded, though not all were lost to enemy—or friendly—shells. The wounded soldier in the hospital chain still had ties to the company. And though for him one war might be over, another had begun.

Back home families waited and wondered. They read the papers, saw the war pictured in *Life*, scanned radio dials, and watched for the postman. Always the question was, were their men safe? The answer was two weeks away, and when it came, it was not necessarily reassuring. This war, the one followed by folks back home, is an essential part of the story.

Finally, there are combat's consequences. Generals measure these in ground gained or lost; citizen soldiers and their families use a more personal rule. K Company's war didn't end on VE Day. Some, especially those who were severely wounded, have intermittently fought the war throughout a lifetime. And for everyone who came back there are memories. These may not be articulated, may be full of contradictions, may sometimes be right at the surface, sometimes buried seemingly beyond recapture. But the traces linger.

This is K Company's autobiography. It is the story of the men in a rifle company, ordinary men, the Willy Lomans of war. They are the men of Company K, but they could stand in for members of other rifle companies across other wars. Look at the historian's situation maps: firm lines and sweeping arrows marking defensive positions and offensive movement. These are remote and comfortable abstractions. But get close to the tip of the arrow and you find a handful of raggedy-assed riflemen, men who have more in common with the foot soldiers at Antietam or Chancellorsville than with anyone half a mile to their rear.

1

MOVING UP

When K Company landed on Omaha Beach there were no heroics and no photographers. The only Germans we saw were PWs. The date was November 2, 1944—five months after D-Day. Along with the rest of the 84th Division, the Railsplitters, K Company crossed the English Channel on a huge tank landing craft in broad daylight. When we arrived in Normandy, the Allied armies had pushed the front back across most of France and Belgium, and the Germans were now fighting along their own frontiers.

Navy beachmasters blinked landing instructions to our convoy. We hoisted our M1s and enormous packs, clambered down the side of our ship on rope ladders, and jumped into small infantry landing craft bobbing alongside. Our boats chugged toward shore, and when the ramps came down, we waded through the surf, rifles held high overhead. The huge pillboxes with their 88s still menaced the beach.

Coming ashore we were thinking about those poor bastards who had landed here on June 6. The camouflaged gun embrasures, the burned-out hulls of tanks, the swamped landing craft rising and falling in the waves, the long rows of underwater obstacles—they were all familiar from the newsreels we'd watched back at Camp Claiborne, Louisiana. Only the confusion and the noise and smells of battle were missing.

The long narrow coastline was crawling with traffic and jammed with supplies. German prisoners were loading American trucks; crates of C rations and jerry cans of gasoline were stockpiled in stacks as long as city blocks. Jeeps bounced up and down rough gravel roads that bulldozers had carved through the bluffs to the beach exits.

Omaha Beach was very much rear-echelon, but it was more than just a bustling supply depot. It was the site of one of the great decisive battles of World War II and the first battlefield K Company ever crossed. And though more than a million men had preceded us, we now felt part of the mighty endeavor, the Great Crusade to free Europe.

That first day in France we marched five miles inland. We did not see a single American grave. The men killed on D-Day lay buried in temporary cemeteries deliberately located out of sight of the new men coming ashore. At Bretteville Farm the company bivouacked until November 5. Our morning report for the date read: "Departed Bretteville Farm, France, 1030 by Motor Trucks. Destination Unknown."

Now that we had at last reached the Continent, we were certain our division was going to be involved in the final push to end the war. In August when Paris had fallen and the German retreat had turned into a rout, it had seemed the war could end any day, possibly before we got overseas. Battle was the last challenge, the payoff of two years of training, the test we had to pass before we could call ourselves soldiers. We had questions about ourselves that could be answered only in combat. After journeying this far and working so long and hard to become soldiers, we would have felt cheated to miss out on the fighting.

On the way to the front, the company basked for an hour in the reflected glow of other men's victories. The division convoy—hundreds of two-and-a-half-ton trucks loaded with GIs, jeeps and trailers, 105mm cannons, antitank guns, and supply vehicles—rolled along poplar-lined roads across Normandy.

In Paris our convoy moved slowly along the wide boulevards toward the east, past cheering crowds waving French and American flags. Caught up in the enthusiasm, we had no misgivings about playing happy warriors. From our open trucks we tossed chewing gum, cigarettes, and K rations to the crowds and blew kisses and yelled raucous propositions to the pretty French girls.

That night we slept under rain-drenched pup tents—the last time we used them—in a muddy field outside Laon. The next day we moved again; another convoy, another unknown destination. When a truck broke down, PFC John Bratten and Sergeant Franklin Brewer went to a farmhouse, where Brewer, listening to a French newscast, learned that Roosevelt had been reelected to his fourth term as president.

On November 8, we reached Heerlen, Holland, seven miles from the German border. The front was less than ten miles away—when the wind was right we could hear the rumble of artillery. For another week the standard statement on the morning report was the same: "Usual bivouac duties." The report did show that Sergeant Klebofski and a detail on temporary duty with the regimental antitank company returned after spe-

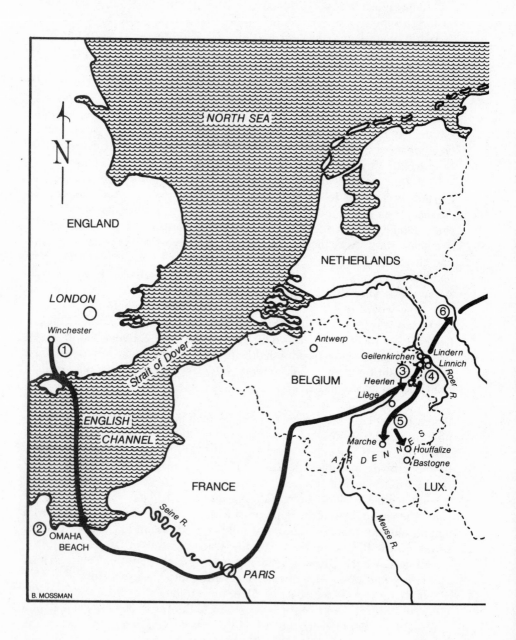

B. MOSSMAN

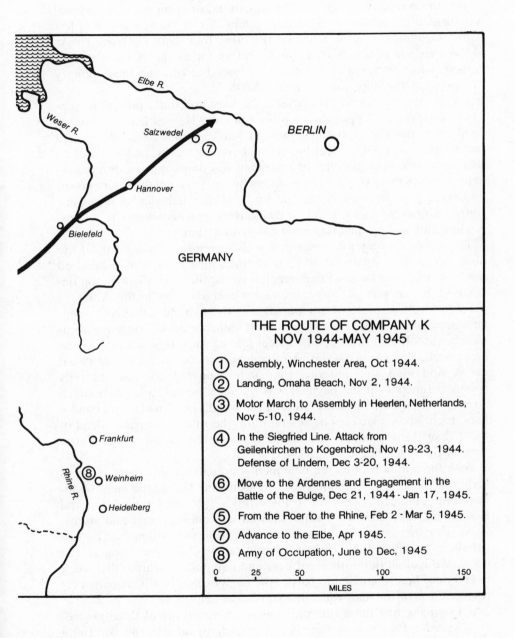

THE ROUTE OF COMPANY K
NOV 1944-MAY 1945

① Assembly, Winchester Area, Oct 1944.

② Landing, Omaha Beach, Nov 2, 1944.

③ Motor March to Assembly in Heerlen, Netherlands, Nov 5-10, 1944.

④ In the Siegfried Line. Attack from Geilenkirchen to Kogenbroich, Nov 19-23, 1944. Defense of Lindern, Dec 3-20, 1944.

⑥ Move to the Ardennes and Engagement in the Battle of the Bulge, Dec 21, 1944 - Jan 17, 1945.

⑤ From the Roer to the Rhine, Feb 2 - Mar 5, 1945.

⑦ Advance to the Elbe, Apr 1945.

⑧ Army of Occupation, June to Dec, 1945

0   25   50   100   150

MILES

cial training in mine detection. Someone at division obviously had a hunch about the skills we soon would be needing.

On the 13th, the 36th Replacement Battalion in Liége sent ten privates to join the company. At division headquarters, or at regiment, a corporal had divided the alphabetical list into groups. Six of the new men had last names beginning with the letter G; the other four, with the letter H. As far as that corporal was concerned, and as far as the Army was concerned, what mattered was not their names but the fact their military occupational specialty was rifleman—MOS 745.

It took about a dozen men behind the lines and thirty pounds of supplies every day to support a front-line rifleman. He was lean and toughened from months of training, and in battle harness, wearing a field jacket and baggy ODs, steel helmet and combat boots, and more often than not smoking a cigarette, one rifleman was pretty much indistinguishable from another. Besides his weapons he carried a canteen, a raincoat, an overcoat, a mess kit, a first-aid kit, a shelter half, and a field pack stuffed with extra socks, toilet paper, shaving gear, condoms, K rations, reading and writing materials, and candy and gum.

The rifleman's only job perk came with his ten-thousand-dollar GI life insurance policy. While his odds of getting killed were several hundred times greater than those of rear-echelon types, the monthly premium deducted from his pay was the same as for everyone else in the Army.

His most basic piece of equipment was the Garand .30 caliber semiautomatic rifle, the M1. His second most valuable possession was his entrenching tool, a sturdy wood-and-steel folding shovel carried in a canvas belt pouch. The gas mask was extra baggage; sooner or later he'd toss it away. And soon after entering combat he would decide that the only apparent function of the bayonet was to add a pound to his M1, which already weighed nine pounds. Adding the weight of grenades and bandoliers, each holding six clips of ammunition, the rifleman carried a load of more than thirty pounds. The company's mortarmen and machine gunners carried even heavier burdens.

With the addition of its ten new men—interchangeable parts as far as higher headquarters was concerned—K Company had all the men, weapons, and equipment called for in the Army's Table of Organization and Equipment. The company roster showed 196 enlisted men and six officers, as close as we would ever come to prescribed strength. The distribution of ranks, from captain to private, was also according to the book. We had all our authorized gear and equipment. During that week in Heerlen, before going into battle, the composition of K Company corresponded man for man with the Army's neat charts.

K Company had three rifle platoons, each consisting of three twelveman squads. The base of firepower for each squad was the Browning Automatic Rifle, model 1908—a BAR. The BAR was twice as heavy as the M1. The rifle platoons' antitank weapon was the bazooka, cumbersome and rumored to be unreliable. The company's weapons platoon provided fire support for the riflemen. Divided into mortar and machine-gun sections, the weapons platoon had three mortar squads, each with a 60mm mortar, the company's heavy artillery. The two machine-gun squads' .30 caliber air-cooled lights were capable of firing four hundred rounds a minute.

In combat our immediate support came from battalion's heavy weapons company, equipped with 81mm mortars and water-cooled machine guns. Regiment had cannon and antitank companies and an entire battalion of artillery on call for support.

In addition to the CO, company headquarters included the executive officer, or second in command, the first sergeant, the communications sergeant, the radio operator, and four runners. The mess sergeant, cooks, supply sergeant, armor artificer (weapon-repair man), and company clerk also belonged to company headquarters, although they stayed in the rear when the company went into combat.

All our weapons were portable; the foot soldier had to be able to carry his arsenal on his back. Although the Field Manual did not spell it out, the essence of a rifle company was that it could go anywhere, anytime, and start fighting. The kitchen stoves were the only company equipment that couldn't be carried by hand.

K Company was one of twenty-seven rifle companies in the 84th Division. Our chain of command ran back through Third Battalion headquarters to the 333rd Infantry Regiment and then to the 84th Division. On the radio nets, our regiment was Doughboy, our battalion was Blue, and K was lengthened to King, making us Doughboy Blue King. As part of the 84th Division we belonged to a largely self-sufficient battle force with infantrymen, artillerymen, engineers, signalmen, and service, quartermaster, medical, and headquarters troops—a total of some fourteen thousand men who could function effectively as a team in battle.

On paper, K Company was identical to every other rifle outfit heading for the front for the first time. The only thing setting us apart was the "K 333" stenciled on the bumpers of our two jeeps and trailers. On our field jackets we wore with honest pride the red-and-white Railsplitter patch, an ax cleaving a log.

K Company was an American mass-production item, fresh off the assembly line, but we thought we were unique. Captain George Gieszl firmly believed we were the best outfit in the division and "just maybe the best rifle company in the whole goddam Army." K Company was yet to be tested, but if morale counted—if an outfit was as good as its morale—then the men in K Company had nothing to worry about.

Gieszl succeeded in communicating his own pride and confidence in the company to the newest private in the last rank. A tough, fair taskmaster, he'd been assigned to K Company during its early days of training at Camp Howze, Texas. He quickly demonstrated he was the sort of officer who never asked his men to do anything that he could not do—and

Gieszl could do almost everything the Army asked of a leader. He was the man in charge; no one ever questioned that.

Gieszl pushed his men hard, but without raising resentment. Most would agree with PFC Bruce Morrell's appraisal. "He was always fair, and that made all the difference. He didn't take advantage of his jeep on marches. He marched farther than the rest of us, moving back and forth along the column." Bruce remembered that on field exercises, "For four or five days we never had more than twenty minutes at a time for sleep, but Gieszl was always out there in front. He was tireless." And Morrell was impressed by the company's lack of disciplinary problems. "Gieszl cared about his men but never mollycoddled them. He didn't want anyone else to chew on them. If they needed it, he was going to do it himself, and he seemed to do it with some regularity."

Gieszl kept his distance from the men and from his lieutenants as well. It would have come as a surprise to most of them to realize the CO was only twenty-two. Blond, blue-eyed, a muscular five nine, he was a man to whom authority came naturally. No one, including his superior officers, tried to push him around.

Having worked his way up from platoon leader to executive officer to company commander, Gieszl was wholly committed to the company. Once he'd made up his mind what was best for the company, he never hesitated bucking headquarters. As he put it, "Battalion didn't exist. K Company existed. Battalion and regiment were just a necessary evil."

A maverick and a ramrod, Gieszl looked for these qualities in the men he picked for positions of leadership. He couldn't always control the selection process—not while the company was in training—but he found ways to get rid of the deadwood. He preferred the direct approach.

When Gieszl took command of K Company at Camp Howze he fell heir to an old Regular Army first sergeant. The sergeant's hash marks filled half his sleeve, and he barely tolerated lieutenants. Gieszl watched him for two weeks before summoning him to his office. "Sergeant, I'm going to have your ass on a silver platter." End of conversation. In less than a week Gieszl caught his topkick selling weekend passes, kicked him out of the company, and made Dempsey Keller the company's acting first sergeant.

Above all Gieszl demanded that his officers and sergeants exert leadership. Since lieutenants tended to rotate in and out of the company during training cycles, Gieszl concentrated on his noncoms, building the company around his key sergeants. To Gieszl, everybody had a yardstick, "and I hung tough on mine." He never went by the book—"that destroys initiative and you're not teaching people to be self-reliant." Before Pearl Harbor, Gieszl had been a sergeant in the Arizona National Guard, and in Dempsey Keller's opinion, "Gieszl always thought more like a sergeant than an officer."

Redheaded, with bristling eyebrows and a short fuse for goldbricks, Keller had the classic gruff demeanor of the typical topkick and shared

Gieszl's insistence on standards. A stickler for Army spit-and-polish, he seemed to some men to be overly strict. Dempsey had commanded a CCC camp before getting his call from the Army, and he had moved steadily up through the noncommissioned ranks. But he was a softer touch than Gieszl. It was impossible for him to hide his deep concern for the personal welfare of every man in the company.

Staff Sergeant John Sabia was one of the few Regular Army men in K Company. Raised as a devout Catholic, Sabia came from the coal-mining town of Hazleton, Pennsylvania. His policeman father was Italian, his mother was Slovakian. When he graduated from high school, it seemed to him a young hell-raiser had two choices: ending up in jail or joining the Army. John joined the Army, trained in the engineers, went to Iceland, and stayed in trouble. By the time he joined K Company he had been busted three times.

When Sabia reported to the division, K Company was in the field. "It was hotter than hell and I was sweating like a horse, and there was this lieutenant lying on the ground under a pine tree with a bottle of bourbon, drinking. That was Gieszl. He asked me where in the hell I'd come from, and when I said Iceland, he broke up. He couldn't stop laughing."

Sabia gave a highball salute and told Gieszl he wanted no part of the infantry; he wanted to get back to the engineers. Although Gieszl appeared sympathetic, Sabia soon became convinced the captain would never let go of him. "Hell, I decided to make the best of it. I liked the Army and loved being a soldier." He admired and respected Gieszl. "That man knew how to run an outfit." Sabia didn't get too upset when Gieszl assigned him a couple of men with disciplinary records. "Sure, he handed me a few eightballs for my squad, but goddammit, I made soldiers out of them." By the time the company entered combat, Sabia was convinced, "mine was the best squad in the whole company."

The company's communications sergeant, the man who stuck closest to Gieszl in the field, was balding, slender Franklin Brewer. A Harvard graduate from a Philadelphia Main Line family, and the company's scholar in residence, Brewer wore wire-rimmed GI spectacles and a helmet that looked two sizes too big for him. At thirty-seven, he seemed elderly to most of the others in the company. He was referred to, always with affection, as Father Brewer, or sometimes as Mother Brewer. Gieszl saw Brewer as a man who could easily have gotten a commission and a safe berth in the rear but who stuck with the infantry because he had something to prove. Only Gieszl knew that Brewer's younger brother, a Navy pilot, had been shot down over Guadalcanal.

K Company's only combat veteran, Mario Lage, was a practicing non-conformist. Tall, lean, and handsome, with a sallow complexion from daily doses of atabrine, Lage had fought on Guadalcanal with the Americal Division. He suffered from recurrent malaria and should have been discharged from the Army. Self-confident and insouciant, Sergeant Lage played the role of the combat veteran to perfection. His reputation was quickly established after he joined the company at Claiborne. As he sauntered down the buckboards on the way to the latrine for his morning shower, Lage sported blue silk pajamas. He studiously avoided digging foxholes on field problems and on occasion simply disappeared. Although as a buck sergeant he was expected to set an example, Mario was not above hitching a ride back to the company area during long, boring marches in the Louisiana backwoods. Sensing in Lage many of his own maverick qualities, Captain Gieszl made it a point to look the other way.

Lage had grown up in North Africa, the Cape Verde Islands, and Lowell, Massachusetts. His Portuguese parents were both doctors. However unusual his background, it made little impression in a company that had become a melting pot from the time the first trainload of recruits unloaded at Camp Howze.

The names on the company roster spanned the ethnic spectrum—Poles, Russians, Irishmen, Cajuns, and all the others. Gieszl's parents had emigrated from Austria. Lucht and Koehler were Germans. Cigar-chewing Mike DeBello was a second-generation Italian. So was Louie Ciccotello, the company barber and mail clerk. Flattop Gonzales, Bruno Ytuarte, and Jose Villagran were Spanish-Americans; and big, taciturn Frank Hair from Oklahoma was an American Indian, a Cherokee. He was called Chief—what else?—just as Lariviere was nicknamed Frenchy.

During two years of training, the company ranks were in constant flux as men left for overseas duty or were transferred to noncombat units. As new men arrived to take their places, names from each of the forty-eight states appeared on the company rolls. Conspicuously missing were blacks, for in 1944, segregation was official Army policy. Otherwise, K Company was an authentic melting pot.

The twin brass dog tags each man wore around his neck were stamped C, H, or P to indicate religion. Max Sobel from New Jersey was Jewish; Adrian Wheeler was an Indiana Protestant; Johnny Bowe was a Massachusetts Catholic. One of several company Mormons, Howard Broderick should not have been in the Army, certainly not as a rifleman; his trigger finger was missing. As the company's agnostic, Brewer argued against indicating religious preference on his dog tags, but he lost the fight to the Army's bureaucrats and settled—with ill grace—for a P.

Education varied. Like Brewer, Paul Coste was a Harvard man. Bruce Baptie came from Yale. Sergeants Erickson and Hadley were college graduates, and Magee had a law degree. Bill Chalmers, a former New York advertising executive, had originated the *Take It or Leave It* radio quiz program. At the other end of the scale were several men who could neither read nor write; friends wrote their letters home.

In April of 1944, the level of education jumped with the arrival of a contingent of men from the Army Specialized Training Program, which had been designed to provide special training for men with high scores on Army intelligence tests. Every single one of them knew it took an Army test score of 120 to enter the ASTP but only 110 points to be elgible for

Officers Candidate School. These men had spent time in college after completing their Army basic training, and when the Army cut back on the program, few were pleased to find themselves carrying rifles instead of college textbooks. Company old-timers called the newcomers ASTP-boys—one word—or the Whiz Kids, and no one tried to conceal the derision in the nickname.

Bruce Morrell thought the new men felt ostracized at first. "We were a bunch of cocky graduates from the ASTP and thought we should all be commissioned officers. We thought we were vastly misused by being sent to the infantry." Typically, they referred to the "dumb sergeants" and looked down their noses at the training operations. Another of the new men, Jim Sterner, remembered, "At first there were two separate companies." But all that changed. By the time K Company was ready to go overseas in August, the so-called dumb sergeants, Morrell recalled, "had thoroughly inculcated a sense of belonging, a sense of purpose, that we were members of K Company, 333rd Infantry, 84th Division. The smart-ass attitude disappeared."

Age came closest to providing a common denominator. Nearly all the men were within a year of their twentieth birthday. The strong bonds of loyalty and friendship developed during those long, grueling months of backbreaking training at Howze and Claiborne became even more important as the Railsplitters traveled toward the front. Wives, parents, and children were on the other side of the Atlantic, an ocean away. K Company was the only family we had. As apprehensions and anticipation grew, so grew the realization that whatever lay before us, we were in it together.

In those final days of preparation for combat there was a new solemnity among the men. Our talk was tough and earnest but with the exception of Lage, our combat veteran, every man in the company wondered how he was going to perform under fire. There were moments of doubt and private fear—but when you are twenty years old, in top physical condition, and Army-hardened, you don't spend hour after hour worrying about what's going to happen.

Nor can you spend all day oiling weapons, waterproofing boots, or writing letters. The principal amusements were the traditional barracks pastimes; poker and all-night crap-shooting sessions. Most men had wads of folding money: soiled dollar bills and funny money—English pounds, French invasion currency, and, most recently, Dutch guilders.

The cardplayers had little difficulty with the intricacies of international exchange. During the nightly games one man might bet a quarter, the second raise the ante by a shilling, the next man call, tossing out a guilder and pulling in a franc so the pot was right—and that was for openers.

When Joe Namey, the third platoon runner, climbed into the back of a diminutive British lorry on November 18 for the company's trip to the

German border, he was flat-ass broke. He had pressed the last of his money into the hand of a little Dutch girl, Anna.

Namey was dark-complexioned, compact, athletic, Catholic, and Lebanese. He had hitched up right out of high school in Jacksonville, Florida. Soon after the company arrived in Heerlen and settled into a comfortable brick schoolhouse, he met Anna. She was standing outside the ornamental iron fence that enclosed the schoolyard as Namey went through the evening chow line. He noticed her long blond hair, braided into a loose pigtail, and her blue eyes.

"Anna was the most beautiful child I'd ever seen." Joe recalls. "I walked over to the fence with my mess kit, and started eating. She watched me take every bite." As Namey later remembered, he did not speak to her at first but pretended he was finished eating and tried to pass a thick piece of GI bread to her through the iron fence. She shook her head. Namey tried to eat the bread, but found it impossible. He could tell she was hungry, and "we had so much." He set his mess kit on the ledge of the fence and lit a cigarette to indicate he had finished eating. "Then I asked her if she could understand English. 'My proo . . .' she said, then laughed. 'Pronunciation?' I asked her. She tried to say it after me but couldn't get it right, and then we both started laughing together. A feeling came over me that I had known her from someplace else, maybe from some former life. Somehow I knew her, I knew all about her."

Namey walked Anna home that night through the blackout. It was after curfew and he missed bedcheck, but none of the sergeants seemed to mind. The next morning when he was in the chow line he saw her hurrying to the fence, trying to pick him out in the crowd. From that time on Namey shared his food with her at every meal. "I gave her soap and sugar and extra GI socks, and I lifted rations from the mess truck for her to take home to her family." He helped Anna with her English, and she taught him a few words of Dutch. "It was amazing how quickly we learned to understand each other."

On K Company's last night in Heerlen, in a mixture of Dutch and English, Anna, not quite thirteen years old, made it clear that she had fallen in love with Joe. She didn't want him to leave. She was searching for a way to repay "Yussef"—she always had trouble pronouncing Joseph—for all he had done for her and her family. Eighteen-year-old Joe Namey thought she was offering to make love. He explained as best he could that it wouldn't be right. He told her what they both knew, that he might be killed.

The next afternoon as the company loaded on the British trucks, Anna stood alone in the schoolyard. She was waving and crying as the company pulled out. Namey never saw her again.

2

GEILENKIRCHEN

K Company crossed the German border during the night of November 18 with thousands of other riflemen from the 84th Division and slogged east through the rain toward assembly areas north of Aachen. The Railsplitters were to take part in Operation Clipper, a joint British-American attack to eliminate a worrisome salient on the boundary between the British Second Army and the American Ninth Army.

The attack had been planned thirty days earlier at a conference of the Allied High Command in Brussels. Eisenhower and his generals agreed it was necessary to maintain unremitting pressure on the German army during the late fall and winter of 1944. Although major battles had been fought at Arnhem, the Huertgen Forest, and in the vicinity of Metz, the Western Front had remained relatively unchanged following the Normandy breakout—shortages of gasoline and ammunition had forced the Allied armies to halt and regroup.

Omar Bradley, the army group commander, outlined the broad strategy: "Hammer the enemy with all possible force, splinter his armies west of the Rhine, and employ every available division in a November offensive to kill Germans and force the Roer River." The British and American generals, cautiously optimistic in October, believed if the German defensive crust could be broken and the Siegfried Line breached, their armies could reach the Rhine within thirty days.

Operation Clipper called for the 84th division's 334th Regiment to attack on November 18 and seize the high ground east of Geilenkirchen. A few hours later, the British 43rd Division was to move against two villages on the left of the town. At dawn the next morning our regiment, the 333rd Infantry, was to attack Geilenkirchen frontally. Able and Baker companies would go in first. K Company and the Third Battalion were scheduled to follow behind and mop up.

Although part of the American XIII Corps and the Ninth Army, the Railsplitters for their first battle came under the operational control of the experienced British XXX Corps, commanded by Sir Brian Horrocks. The British general had mentioned to Eisenhower over dinner one evening that he lacked sufficient troops in his command to mount the attack in adequate strength—he was pleasantly surprised when Ike offered him the newly arrived 84th for the operation.

The British connection provided immediate benefits for the 84th's GIs, as K Company's Ray Bocarski noted: ". . . attached to British XXX Corps. We received our first rum ration this morning—about half a canteen cup."

It was to be the first attack not only for K Company but also for the XIII Corps and the Ninth Army, which had just entered the line between the British to the north and the American First Army. Bradley suspected that Field Marshal Montgomery would attempt to wangle control of several U.S. divisions for the November offensive. So rather than place his veteran First Army or Third Army within Monty's reach, he inserted the newest of his armies next to the British.

But this was high-level stuff. None of the Railsplitters knew of Eisenhower's dinnertime generosity or Bradley's suspicions of Monty's motives, which determined our location along the battlefront.

Situated twelve miles south of Geilenkirchen, the city of Aachen had been captured by the Americans late in October. Now in November attention focused on Geilenkirchen, a minor road and rail center in the middle of a dreary, drab, coal-mining district. As far as we knew, not even Charlemagne in his heyday had paid any particular attention to the city. But in 1944, Geilenkirchen was of major tactical importance to the Allies. Its location athwart the Siegfried Line made the city one of the prime objectives in the November offensive.

The Siegfried Line—or West Wall, as the Germans called it—was an elaborate chain of massive concrete fortifications and antitank defenses stretching along much of Germany's western frontier. It consisted of interlocking pillboxes, gun casements, bunkers, and observation posts constructed in the late 1930s before the outbreak of war.

In the Ninth Army's narrow sector, the fortifications were concentrated between the Würm and Roer rivers and had been hastily refurbished as the American and British armies rushed across France. New communication links were installed, and miles of connecting trenches between the concrete forts were dug by civilians and slave laborers so that troops could move between threatened strongpoints. Ground in front of the pillboxes was graded so the defenders could deliver maximum grazing machine-gun fire. According to General Bradley, the Siegfried Line provided the Germans considerable additional defensive muscle—the equivalent of numerous combat divisions.

By the time the Railsplitters reached their assembly area, Geilenkirchen was already in ruins. Its seven thousand civilians had long since been evacuated to relocation areas beyond the Rhine. Allied artillery had been methodically bombarding the town for weeks, and British and American fighter-bombers added to the wreckage, conducting hundreds of rocket sorties and low-level strafing attacks on pillboxes and strongpoints in the vicinity. A napalm air strike on November 8 had caused even more damage, and specially equipped night bombers dropped several million propaganda leaflets over German positions in the Ninth Army's sector.

Geilenkirchen was defended by a battalion of the 183rd Volksgrenadier Division and support units. Deployed behind the town and on its flanks were the balance of the 183rd, the German 176th Division, and the XII Panzer Corps artillery. The battle-hardened 9th and 10th SS Panzer divisions, two of Germany's finest, were in reserve.

During K Company's week in Holland, British liaison officers conducted special briefings on Clipper for the 84th's officers and senior noncoms. One of the company sergeants, Al Oyler, was impressed at first. "They made everything sound so simple, so easy. We move from this point to that point, a distance of five miles. We'll reach our objective by nightfall." But after returning to our Dutch schoolhouse to brief his squad, Oyler had second thoughts. "It seemed so simple, but then my men started asking questions. 'Are we really going to be able to do that?' And I began to have my first doubts."

Lorries hauled the company on the first leg of its trip to the border, and the men dismounted in the rain. As Ed Stewart remembered, "It was pitch-dark—no smoking was allowed." The artillery became more distinct, and flashes from big 155s and 8-inchers lit up great portions of the night sky. "The countryside was practically desolate, a bare tree now and then or a battered solitary house breaking the wind blowing across the fields. The sky constantly flared with the vivid orange of the artillery."

On Sunday morning, as K Company waited for orders, George Gieszl watched the town through his field glasses from a low ridge south of Geilenkirchen. John Sabia was feeling guilty about missing Mass. George Lucht, whose parents were born in Germany, wondered if he might have cousins in the ranks of the troops garrisoning Geilenkirchen. Mario Lage knew it was irrational, ridiculous, completely senseless, but he found himself looking forward to returning to combat. Brewer oriented his maps and checked his overlays. On previous trips to the Continent he had traveled in literary circles. His friends in Paris, particularly Miss Stein, as he referred to Gertrude, would never believe he was back in Europe as an ordinary foot soldier, a sergeant in the infantry.

*   *   *

In the small hours of Sunday morning as K Company formed up along the main street of Zweibruggen, Joe Namey was still thinking of Anna, but there were other things on his mind as well. Back in Heerlen a British briefing officer had told the company the attack would be supported by five miles of artillery lined up hub to hub. Five miles of artillery—it sounded fishy to Joe. But as thousands of British and American artillery rounds passed overhead and plummeted into Geilenkirchen, the roar was continuous.

When the barrage ceased at first light, four hundred GIs from the 333rd's First Battalion jumped off in the attack. They moved quickly into Geilenkirchen's outskirts and advanced along rubble-strewn streets, meeting only occasional resistance from machine-gun nests and snipers. American Sherman tanks, belonging to the British Sherwood Rangers Yeomanry Regiment, wheeled in behind the GIs, using their 75s at virtual point-blank range to silence stubborn areas of resistance.

K Company, leading the Third Battalion, moved up the road closer to Geilenkirchen and waited. The men talked in subdued voices, fished cigarettes from helmet liners, fiddled with their bayonets and trench knives, and took short swigs from their canteens. The radio operator, the machine gunners, and the mortarmen put down their heavy loads. Fred Flanagan pulled a paperback from his pack and tried to read. Mike De-Bello lit his second cigar of the morning. Platoon Sergeant George Pope took a critical look as the first batch of prisoners from Geilenkirchen passed between our columns on the way to the rear: "These fucking supermen are the lousiest-looking troops I've ever seen in all my years in the Army."

Not until noon did regiment order the Third Battalion forward to consolidate and mop up. It was our turn now.

At the railroad embankment at the edge of town, Captain Gieszl gave the order to fix bayonets. John Bratten wondered if that was supposed to intimidate the Germans. "I don't know, maybe it did; but the order to fix bayonets sure scared the hell out of me."

K Company was to play a minor role in securing Geilenkirchen, but that walk into the town was nevertheless the beginning of our war. The company's third platoon, in the lead, cleared the railroad underpass at the edge of Geilenkirchen. The men were crossing an open space heading for the first houses when an engineer yelled, "Christ, they're Krauts!" Planes—two of them, dull-black fighters with huge crosses—bore down toward the men at treetop level. The pilots' faces were clearly visible. The platoon leader was certain most of his men were going to be wiped out. Leinbaugh had never been so frightened, "but before hitting the pavement I was trying to decide if those planes were ME 109s."

The fighters barreled away without firing a shot. Were they out of ammo? Photo recon planes? Nobody knew. The platoon got shakily to its feet and with the rest of the company fanned out to begin a house-to-house search of the city.

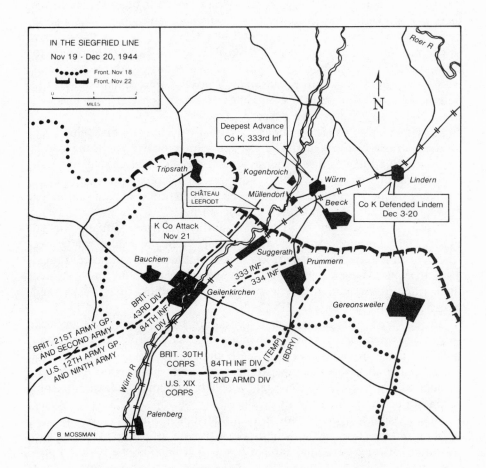

IN THE SIEGFRIED LINE
Nov 19 - Dec 20, 1944

●●●●● Front, Nov 18
Front, Nov 22

0   1   2
MILES

N

Roer R

Tripsrath

Kogenbroich

Deepest Advance
Co K, 333rd Inf

Würm

Lindern

CHÂTEAU
LEERODT

Müllendorf

Beeck

Co K Defended Lindern
Dec 3-20

K Co Attack
Nov 21

Bauchem

Suggerath

Prummern

333 INF

334 INF

Geilenkirchen

Gereonsweiler

BRIT.
43RD DIV

84TH INF
DIV

BRIT. 21ST ARMY GP.
AND SECOND ARMY

U.S. 12TH ARMY GP.
AND NINTH ARMY

BRIT. 30TH
CORPS

U.S. XIX
CORPS

Würm R

84TH INF DIV (TEMP.)

(BDRY)

2ND ARMD DIV

Palenberg

B. MOSSMAN

Few buildings remained intact. Holes had been punched in roofs and walls for firing ports. By knocking holes between cellar walls, the defenders had created block-long tunnels to connect strongpoints. Household goods—clothing, books, cookware, furniture, children's toys—spilled through gaps in the walls. Alleyways and streets were blocked with jumbled piles of bricks, roof tiles, charred beams, electric cable, and telephone wire. Mud churned up by bombs and artillery seemed to cover everything. Fires smoldered, and the stench of wet-burned wood and dead horses clung to the city. Then we saw our first dead German soldiers; we studied them curiously from a distance and gave them a wide berth.

The mop-up operation proceeded slowly, cautiously, and according to the manual. Sabia positioned BAR men in doorways across the street from each other, backing up his squad. Two at a time, men entered the houses, kicking in doors of the buildings that were locked. They checked every room, particularly the cellars.

Sabia decided to check one house personally. "The very first thing I see on the wall is a picture of St. Theresa and a big crucifix. The thing stands out in my mind to this day. Honest to God it does. You know you heard about everyone being persecuted—the Jews, all the others—and here's St. Theresa and a crucifix. We hadn't seen any fighting yet, but that made me start thinking. What the hell's going on here?"

Prisoners were soon coming in. Charlie Sullivan's squad rousted twenty-eight Germans from a single cellar. "They waved a white flag when we came down the street. They were definitely second-rate troops, a mixture of old men and youngsters. We searched them and smashed their rifles. Two men lined them up, hands behind their necks, and marched them back to the MPs."

Having been warned to watch for booby traps, Steve Call became suspicious when he peered in a window and saw a rifle, bayonet, and potato-masher grenades arranged neatly on a table. "Sergeant Clark and I figured it had to be a setup, so we took cover and tossed a grenade through the window. Sure enough, we had a second explosion a split second after the grenade went off."

Sabia's crew stopped outside a local beer hall. "The place was locked up, but looking through the windows it seemed a little too inviting. I had a confab with my guys, and though it was sacrilegious, we tossed a grenade inside. There was a good loud blast—so the place was wired. Then we went in and found some survivors: bottles with good-looking labels."

Stewart recalled, "At first we were all a little edgy and nervous. Fred Flanagan almost shot Joe Namey. Flanagan stuck his head in a door and yelled, '*Kommen Sie heraus*,' and just then Namey stuck his head out of a second-story window. Fred was taking a bead when he realized who it was."

Bob Martin and his partner became a little careless. "Our platoon set up a command post in a building off Geilenkirchen's main street, and I was covering the squad going down the street with my BAR." Once the street was cleared the two leaned their rifles against a wall and broke out their K rations. "All of a sudden the door opens and two German soldiers come in. The Germans looked at us and we looked at them. Thank God they turned around and left in a big hurry."

Other GIs got carried away—shooting locks off doors and firing indiscriminately at abandoned German emplacements. "This was the first time the men had live ammo off the rifle range," Len Erickson recalled, "and some of the fellows got a bit out of hand. Lage and I kept cautioning them to think before shooting. One of our guys did react instinctively, the way he should have. We were checking out an old office building and Mike DeBello, puffing his cigar as usual, stuck his head around a corner in a dark hallway. Seeing this rough-looking character at the far end, he gave him a full clip from his M1. The first platoon took credit for destroying one full-length mirror."

Don Stauffer and Jim Sterner, friends from Wilmington, Delaware, heard a familiar tune as their squad neared the center of town. "Someone was playing a piano," Jim explains, "so Stauffer and I went to investigate. Inside this house we found Captain Gieszl with several of our guys and a young British lieutenant who was playing 'Lili Marlene.' First we were surprised. Everybody had been alerting us about booby traps. They even warned us about not touching pianos. But here was this Englishman just having one hell of a good time. Our guys were laughing and singing along with him. What I remember most is a feeling of total exhilaration. Boy, this is really great—the way a war ought to be. It was like a scene out of an old World War I movie."

Near the town's center, two men emerged proudly from a cellar herding half a dozen elderly Germans. Erect and dignified in long uniformed coats and polished black boots, the Germans had surrendered docilely. Our men were convinced they had captured an entire German general staff, but when Brewer scanned their documents, he announced that K Company had just distinguished itself by capturing the entire Geilenkirchen police force.

It was nearly dark when a sergeant came across the main square to report to Gieszl. He had left two men guarding the entrance of an air-raid shelter. Probing down the steps with their flashlights, they had spotted a German peering around a corner.

When the captain and Brewer went to investigate, a frightened German private came up the steps waving a white handkerchief over his head. Brewer calmed the man down long enough to learn that fifty or sixty soldiers inside the shelter, realizing they were trapped, wanted to surrender. The bunker had been the battalion headquarters for the German garrison. Gieszl told Brewer to send the man back and bring up the others. "Warn him not to try anything. Tell him he's got five minutes, no more, or we'll come down and haul their asses out of there."

A crowd of Germans soon came stumbling up the steps, bareheaded, hands in the air. The last man out of the bunker was older, wearing a neatly pressed uniform with medals—obviously a senior officer. Carrying his holstered pistol in his left hand, he marched over to Gieszl, saluted, handed over his sidearm, and waited uncomfortably at attention.

Gieszl took the pistol and tossed it to his runner. He took a jaundiced view of colonels, regardless of nationality. He looked the German over carefully, taking his time. He finally returned a casual salute and looked to Brewer. "What did he say? What's his problem?"

Brewer took over, firing off a string of questions. The colonel, it turned out, was in command of the Geilenkirchen garrison, and the prisoners belonged to his headquarters staff. Although he had ordered his men to surrender, four junior officers had refused. They were still in the shelter.

Gieszl wasn't unhappy, he was delighted. "Well, how about that? We'll just go down and haul their asses out of there." He motioned Leinbaugh and two riflemen to the entranceway. They felt their way slowly down the steps and eased along a cement corridor littered with rifles, helmets, and grenades. Reaching a final flight of steps, the men opened fire. Long flames burst from their rifles, and bullets ricocheted wickedly around the bunker. Over the din they heard frantic shouts in English: "We surrender! We surrender!"

Sabia's squad added to the haul of prisoners. Given the task of clearing a battered hospital, the men started in the basement and worked their way up. "We heard this noise in one of the wards on the first floor. We couldn't see anything, so we took a flashlight and slid it through the doorway. We heard one shot and fired back through the doorway. Then we heard a whole bunch of them hollering, '*Kamerad! Kamerad!*'" The men found fourteen Germans in the ward; several had been wounded. "The rest probably figured it was a good place to surrender." The wounded Germans were placed on litters, and healthy prisoners, under Jess Canchola's watchful eye, carried them to a prisoner collecting point.

Ray Bocarski, who spent most of the afternoon interrogating prisoners, found the mop-up operation slow, tedious, and frustrating. "We had a job to do, but a lot of time was lost by men pawing through the closets and chests of drawers looking for souvenirs. Both the officers and noncoms were lax in allowing the clean-up operation to turn into a treasure hunt."

By evening, half a dozen men were sporting top hats in place of helmets. Several strolled casually down the streets twirling canes. A few were obviously tipsy. But a celebration was in order: K Company had rousted more than a hundred Germans from their hiding places and had not suffered a single casualty.

Marching out of Geilenkirchen, the third platoon discovered a large cache of German weapons in a stone farmhouse. Crowding in with flashlights, they found twenty new light machine guns, Panzerfausts, rifles, stacks of ammunition boxes, field phones—more than a truckload of booty. Leinbaugh decided that the company could use several of the phones and four machine guns.

The next morning, in the company's new positions beyond Geilenkirchen, the men set up their new weapons, pointed them in the general direction of the German army, and fired a few bursts for practice. Within moments a British lieutenant was on the scene screaming, "You bloody fools! Stop that firing!" When he realized how green K Company was, he calmed down and explained that it made his tank crews nervous to hear German weapons fired within our own lines.

We tossed our new guns into the Würm River.

While K Company was mopping up in Geilenkirchen, Baker and Charlie companies were pressing forward another mile, only to meet strong resistance at the edge of Suggerath. Fire from pillboxes and machine-gun nests brought their attack to a standstill. The battalion commander was wounded, contact with regimental headquarters was cut, and the lead platoons became disorganized.

After clearing the last houses in Geilenkirchen, K Company moved forward another mile to its assembly area, digging in across the road from Able Company. At the nightly meeting of COs held in Geilenkirchen, Gieszl received an order to send a patrol across the Würm to establish contact with B and C companies and determine their exact location.

It was after midnight when the captain returned to the company. The company had dug in as best it could in the darkness. German artillery and mortar shells were falling on Geilenkirchen, and small-arms fire, constant at times, could be heard from the direction of Suggerath. Supporting artillery blasted away at distant targets to our front. The lieutenants and sergeants paced from hole to hole, as restless and keyed up as the men. Hoarse whispers were exchanged between men in the foxholes as they watched moving shadows and listened to strange sounds. No longer was there doubt whether we'd see combat—we were in the middle of it.

Hundreds of British bombers passed directly overhead, and German antiaircraft guns opened up. In the distance we saw two bombers hit and go down in huge explosions. When the British dropped their bombs, the ground vibrated.

Sleep? Forget it.

Gieszl had an uncanny knack of picking the right man for a job. Choosing John Sabia to head K Company's first patrol made good sense. His self-confidence and natural aggressiveness were tempered by a professional's shrewdness and caution.

"Big John" picked his own crew for the patrol—seven men from the second platoon. "We darkened our hands and faces with mud, taped our weapons, dog tags, and anything that rattled, and left our wallets and extra gear in the CP. The captain gave us a nice snow job about being good men, and then we headed out through Limey lines."

It was 1:00 A.M., November 20.

Sabia and his patrol were heading into strange territory with no knowledge of the location of German pillboxes or minefields. Making contact at night with friendly troops in the middle of a firefight was next to impossible—veteran troops would never have tried it.

The patrol felt its way cautiously through the dark, crawled under three barbed-wire fences, and froze when parachute flares went up across the Würm. They found a farm road, turned right, and followed it to a blown-out bridge. Sabia led the men downstream. "We crossed the Würm on a large tree, just like in those old war movies." Inside Suggerath the patrol found nothing but Germans. "They were everywhere. We went right up to the buildings and heard them talking. Their equipment was all over the place. There was no sign of friendly troops."

Sergeant Johnny Freeman was Sabia's second-in-command. "We got to the village and it was full of Krauts. Chief Hair and I walked right up on a German chow line. Hell, if we'd had our mess kits they would have fed us." Freeman and his buddy Chief had found several bottles of rum in Geilenkirchen. "The truth is we both were so plastered I can't figure out how either of us got back to the company."

Having verified the Germans held Suggerath in strength, Sabia and his men recrossed the river. They returned to our lines—only to be sent out again.

As Bob Martin recalled, "Battalion wasn't persuaded we'd gone to the right place. I'd been the point man the first time out, so they needed me because I knew the route." Gieszl designated the same men for the second patrol, with Lieutenant Dillingham as patrol leader.

As Martin tells it, "We crossed the river, and went right on past the first village where we'd spotted the Germans on the earlier patrol. Whitson and I were the point with the rest of the patrol twenty-five yards behind us. All of a sudden firing broke out to our rear." Martin and Whitson hit the ground and fired back in the general direction of the commotion. "It was dark and drizzling, so we couldn't see anything and we didn't know what in the hell we were firing at. Then we realized nobody else was around. We were all alone out there, just two nineteen-year-old kids out there in the dark."

The shooting behind Martin and Whitson erupted when the main body of the patrol ran into a German outpost. "We were being as quiet as possible," Sabia says. "The area was lousy with Krauts, and we went maybe five minutes when Chief Hair heard a noise." Sabia whispered for the men to hold up. "Suddenly this German stuck his head up alongside the road and started squawking—then seven or eight more stuck their heads up out of this pit." Sabia reacted automatically. "I pull the pin on a grenade, toss it, and open up with my submachine gun. Another Kraut sticks his head up right in front of Chief Hair, and the Chief let him have it. It just blew this German's head away."

Don Phelps hit the ground next to the Chief. "I could see a German sentry down this ramp leading to a concrete pillbox. Someone started firing, and I emptied my M1 down the ramp toward the German. If I ever killed a German this would have been the time. He was awfully close. When it was over, we ran like hell."

The encounter lasted less than a minute. After hightailing it down the road, the men stopped to reorganize. When they realized that the lieutenant, Martin, and Whitson were missing, they hugged the mud next to the road hoping the three would show up. Sabia gave orders to head toward the rear. J. A. Craft was in line behind Sabia. "John whispered he heard hobnails and told us to get in the ditches. We did. A full platoon of Germans came marching down the road between us. I had a lot of confidence in Sabia. He was very thorough. I trusted him completely."

After the Germans passed, Sabia led the men toward Suggerath. "Krauts were all around us in buildings, and just as we sneak across the river they start throwing a lot of lead at us. Then some of our own artillery comes in on the buildings."

Freeman dove in a crater for cover. "The bottom of the hole was covered with phosphorus from one of our shells. This stuff got all over my pants, and when I got out and started moving, both my legs were glowing in the dark. I brushed and brushed, but I never could get all that crap off. I was lit up that night in more ways than one."

While the men waited for the shelling to ease off, Lieutenant Dillingham located them. He told Sabia to take the others back to our lines while he hung around to see if Martin and Whitson would show up. "The Germans tried to pepper our asses with mortars," Sabia says, "but thank God we made it in. I reported the situation, chiseled a drink or two of whiskey, and sat down to rest."

The Chief and Freeman were separated from Sabia on the way in. Near friendly lines, machine guns opened fire on them. "I yelled, 'You fuckers turn that thing off,'" Freeman recalled. "And then this Englishman yells, 'Is that a Yank out there?' And I yelled at him, 'Who the fuck you think it is?' Well, I guess the way we were swearing he knew we had to be okay, so he let us on through. About that time the rum and fatigue caught up with me and I passed out."

During the patrol's firefight, Martin and Whitson stayed put. They were still crouching in a ditch when two German tanks came down the road, so close the two GIs could have touched them. In time they became convinced the tankers had captured the rest of the patrol. Their best hope, they decided, was to find a safe place to hide and let the company catch up with them in the morning.

"We kept our helmets off," Martin explains, "because they had a different profile from the German helmets, and we held our guns down low in one hand like the Germans carried theirs. And so the two of us walked right into Würm, beautiful downtown Würm, looking for a place to hide until the next day when K Company would move in." Germans were all around, walking up and down the streets. The two hid beneath a bathtub in a vacant lot.

Once they crawled under the tub, they had to stay put. "Our shells were coming in heavy, and every once in a while a piece of shrapnel would ping off our tub. We had to stay under there and piss in our pants. Here we are, crammed up together under this goddam bathtub, with a BAR and a rifle, ammo, grenades, and nothing to eat but a few lemon drops I had in my pocket." As night came again, Martin recalls, "We crawled out and took a quick crap. We were getting horrible leg cramps. Christ, there wasn't room to breathe."

The men had to find a better place to hide. Creeping into a ruined house, they crawled under a bed. Germans kept coming in and out, even sitting on the bed. Later they slipped downstairs and hid in the basement, where they found a pile of old potatoes, their first food.

"That next night, just at dusk, we heard English. Someone yelled, 'Where is that fucker?' So we took off up the steps and saw GIs in the street. Whitson knew this one guy from Item Company. Fortunately they recognized us and didn't shoot. There were about twenty of them. They were the point who had pushed through into town, and so I'm thinking, Hot damn, by tomorrow I'll be back with the company eating K rations."

But as the two men soon learned, they were far from safe. The lead platoon from Item had no communication with the rest of the company. "Finally it was decided a sergeant and two men would go back and pick us up with the rest of I Company in the morning." But Martin heard later that the sergeant and his two men were ambushed.

"Now this group of us are together in the cellar, dog-tired, filthy dirty, covered with slime, and hungry, and not sure what's the situation. Then we hear tanks and other vehicles. I think, This is great; won't the guys in the company be surprised to see us." At first light two GIs went upstairs, and the men in the cellar heard firing. "These Item Company guys thought they had a batch of German stragglers and started knocking them off. What we didn't know is that the Germans had moved back into town in force during the night. German tanks and infantry moved up on our house, and the tanks just pulverized the upper level."

In the basement the little group of GIs were blinded by dust and smoke. The Germans fired a Panzerfaust down the stairs; Martin was wounded. "Some fragments knocked out my front teeth and ripped up my forehead and hands. I was out of it, but they told me one of the tanks lowered the muzzle of its 88 right down the cellar steps. There was no way to get out. We were trapped with a bunch of wounded. So everyone was captured and that was the end of the great patrol."

The sound of battle slacked off on Monday morning, the 20th. The company deepened its foxholes and cleared fields of fire for the machine guns, Bert Christensen and Lance zeroed the mortars, and Ashby and Chapman ran wire to the battalion CP. Barnes and J. O. Smith brought up hot food and coffee from the kitchen in Zweibruggen, and Gieszl sent his third platoon leader across the road to Able Company to coordinate defensive fires of the two companies.

It must have been a dull morning for the German tank crew parked half a mile away, but they perked up when they saw Leinbaugh sprinting across the road. They wasted six 88 rounds trying to anticipate the lieutenant's next move. Leinbaugh assumed Lieutenant Doyle, his old college chum in A Company, would be glad to see him, or at least congratulate him on outguessing the German gunner, but Doyle was less than cordial—he was throughly pissed. "You sorry son of a bitch. You've given away our positions."

An hour later, after returning to his platoon, Leinbaugh heard that same 88. This time the blast, the cloud of smoke and dirt, erupted on the embankment close to the road. Adrian Wheeler was standing in the middle of the explosion; he crumpled to the ground. Leinbaugh crawled over beside Wheeler and yelled for the medics. "I pulled Wheeler's aid packet from his belt pouch, but he was ripped up so badly I didn't know where to begin. Doc Mellon came running up and we just looked at each other—both of us thought Wheeler was a goner."

Wheeler's head and chest were covered with dirt and blood. His left eye had been blown out of its socket and was lying on his cheek still attached to the optic cord, and his neck gushed blood.

The lieutenant held compresses while Doc tied pressure bandages. Doc kept talking to Wheeler, telling him he was going to be okay, telling him to hold still. After pushing the eyeball back into its socket and bandaging the head wounds, Mellon slit open Wheeler's field jacket and dusted the wounds in his chest and neck with sulfa. He tied more bandages and checked for bleeding while Wheeler slipped in and out of consciousness. Two company medics came up dragging a stretcher and eased Adrian down the hill to a shed near the road. When Wheeler started choking in his blood, Mellon took the top of a pen, broke off the end, and stuck it through the hole in Wheeler's windpipe to keep him from suffocating.

"What I remember is the bad wounds in the throat and neck," Doc said. "He'd swallowed his tongue and was strangling in his own blood, and I remember looking at my muddy hands before I stuck a finger through the hole into his voice box so he could get some air. But I have no way of really knowing how much I might have helped him pull through. We didn't get any reports back. We never heard whether any of our wounded guys even made it to the field hospital."

Wheeler remembers he was close to the crest of the hill when the round hit. "It's hard to explain—I knew there was an explosion; I was aware of it, but I didn't hear a thing. The shrapnel hit me in the head, the throat, and the mouth, and I went down. The worst part was I couldn't breathe, and I must have passed out. The letter I got from John Sabia in the hospital said he thought they got me evacuated on the jeep in the afternoon, so I must have lain there for a couple of hours. Then I went back, evidently to regimental aid, because Major McArthur was there and he cut off my dog tags. I never did understand that—maybe he thought I was already dead."

News the company had taken its first casualty sped along the line. Ed Stewart was in a barn when the solitary round exploded. "We heard someone yelling that Wheeler had been hit in the throat and needed Doc. Then we heard Wheeler didn't have much of a chance." Sergeant Hadley, one of the squad leaders, became very grim and angry, according to Stewart. "Hadley was a good typical American on the verge of battle; but he had to have one of his closest friends critically wounded, a man with whom he had played, worked, trained, suffered, before he was deeply moved by the war."

3

THE CHÂTEAU

At noon on Tuesday, November 21, K Company jumped off in its first attack. We had been through this drill before, time and again on maneuvers, and it was hard to realize this time it was for real—not just another one of those Louisiana practice sessions.

From a low hill behind the line of departure, First Sergeant Dempsey Keller watched the company climb out of roadside ditches and foxholes and form up as skirmishers. These were the men the first sergeant had helped train and had worried over for two years. "They were the finest men in the world, the very best. I choked up with pride, but I felt cold chills not knowing what was out there waiting for them. It was the one single moment of the war I can never forget."

The third platoon's aidman, Doc Mellon, also wondered what to expect: "We had no idea what was out in those fields—I felt like I was back in Alabama on a rabbit hunt." And Ed Stewart remembers the man from A Company with "that strained and startled look in his eyes that was to become so familiar later on."

Keller watched as the men opened fire. "I kept waiting for the Germans to start shooting back. I was saying silent prayers for every single one of those guys that morning."

The company had moved into A Company's positions while waiting. Stewart remembers "shells coming in thick and fast. One of our guys jumped in a foxhole and realized the A Company man in the hole was dead. The command came to move out and as we got to our feet a sergeant from Able Company yelled, 'Good luck.'"

Stewart, the flank man for the company, was guiding on the road to his left. Following behind the company, down the middle of the road, came three Shermans from the British Sherwood Rangers Yeomanry Regiment. The tanks commenced firing at buildings to the front. "Someone yelled for us to hold up, and I hit the ground. The lead British tank must have spotted something—it moved up closer and fired tracers that were hitting twenty or thirty yards in front of us. The fire was just over our heads. If one of our guys had gotten to his knees or stood up he would have been cut in half."

At breakfast the men had received their daily British rum ration, but Howard Broderick gave his share to other members of his platoon, discovering that "all of us Mormons were awfully popular that week." The lead platoon's second scouts, Broderick and his partner, were slightly in front of the main line of skirmishers. Like Stewart, they worried about the tank fire. "Once in a while their angle was wrong and we realized the fire was not going over our heads but past our ears."

Another Mormon, Steve Call, the third platoon guide, also began his morning without the warming effects of the strong red rum. A staff sergeant and the platoon's second-ranking noncom, Steve was a clean-cut blond six-footer from Utah. "We went through several fields firing at the hedgerows and farm buildings, and a few shells came in, but most exploded well behind us." Up ahead through barren trees the men saw a larger building, a château, and Steve spotted a rapid blinking red dot from the upper floor. "I don't know why it took me so long to realize it was machine-gun fire. I couldn't hear it and I wasn't aware of any bullets hitting around us. I'm sure none of our guys were hit, and a lot of the men didn't even realize we were being fired on."

When the skirmishers came within a hundred yards of the building, tracers ricocheted off the ground in front of the company scouts. Ducking instinctively, the men kept moving and firing, hitting the ground, zigzagging, yanking M1 clips from their bandoliers, and pouring heavy fire in the windows of the château.

A machine-gun squad leader, Frank Gonzales, had yet to see a German, but he did see a stranger. "He was behind a tree with a big camera and was in uniform but he wasn't wearing a helmet. I asked him what in the hell he thought he was doing, and he told me he was taking pictures. I was really astonished to see him—I thought the guy was crazy."

The gunners set up the light .30s and sprayed covering fire for the riflemen. Hesitating at a wide moat full of green, scummy water, the lead squads flanked the building and reached the château's entrance. Sergeant Hadley and the platoon lieutenant tossed grenades through the gatehouse windows. Jimmy Clark's squad, hugging the brick walls, worked its way cautiously into the courtyard. The place seemed deserted.

According to Brewer's map, K Company had captured Château Leerodt, a large three-story brick complex surrounded by leafless poplars. The big square courtyard was empty, but coals were smoldering in the kitchen fireplace, and we found the usual soldier's litter—empty ammo cases, dirty blankets, rolls of field wire, broken wine bottles, letters, a broken rifle. The rooms off the courtyard reeked of urine and stale cabbage. Proud of ourselves, feeling a bit possessive, we searched cautiously for booby traps and gaped at the massive brick quadrangle. The company had captured its first objective, and the château, like Geilenkirchen, had been a pushover. For us it confirmed the Germans were beaten and on the run—nothing had happened so far to make us question our optimism. We were buoyed up and cocky. In another hour we should be digging in around our objective in Würm.

Gieszl was pleased, but he was concerned by tactical considerations. The château was a natural defensive position. It had been handed over without a fight—why? He looked again at his map, trying to decide where the Germans would dig in and hold. "I was very worried about our flanks—we hadn't seen any friendly troops on either the right or the left. I didn't like the situation, not one damn bit." Gieszl felt sure the companies across the Würm were half a mile to the rear. K Company was now very much on its own—a new experience, but to be repeated.

Two Germans, older men in worn and dirty uniforms, were found hiding in the château's cellar waiting to surrender. Others, we knew, had pulled out as K Company advanced. Only a few scattered foxholes had been dug around the château, but the abandoned field phones and spotting scopes meant the building had been used as an observation post. Muddy tank tracks, fresh ones, left a trail along the road toward Würm.

Billy Waddle's squad had fired at several Germans hightailing it beyond the château. "That was the first time, I guess, that any of us had fired at an enemy we could see, but I don't think we hit any of them." And the souvenir hunting continued. While searching the upstairs rooms, Billy found a Luger. "None of the other guys wanted it because of a rumor if you got captured and they found a German weapon on you, you'd be shot." Waddle stuck the automatic inside his field jacket for emergencies.

Half an hour was spent checking out the main buildings and the area between the château and the river. While Gieszl tried unsuccessfully to get through to battalion on the radio, the sergeants rounded up their squads and the platoons formed up beyond the moat, ready to continue the advance toward Würm.

Gieszl gave the word. The third platoon moved forward, the first platoon following closely. The Germans were watching. They let K Company move fifty yards beyond the château—no more. Then all hell broke loose.

When the first two flat-trajectory rounds hit seconds apart, nobody grasped what was happening. The rounds were close, and several men were sprayed with mud. We hit the ground and were scrambling to our feet when two more rounds came in with an incredibly sharp fast crack—skidding explosions—and this time two men were nicked by shrapnel. Then the mortar barrage commenced in full fury.

While the company had been forming up, Steve Call had watched the British tanks on the road softening up the area with machine-gun fire. "The bullets were hitting too close in front of our guys—we would be walking right into their field of fire." Steve ran to the road and pounded on the side of the lead tank with his M1, yelling for the gunner to stop firing. It was this same moment the Germans let loose with their barrage. The area around the tanks erupted with explosions. Steve was hit. "It was like getting slugged in the rear end, hard, with a two-by-four. I was blown clear off my feet but managed to crawl over to the ditch. I was bleeding pretty bad, but finally got my pants down and wrapped bandages around my rear end." Call stuck his rifle in the ground and hoped somebody would find him in a hurry.

Leinbaugh, convinced friendly artillery was hitting the company with short rounds, ran forward and tossed a red smoke grenade in front of the line of riflemen—the signal for our artillery to lift its fire. Too late, he realized these rounds weren't coming from the rear. Now the Germans had the benefit of a billowing red smoke cloud marking K Company's forward location.

Within the next few minutes we received an on-the-job training course in the different sounds made by German shells. Artillery rounds gave enough warning to take three quick leaps for the nearest hole. Mortar shells gave only a split second to tighten your gut, wrap arms around your neck, and cram as much of your body as possible into your helmet. And there was really nothing to worry about with 75s and 88s, since their rounds traveled faster than sound. They were behind you when you heard them. (Throughout the war we referred to all incoming flat-trajectory rounds as 88s—the best ear in the company couldn't tell the difference in the size of an explosion from a 75 or an 88 round.)

Flat on his belly, digging into the soft ground with his helmet, Leinbaugh learned how close an 88 could hit without lethal damage. "My radio at arm's length took a direct hit—the only thing left was the bent antenna."

Doc Mellon had positioned himself midway in the skirmish line. "None of us who made it through that first barrage will ever forget it—heavy tank fire and mortar rounds. We hit the ground and started digging like mad. Fortunately the ground was soft." Within minutes most men had carved crude slit trenches a foot in the soft soil—deep enough to give protection from 88 fire.

J. A. Craft, a Mississippi farm boy, was told to pull back across the moat. "All of us were supposed to have learned how to swim back at Camp Claiborne, but I never got the hang of it at all. I couldn't swim a stroke. Somebody had rigged planks across the moat, and we crossed okay, but after that first heavy barrage the planks had been blown to pieces and all hell was breaking loose. I figured I could walk across the bottom of the moat, and that's just what I did. The water was over my head, so I just marched across the muddy bottom and climbed out the other side. I was lugging my rifle, half a dozen bandoliers, grenades, and they weighed me down."

After the company pulled back inside the château, Mellon heard a call for an aidman. "I had to wade and paddle across the moat to get to him; the water was icy-cold and up to my chin. Suddenly I realized a guy, one of ours, was shooting at me. I yelled, 'Hey, I'm on your side.'"

"After I got the wounded man patched up I scrounged around and found some old gray German underwear in the horse stable and put that on to keep from freezing. Most of the foxholes around the château were filled with water and it was raining most of the time, which made it awfully rough on the wounded."

After waiting behind the château, Sergeant Lance and his mortar squad decided it was time to move up nearer the rifle platoons. They picked up the baseplates and tubes and began advancing during that first devastating barrage. They found Steve Call in a ditch and stopped long enough to rebandage his wounds. Farther on they found Broyles, sprawled and bleeding, his leg badly ripped by a tree burst. They gave him first aid and carried him to cover.

Lance, a lanky ex-bartender from Idaho, wanted to catch up with the rest of the company. "Steve Call told me the company should be on ahead of us, so we really shagged ass. Two of those British tanks pulled out and followed us—we didn't ask them to follow us, they just did it." German mortars were zeroed in on the road, and it was a small miracle none of the men in the squad was hit. Each man carried five or six mortar rounds weighing five pounds apiece, in addition to the tubes and baseplates. They hurried along the road, passing the château without seeing anyone. The entire area was covered with explosions and smoke.

After going several hundred yards, "we started taking machine-gun and rifle fire from a stone farm building off to our right," Lance recalls. "We spread out and began firing, hitting the ground, moving in closer—fire and movement. We couldn't use our mortars. All told we had three or four M1s and carbines, and a couple of .45s—not a hell of a lot of firepower. Every time one of us raised his head or tried to move up, the Germans sprayed the field. We were wondering how to get out of this mess when behind me I heard this British voice asking if we could use a bit of help.

"It was a goddam British officer—here he was standing up in the middle of a firefight without a helmet. He had climbed out of his tank and walked across the field behind us. I told him, 'Lordy Jesus, yes, we need some help.' It seemed pretty obvious to me, but I guess he was just being polite."

The British officer ran back to his tank and gave the building three quick rounds from his 75, one in each window. Thirty or forty Germans poured out waving white flags and yelling, "Don't shoot." The GIs moved in, tossed the Germans' weapons and helmets in a pile, and lined them up.

While advancing across the field with bullets kicking up mud around his feet, Jim Sterner, instead of being frightened, was thinking, "Jeez, this is just like in the movies." When the Germans ran outside to surrender, Jim and the other men began searching them. One prisoner pulled several snapshots out of his wallet. "Here we are, right in the middle of a battle, and this guy wanted to show me pictures of his wife and kids back home."

"We felt pretty pleased with ourselves, with the big haul of prisoners. But then," Lance says, "our troubles began all over again. The Germans called in enough fire on us to wipe out a regiment. With all that shelling some of the prisoners were wounded and started to panic. Four or five tried to run. We yelled for them to stop. The ones that didn't got shot."

It was no easy trick to herd the Germans back toward the château. Mortar rounds followed the GIs and their prisoners every step of the way. More prisoners were wounded. One episode remains with Lance: "This thing has always bothered me. A German with a bad compound fracture of the arm panicked and refused to wade the stream. I finally poked him in the rear with my bayonet—that got him across the creek in a hurry. But I knew I shouldn't have done that, not to a wounded man."

The mortarmen finally saw men from the company in front of them getting ready to fire on their German prisoners. Not until then did Lance and his crew realize they'd been far out in front of the rest of the company.

Over the years the mortar squad's sortie against the German army became something of a legend at K Company reunions. Gieszl enjoys needling Lance about the escapade. "It was Lance and the mortar section that caused all our problems. They came bringing this big batch of prisoners back to the château, and that started the whole goddam war. That was exactly when the Germans really got pissed off at K Company."

The three rifle platoons had been thoroughly clobbered trying to advance beyond the château. The concentration of German firepower was absolutely overwhelming with its violence, surprise, and intensity. Artillery fire, 88s and 75s from hidden tanks, and 120 mortars with apparently limitless supplies of ammunition hit us. Machine-gun fire whipping in from pillboxes across the Würm seemed almost an afterthought. The noise, the shock, the sensation of total helplessness and bewilderment, the loss of control, the sudden loss of every familiar assumption—nothing in civilian life or training offered an experience remotely comparable. The barrage went on and on. The company had lost the initiative and taken several quick casualties. Men scooped slit trenches in the mud; others grabbed cover wherever they could find it. Our new-boy illusions of the past two days dissolved in a moment.

An hour earlier Doc Mellon had felt as if he were on a rabbit hunt—now it occurred to him we might be the rabbits.

"We got frustrated." Gieszl explains. "We had nothing to shoot at and no room for maneuver. We were canalized in this little valley a few hundred yards wide. Everything to our left beyond the road was in the British zone. It was the division, corps, and army boundary, a no-fire line. We weren't even supposed to shoot across that road, and everything across the Würm River on our right belonged to I Company. The Germans had the best of all worlds—good observation, grazing fire from the pillboxes, and plenty of time to prefire the entire area."

K Company had no choice but to pull back around the château. The company had tried to form up in the middle of the Germans' main line of defense, lost its momentum, and took a dozen casualties—but there was no panic, no loss of discipline or of determination. During lulls in the shelling, men pulled back a few at a time, bringing the wounded inside.

An ASTPboy who had come to K Company in April, Bob Schiedel, was one of the few men to spot a legitimate target that afternoon. He fired one single round from his M1. The problem was locating the German positions across the stream behind the château. The pillboxes were well camouflaged and covered with earth, blending perfectly into the landscape. "I kept watching and finally spotted a machine-gun-firing slit and squeezed off one shot, a tracer. That was a mistake. Every German for miles around must have spotted me, and they kept me pinned down for the next hour. I couldn't move."

Howard Maddry's machine gun was also quickly spotted by the Germans. An engineering student from North Carolina, Howard fired only a few brief bursts before a German mortar crew zeroed in, destroying the light .30 and wounding him in the legs.

Floyd Reed and his squad were close to the river firing at embrasures in the German pillboxes. "We were getting hit with everything in the book. It was hard to pick up targets, and I was trying to spot muzzle blasts." In the middle of a mortar barrage, Reed was hit. "The explosion was right on top of me, and a big hunk of hot metal tore into my back and BAR ammo belt, exploding the .30 caliber rounds. It really messed me up. For a while—I don't know how long—I was blind. Then I remember some guys working on me. I think they got me back into the château on a door, but I was pretty much out of it."

While most of the men in the company were wearing field jackets, George Lucht had decided to wear his heavy GI overcoat on the first attack. George found his coat soaked up the rain like a sponge, burdening him with pounds of extra weight. "We were hit by heavy fire, and I was half in mud, half in water. The cold was terrible. I'll tell you the truth, I felt like giving up the struggle."

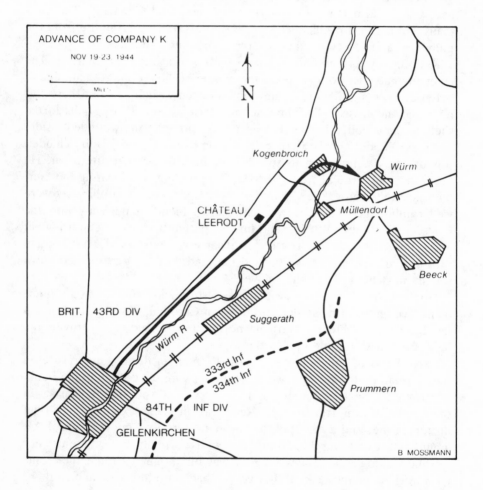

ADVANCE OF COMPANY K

NOV 19-23 1944

MILES

N

Kogenbroich

Würm

CHÂTEAU
LEERODT

Müllendorf

Beeck

BRIT. 43RD DIV

Würm R

Suggerath

333rd Inf

334th Inf

Prummern

84TH INF DIV

GEILENKIRCHEN

B MOSSMANN

*   *   *

The wiremen finally got a link through to battalion, long enough for Gieszl to receive new orders before shelling broke the line. K Company was to push off again at 4:00 P.M. and not to worry about its flanks. Gieszl remained concerned. "We were going to be in limbo, but I felt we had a better chance of breaking through at dusk."

The captain took a man and made a fast reconnaissance on the high ground across the road in the British sector. A couple hundred yards beyond the château the two picked up movement, an observation post. "It was two Krauts with glasses and a field phone. We were lucky—there was so much noise from the shelling they didn't hear us and we picked them off without any trouble."

K Company profited from the lesson learned in its first attempt to attack beyond Château Leerodt. Following the artillery preparation, the platoons moved out again at four o'clock. The squads climbed from their foxholes and slit trenches, forming up on the move. As they hurried across the first field, German mortars coughed out shells, but too late this time—the line of explosions trailed behind the attackers. Gieszl had made it clear: Run, don't walk, organize on the go, spread out, keep moving. K Company passed through the heavy protective fire zone before the German gunners could adjust, but then they shortened the range.

"After a few hundred yards we came under continuous fire," Stewart says, "but we kept moving. I remember our lieutenant being thrown from one end of a shell crater to the other by a near miss. I remember the wet cold slippery mud, a curious elation and mixture of fear, determination, and a desire for violence as I was captured by the frenzy of the attack. My M1 kicked in my hands as I pulled the trigger time and again, the empty casings and clips arching through the air."

K Company cleared three fields, and then a fourth; no longer running, the men pushed doggedly ahead, walking a steady pace, firing from the hip into the approaching woodline. "It was nearly dark when we entered the treeline and an area of marshy underbrush," Stewart says. "They had been waiting for us again—we were met by a murderous combination of machine-gun fire, artillery, and mortars. Suddenly the air was filled with bands of crisscrossing tracers. The impact of wave after wave of shells was maddening."

Pope and his men advanced in short dashes. "You could light a cigarette off those tracers. When we hit the little marshy area we were right in the middle of the Krauts' main line of resistance."

Gieszl sent word to hold up so that the reserve platoon could be brought forward. As the men sought cover in the heavy muck, a series of giant orange-red explosions suddenly ripped through the approaching dusk, tossing up huge fountains of muddy water in the river. And in the brief seconds between blasts, a loud, unearthly, chilling scream—"Help me, help me, oh my God, oh my God, help me!" It started at a piercing crescendo, trailing off into a despairing gasp, stopping, and then again, "Oh my God, help me!" No one who heard those anguished cries will ever forget them.

Tracers kept ripping overhead in long red swaths two feet off the ground. Word was passed to keep low—the Germans were firing live rounds beneath the tracers. Williams was hit in the belly by machine-gun fire. Mellon crawled over to bandage him. A runner came crawling up to report the tankers were pulling out. With darkness approaching they were helpless against the mines in the roadway and could no longer support the GIs with fire.

"I didn't like it when the tanks pulled back," Gieszl recalls, "but it was understandable—tanks need protection just like people do. The Germans shelled the shit out of them and knocked out one tank. Those tankers did everything I asked them to and a little bit more. I had no qualms about any of those British. The fellow who was in command of that outfit—he was the calmest son of a bitch I ever ran into."

David Render, a British tank officer in A Squadron, which supported the 84th's GIs along the road north of Geilenkirchen, got up a bit late the morning of the attack. "I was wearing pajamas under my tank suit. We always referred to you chaps as the PBIs—poor bloody infantry. And if it wasn't for some of the actions and help of the Americans, I, for one, wouldn't be here. Your gallant chaps certainly gave a very, very good account of themselves in those wet and rotten cold conditions."

Lieutenant Render's tank, *Aim,* which he had had from Normandy, "a good diesel," was lost when it hit a mine. The tanks had started down the "ominously deserted road" and were firing away at a pillbox when the mine went off. "Lots of sparks and black smoke resulted, but we were able to carry on firing away for a bit. The Jerries then wheeled up a gun and hit our tank, which fired back, and then it was time we were away." None of Render's men was wounded, but the driver was killed. "We then met your chaps and we were stonked to quite an extent, but got back by nipping along in the crouched position. The GIs made a fuss over us and we did help a poor wounded American chap back so that the stretcher bearers could take over. It was all a bit hairy."

"I worked on so many badly wounded guys that night," Mellon says, "that I couldn't keep them all straight. Most of the time when I patched a guy up I never knew whether he made it. There was just no way to know. A lot of the time I had no idea who I was working on, particularly if the guy was unconscious. You felt around in the dark for the blood or the wound and just did the best you could." While all the men in the company had received first-aid training, they weren't confident of their skills, not on that grisly night. But the squads tried to evacuate their own wounded as quickly as possible.

The German mortar fire leveled off to a methodical pounding; shells walked back and forth across the swamp. Green flares lit the sodden battlefield, swinging and jerking in the gusty wind. Enfilade fire poured across the river—tens of thousands of rounds whipping through the canes and underbrush above the men's heads. Getting the company to its feet and continuing the attack was totally out of the question. K Company was pinned down.

Gieszl went to the château and contacted battalion for permission to withdraw. For half an hour the men hugged the marshy ground and waited. The cold became intense, and the wind increased, bringing with it scudding bands of rain. The distant searchlights reflected off the banks of the low-lying clouds. (A British unit, Drewforce, provided "artificial moonlight" for the operation. Four huge searchlights afforded enough light to help attacking forces identify objectives during nighttime.)

Men began digging but struck water just below the surface. "An overpowering feeling of fear and of despair enveloped me as I tried to bail water out of the hole with my helmet," Stewart recalls. "The shells continued to explode in the midst of us. It was dark and cold and miserably wet. We were taking terrific punishment." Finally word came whispered down the line to pull back. "In small groups we found our way back to the assembly point. We brought in Williams on a stretcher crudely fashioned from rifles and raincoats; one arm was dragging on the ground."

After Broderick hit the mud several times, his rifle jammed. "I looked around for a casualty, got his M1, and fired my first shot." Then Broderick had the wind knocked out of him by a big piece of flat shrapnel that hit him in the back. "We lost two good men in my squad, David Muniz, the young Indian boy from New Mexico, and Williams, Johnnie Radovich's ammo bearer. Williams took a full burst of machine-gun fire in the stomach. Four of us carried him back, but he was dead by the time we got him inside the building."

Stewart remembers the château offered protection for company headquarters. A smoky fire was started. "The platoons didn't have any convenience of this sort, but began the tedious job of digging, in an effort to hold the position. I found a large feeding trough and painfully dragged it over my hole—just then one of the top floors of the burning château fell with a mighty roar of flames. The German rounds came in threes; one came in right in front of my position, the second round halved the distance, so I took a breath and my head goes under the water in my slit trench, and then that thing explodes right above me. I had this feeling—it was a very sensuous feeling actually, just kind of drifting, swimming." Stewart was knocked unconscious. "I remember coming out of it and after going inside around a fire, I came back to my hole and at daybreak I looked at my rifle, a muddy mess. I tried to find Moose in the next hole and went to another hole, then I realized I was the only guy out there."

A hefty third platoon BAR man, Paul Coste, who had arrived in K Company by way of Harvard and the ASTP, dug a hole close by the château with a tall Irish boy. "He was even younger than me, and more frightened than I was. I was torn between sympathy for his terror and disdain for his fear. I tried to reassure him, but it was way beyond me. He broke down completely; we never saw him again."

That night at Leerodt, Gieszl swears, was the most miserable one of his entire life. "I kept running around—trying to do something. The rain was pretty continuous, everybody was soaked, tired, hungry, and then everything gets exaggerated—you use up all your calories. The intensity of that barrage was just unreal. There wasn't anyplace to go, they just saturated the place. There was so much fire the Germans started hitting foxholes, not because they were aiming at them—they just dumped that many shells in there. Those guys didn't have anything to do except lob rounds down the barrel. They must have kept six trucks running shells to those goddam mortars all night long."

Gieszl was checking the perimeter by the river, and was on his belly in the water when he heard a crash as a round came through the trees. "There was light from the fire in the château, enough to see by. And there were these mortar fins—that was all that was sticking out of the mud—vibrating about two feet from my head. I was right pleased that thing didn't go off."

Broderick had to dig his hole by himself. "Henderson and I were teamed up, but for some reason he wouldn't help. Heavy shelling hit our area, and Henderson got in the hole with me, but it bothered him so much he hadn't helped dig that he climbed out and took his chances. He was killed the next day by a mortar round."

A third platoon squad leader, Charlie Sullivan from Horse Cave, Kentucky, was sent to establish an outpost beyond the château. "When we headed out about 11:00 P.M., it was raining and pitch-black, but the searchlights gave us something to guide on." The men slipped quietly into an empty house several hundred yards in front of the company and heard activity over the back fence. "The Germans had a mortar position right behind the house, so close we could hear every round go down the tube. We came in at four in the morning and pinpointed the location so our artillery could go after them."

During the night, Pete Visconte, a mortar-section sergeant from California, was killed by a direct hit on his foxhole. After Pete's body was carried inside the château's gatehouse, Lance returned to his foxhole. "I was in a hole with a good Catholic boy from upstate New York. For some reason, I'll never know why, I went over to the next hole to check on the guys, and I no more than got there than they dumped a round right on my old hole, burying the poor guy. He was wounded, but we hauled him out of the mud alive. It could have been he drove me out because he 'Hailed Mary' all night. After taking so many hours of that, I probably left to get away from those Hail Marys."

Some men got foxhole religion, but Lance didn't. "I'd pick out the religious ones and trade them my candy bars for the rum ration. That way I could get the courage to go on."

During the nonstop shelling, fear hit Al Oyler for the first time. "I had a pocket New Testament, one that had a little thin piece of metal backing you were supposed to wear in your breast pocket over your heart. I pulled it out and read a few passages. The château was burning, so there was plenty of light. I asked the old guy upstairs—and I wasn't overly religious—if he meant to see me through this I would like it, but if not, do the best you can."

One of the night's casualties received a massive head wound. Mellon propped the man against the side of a wall to bandage him. "Part of his brain sac was pushed outside his left temple. It was incredible, but the guy lived for thirty or forty minutes. I know that because I kept getting a pulse." Doc never knew the identity of his patient since "his face and head were so messed up I couldn't tell who he was."

Len Erickson, the first platoon's guide, spent most of the long night rotating men between holes and the buildings. "I was slopping through the mud checking the line of our foxholes, and heard a noise right behind me. It was raining, black as the devil, and there within ten feet of me was a four-man German patrol. Before I could react, they took off and I didn't fire a shot."

Later, past midnight, a big fellow in Erickson's platoon shot himself in the leg. "He was trying to hit his foot, but got a bit of the shinbone and really messed himself up." Then a new aidman assigned to the company cracked up. He begged Erickson, "Do me a favor, sergeant, shoot me in the leg."

Barnes returned from Geilenkirchen after delivering the most recent load of wounded. He brought back a load of ammunition and three replacements: Leslie Carson from Truman, Arkansas, and Browning and Butler. "I guess we were the first combat replacements to join K Company," Carson says. "Browning didn't last long; he got hit the very next day and was evacuated with blast injuries, and Butler got killed at Christmastime."

After being assigned to John Corkill's squad in the first platoon, Carson was quizzed by another sergeant. "He didn't recognize me and thought maybe I was a German in a GI's clothing, but there was no problem fitting in and being accepted—we were too busy up there, there was too much going on." Carson, an older man with an eleven-year-old son, was put right to work. "My first job was getting a door and going out with four other guys to bring in a wounded man. I was told to carry the other men's rifles and provide protection, but lugging five M1s, I couldn't protect anybody."

Mortar rounds plunging into the burning wing of the château sent spectacular fireballs flying through the air, showering nearby foxholes with burning embers, but the heavy rain kept the other wings of the complex from going up in flames. Gieszl and Leinbaugh set out to check the perimeter. They found one man, a reasonably cheerful fellow who had needed to take a leak, but who hadn't dared leave his hole. He reported it felt so nice and warm he'd done it again.

The captain and the lieutenant were caught in the worst shelling of the night. "We were covered with chunks of mud and lifted off the ground by rounds exploding yards away. Gieszl got nicked in the leg and his pants were ripped by shrapnel," Leinbaugh recalls. "When it slacked off we made a dash for the buildings. We pulled off our helmets and took out cigarettes, but we were shaking so hard from the cold and shelling we couldn't get them lit. We realized we hadn't eaten a bite the entire day."

"The rain and cold were a hell of a problem," Billy Waddle says. "We were all soaked through with no chance to dry out. I was wearing a field jacket but gave up on the overshoes. You couldn't run in those things— they were too heavy. In some of the foxholes the water was knee-deep, so the overshoes wouldn't have helped anyhow."

In the château's cellars the men took turns trying to get some sleep. Waddle was in a basement room where they stored jars of fruit. "Every time a shell came in jars fell off the shelves, waking us up."

It was 3:00 A.M. when Bob Schiedel was wounded. "I was getting into my hole when there was a tremendous blast and I was hit by a big chunk of shrapnel in my thigh. It would have been worse, but the mud absorbed a lot of the explosion." Bill Sanders in the next hole came over to give a hand. "He was helping me toward the château when another round came in almost on top of us. I was trying to hold on to my M1, but was having so much trouble Sanders told me to drop it. When we got inside Sergeant Keller wanted to know how I lost my rifle." Schiedel was bandaged and carried outside. "They were tying me on a stretcher on the jeep just as we got another barrage. Everybody took cover, but I managed to untie myself and crawled inside the gatehouse on my hands and knees." When the shelling eased, Schiedel was evacuated.

Most men in the company had been in water-filled holes for three or four hours. We started rotating, half the men going inside for an hour; but the damage was done. In addition to the dead and wounded, the company lost a dozen men that night from immersion foot.

Latherial Barnes and John O. Smith spent most of the night shuttling wounded between the château and the battalion aid station. "We were shelled every trip. Sticking to the road was a real problem, but the searchlights behind Geilenkirchen gave us something to guide on." On his last trip of the night, Barnes dropped off more wounded. "Then I met John O. at the kitchen, where we picked up more ammo, K rations, and jerry cans full of coffee, and we headed for the company." It was raining hard, and though Barnes had made the trip several times, somehow in the shelling and the rain he missed the turnoff to the château and kept on going. "I knew something was wrong, so we eased to a stop at a group of brick houses. I figured we were in some kind of trouble, so I stepped out of the jeep to listen and look around." Barnes heard men talking back and forth in German. "We got back in the jeeps and turned around very slowly, and took off nice and easy."

More than three thousand riflemen from the eighteen rifle companies in the 84th's 333rd and 334th regiments were involved in the fighting around Geilenkirchen. By the night of the 21st the majority of companies had lost a third of their men. The two regiments were trying to capture five German villages: Würm, Müllendorf, Leiffarth, Beeck, and Lindern, located in a crescent-shaped cluster northeast of Geilenkirchen. The villages, each an individual strongpoint, were surrounded by hundreds of massive Siegfried Line pillboxes. And the muddy terrain, ideally suited for defense, was defended by two veteran SS Panzer divisions that fought stubbornly for every yard. The battle had degenerated into a bloody draw by the night of the 21st and the morning of the 22nd, but army, corps, and division decided the attacks would continue.

4

KOGENBROICH

During the night Gieszl brought word from battalion that the attack was on again for the next day. The division commander had ordered that Würm must be taken "at all costs." Battalion had promised more artillery, more support across the river with I Company being joined by L Company, and more tanks to help neutralize the pillboxes. We were not surprised by the new orders; we simply accepted them. We were far too new at the game to know if they made sense.

Gieszl also passed along a new directive from division. "Henceforth all commanders are prohibited from using the term 'pinned down' in situation reports." Gieszl laughed when he gave the word to the platoon leaders. "This crap could be based on my report last night that we were pinned down in the swamp and couldn't stick our heads out of the mud. This is brilliant, just brilliant."

The British tank commander in clean, pressed battle dress came to the CP to coordinate plans for the new attack. One glance reminded us of our own appearance. We were covered with mud and slime, red-eyed from lack of sleep, our faces layered with dirty stubble.

While the officers were going over the maps, three heavy explosions shook the château, filling the room with plaster dust and knocking over the candle on the table. "Those were extra-heavy-caliber," the tanker explained. "I suspect the Jerries are after my tanks."

Somebody yelled for the medics—the heavy salvo had cost another casualty. A GI was brought into the CP with massive chest and head wounds, but as Keller recalls, "by the time we cut open his field jacket it was obvious he was dead. He was unrecognizable, and Mellon and I had to feel around in all that flesh and bone to find his dog tags."

During the nightly meeting at battalion, Gieszl had persuaded headquarters the pillboxes in front of I Company would have to be neutralized before K Company advanced, so in the early-morning hours of the 22nd we sat tight. Although the shelling eased off, the casualties continued. Pilgrim was brought in from his foxhole doubled up in a knot; his cartridge belt had to be cut off. Sutton was disabled with an ugly shrapnel wound in his hand. Lafreniere was carried inside the château with frostbitten feet and legs. Stewart could barely stand. "We hardly understood how we would be able to attack again, but when the time came we did. Sergeant Dulin asked if I could make it and Leinbaugh asked me if I could walk. I told them yes."

The supporting artillery barrage was twice as heavy and twice as long as on the previous day. Big guns—155s and 240s—joined in blasting the swamp area, Würm, and the adjoining roads. We felt a grim sympathy for the Germans out there waiting for us. The ground shook and the air vibrated as the rounds whirred and screeched overhead. Trees were splintered, huge waterspouts rose from the Würm, the entire front disappeared under clouds of smoke and mingled orange-red blasts of the explosives.

When the artillery lifted, K Company attacked for the third time up the river valley toward Würm.

For the first several hundred yards, crossing the ground we'd tried twice before to take, it seemed as if the artillery barrage had worked. The Germans fired airbursts from 88s, a new experience, and machine guns from pillboxes across the river opened up again, but the fire was sporadic. We waded through the swamp, with the black muck more an inconvenience than a barrier in daylight. Reaching firm ground, the company regrouped in an orchard. The line was straightened, the laggards caught up, Gieszl and the platoon leaders checked the terrain with their binoculars. Brewer made the most of the interlude. Gathering an armful of apples from a shed, he distributed them along the line as if we were on a picnic excursion.

So far it had been easy. Why so simple? Were the Germans sucking us into a trap? Had the artillery preparation stunned the Germans and knocked out their guns?

The ground in front of the company looked empty. Beet fields divided by hedgerows were all that separated us from a cluster of red brick houses and farm buildings. Gieszl tried and failed to reach battalion on the 300 radio. He restudied his map and again scanned the area with field glasses. Nothing happening out there. He gave the order to move out.

The Germans had pulled back, prepared a new line of foxholes and log emplacements, and waited for us. Enemy rifle fire increased. A man was hit. After we plowed through a hedgerow, German burp guns opened up, slowing our advance. Men looked for targets, hit the ground, and advanced in short rushes. A barn and a shed dead ahead concealed several riflemen.

"Gieszl got out in front of everybody, but I finally caught up with him," Leinbaugh recalls. "We ran around the barn from the left and saw three Germans hightailing it out the back. They never saw us and we were so close we couldn't miss. Then I hollered at the captain we'd better hold up and wait for the rest of the company."

Oyler's machine-gun squad was stretched flat along the side of the road. "The firing was awfully heavy. Lage came walking up as calm as anything, stopped, got down on one knee, and we talked. He said those Germans weren't shooting at my squad but at the guys farther on up the road. He told me this wasn't my time, and I felt a lot better. He really helped me."

Freeman's men rushed a house next to the road to clear it so the British tankers could move up. They took three German prisoners. "We were shaking them down, frisking them for weapons, and I pulled this pen from one of the Germans' pocket. The guy spoke pretty good English. He was upset and screamed his grandmother gave him the pen, and then he spun around and tried to run out of the house." Freeman yelled twice for the man to stop. "I hated to have to get him in the back."

The Germans poured more mortar fire into the area along the road. Lieutenant Dillingham was wounded; shrapnel broke his arm. Fred Long was hit and Sergeant Klebofski was killed sweeping the road with a mine detector in front of the British tanks.

The next line of hedges was infested with Germans. Sergeant Hadley and Sergeant Clark of the lead platoon were killed by snipers within seconds of each other. Leinbaugh, between the two sergeants, hit the ground six feet from the hedge. "My M1 was jammed; the Germans must have written me off and were firing over my head. A BAR man, Coste or Radovich, moved up, fired several bursts, and took care of the problem." More men were wounded. Then word was shouted to hold up. Mines had been found in the road in front of the tanks and had to be removed before the advance continued.

Joe Namey had been close behind Sergeant Hadley when he went down. "Flanagan and I rolled him over. He must have been dead before he hit the ground. We stuck his rifle in the mud and put his helmet on it." Two men crawled over to Clark. He was dead too; hit in the head by a sniper. Joe and the rest of the platoon laid down heavy fire on the next hedgerow. "I was next to a fellow we called Combat, because he always swore he would never go overseas. I kept yelling at him to use his rifle, but he just stuck his head in the ground and said, 'I'm not shooting.' When I ran out of .30 calibers I made him throw me his bandoliers." When Combat received a shrapnel scratch and yelled for an aidman, Namey looked at the minor wound and made the fellow shut up.

"In the next field," Joe remembers, "we got near a German log dugout and one Kraut tried to sneak out and get to a nearby concrete pillbox. I fired off a whole clip, but missed. I'm pretty sure it was Paul Coste, the big fellow from Harvard, our company packrat, who got him with his BAR."

If Coste did hit the man, he wasn't aware of it. He remembers, "I finally got to fire my BAR, but I never had a target. I laid down fire when someone told me to, but I literally never aimed at anyone. I carried that damn monster gun out of some sentimental attachment to my father, who had a wartime job in a factory making BARs. I lugged it all over Louisiana and Europe, but never did anything to help our cause."

Men from the company continued to creep and crawl forward, building up a heavy base of fire, and several Germans broke and ran for it. They were mowed down at such close range that we heard the strike of bullets, like the thwack of a rotten tomato hitting a board fence. A dozen more Germans surrendered in their holes and were ushered toward the rear. One man whose best friend had just been killed took revenge on four prisoners. He said they had jumped him and tried to escape—maybe they had, but he got no more escort duty.

After breaking through the line of German defenses in the hedgerows, the company took more prisoners in Kogenbroich—a village of a dozen or so brick houses and outbuildings. It was approaching dusk by the time the last house was cleared. Gieszl sent the first platoon leader to check the best place to cross the river. He watched a man coming toward him and thought it was his lieutenant. "I yelled at him, but didn't make out the shape of his helmet until he turned. He cut loose with one of those German machine pistols, and I dropped. There was a little wall there, and it seemed like those bricks fell for about thirty minutes. He just sawed it in two. He sure knew how to handle that gun. When I came back up, he was gone."

The company headed for the river and Würm. Our final objective was only a few hundred more yards. But more dug-in Germans were waiting, and they forced the lead squad from the third platoon into a shallow ditch. "We tried to keep going, but were pinned down with point-blank fire only thirty or forty feet away," Leinbaugh says. "The fire was constant, blasting our eardrums, spraying the lip of our hollow with sheets of mud. We couldn't get off more than one shot at a time. We were trapped; we couldn't move forward or backward. I figured that was the end. We'd had it." He remembers a strange altered-state experience. "I was looking down from above and watching the episode unfold in slow motion. I remember feeling completely detached, but terribly sorry for the guys spread-eagled in that little muddy ditch."

The men yelled for the machine gunners, and somehow Gieszl, Brewer, and a couple of other men worked their way into the swale. Radovich, the BAR man, remembers Gieszl was pissed. "He yelled a remark over the noise of those machine guns, something about letting a couple of Germans and a water pistol stop us."

Before anybody could reply, the captain raised to a half-crouch and charged full-tilt for the Germans in the hedgerow. He ran twenty feet before being spun down in a stream of bullets. His helmet sailed through the air; his carbine somersaulted in a wide arc.

"We were in a little swale," Gieszl recalls, "and the Germans were spattering us pretty good. There wasn't any cover at all except in this piece of low ground. I knew where the fire was coming from, and what I was trying to do was to get a lot of concentrated fire on the corner of the hedgerow. I felt if I got over there I would just be there, and I thought I'd go head-on. It would push the Germans' heads down and then I'd be in the same hedgerow with them.

"When I got hit I felt I was falling to the ground, and then I lost consciousness. The next thing I knew somebody was dragging me, and then I passed out again, but I wasn't unconscious for long. I got one grazing round under the ribcage that went in and out. The second bullet caused the damage. It went in my upper arm and out through my chest. And the third round nicked my little finger.

"When they got me back to the ditch and were bandaging me I told Leinbaugh to take over the company—it was just a matter of making a decision and I had confidence he would do okay."

"We'd been crawling forward on our bellies," says Frenchy Lariviere, "with German machine-gun fire strafing the field over our heads, and tracers were lighting the area, so I could see clearly. Gieszl was hit hard; he was spun around and tossed down by the bullets." Gieszl's radioman, John Bratten, was on his belly behind the captain. "Someone yelled the captain was hit and asked if I'd been hit too. I yelled, 'No, not yet,' and wiggled back on my stomach to cover."

When the captain went down, Bill Masters, M Company's mortar observer, crawled over next to Leinbaugh, asked him to hold his carbine, and said if he could get enough covering fire he thought he could pull Gieszl in. The odds of getting either the captain or himself back weren't very good, but he did it with the help of Franklin Brewer, who crawled out behind him. After the two pulled Gieszl in, Leinbaugh saw blood on Masters's shirt collar. "He had two bullet holes in the side of his neck an inch apart, but he insisted it was just a scratch and tied a dirty handkerchief around his neck to stop the bleeding."

Claudie Daniell and his machine gun provided the extra firepower to make the rescue possible. The big machine-gun section chief from Oglesby, Texas, came plowing up through the mud with his gun in one hand, a box of ammo in the other. "The Germans had a lot of men with burp guns dug in there. Most of my men were casualties already, so I was carrying our one good gun by myself." Daniell stuck the barrel over the lip of the draw far enough to cover the base of the hedges hiding the Germans. "I didn't have a loader, so the lieutenant was feeding the belts. The Germans were spattering us with mud, but we kept pouring in rounds till they quit firing. Some of those Germans made the fool mistake of trying to climb out of their holes and take off."

The heavy bursts from Daniell's machine gun added to the fire from the Brownings and M1s routed the Germans—the fighting turned in our favor and the enemy broke. They tried to get away. A few were killed in their holes; more were shot down when they ran. The brutal little exchange occurred in a small area, less than half the size of a football field, and the firing quickly tapered off to occasional rounds.

It was now completely dark. The Germans flooded the area with green parachute flares, and K Company's new CO had to make a number of decisions in a hurry. "The first thing was to get Gieszl to the rear. Then I sent men out to find the platoon leaders so we could talk things over." Bratten and the lieutenant tried reaching battalion on the radio without luck. "I knew trying to cross the river and capture Würm in the dark was out of the question. All three platoons were committed, we had no reserves, and our own artillery was still hitting the town. Without the radio we had no way to stop it."

Erickson and five men were given the job of carrying Gieszl to safety. "I decided to head back for that little village and find a door to carry the captain out. We ran into a lot of machine-gun fire and heavy shelling but we were lucky and didn't bump into any Germans."

After Gieszl was started back, the officers and senior noncoms came up and met with Leinbaugh. "I told Lage to take over the third platoon—that was an easy decision." Leinbaugh then told the men the company was not going to continue the attack and outlined three choices: dig in and hang on where we were, pull back several hundred yards to Kogenbroich, or fall back to the château, where we could be in touch with battalion, and regroup there. The consensus: to defend Kogenbroich. Taking a vote, Leinbaugh realized, was not the approved way to make a military decision, but the men taking part in the impromptu council all had the same thing in mind—the company's welfare.

By twos and threes, K Company began pulling out to the rear. Some men, totally exhausted, had fallen asleep in the mud when the firefight broke off. Stewart recalls the order to withdraw, "which we did without much semblance of order, in the manner that all actions are fought. The pillboxes had the terrain perfectly zeroed in. All the way back we ran this murderous gauntlet—machine-gun fire followed by mortar shelling." To avoid being silhouetted on high ground the men headed through the swampy area next to the river. The water was knee-deep, the underbrush so thick it was almost impassable. Spray from bullets spattered muddy water. Some men stopped, too tired to go on. It seemed an eternity, but finally the ground firmed and from the light of explosions we glimpsed the ruined houses in Kogenbroich.

Morrell found another man in the dark. "We stuck together like brothers. We got hit with heavy machine-gun fire from a pillbox, and the company got pretty well separated. We wandered on back and found a few buildings, but no one else was there. We decided I would stay there to intercept anyone who wandered by, and my partner would go looking for other members of the company. Most of the men filtered in, and we split up among several houses. Four of us tried to get some sleep on a bed, but it overloaded and collapsed during the night. There was considerable joking about what we'd done to the lady of the house's bedroom."

Paul Coste also remembers the uncertainty of that night. "We got into a building, where we huddled in silence, thinking the Germans were just outside. I had no idea of the situation; I was totally dependent on being told what to do. After some hours I offered to go out to look around, a ludicrous thought when I could see so little. I wanted to know what we were doing, but perhaps no one knew. It's still a huge mystery."

The CO found Brewer, Erickson, and Doc Mellon waiting with the captain. Lucht and two men headed to the château to find a stretcher. The men were past exhaustion; they moved inside the houses and slumped to the floors. Most were asleep within minutes.

Pope, groping his way through the dark, finally located the house being used as a CP. "The men were beat out and scattered, and when I came in, here were these two lieutenants arguing who's commanding the company and Gieszl was passed out right down at their goddam feet. The first lieutenant was pissed because he outranked Leinbaugh, who was just a second john, but Leinbaugh says, 'The captain gave me the command of the company, and I'm taking command, that's all.' And I said, 'Will you two sons of bitches finish arguing who's commanding this fucking outfit, so we can get organized.'" Pope started from house to house whispering, "First platoon, first platoon, over here." "Finally I got whatever guys I had left and we dug in."

Lage and Leinbaugh shared a drink of rum and made the rounds of the houses. "We had to shake people to get them back on their feet—most everyone was numbed from exhaustion and no longer able to function. We covered the road with a bazooka team and tried to dig in, but gave up when the holes filled with water and organized a defense from the houses. If German tanks had moved in that night, K Company would have been wiped out."

After Lucht and his crew returned from the château with a stretcher, Gieszl was evacuated. "I think I was conscious for most of the trip, but with the morphine I was in dreamland." At the château a jeep was waiting, and the captain was driven to the battalion aid station.

Dr. Grizzard was expecting Gieszl. "I'd heard George had been hit and was being carried back. I knew George real well from Claiborne days and I was able to get to him right away. Of course, I was primarily concerned with his chest wound." When Gieszl was brought in the doctor noticed the pupils of his eyes were dilated. "I knew he'd been given morphine, and I'm sure it wasn't by one of the company aidmen, because they had strict orders not to administer morphine to men with head or chest wounds." Grizzard gave George plasma. "Then I stuck three-inch adhesive tape over the bullet holes—that was standard procedure." The doctor twisted an empty syrette through Gieszl's collar lapel to alert the doctors at the hospital that he had received morphine. "I put a tag on him noting my original impressions and treatment. George stabilized pretty quickly, and we got him back to division clearing on the next ambulance."

Lucht brought word to Kogenbroich for the new CO to report immediately to battalion. Leinbaugh took Lage with him on the way to the CP. "I carried my M1 and followed along behind Mario, trusting he knew what he was doing. When a flare went up I noticed he didn't have a rifle but was strolling along with both hands in his raincoat pockets. It was a nerve-racking trip, but I felt better when we got to the CP and found Lage had a cocked .45 in one pocket, a Luger in the other."

Fortunately, the Germans did not counterattack during the night, but patrols probed the company's perimeter, and harassing mortar rounds hit the houses. Before dawn the CO returned to the company with orders to hang on. Charlie Company from the First Battalion would come up by noon, and the two companies were to mount a joint attack across the river and then wheel back toward Item and Love companies, hoping to pinch off the pillboxes frustrating I Company's attack. The idea of rifle companies attacking toward each other was absurd—but those were our orders.

Morris Dunn, a Californian who hated cold weather, and Mothershead, automatically dubbed Pop because he was older, joined the company at Kogenbroich. They'd been waiting in a replacement depot in Liége for weeks. "We were just numbers, we didn't know anybody, and I've never felt so alone and miserable and helpless in my entire life— we'd been herded around like cattle at roundup time," Dunn remembered. "On the ride to the front it was cold and raining with the artillery fire louder every mile, and finally we were dumped out in the middle of a heavily damaged town."

The two were told they were now members of the 84th Division. They were put on a jeep, dropped off at a shed, and told to wait for another jeep, which would take them to the front. "Pop and I waited there all alone. We could hear rifle fire and a lot of artillery, but we didn't know if it was ours or theirs. We just waited. Finally a jeep picked us up and we drove to a barn, where we picked up boxes of ammunition for the company. One of the men warned us not to step on the dead German next to the door and told us to dump the gear we wouldn't need, like gas masks and shelter halves. Then we loaded up and made a mad dash, no lights, to another shed. We were told to wait for daylight. Neither Pop nor I had ammunition for our M1s." Just before daybreak a sergeant came running to the shed looking for a rifle. "His was jammed and he pleaded for one of us to trade M1s, but we had the good sense to tell him nothing doing. I found out this guy was Sergeant Smart, and an hour later I was assigned to his squad."

At daybreak Dunn and Mothershead were guided to a small group of brick farmhouses. "You could tell things had been mighty hot. Most of the roofs were gone, all the windows were shot out, two of the houses were burning, shell casings were scattered around the rooms. Lieutenant Leinbaugh came in, took our names, and told us we belonged to K Company and assigned both of us to the third platoon. A sergeant gave us bandoliers of .30 caliber and a couple of hand grenades, making me and Pop feel a lot better."

Minutes later Dunn received his first assignment. "The lieutenant took me to a window and pointed out three houses and told me to go and bring back casualty reports and find out about each platoon's ammo supplies. In the first house I saw my first dead GI—most of his leg was blown off. Several wounded men were waiting to be evacuated. I ran to the second house past dead Germans crumpled in the road and talked to the platoon sergeant. I don't think I ever did make it to the third house." When Dunn reached the company he was cold, tired, and hungry. "But these guys were really in rough shape. They were covered with mud, red-eyed, soaked through, shivering from the cold—they were so tired they could hardly stand."

Bratten spent the night with his SCR (Signal Corps Radio) 300 handset glued to his ear. "The company commander kept trying most of the night to get in touch with battalion. The two of us would crawl out along a ditch away from the houses and try to transmit. Most of the men thought the Germans were triangulating on our radios, but our signal was so weak due to poor batteries that battalion couldn't receive our calls, so I didn't have this fear—if battalion couldn't hear us, how could the Germans? We heard the battalion operator saying, 'Come in, King Company,' but they couldn't hear us."

Sterner, Brewer, and two other men spent the night in a crawl space underneath a house in Kogenbroich. "We had some cover and a decent field of fire, but we were pinned down overnight, and I think Brewer was the only guy who really kept his head," Sterner says. "Brewer was the pacifying effect, he was an atheist, agnostic, whatever you want to call it, but one of the things that has stuck with me all through my life—Brewer was the calmest, the man who kept all our morale from breaking. It has always bugged me; the Christian was supposed to be in control in times of crisis because he had the road to salvation, and then you have to think about Brewer's example. As far as religion is concerned, I think that experience that night with Franklin Brewer under that house made me more of a doubter than anything else in my life."

Stauffer agreed with Sterner's opinion of Brewer. "He was the guy who was coolest under fire. He was a calming influence on everyone. An 88 hit the wall right next to Sterner and myself and then a mortar shell came in a few feet from the two of us—that was the one that got Claudie Daniell, our machine-gun section leader, and killed Henderson. Right afterward the platoon leader came over and said to Daniell, 'Come on, Danny, we're going over here.' And Danny said, 'I can't, sir, I'm wounded.'"

Claudie Daniell was surely the biggest man in the company. "I was around six two, and weighed at least two-twenty. When I got hit pretty bad with mortar fire it took five or six of the guys to haul me out on an old door. I felt sorry for them having to carry me through all that mud and shelling back to the château. When they got me to the aid station and patched me up the medics had to cut my boots off. My feet and legs were black up to the knees. Besides being wounded, I had a real bad case of trench foot."

"The CO," Stewart remembers, "called for volunteers to help evacuate the wounded. We tore down doors, anything to make an improvised stretcher, and a party at a time moved out along the road praying to God the lull would last till we reached the château. The medic we were carrying—hit in the lung—kept moaning and accusing himself of failure because he was not able to treat the wounded and was himself being carried to the rear."

On Thanksgiving Day, November 23, 1944, the battle to capture Würm continued to be orchestrated from Third Battalion headquarters, located in a captured German pillbox on the outskirts of Suggerath. A log kept in the CP during the battle furnished highlights: "After two full days of striving to capture Müllendorf and Würm against heavy odds and without adequate support, the 3d Battalion of the 333d was a battle-weary organization. On the 23d, the plan of attack on Würm remained essentially the same. Company L, however, was to pass through Company I and assume the main effort. Company K on the left was to continue the advance. H hour was 0700A."

Extracts from terse situation reports on Thanksgiving Day reveal the frustrations faced by the British and American commanders.

"0700. In an attempt to support the attack, two British tanks sent up the road toward K Company were disabled by mines.

"1048. Battalion switchboard operator reports no radio communication with the rifle companies.

"Major Simpkins, British liaison officer, says, 'I had to pull my tanks to hull down. What we are doing is waiting for the company commander on the left, K Company, to contact the enemy from the left. I have report there are six German self-propelled guns at coordinates 884666. If there are, we will never get in. We are going around to the left with the infantry and run the absolute risk of being utterly trapped in Müllendorf.'

"British ordered to take their tanks, proceed up the road to Kogenbroich, and make contact with K Company.

"Bn CO asks British major what tanks are doing. Simpkins replies, 'They are parked up there amusing themselves and the Germans are out walking around their pillboxes.'

"1310. Still no communications exist forward of battalion command post. Coordinated movement of tanks and infantry on the left flank has begun. Simpkins reports: 'The leading tank is stuck, has wounded aboard. They want to turn around and get the wounded back, but the tank won't move. We are receiving extremely heavy fire on our left flank from artillery and self-propelled weapons. One tank has been knocked out and the commander killed.'

"1340. Note received from Captain Mitchell I Company. 'Am pinned down. If don't get support won't have any men left!'

"1540. Message intercepted over SCR 300. From C Company CO to CO Company K. 'Everything being held up because the tanks aren't here. See if you can move them.'

"1600. Bn CO to Regiment: 'K Company and C Company are in water to their waists and receiving grazing fire from three pillboxes. One tank knocked out and they are not committing any more tanks there. We gotta have something to knock out these pillboxes, foot troops can't knock them out.'

"Bn CO: 'I'll be commanding a Headquarters Company and part of M Co. pretty soon.'"

Sterner and Stauffer were in an alleyway in Kogenbroich when the British Yeomanry tank pulled up. "The British commander was standing in the turret directing fire at a pillbox; we could see them firing at each other," and then Stauffer saw the Englishman killed. "It just took the top right off of him." The rest of the crew bailed out of their tank unharmed.

At best K Company had been able to round up seventy men for the attack across the Würm with Charlie Company. We had no time for planning, no opportunity to reconnoiter, no satchel charges to use against the pillboxes, no smoke grenades, no artillery observer, not the foggiest idea of the number or location of the German emplacements. We did have seventy muddy M1s and hand grenades.

The Germans let Charlie and King companies get halfway through the swampy river before opening fire. Steady streams of bullets cross-stitched geysers of muddy water across our path, and shrapnel whined through the underbrush. We fired at the pillbox embrasures. Men ducked their heads underwater, trying to escape the fire.

Before a single man reached the far bank of the Würm, Charlie Company's CO yelled across the swamp to Leinbaugh to hold up. He had a working radio and had persuaded the colonel the attack had no chance of success and got approval to pull out. We backed off slowly and retreated again to our little group of houses. Casualties in the two companies were mercifully light. Charlie Company's commander got the okay from his battalion CO to return to Suggerath, and K Company was alone again.

We peered out the windows of our battered houses and waited for the Germans to come after us.

At battalion headquarters, more than a mile to our rear, a rumor started that a German counterattack with tanks was heading toward Suggerath. The regimental log gave details: "3d Bn reported being forced back. A counterattack of tanks and infantry is reputed to have broken through L Co.'s defenses. Excitement terrific: 3d Bn Hq. and Hq. Co. retreated through Geilenkirchen but when situation was cleared up— found that one tank and 15 infantrymen made a counterattack and were forced back—our lines held. Remnants of 3d Bn Hq. and Hq. Co. assembled and taken back to positions in Suggerath. Counterattack beaten off."

Captain Wooten from battalion came up to K Company's perimeter not long before dark with orders to withdraw—not to the château, but all the way back to our starting point near Suggerath. Pope was in the company CP. "The captain was a bit excited, and said, 'We gotta get you guys out of here, you're going to be trapped, you're going to be surrounded.' And I said, 'Shit, captain, let's go—you're telling us what's around here?' We kept off the road, but every fucking place we moved we got shelled on that withdrawal, and I was thinking, We may have a Kraut in this line."

Wooten held no brief for either the battalion or the regimental commander's conduct of the battle. He called the battle a bloody, inexcusable disaster. On the trek back, beyond the château, the Germans loosed a farewell barrage in K Company's direction. Stewart recalls flinging himself to the ground next to the base of a large tree and finding himself face to face with Cal Pahel. As they hunched down together they both realized the explosions no longer frightened them—the shells were landing at least thirty yards away.

5

AFTER ACTION

Our losses were worse than feared. Before dawn on the morning after our withdrawal, we took our first head count. We could locate only forty-eight men from the line platoons. Keller and the CO quizzed the sergeants and concluded that twelve or thirteen men had been killed and at least forty wounded. Thirty men had been sent to the rear with trench foot. A dozen more were simply missing.

Sabia and four men, sent on patrol during the night, had not returned. Martin and Whitson had been missing since the 19th—we now assumed they were dead. A number of men had been sent to the aid station to have their feet examined, and we had no idea how many would be returning to duty.

The company's lost patrol returned at midmorning. They had been spotted and fired on, and Sabia and one of the men had spent the night in a water-filled foxhole. "We sat there, God knows how long, and both fell asleep." It was light when Sabia awoke and stuck his head up to have a look. "A few slugs kicked up dirt around the hole, so I slid down and had a can of C rations." Later the men decided to make a break for it and headed down a road for the American lines. "A Limey halts us and then his sergeant takes us to our own CP. We see our guys and start hugging each other like relatives who hadn't seen each other for years—they figured we were killed or captured."

Hobbling on swollen feet and exhausted, Sabia had lost not one ounce of his bristling self-confidence. He gave his report and argued with the CO he'd be fine after a little sleep. Not until the next day did he agree to go to the aid station, where the medics took one look at his feet and evacuated him. During the day K Company's numbers continued to improve—to about seventy—but half a dozen men were still unaccounted for.

K Company's casualties during the three-day attack cleared through a separate aid station headed by Doc Grizzard, a tall, lanky Virginian, who was the assistant regimental surgeon. Because of the lack of bridges across the Würm, Grizzard's aid station was established on the left side of the river to handle the wounded from both Able and King companies. "On that first day, going through Geilenkirchen, casualties weren't too heavy," Doc remembers. "We took care of a few men from A Company and a number of wounded Germans. Then when K Company attacked, the aid station was moved forward to a farmhouse alongside the road dividing the American and British zones."

Forty years later Dr. Grizzard still remembers K Company's attack up the Würm valley. "For the medics that was the worst single experience of the entire war. As far as I'm concerned K Company was wiped out."

Grizzard tended his patients on the floor of a battered farmhouse. "We didn't even have a table to work on and not enough bandages, splints, or plasma. I had three enlisted medics helping; one held a Coleman lantern over the patient so I could see to work. We tried to stabilize the casualties, perform skilled first aid, and then get them back as quickly as possible to the collecting company on the far side of Geilenkirchen. Depending on the man's condition, he would then be sent further back to an evac or field hospital with X-ray machines and operating facilities."

The wounded, Americans and Germans alike, were treated on a priority basis. When the number of casualties increased, Grizzard asked regiment for help. A New York dentist, Dr. Spielman, came up to assist, along with Blackmon and Cowsert, the regimental chaplains. Their jeeps, with litter racks, began shuttle runs between the aid station and division clearing.

The British gave vital help. "They set up machine guns around the aid station to provide security, and at night when their tankers were heading back to gas up, they stopped and picked up a load of wounded." The British also brought back dead GIs on the rear decks of their tanks. "I had to certify and tag the dead men and then the Graves Registration teams would pick up the bodies and take them to a collecting point. The aid station was shelled regularly, but none of the patients was wounded a second time that I remember."

During the second night of the battle the regimental surgeon, Major McArthur, came across the river to check on Grizzard's situation and left "deeply disturbed by the number of casualties. He said he was going to persuade the regimental CO to come up and see for himself how bad things were."

The regimental commander drove to the aid station the next morning.

"He looked me over. 'Captain Grizzard,' he said, 'you haven't shaved.'"
Grizzard told the colonel he'd been working three days and nights without sleep, and hadn't had time to eat, let alone shave. "Then the colonel chewed me out because the aid station wasn't properly located." The colonel seemed unsure of the location of the front-line companies. "He asked me where K Company was located, and I told him Leinbaugh and about twenty-five or thirty men—all that was left of the company—had been ordered to pull back and were on the next hill with the British."

The doctor had just returned from a visit to the company. "I told the colonel I was terribly concerned about the trench-foot problem—something had to be done right away. I suggested as diplomatically as possible that the colonel might want to talk to the K Company CO and see the condition of the men for himself. He gave some excuse about having to get back to his CP—he never did go beyond the aid station."

During his visit to K Company, Captain Grizzard had carried an armload of dry socks. "I looked at the men's feet. Some of those men had been in water-filled holes for two or three days. It was demoralizing—I saw no more than twenty or thirty guys that could be called fit for duty. Some could barely walk and had to be sent back right away. Most everyone was in bad shape, but just couldn't be spared. Leinbaugh asked me if I had any idea how he could get replacements for the company. Looking back, it seems a strange question, but none of us had confronted that kind of problem before."

A most unlikely partnership was forged for the attack on Geilenkirchen. The newest, rawest American division in all of Europe was paired with the Sherwood Rangers Yeomanry Regiment, seasoned veterans who had fought at Tobruk and El Alamein. If at first the British were concerned about the Railsplitters' lack of experience, they carefully concealed their reservations. When the battle was over the rangers called the brief alliance with the Americans at Geilenkirchen "a great and proud partnership."

The men in K Company found the Englishmen casual, competent, and remarkably cool under fire. Late Thanksgiving afternoon when K Company pulled back near Suggerath, the rangers' CO motioned Leinbaugh aside. "Your fellows are making my chaps nervous; they hit the ground every time a shell comes in."

"I admitted we were a bit nervous," Leinbaugh recalls. "I told him the company had lost more than half its men and nobody had had a minute's sleep during the past three days, so we were a bit edgy." The British officer was sympathetic. "Remember you chaps can't win the war all by yourselves. There's an awful lot of hills between here and Berlin. You're going to find good days and bad days for killing Jerries—if it's a bad day you just have to wait for a good one."

Back at Regiment a replacement officer, John Campbell, had volunteered for K Company when he learned that Leinbaugh, an old friend from Knox College, had taken over as CO. Late Thanksgiving night a jeep dropped Campbell off at the company area. He edged into the shelter carved into the hillside—K Company's CP.

The Coleman lantern picked out faces. Leinbaugh looked older, years away from a college campus. He drew rapidly on a cigarette; another burned in a C-ration tin beside him. He looked up, astounded and pleased. "Johnny Campbell, what are you doing here?"

After greetings Campbell had a jumble of thoughts about the men in this crowded little hole in a hill. Leinbaugh and the NCOs looked worn out and worried; they told him about their losses. But the situation seemed under control. Two noncoms made an immediate impression: Bert Christensen, the platoon sergeant for the fourth platoon. "For some strange reason I thought, I'll bet he's a good tennis player." And Franklin Brewer, a lot older than anyone Campbell expected to meet in a rifle company.

Campbell knew that in the safety of the CP, he wasn't afraid. But could he handle what was ahead? He figured he was lucky to have other people to worry about, to keep him busy, so he wouldn't have so much time to worry about himself.

Later that night a trip with Leinbaugh to the pillbox serving as battalion CP further complicated his thoughts. To Campbell the battalion commander looked like a tired, haggard old man. And the CO of I Company, Captain Mitchell, looked even wearier. But somehow Mitchell appeared to have a reserve of strength to draw on that was unavailable to the colonel. "I didn't have any basis for making those judgments, let alone any right to do so. I don't know what led me to those conclusions. But that was what was in my mind when we left the pillbox to go back to the company."

Campbell's new platoon was less than half strength. The platoon leader and platoon sergeant were gone, but Sabia was there. Campbell figured he was lucky to wind up with John, but the luck didn't last long. It was the next morning that Sabia was evacuated with trench foot.

None of the men in the 84th had the necessary experience to evaluate that first battle, but the British tankers agreed the fighting beyond Geilenkirchen in the Siegfried Line was as violent as any in their long experience. Their regimental history describes the country as difficult, "and it was not possible to get the tanks off the road; progress was slow. The American infantry were pinned down by fire from pillboxes and the Americans found it difficult, even at night, to supply their forward troops, or to evacuate the wounded. We were plagued by the appalling squishiness of the ground. It was almost impossible to manoeuvre."

The tankers, out long before first light, "did not replenish till long after dark—the replenishment often being carried out by artificial moonlight." The history continues, "Everyone was dead-beat from lack of sleep. By the 23rd our composite Squadron had only five tanks left. The weather was getting worse and worse. Every inch of the ground where our tanks were bogged was covered by enemy machine guns firing at night on fixed lines."

Lieutenant General Sir Brian Horrocks, the British corps commander in charge of the operation, noted that in order to take Geilenkirchen, the Allies would have to break through the heavily defended Siegfried Line. He felt this was a lot to expect from troops who had no previous battle experience. "The 84th was an impressive product of American training methods which turned out division after division complete, fully equipped, and trained for war."

But Horrocks was sharply critical of the American commanders. "Their staff work, however, was not yet geared to battle conditions." When the 84th came under his command and was positioned in the line prior to its attack, Horrocks went forward to "smell this new American battlefield and have a look at their objectives." It became obvious to the English general that U.S. corps and divisional commanders rarely, if ever, visited their forward troops. "This was something I had to put right without delay because of the appalling wintry conditions which the 84th were likely to meet in this, their first experience of battle, opposed by experienced, battle-hardened German troops."

Horrocks was deeply impressed by his contacts with the Railsplitters' GIs. "The 84th Division, though completely raw, was composed of splendid, very brave, tough young men. I knew from past bitter experience that they were faced by a very, very unpleasant introduction to war. After capturing the heavily defended Siegfried Line they would have to stand up to vicious counterattacks by two first-class German divisions, the 15th Panzer and the 10th SS."

Determined the 84th should have all possible assistance in its first battle, the British general "gave them my most experienced armoured regiment, the Sherwood Rangers Yeomanry, commanded by Stanley Christopherson, some flails, and flame tanks from the 79th Division, and above all the support of my superb Artillery Corps."

Senior American officers, Horrocks observed, did not seem to worry much about the welfare of their troops; and regimental *esprit de corps* was largely absent or at least not obvious. He was greatly concerned to find that the American troops in the front line were not getting hot meals in contrast to the forward units of his British 43rd Division.

After K Company pulled back to its original position and was resting in farmhouses shared with the British, General Horrocks came forward to confer with his tank commanders. None of our American commanders, not even our own battalion commander, ventured that far forward.

In Horrocks's opinion, the battle of Geilenkirchen was one of the hardest-fought actions of the whole war at the battalion, company, and platoon levels. "I was filled with admiration for the extreme gallantry displayed by the raw GIs of the 84th Division. If only their administration and staff arrangements had been up to the level of their courage, the veteran German troops might well have had a bloody nose."

Horrocks was not alone in his criticism of the conduct of the battle beyond Geilenkirchen. A tall young Irishman, a captain from the Ninth Army's historical section, observed the battle's progress from our Third Battalion's CP located in a pillbox near Suggerath.

His name was John J. O'Grady, and after the battle he prepared a lengthy memorandum to his headquarters. "On the 21st, 22nd, and 23rd of November, the Third Battalion, 333d Infantry Regiment repeatedly launched unsuccessful attacks from the vicinity of Suggerath, Germany, toward the village of Würm, Germany. One fact became obvious from the start. The battle was being directed by telephone and radio and at the close of the three-day period I found my knowledge of the battle to be much more coherent than I dreamed it could be."

Captain O'Grady noted that the actions of the 333rd Infantry Regiment in its venture up the Würm valley were most successful through the city of Geilenkirchen and into the town of Suggerath. "But after that time they were doomed to failure. For three days the Third Battalion, 333d Infantry knocked its head against a stone wall." O'Grady became persuaded that the battalion commander was in a hopeless situation.

"The battalion," O'Grady pointed out, "was attacking up a river valley with an extremely narrow sector. The battalion went into action with its companies at full strength, 186 riflemen, and after the first day these companies consisted of one-half that, and on the third day it was necessary to count supply personnel and cooks to record 50 names on the company rosters."

O'Grady's report continued, "Trench foot was a factor, but the important point is that when the 23rd of November arrived the battalion was attacking a superior German force entrenched on an excellent position. The only thing that higher headquarters contributed to the debacle was pressure, and God only knows where the pressure started, perhaps Corps or perhaps Army. It had the effect of ordering men to die needlessly."

The report concluded: "Tactics and maneuver on battalion or regimental scale were conspicuous by their absence. It never seemed to occur to anyone that the plan might be wrong; but rather the indictment was placed on the small unit commanders and the men who were doing the fighting. The companies went into battle against the formidable Siegfried Line with their T/O weapons and nothing more. Hand grenades and rifle bullets against pillboxes. The 84th Division walked into the most touted defensive line in modern warfare without so much as the benefit of a briefing by combat officers who had been fighting the problem for some months and had found workable solutions."

*   *   *

The home front's version of the battle in *Time* magazine's "Western Front" section of November 27 differed considerably. "From behind Geilenkirchen to the Aachen-Duren hills the German sky throbbed to the thunder of more than 4000 aircraft, the German earth shook under the bolts of 10,000 tons of bombs, the blows of 20 tons of shells a minute. How any German could stand up to battle after the opening blow was beyond the belief of those who watched. But Germans did stand up to fight and die, to cling tenaciously to the German soil, to patch the breaches with more men against a grinding weight as the battle went through three smoke-clouded days and fiery nights.

"Geilenkirchen was a classic of teamwork; Germans were trapped between U.S. and British units. Within a few hours American GIs riding British tanks had pushed on into the Würm valley for three miles. The crust had softened. There were signs of limited German withdrawals."

The Associated Press story on the Geilenkirchen battle appeared under the headline: "Railsplitters, in First Battle, Chalk Up 'Perfect Operation.' "

A less Olympian view of the battle came from K Company's Bruce Baptie. "That attack up the Würm valley was balls-ass stupid."

The Army's official history, *The Siegfried Line Campaign*, reported that the 333rd and 334th regiments, which were involved in the Geilenkirchen battle, suffered more than 2,000 casualties in less than a week. The history reports 169 men killed, 752 men missing, more than 1,000 men wounded, and another 500 evacuated as nonbattle casualties, primarily from trench foot.

George Gieszl

Robert J. Martin

George Pope

Adrian Wheeler

John Sabia

Franklin Brewer

Don Phelps

Ed Stewart

Doc Mellon

Dempsey Keller

Dr. Sam Grizzard   Jim Grafmiller

Keith (Doughhead) Lance

Jimmie Clark (left) and Mutt Tomlinson. Both were KIA.

Mario Lage (right, on Guadalcanal) and with granddaughter

Norman Long

6

BACK TO GEILENKIRCHEN

Late on Friday, November 24, K Company got the word to pull back to Geilenkirchen. Orders were to complete the move soon after midnight. So the remnants of the company slouched through rain and mud, back toward the town's derelict buildings. When the relief began, the tactical situation was confused. But one thing was plain. On beyond Suggerath was a piece of ground that two days ago K Company had been told to take and hold at all cost. We had taken it, and the cost was high. Now we were giving it back. The ground, like the men who took it, was expendable.

K Company, the last unit in the battalion to close back to Geilenkirchen, approached the company area—six or seven brick and stone houses across from the gutted shell of a church. From a doorway an MP sounded off, "Put out those cigarettes." A few men glanced up curiously. The MP repeated, louder now, "Put out those goddam cigarettes!" Pope waited until he was almost opposite the man, then suggested, "Why don't you shut your fucking mouth?" That exchange marked the company's new attitude toward the rear echelon, that part of the Army defined by J. A. Craft as "any son of a bitch behind my foxhole."

The first men in each house moved into the safety of the cellar. Stragglers took the first floor. The roofless upper stories remained vacant. No platoon needed much more space than that of a single building. Even before guards were posted, the men had slumped to the floors, sacked out at last.

*   *   *

The kitchen crew, farther to the rear, packed to join the rest of the company. J. O. Smith waited with his jeep and trailer while Burkett, the mess sergeant, and First Cook George Gehrman checked to see that the stoves were securely lashed on a two-and-a-half-ton truck from the motor pool. Then the whole kitchen crew picked up their M1s and mounted the truck.

This was their first trip near the front. The sky held just enough light for Gehrman to catch glimpses of strange pyramidal profiles in the fields—the West Wall's dragon's teeth. In Geilenkirchen, the trucks nosed through rubble, then stopped near the church and the row of buildings where the company slept. Gehrman climbed down and checked out possible locations for the kitchen.

He could see the church was a shambles, with "roof.and walls shot up, bricks, stones, plaster all over." Then he noticed a ladder against the church wall. "The Germans left it there for a trap," Gehrman thinks. "Zeroed in on it. If a GI climbed it they could see we were there. Inside was an organ. Hadn't been hit, but beside it was a big shell—hadn't exploded. I told my men, 'Keep the hell away from it. Don't touch it.' So we set the kitchen up in the churchyard. Muddy? Maybe even worse than that goddam mud-in-your-ass company street back in Camp Howze."

Men plunked the stoves down in the mud close to the church and pitched a tarp to screen off the kitchen. Cooks pumped up the tanks, lit the stoves. Coffee on to boil, then with a single chop of a cleaver Gehrman opened a tin of bacon. The bacon was salty as hell. He had to soak it to make it edible. The rest of the rations: powdered milk and powdered eggs. "We'd mix a batch of scrambled eggs from that stuff and hold our breath when we were cooking them," Gehrman says. "Terrible smell."

Gehrman had been hearing casualty reports. He knew that Gieszl had been hit, and Jim Grafmiller, the company clerk, had given Gehrman other names. Before drawing rations at battalion, he and Burkett had checked morning-report information on company strength. A lot of good men gone, Gehrman thought.

But he wasn't prepared for the sight of the ones who did drift in for their first hot food in days. They hardly looked like the same men. And so many were missing—there would be a lot of food left over after that meal. "Oh-oh," Gehrman said to himself as what was left of the company passed through the chow line, "somebody fucked up."

Maiuri, the supply sergeant, and Zilliox, his armorer-artificer, had trucked the company's field packs up to the men. Then in midmorning, Keller sent word that Louis Ciccotello was waiting in the church.

Chick was the mail clerk. When he left Philly for the Army he brought along the tools of his civilian trade—scissors, brush, clippers, comb—and doubled as the company barber. Friendly and cheerful, he used to sing, "I met her in the park one day, in the merry, merry month of May."

Gehrman, who had to listen to him, thought Chick "couldn't sing for shit, but it was fun, and he was always trying."

Chick had brought up a sack of mail, the company's first since entering combat. In minutes the men clustered near him. Someone called out, "About time, Chick." Another did the usual singsong "We've been waiting for you." But most were quiet as mail call began.

Names of a handful of early casualties had reached Chick, and he'd made an effort to remove their letters when, before coming up, he'd sorted the mail by platoon. Looking at the assembled company, he saw how the ranks had thinned, and he was shaken. Still, he pulled out the stacks of letters and began tentatively calling out names.

John Bratten had several letters to open. "One was a note from my sister Sue informing me that she was buying me a twenty-five-dollar War Bond every month. Then she added that she was to be the beneficiary in the event of my death."

The unclaimed letters accumulated. Chick was bothered, but pressed on. His face showed relief when Brewer accepted his mail. But too many of the letters to the other noncoms, the men Chick had known the longest, couldn't be delivered. Leinbaugh, leaning against a church pew nearby, had to break the news.

Then came the packet of letters for one of the sergeants who'd been killed. Chick's eyes welled with tears. He turned and with the slight stammer that sometimes came into his speech said, "I'm sorry, lieutenant."

"That's okay, Chick, we'll take it from here." And Leinbaugh and Keller completed the task.

Back at division those who worked on the after-action report for that period began their narrative of operations with this movement report: "When the month of November 1944 opened, the 84th Infantry Division was still in southern England. When it closed, the 84th Infantry Division had been fighting in Germany for thirteen days." For the final sentence they wrote: "The combat teams lived up to their name. Officers and men, almost all of them in action for the first time, made history."

Morning reports show that making history at the company level was a costly business. The company clerks did their best to keep the records up to date, but they were sitting back in Holland and only got the word in bits and pieces. "The first day or two," Jim Grafmiller, K Company's clerk, says, "it was quite a mess when we got information on all the casualties up there. Of course, we knew that something was definitely happening. And yet when it did come it was quite a shock to me."

Keller tried to keep Grafmiller posted on each day's events. Information also came to him from regiment's medical detachment, the division clearing station, and Graves Registration. British sources relayed names of casualties who had filtered back through their lines. One thing for sure—there was no Claiborne barracks bed check to help simplify the count. So the statistics were rough, and the numbers overestimated company strength.

On Sunday, Leinbaugh and Keller jeeped back to Palenberg to have a session in a further attempt to straighten out company strength for the morning report. They'd each heard that the division had over a thousand men in limbo—missing or not otherwise accounted for—and they felt extra pressure to get accurate information. Before the company jumped off, Keller and other first sergeants had been told one of their primary jobs was "accounting for every person in the company. If we didn't— well, that was a good way to become a rifleman." And Leinbaugh had gotten the impression that if the problem of missing men wasn't straightened out, both company commanders and first sergeants would be courtmartialed.

As Keller quizzed Leinbaugh about the men, they began to grasp just what a beating the company had taken. Keller said another three days like that and that would be it. There'd be nobody left. Grafmiller later came up to Geilenkirchen to make a further check, but his visit didn't solve the "bookkeeping" problems. The totals, though, were becoming clearer.

Those records, as inaccurate as they were even after many corrections, show that between the 19th and 24th of November, eleven men from K Company had been killed and forty-two wounded. Two were MIA. After the names of eighteen others the morning report showed the abbreviation "LD NBC," meaning "line of duty, nonbattle casualty." These included hemorrhoids, hernia, acute appendicitis, trench foot, exhaustion, and two self-inflicted wounds. One SIW appeared on the morning report as "Slightly wounded, gunshot, accidental." That bothered Al Oyler, but he holds no grudge today. "It wouldn't be all that difficult if I saw him now," Oyler claims. "It's a mental thing more than anything else. Besides, he might have been more harm to us in the field if he'd stayed. It's just that there were some who could take it, some who couldn't."

No ranks were spared. The captain and one lieutenant had been wounded. Two of the four original platoon sergeants were out, and the men who had replaced them were also gone. Seven of the fourteen combat staff sergeants had been killed, wounded, or injured in action. With six buck sergeants gone, PFCs were now squad leaders. One aidman had been seriously wounded. And nearly half the privates who had swung out toward the château three days earlier didn't make it back when the company returned to Geilenkirchen near midnight on Friday, November 24.

K Company had been just one among many. In Operation Clipper, the fight to eliminate the Geilenkirchen salient, the division and other components of the Ninth Army had taken heavy casualties. This had been anticipated. On November 14, a Ninth Army report informed the commanding general that a cemetery for the Army had been located near Margraten, Holland: "The new cemetery will have an initial capacity of 7,200. This site can be developed into an excellent cemetery properly befitting the burial of Allied dead." A steady downpour had, however, turned the area into a sea of mud. There, in the last week of November, the bodies of eleven K Company men—Leroy Goats, Lyle Williams, Thomas Hogan, James Clark, Lewis Goins, William Hadley, Robert Henderson, Raymond Klebofski, Pete Visconte, Bruno Ytuarte, and John Gima—were placed in temporary graves beneath rough, unpainted crosses.

In Geilenkirchen the men cleaned weapons and repaired equipment. Then some checked on friends in other platoons. In the street they picked up Allied propaganda leaflets still plentiful there. These warned in German that Geilenkirchen was surrounded and advised the enemy to surrender. The message on the flimsy sheets ended with the threat: "Only as prisoners of war can you escape annihilation."

Diaries were forbidden, and letters home were censored to make sure they didn't give away any military secrets. Still, in basements, working by the light of candles, or lanterns, or improvised torches—gasoline-filled bottles with rags serving as wicks—they did write. And what they couldn't say is felt in their restraint.

After that first mail call, a third platoon rifleman, John Bowe—Johnny in the company, Jack to his family—wrote home:

Dear Mom, Dad, & Bob,
Hi everybody, it's me again, after a short pause for station identification. . . . I'm still okay and going strong and hope that you are also. The mailman came through with eight letters for me. Boy, everyone reported—you, Dad, John Sweeny, Mary, & Eve. . . .

Dad, it's a month from Christmas now and quite a bit different than last year, but do everything you can to make things good for Mom and Bob. Take care of them both and yourself for me and I'll make out okay. . . .

That's about all there is to say for now—except how was Thanksgiving. I know you'll write about your turkey and all, but we had ours too. It wasn't quite like any other Thanksgiving I've ever had, but the idea and the turkey were both there so that's what matters most.

Mom, I'm going to sign off for now. I'll write again when I have another chance. Until then take care and don't worry about me cause I'll be okay. Until the next time.

Love to all,
Jack

Even Leinbaugh found time to write his parents that he was "now commanding a rifle company . . . busy and working hard, but okay." And naturally he reported the Stateside link. "Amazing thing happened. Was in my dugout and a new officer walked in—Johnny Campbell from school. . . . One of my best friends!"

*　　*　　*

The key questions that many of the men asked themselves—how did we do? how well did *I* do? and what about the future?—did not show up in letters home. Even now, though, thoughts linked to these same questions persist.

For Al Oyler, everything started over. "In the first few days we threw the book away. It didn't work the way we'd been taught. In combat we learned from what was going on at the time."

Doc Mellon thought the company was "green as goose shit. We knew the manuals, but we didn't know what was happening because we'd never been under fire before. Company K was an okay company, but it didn't have a horseshoe." He took some satisfaction in his own performance: "A person really don't know what to expect until he gets that baptism of fire. Knowing you can keep cool, that you have the initiative—that's pretty good. You learn that in a crisis you can do the things you were supposed to do and come through okay. It's pretty good knowing you could get scared as hell and yet still cope."

The company was "reasonably competent, not lost or inept," for George Lucht. "But how do you judge this, what do you compare it with? I had a blind faith in what was going on." To make combat more manageable, Lucht concentrated on his own immediate concerns, "like football back in college. Like playing weak-side halfback on defense—I did my job and didn't worry about anyone else. It was zone coverage, and I covered my zone."

The company's Guadalcanal veteran looked at it from a broader and more stoic perspective. "The casualties were a little higher than normal," Mario Lage says. "That was to be expected in a new outfit. The men had a lot to absorb quickly. One thing they had to learn, casualties come in bunches—like grapes. We didn't get the artillery support we needed. And maybe our own weapons training wasn't really that good. If I were hiring mercenaries, I would pay BAR men two or three times as much as ordinary riflemen."

This had been the first action for the first platoon's sergeant, George Pope. After that first night of shelling beyond Geilenkirchen he thought, "If I live through this goddam thing I'll live through anything. They were concentrated in the area and came so close they would just raise you off the ground. And there was no hole to hide in." Pope's experiences in a later war provided a benchmark for comparison: "That was the worst shelling I've ever been in. That includes Korea. To me World War II had to be the roughest. I don't give a shit what they write in the books. But Korea or Europe—it's the same. It's a matter of survival. To dig a hole, or not to dig a hole. Or you're too tired to dig a hole, or you don't give a shit."

A delayed reaction to a tree burst caught up with Jim Sterner when he got back to Geilenkirchen, but that may have been a turning point for him. "I had a real shaking spell outside the church there after we came back," he remembers. "I squatted there and leaned on the church. And I shook all over for a few minutes. I figured, 'My God, I'm goin' nuts, I'm breaking.' Then I said to myself, 'Nah, you're not going to break.' That moment is when I decided, 'Hey, I'm going to be all right!' That was probably it.

"In the down times of my life, the rough moments, of which I've had a few, that bottom line I've always come up with, 'Christ, this isn't so bad. You could be back there under a tree burst.' That was when I was most miserable, when I came closest to saying, 'What the hell, I'd give it all up.' But it was a bad day."

There probably wasn't a man in the company who didn't make his own private reckoning. What it all meant, that first combat, was by no means clear. Each man tried to add it up in his own mind, but there was no settled agreement on the sum. Except for efforts by company headquarters, nobody had made a head count. But they didn't need to; they'd all lost friends. Near the back of the mind was the thought "I survived." Just behind that, and not very well concealed was the question "Yes, but for how long?"

K Company's war was very different from the one we'd been trained to fight back at Claiborne. Though it was too soon to size it all up, some things had definitely changed. Gone was the blind faith in the manuals, in the infinite wisdom of senior officers. What counted instead was experience, sheer bloody experience. K Company had begun to learn the simple skills of the infantryman the hard way.

The job of getting K Company back up to strength now began. Battalion, regiment, division—in fact, the whole Ninth Army—faced the same task. Ninth Army brass tried to speed up what they referred to as "the requisitioning process for replacements." A request to the headquarters for American troops in Europe brought this teletype:

COMBAT UNITS ARE AUTHORIZED TO BASE DAILY REPL REQUISITIONS ON ANTICIPATED LOSSES FORTY EIGHT HOURS IN ADVANCE TO EXPEDITE DELIVERY OF REPLS PD TO AVOID BUILDING UP OVERSTRENGTH ESTIMATES SHOULD BE MADE WITH CARE PD AUTHORITY WILL NOT REPEAT NOT BE EXTENDED TO ANY UNIT NOT ACTUALLY ENGAGED IN COMBAT

SIGNED: EISENHOWER

This requisitioning based on anticipated losses was, however, SOP only from the 14th to the 22nd of November. The change on the 22nd stemmed from "the critical shortage of replacement personnel throughout the Ground Forces Replacement System."

On the 25th and 26th, K Company's shortage was partially solved. Twenty-two replacements came in on the 25th, another thirty-two on the following evening. This scene would be repeated more than half a dozen times in the months that followed. But never again would as many arrive in a single shipment as came in on each of these two days.

Two or three men in the doorways of the K Company houses greeted the first arrivals. "Go back!" they called. "You'll be sorrreee!" Most were too dispirited to pay attention to the newcomers. Carrying M1s and packs, the replacements climbed down from the canvas-topped trucks, looked about them at the devasted area, and clustered in a loose formation in the churchyard. "Sound off when I call your name," Keller growled at them.

Anybody could see they were needed, even though there wasn't a single noncom among the new arrivals. The little guy with the glasses, Walter Roman from the Bronx, was the only PFC. The rest were privates. They would all start at the bottom, but there was plenty of opportunity for advancement.

For these new men, K Company was the final destination of a journey begun months earlier. All had come through replacement channels, though not all had followed the same path. From the time their routes forward began, they hadn't had a chance to feel they belonged anywhere, but now they belonged to K Company. They would look around at the men who'd already been in the fight, size them up from their own perspectives. And they would wonder how they themselves would fit in and how they would do when the time came.

For Clayton Shepherd, who came up on Sunday, the routine back at the repple depple was a familiar one. They had assembled outside the barracks, and then a clerk turned to his roster. Shepherd, one of ten prospective K Company men whose last names began with S, had come to England as an artilleryman, but left in September an infantryman. Each replacement depot since then had brought this wiry nineteen-year-old from Alexandria, Virginia, closer and closer to the front. He knew that one near Liége was the last. "They had our names on long sheets," he says, "in alphabetical order. If your last name began with A, buddy, you'd had it. You were gone. But I was glad to climb on a truck and get away from there. Those buzz bombs the Germans had been shooting over were landing so close that they put out the window lights. It's almost as bad to go through the replacement centers as to get up there fighting. I'm telling you, by the time I got up to the front line I was about dead. And here all I wanted to do was get over there and shoot.

"I trained in the artillery in Mississippi for thirteen months. Then they sent us overseas to a place called Codford, England, and they handed me an M1 rifle. I didn't even know what one looked like. I always carried a little carbine as an artilleryman. But they give me that M1 gun, give me the nomenclature of it, made me shoot it, disassemble it. And then they said, 'You're a doughboy now.'

"They took us out and showed us a mortar which another man shot. We sat and watched him; we didn't drop the shells in the tube. But he says, 'All right, you're a mortarman now.' I thought it was awful strange, but what the hell, I didn't know nothing about this infantry training."

On his first night with the company, Shepherd was hungry, so he walked to the churchyard and peered around the tarpaulin protecting the stoves. Shepherd had a slight hearing problem, but he got the message when the man behind the tarp leveled a rifle at his stomach and said, "There ain't nothin' to eat 'round here." Shepherd took off.

Back at the fourth platoon he laid out his gear for the night. Then he studied the K Company men who had come back from the line. Nobody had any insignia on, he noticed. He couldn't tell officers and noncoms from privates. But he could tell they had been in a fight: "They were all shook up. Nervous. They said, 'This man got his head blowed off, this man his arm blowed off,' and all that. And I thought, Jesus Christ, what am I getting into here? They shouldn't have told us new guys that. They scared the hell out of me before I even got started. We was kind of scared of them, too; they were combat men. We figured, you talk too rash to them, they'll knock hell out of you. I thought they'd been up there two or three months. And they told me all that stuff, and one man was crying, and I thought, Jesus Christ, is this going to happen to me too? I was more scared than anybody in all the damn branches of the service."

Walking into the church in Geilenkirchen that Sunday, Gene Amici thought it was like a barn: "Just bare floors with guys stretched out on both sides, laying down on blankets, and I—the new man—just sat back and watched." He was a long way from New York's Fulton Street, where, before the Army, day in and day out he'd cut and polished diamonds.

When he'd been inducted nine months earlier the Army acknowledged his craftsmanship by training him as an armorer-artificer. But in K Company Zilliox had a lock on that relatively safe slot, so Amici filled one of the First Platoon's many vacancies for riflemen. He'd watch and listen and figure things out: "Everybody was talking about the first big combat and how 'we shot these guys and put a knife in them' and all that jazz. Being only twenty-two, I thought they were the big-time pros. Later on I could see the true colors of some of the fellows come out. On the average, though, they were pretty quiet. You had a few loudmouths that exaggerated. When you bring in a bunch of recruits, the talk gets louder and more boisterous to make an impression. So naturally you're going to be impressed. You sit back and listen. You think, Oh, God, these are the old pros. So you listen to what they've done."

Even though some of them laid it on a bit thick, these old hands were the ones with experience, the ones who could give some clue as to what this new situation was all about. So new men figured it was worth sticking close to them. One third platoon newcomer bedded down on a pile of coal in a room with the veterans. He preferred being with the old hands, rather than in more comfortable quarters occupied exclusively by replacements.

Another new arrival, older and more experienced than others, maintained a greater distance. Jerry Dunne's MOS was for antitank gunner, but he wound up in K Company. He'd had six years in the National Guard, had been a noncom regimental recruiter in New York's old 69th—the Fighting Irish. Jerry would have stayed with them, but he got married. He'd worked in New York City through the Depression and had just made the big move to Connecticut. He and his wife Kay had been there nine months, his son was just nine months old, and Jerry was twenty-nine when he got called up. He was pissed off because of his age and because he was just getting going after the move when they called him up.

Jerry arrived in Geilenkirchen a buck private. He looked around him and didn't like what he saw. "The company's morale was gone. They looked like they needed men. They'd got beat, I'd heard that. But I wasn't one to try to find out, and anyway I didn't have time to find out. Everybody was young. Everybody except Mario; he didn't seem young. But they looked like a bunch of kids to me. And the officers looked like kids."

In the third platoon Jerry told Lage, "I'm an antitank gunner. I don't belong here. I don't want to be here." But Lage said, "You're stuck here, and we need you."

Mario started Jerry as a runner, told him about the possibility for stripes. He's trying to con me, Jerry thought, but he took a liking to Mario anyway; Lage knew what he was talking about. But Jerry didn't feel he belonged to K Company. From the start he decided to be a loner, didn't want to latch on to anyone. He made the decision not to get too close. He told himself it was a selfish decision, but a guy could get hurt if he got too close to a buddy.

Dunne and the others who came up to K Company that weekend had been simply numbers on a "Replacement Stockage Report" in Ninth Army's G-1 section, just pegs to fill a lot of empty holes. When the men were in the replacement channels their movements had at times appeared haphazard. Now, no matter what their route, they had completed a trip, had reached a destination. The company now was their job and their home. And for these men there were new things to be learned and old habits to be forgotten.

Lieutenant Wilson greeted the replacements for the first platoon with this instruction: "Don't call me Lieutenant Wilson, just call me Willie. And *don't* salute." Leo Topel remembered basic training back in Fort McClellan. There everybody bore down on military discipline, so he wondered what the hell kind of officer this Wilson was. But Wilson made him feel at home and also gave him practical advice about German pistols: "Don't get caught with a P-38. If the Krauts get you, they'll shoot you right then." And Topel also got a job. Someone gave him a bazooka. Bazookas and BARs went to the new men—nobody wanted the things.

Then on his first night he stood guard, sharing a post with Sworen, another new replacement. One shell came in that night and knocked Sworen flat, but did no damage. "My God," he said to Topel, "those things are dangerous."

Among Sunday's arrivals, two were buck sergeants and three were corporals. Then on the 28th two officers were transferred out and three replacement officers came in. Lieutenants Zadnik and Meek went to platoons. Captain Bradford took over as company commander—the third CO in a week. The new noncoms and officers brought rank, but no combat experience.

The company stayed in Geilenkirchen until the following Wednesday. The men worked on their weapons, and some went to Maiuri, the supply sergeant, for new ones. As the weather turned colder, Maiuri also told men who were lacking GI overcoats to help themselves from the packs of the men who were no longer with the company—just not to take any personal items. In the church Father Sullivan served Mass; Joe Namey helped as altar boy. Then the church became a theater. The special service people showed a movie that Richard Heuer, one of Sunday's replacements, had seen just a month before in California. All the men had cleaned up by now, and, at a glance, you couldn't tell the veterans from the newcomers.

But it was easy to tell in the middle of the feature when the projector let out a screeching noise. Those guys who hit the floor—they had to be veterans.

7

THE HOME FRONT

For the folks back home there was a two-week delay in the mail. Families could only wait for news from the company—and hope that it was good. By now, though, Mary Long in Arkansas, Susan Keller in Indiana, and Jeanette Tomlinson in Idaho were accustomed to waiting. The first links in the chain binding their lives to K Company had been forged two years earlier, when the Army activated the 84th Division. By early December 1942, their husbands had arrived at Camp Howze, near Gainesville, Texas, part of the first contingent of draftees to begin training with the division. There the Army now told the men what to do and how to do it, but their wives received no guidance whatsoever. To stay with their husbands they had to shift for themselves. Following their men to Texas and later to Louisiana, they took their training catch-as-catch-can.

Mary and Norman Long had just come back from a Thanksgiving trip when Norman's induction notice arrived. Mary had "a numb feeling, a feeling of trying to capture everything, to hold on to everything we were going to do in a very short time." She taught dancing, and as soon as Norman's orders came she thought, "What will I do with the dancing class? Because I know I'm going to go and be with Norman as long as I can."

The Army shipped Norman to Howze. Mary was determined to stay with him in Gainesville that Christmas because she knew he wouldn't get home. "My dad called the hotel manager there for a room, so I felt set up. But I got there and found they hadn't heard of me. So I spent Christmas in the guesthouse at the camp. It was festive; there was a lot of friendship. Friendships formed rapidly during the war."

After Christmas, Mary got a job in the PX, selling cigarettes and candy. "I'd never worked a cash register before. The first day the register was off a lot, but by the next day I felt I was a pro. The PX jukeboxes played 'Deep in the Heart of Texas.' Remember, this was Texas and most of the soldiers were young, not as sentimental as us older ones. And honky-tonk music blared away all the time there. I'd always hated it. After a while, though, I decided it was the prettiest music I had ever heard."

Mary faced a rough Texas winter. "You could begin putting out laundry on the line, and by the time you'd come to the end of hanging it all up, the first that you'd put on the line was already frozen." Later, when the division went to Louisiana, the problems were different. "I got an apartment in Alexandria on a lower floor. One time a man looked in the window there. I felt pretty brave, I just got up and told him to get away, and he left. I felt very worldly then. You see, I had gone to Chicago every summer for several years to study. And even though I stayed on the Near North Side there, which was supposed to be a trouble spot, I was never bothered. I wasn't all that worldly, but I felt in better shape than many of the others."

Susan Keller had just given birth to her first child and was still in the hospital when Dempsey broke the news—his orders for induction had arrived. Before Christmas 1942, he'd left for Howze. In Nashville, Indiana, Susan was glad little Mickie, the baby, was there to keep her mind occupied. She and Mickie didn't reach Texas until the day after Dempsey finished basic training. She moved into a tiny apartment. "It was one room," she says, "a living room, bedroom, and kitchen combined. There wasn't any air conditioning in Texas then. But we did have our own bathroom."

Texas people took the Kellers under their wing. "We didn't have a car, so Dempsey hitchhiked to camp and back. I needed to get out with the stroller and take the baby for a walk. People always stopped and asked if they could take us somewhere in the car. When Dempsey got a weekend pass and we had enough money we'd splurge and eat out at Mrs. Crain's Café. While we enjoyed a Texas-size steak dinner, Mrs. Crain entertained Mickie by letting him play with the money in the cash register. Our son down there had many grandmas."

When Dempsey and Susan learned that after maneuvers the division would move to Camp Claiborne, Susan went on to Alexandria. "But as far as getting an apartment there," says Susan, "we made out terribly. I looked through the apartment listings in the newspapers. There were a lot of them, but so many said, 'No children.' Then I'd go to look at an apartment and the landlord would see that I was pregnant again. I was ready to give up. Finally I read about an apartment that was one mile from a bus stop. I walked the extra mile to the house. You see, I was a country girl and felt pretty brave because I wanted to be with Dempsey so much.

"When I talked with the woman about this apartment, she said, 'Honey, I don't think you want what I have.' That just hit me, and I began to cry. She said, 'Come in and rest, honey.' So I went into her living room and sat down with this woman and her three little children. She asked me how I'd gotten out there. I told her I'd walked from the bus stop. Then she gave me a cold drink, and after a bit I pulled myself together and got up to leave. The woman was still sitting down. When I got to the door she called me to come back. Then she took me into another room and said, 'This is the bedroom. Do you think you can manage?' I broke down again in tears. But I'd do it all over again so Dempsey and I could be together.

"We shared a bathroom with our landlord and landlady. One day she said, 'Susan, I hate to clean up the kitchen but I love to cook.' So that's the way we shared the kitchen. All the while we were there we got along famously. Also our only close neighbors sure did help when needed. They took me to the hospital when our daughter was born in April and took care of Mickie when Dempsey couldn't be home to help."

Susan remembers every one of Dempsey's promotions. "The first chevron he ever got I feather-stitched on just the way he wanted it. With each promotion I was so elated and proud of him. I laundered all his uniforms and ironed them just the way he liked them. I put the three creases down the back and the two creases in front for each shirt and there was real joy in doing them."

Uncle Sam's "greetings" reached Emmett Tomlinson in Twin Falls near the onset of Idaho's 1942 winter. Despite the orders for Mutt to report for a pre-induction physical, his twenty-one-year-old wife, Jeanette, felt confident he wouldn't have to go. After all, they'd been married more than three years, and Mutt was almost thirty-five. So they would stay on in Twin Falls and Mutt would continue in his job as steward at the Elks Club. But when the bus brought Mutt and others back from their physicals, Jeanette learned that wasn't in the cards. "They were certainly celebrating *something,*" she says. "That was the drunkest busload I've ever seen, before or since. Needless to say, Mutt passed the physical."

The Tomlinsons sold most of their furniture and stored the rest in Mutt's sister's basement. Then Jeanette found a job in the local beauty salon and rented a room in her ex-landlord's home. "I spent most of the time the next few weeks with Mutt's mother," she says. "And he spent most of his time in the local pool hall playing cards. His luck wasn't very good there either."

Mutt left for Camp Howze in early December. Jeanette spent Christmas in Idaho. "I felt real sorry for myself and I'm sure I made everyone miserable. I worked, worried, and cried for a couple of months and finally decided to be a 'camp follower.' I must've made eight or nine trips from Idaho to Texas or Louisiana and back.

"My first trip I went about eighteen hours without eating because I was too shy to go to the diner on the train. When they came around selling sandwiches I almost ate the poor fellow's arm off. One trip I stood up from Grand Junction, Colorado, to Salt Lake City, Utah. After a few of these experiences I learned to push and shove with the best of them. I could get on a bus and fall asleep until time to change buses or I reached my destination. I grew up a lot in those days."

When she reached Gainesville, Jeanette found a room in an old hotel. "What a room. I don't think the third floor had been opened to the public for years—a real antique. The carpet was in shreds. I ripped it up so I could scrub. Later, we rented two second-floor rooms with a private bath. We shared this luxury with another couple. It cost us something like twelve dollars per week per couple.

"We really had to scrimp to make it. I had to save one allotment check ahead so I could get home when necessary. We didn't go anyplace that cost money. I can't recall even attending a movie during all that time. The hotel was full of wives and sweethearts—so we were all in the same boat. And we lived for our soldiers coming 'home' for the night. We had a lot of company on weekends. When the single men weren't busy chasing girls, they spent time with us."

After the division moved to Camp Claiborne, Jeanette followed her husband to Louisiana. "I lived in a shack—one room, electricity, but no water. I'll never forget the big wooden water bucket I had. That thing weighed a ton when full. I washed clothes on a board, boiled them in a big black cast-iron kettle in the backyard, and hung them on a clothesline strung between the shacks. There were four or five such shacks—slave dwellings at one time—in the landlord's yard, all occupied by camp followers like me. We all shared a big community icebox, and we would take turns getting up at dawn to go get a block of ice. We would have to go before it got too hot or the ice would melt before we got back. Two of us would go. We walked and carried the ice—by means of a stick stuck through clothesline rope wrapped around the ice."

Jeanette and other wives spent about a year in Louisiana. "Winter was cold, wet, miserable, sitting around an oil heater that was on its last legs. Summer—so hot you had to get up at dawn and get settled under a shade tree. It was so hot and humid one couldn't stand the shack. There was really nothing to do but sit and wait. Sounds miserable, but those were happy times. We didn't have an extra quarter for a magazine, but we had each other and lots of good friends."

From time to time during training, new men came in to replace those who'd been transferred out. Most were unmarried. But for those who were married and for others who contemplated marriage, the war's momentum had influenced courtship and marriage plans. George Gieszl reached K after its first few months. Adrian Wheeler arrived later on. And young Jim Sterner was a part of the last large packet of men that came to Claiborne. Both Gieszl and Wheeler were married. Sterner, still single, had high hopes.

George Gieszl and Betty Anderson had begun dating as freshmen at Arizona State. In their sophomore year George went on active duty. That finished his college education for a while, and after the attack on Pearl Harbor, Betty's plans changed too. They decided to get married. "We were such kids," Betty says. "We wanted to sleep together but were old-fashioned enough to think we ought to be married first. I was twenty, George nineteen, so we needed his mother's consent. At the courthouse in Abilene, George forgot to lie about his age, so we couldn't get a license. Then in Sweetwater the courthouse was closed. But someone came down."

A week after their marriage, George shipped out for Panama. After nine months there as a platoon sergeant, George came back for OCS at Benning, earned his commission, and joined the 84th Division.

Becoming an officer didn't change his set. George had his own priorities for military life; teas for officers and wives weren't on the list. When Betty finally dragged him to one, she was almost sorry—he was a perfect lout. George must have been doing something right, though. In a year with K Company he moved from platoon leader to executive officer to company commander.

In April 1944, the Gieszls' son Scott was born. Just over a month later George made captain. In less than four months Company K would head for Europe.

The Wheelers already had a son when Adrian joined K Company late in 1943. Both Adrian and Lib came from Shirley, Indiana, but they made their wedding plans in Mississippi. Drafted in 1941, he was training with the 38th Division at Camp Shelby near Hattiesburg. Lib drove south with friends. There, according to Lib, "Ade decided he'd better marry me because otherwise, he thought, all of the girls would be gone before he got home."

Adrian claims, "Lib chased me down to Hattiesburg." He says he risked his corporal's stripes to sneak out of camp when they were married: "The company was on alert—I wasn't supposed to leave camp. So I told Lib she'd have to get the license. But the woman at the courthouse wouldn't give it to Lib, she had to have a man. The next night I slipped out again and went into town. The clerk brought her book home from the courthouse so we could sign. The Methodist minister in Purvis married us. I gave him a five-dollar bill and waited for two dollars in change. But the minister put it all in his pocket. It cost so much to marry her then, I couldn't possibly get rid of her."

Marriage and the Army agreed with Wheeler. He made buck sergeant, and in January 1943, their son Tom was born. But when the 38th Division shipped for the Pacific, Wheeler stayed behind. The medics had discovered a spot on his lung. After Christmas 1943, he was transferred to K-333 in the 84th Division. The following July he made staff sergeant. Lib was proud of him, but overseas shipment was closing in.

Stella ("Sis") Ward had never heard of K-333 before Jim Sterner and two thousand eight hundred other ASTPboys came to the division in the spring of 1944. She and Jim, both from Wilmington, had met a year and a half earlier at the University of Delaware when Jim, a sophomore, engineered a pickup on Sis's first day there as a freshman and "fell in love with her right away." The two went together until Jim left for the Army. But then, he says, "while I was down in Camp Walters taking basic training, she began dating a sailor. Then I went to the ASTP program at Drexel University. Once I got back to Wilmington that sailor didn't have a chance.

"Sis and I got engaged, sort of, when I was home on a pass. That's the night her father and I made a contract. Mr. Ward was a gentleman of the old school, so I had to ask for her hand. That night in his library he outlined the conditions for getting engaged. I made a verbal contract with him—he was a lawyer—that Sis and I wouldn't get married until the war was over and I was out of the army and had a college education and a job."

When the ASTP folded, Sterner went to the 84th Division. ("We hit Claiborne on April 1. Some April Fool's joke.") He and Sis kept in touch by mail and telephone. When they said, "Let's get married," her father said, "But you have a contract." It was on again, off again. They said, "We won't get married because we know the circumstances."

Then circumstances changed; overseas duty loomed. Sterner got a furlough, and they thought the wedding was on. But the night Jim arrived in Wilmington, "Sis's father was still trying to talk us out of getting married. He had me up at the University Club and sat me down on the porch there, a members' room with big overstuffed chairs. And here I am just out of the jungle and chiggers of Louisiana—a real big shot—but the two of us sat on the porch that night and talked about the decision Sis and I had made to get married right away. I guess he thought I was being conned into the wedding. So he said, 'You know, you can still get out of it.' I said, 'No, I don't want to.' Had quite a time. But talk about being intimidated—this was a long way from Louisiana."

They scheduled the wedding for July 1. For Sis Ward the rush was on. "That wedding was almost a blur. We had to do everything within that week. And there was a bit of parental opposition. It was scary, but we knew we wanted to be together, and in those days marriage was the only way to do it. The wedding was at St. Stephen's Lutheran Church and the wedding reception at the University Club. Everybody had a ball at that reception."

The young couple even managed a honeymoon before Jim went back to Claiborne. "Friends of Jim's parents were going to Canada for a week, so they let us use their house. When they left, they took their dog. The dog had fleas that stayed behind and multiplied. Jim and I kidded about that. We said we couldn't get out of bed for four days—because of the fleas."

Summer 1944. The Allies landed in Normandy on June 6. For the people in Claiborne the question shifted from *whether* the division would ship out to *when*.

The Kellers now had a second child, a daughter, Jackie, born there in Alexandria. Both Susan and Dempsey knew that they had to make plans, but for some time they couldn't bring themselves to talk about this. They didn't decide that Susan and the children would return to Indiana until just before the division's shipment orders came through.

Betty Gieszl had been washing George's khakis—soaking them in the bathtub, stepping on them to get them scrubbed, rinsed, and wrung out—when a friend came with the news: The men had their movement orders. Betty picked up Scott, hopped in the battered old blue Plymouth—the one George had partially wrecked after the last party—and headed out to the post to kiss George goodbye. She found George by the officers' hutments in the Third Battalion area.

At some point as they talked she handed five-month-old Scott to her husband. It was this family portrait that Leinbaugh, walking into the area, stored in his mind—Betty, George, and the baby, with the blue Plymouth and the officers' quarters in the background. For Leinbaugh it had always been George Gieszl, company commander. Now for the first time he saw George holding Scott in his arms. Suddenly it hit him—the company commander was also a husband and father: When you're shipping out, it's the ones with families who have the burden.

With the division scheduled to leave Claiborne on September 4, the men were restricted to the post. But Jeanette Tomlinson's husband managed to slip away briefly. "The last night before the boys were shipped out," she recalls, "Mutt sneaked home for about an hour. They were on alert, but he could climb over the back gate and walk to our shack. That was the advantage of living as we did. That night he tried to tell me that he wouldn't make it home. But I wouldn't listen. I was so sure he would come home."

Sergeants checked rosters one last time, men climbed aboard coaches, moved down aisles, pushed windows open, and said goodbye to Claiborne. At 1:00 P.M., September 4, the troop train pulled out for Camp Kilmer, the staging area. It was a slow haul, more than two full days to reach the New Jersey destination.

The train followed the B&O tracks right through Newark, Delaware, the university town where Jim Sterner and Sis had met. Then in

Wilmington, Jim looked out the window, saw his father-in-law's house, and really wanted to jump the train. The two-week wait at Kilmer, though, gave Sterner a chance for another farewell. He wangled a couple of twelve-hour passes, and Sis dropped everything to come to Trenton. They spent Jim's two passes in the Hotel Hildebrecht.

Adrian Wheeler wired his wife, back home in Indiana, and asked her to come to New York—one last chance for him to see Lib. She headed east. "Ade said to go to the Governor Clinton Hotel near the Pennsylvania Station. I got there and the hotel was full. So I sent Ade a telegram that I was at a different hotel. Getting the telegram really scared him at first, because no one outside was supposed to know the Camp Kilmer address. But I just sent it to his APO address, and that was okay.

"I was there about a week, and Ade came in most every evening. Then I took a bus back to Shirley. This stopped at Niagara Falls. I felt very lonely there, all alone, since that's where so many couples went on their honeymoon."

In New York harbor the troop ship *Edmund B. Alexander* weighed anchor on the morning of September 20, and K Company joined a convoy bound for Europe. For a while mail deliveries in either direction were nonexistent. Then the trickle began.

At the University of Delaware, Sis Sterner returned to the classrooms. It wasn't easy being both a coed and a bride with an absentee husband in a rifle company overseas. "I couldn't settle down to do my homework until I wrote him. He wrote me, but everything was censored. It was scary. I just didn't *know*."

Susan Keller and the children left Claiborne for Nashville, Indiana. She located a house half a block from her parents, moved in, and "tried to keep up with what was going on in Europe. I listened to all the news on the radio. I just heard the radio because I couldn't afford to buy a newspaper.

"Those times were terrible. I'd just have to get out of the house. In almost every kind of weather I'd have to walk. I'd put both children in the baby buggy and go out.

"I had the worst thoughts that I might never see Dempsey again. My neighbor could see how this was getting to me, so she asked if her minister could talk to me. I agreed, and after talking with him I could see the light of day. I prayed with Dempsey's picture every night and the kids and I kissed his picture before we went to bed. That minister must have really known the right things to say to me."

At first Jeanette Tomlinson couldn't settle down. She went back to Twin Falls, then to her parents in California, then back to Idaho again. "I moved to Gooding. Friends of Mutt's had leased a service station, bulk plant, grocery store, and cabins there and asked me to work for them. I don't remember my wage, but I got a two-room cabin and my board. I worked hard, but I was at last content—fixing up my little house and being with people I learned to love dearly."

Jeanette wrote to Mutt every day, but no letters came from overseas until after the first of December. The press and radio were her lifeline to Europe. Then one evening the news came. "I was standing between the kitchen and the utility porch," she says, "had just finished dinner dishes and picked up the evening *Times News*. When I saw the article, '84th Division Attacks at Geilenkirchen,' those headlines jumped to a foot high. I grabbed the mop and scrub bucket and gave that utility floor a first-class scrubbing while tears were streaming down my face. I've always been that way. I work when I'm worried or upset, doing anything physical.

"I was so upset. I don't know what I'd thought had been going to happen. Maybe I thought, They'll go over there, and the war will be over, and so they'll come right back.

"I read everything I could get hold of to try to find out about the fighting—*Newsweek, Life,* and *Look.* Every night I listened to H. V. Kaltenborn. He came on the radio about nine or ten.

"Then Mutt's letters began to arrive. Each letter I got I was thankful he was still alive, still able to write me. One thing did bother me, though. Mutt was always so immaculate, kept his clothes just so. I knew that when the company went into combat it must have driven him out of his mind to have to live in such conditions and not be able to keep his things better."

One of the first Army telegrams came to Mary Long in early December. "I've been a positive person all my life," she says. "I've been sure something *is* or *isn't* going to happen. I have positive feelings. I thought God was not going to let Norman *not* come back. But man, not God, singles people out one way or another. Norman was hit. The telegram said 'slightly injured.' My immediate feeling was one of relief. Then in the papers I began to see the big headlines about the V-1 rockets destroying a hospital in Belgium, and I began to wonder and worry again."

Mary didn't get a letter from Norman for two weeks. Then she learned that he had gotten shrapnel in his eyes. "That could have been very serious, but Norman was sent to a hospital in Paris where they did excellent work on him. It turned out that the shrapnel was made of iron. If it had been something else they might not have been able to get it out. But they'd just perfected a technique using a magnet, and the operation got all the metal out. His being hit didn't affect his eyesight at all."

In Shirley, Indiana, Lib Wheeler waited. The V-mail letters from Adrian began to arrive. Then one day a man from the depot walked up the street with a telegram; Adrian had been seriously wounded.

A C-47 flight from Paris took Adrian to England on Sunday, December 3. Near the middle of the month, Lib got her first mail from Europe since Adrian had been hit, a letter written by the soldier in the bed next to Wheeler's. "Adrian had the man tell me he couldn't write on account of his arm," Lib remembers, "since he didn't know the extent of the damage to his eyes and thought they could fix his right eye so it would be all right when he got to the States."

But no new technology could save his sight. So for Adrian the picture of Lib is still the dark-haired young woman of 1944.

Betty Gieszl returned to Arizona. With George gone she decided to try college again. She'd gone back to Flagstaff for long enough to know that she couldn't easily handle both motherhood and college while George was somewhere in Europe, so she had just withdrawn from school. But she hadn't known George was in combat until Western Union forwarded this telegram:

TTFN 8 55 GOVT
    WASHINGTON DC 845P DEC 5–44
MRS BETTY J GIESZL
    BOX NO 1326 COOLIDGE ARIZ
REGRET TO INFORM YOU YOUR HUSBAND WAS SERIOUSLY WOUNDED IN ACTION IN GERMANY TWENTY TWO NOVEMBER UNTIL NEW ADDRESS IS RECEIVED ADDRESS MAIL FOR HIM QUOTE CAPTAIN GEORGE S GIESZL SERIAL NUMBER (HOSPITALIZED) CENTRAL HOSPITAL DIRECTORY APO 640 CARE POSTMASTER NEWYORK NEWYORK UNQUOTE YOU WILL BE ADVISED AS REPORTS OF CONDITION ARE RECEIVED.
        WITSELL ACTING THE ADJUTANT GENERAL
        945P

George wrote ten days later. But after the telegram arrived she didn't hear from the War Department for three more months. There must have been some snafu in the central hospital directory as well, for none of Betty's letters reached George.

Morris Dunn's mail from home still drifted around in the replacement channels. Since leaving the States two months earlier he'd been eager to hear from his wife, Dorothy. Was their first child a girl or boy? It was December now and Dunn still didn't know. And although he'd written home regularly, several weeks passed before Dorothy knew her husband's whereabouts. He'd been on a troop ship headed for Europe when the nurses on the maternity ward asked where her husband was stationed. All she could tell them was that he was "someplace on the high seas."

Dorothy and the baby went home. Then she took all of Morris's clothes, had them cleaned, and put them in a trunk. "Before I had them cleaned," she remembers, "I wrapped myself in them on the bed and cried and cried and cried. And I made my peace, I had settled it. If he never came back it would be all right; somehow I would make out with that child. But I had his clothes cleaned and put them in a trunk and locked it. Had he never come back I would have saved them for the child and told him that these were his father's clothes.

"I didn't sleep well. I'd pull back the blinds and look out at the moon and wonder, Is it shining down on my husband? If that moon could only talk it could tell me where he is.

"Then when he wrote from the 84th Division, I bought a big map of the world and put it on the wall over the dining table. I'd put pins in the map from day to day as I would hear the news of where the division was."

8

CELLARS AND HOLES

The K Company that left Geilenkirchen near dusk on Wednesday, November 29, was a very different outfit from the one that had begun combat ten days earlier. Replacements, now nearly half of the company's combat strength, had altered its composition. Experience had altered its perspective. Men who'd been at the château were no longer green and impressionable; some were downright cynical. Ed Stewart expressed the attitude of the veteran when he described the battalion CO, watching from the side of the road as the company headed out. There stood the colonel, "giving orders in all the military glory of an officer 'commanding'—now that shells were scarce and far between."

Stewart was one of sixteen, ten of them ASTPboys, who would be promoted the following Sunday. Now these men would have the rank that went with the duties they'd already assumed. All had been with the company from Claiborne days or before. Replacements looked on them as veterans—as they were. These and other noncoms forged the character of K Company as a line outfit, a character still shaped in the image of George Gieszl, with a crucial tempering ingredient added—combat experience.

The move took us to Prummern, a mile behind the front. There, as division reserve, we sat tight with the rest of the battalion and sweated out the Railsplitters' new attack, which had begun that morning before dawn. Rear-echelon—but not far enough to the rear to be safe. On Thursday the Germans dropped a few random shells in the area. Three men wounded then were replacements who had joined the company the preceding Sunday.

Friday and Saturday, the first two days of December, the shelling of Prummern stepped up. Shells came in on the noon chow line. Replacements followed the vets' lead—filled mess kits, clamped them shut, and dashed for cover. The first platoon's Willie Wilson was wounded in the Saturday shelling, so of the five officers who had jumped off with the company only Leinbaugh remained. Someone in the battalion aid station made this note for the day: "Not enough room in aid station to accommodate all casualties. As we treated them outside the mortar shells burst, hitting us with mud and shrapnel. One wounded soldier asked to receive an excessive dose of morphine to end his suffering."

A self-inflicted wound ended the war for one replacement. The morning report left it indeterminate whether the wound was in line of duty. Another replacement, Leslie Carson, scrounged the SIW's pack. During the shelling he may have earned a small reward. When the next hole over took a hit, a man cried out that he was blind. Carson crawled over and pushed the man's helmet up. Sight restored!

On Sunday night the battalion began its muddy march to Lindern. The 335th Infantry had taken the town while we sat in Prummern. We were moving up to relieve their First Battalion, which now held the town. A note from our battalion aid station reported that mud and rain made the move exhausting: "Numerous soldiers stumbled and fell in the mud and could hardly rise. Lost several litters and other supplies running gauntlet over high ground."

K Company's more laconic morning report reads, "Marched app 5 miles thru mud." The men were already connoisseurs of that substance. Campbell, writing to Nelle Laughlin at Knox College, had delivered what he thought was the definitive opinion on the mud: "Georgia has the red clay kind, slippery going uphill. (I've never met anyone going in any other direction in Georgia.) Florida's mud is wet and sandy, packs well and is good for cleaning mess kits. England has soupy mud that doesn't play square. If you're on a brick walk, at some point where bricks come together you'll cause a geyser of brown mud to shoot up and spatter your clothes. French and Belgian muds vary from thin paste to huge chunks. They peel easily in strips like dough for pie crust before it's been baked."

But this mud between Prummern and Lindern—dense, heavy, sucking—was serious. It demanded respect and ingenuity. Johnny Freeman and a few other second platoon veterans coped by "requisitioning" a swaybacked horse. Putting the platoon's equipment on it, they transformed themselves into K Company's cavalry.

For the replacements, this night march, their first trip to the line, was a journey into the unknown. Gene Amici had never seen it that black in his life: "It was raining, no stars, no moon, no nothing. And not knowing where you're going. Everybody hanging on to the guy in front—hanging on to his belt and just walking. You just kept walking, and once in a while you'd see a burst of gunfire, and that was it. Then all you'd see was a head up there in front of you."

Clayton Shepherd also saw little, but he took a lot in: "We walked a long ways. In among those dragon's teeth. Mud up to our knees. Going through that rain and mud some fellow said he'd like to get his hands on the guy who wrote that song 'The Wind and the Rain in Your Hair.'" Then the searchlights came on, and their beams bounced off low clouds and onto the men. "I wondered what the hell was this," says Shepherd. "I knew we was right around where the Germans was. I says if they got the lights shining on us, they're going to see us and shoot us anyway. That's what goes through your mind. But they must have gotten to somebody to turn the searchlights off. So we went on."

Mud took its toll. First, men jettisoned unwanted equipment. John Bratten pitched away his gas mask, "even though it was equipped with special-made lenses to correct my nearsightedness and astigmatism." People got mired. Paul Cote, weighing in at 208 pounds—excluding his BAR, ammo belt with eight clips, three additional bandoliers of ammo, and six grenades—sank to his crotch. A couple of men hoisted him out. Cote then watched Leinbaugh help the next one who couldn't keep up. To ease the burden Leinbaugh took the fellow's pack—awfully heavy. The guy had picked up a small cast-iron stove and didn't want to give it up. Leinbaugh threw the stove in the mud, and we went on. Then Don Stauffer and Jim Sterner tried to pull another GI out while all the time he was saying, "Go. Leave me. Please leave me! I want to stay here! You guys, go!"

Long after midnight the company, in an extended column, a file on each side of the road, headed up a slight rise and moved into Lindern, a few hundred yards from German troops. Still, we didn't take cover immediately. "There according to the best Army tradition we stood, seeking shelter against the buildings, while the next step was pondered by the officers," Ed Stewart noted. "After being billeted once and then moved, the squad settled down in a comfortable cellar for the night, with a dead German outside, a grim sentinel. We built a fire which produced more smoke than heat, ate K rations, and wore out the rest of the night."

The two platoons that were going to be on line picked up guides who led them to their holes, while the other two platoons made for the safety of the cellars. As Shepherd started down, he thought it "looked like a dungeon." But he appreciated its solid construction: "It looked like they had been preparing for that war for years, the way them basements was made. I got to figure you was safe if you got in one of them." J. A. ("Strawberry") Craft, tired and worried, just headed into one of the battered houses. All he wanted was to stretch out, relatively dry and safe on a cellar floor, because he was "shaking like a dog shitting peach seeds. A lot of that was from sweating, marching so fast."

Amici, too, was ready for some sack time, but he had a couple more hours to go: "It was 'Amici and Charlie, out on guard duty.' The others just plopped, but in a couple hours they got to get up and relieve you. It was quite a night. But you did it. You didn't bitch about it. You didn't stop to think whether you were tired or wet. You did it, period. Nowadays, walk in water three feet deep—you couldn't do it. But you were young then, and you just did it."

Lindern was an essential building block for XIII Corps's objective—a bridgehead across the Roer River at Linnich. But German forces still held Würm and Müllendorf, two miles to the west. Until these two towns had fallen, the division would not attack beyond Lindern. The battalion, with K and L companies on line and I in reserve, would defend the town.

At daybreak we sized up the situation. The company sector looked out on flat fields bounded by the higher ground of Randerath to the northwest and Brachelen to the northeast. Between the two villages a rough semicircle of pillboxes dotted the area like raisins on a cake. K Company's holes on the edge of town spanned a flat arc four hundred yards from flank to flank, anchored at either end on a deep railway cut running from northeast to southwest.

With Germans to our front and the rest of the battalion sharing Lindern with us, we weren't isolated. Still, our contacts, with GIs or Germans, were limited. As long as the battalion defended Lindern, K Company's life would be confined to cellars and holes. This fact influenced routines, shaped the course of friendships, and had a direct bearing on matters of survival.

For the fellow who thrived in the service, GIs had a stock expression: "He found a home in the Army." In some crazy way the company found a home in Lindern. We were on our own, with a job to do and no one but ourselves to depend on. An ASTP boy in the third platoon noted, "Few days stand out from the montony of shelling, of shifts by night, of K rations for meals, and the discomfort of diarrhea, which everyone had in one stage or another." But those early days in Lindern continued the testing that had begun two weeks earlier for the old hands and marked the initial battlefield indoctrination for the new. We were fortunate that in our first two or three days there the challenges did not go beyond the "monotony of shelling."

The veterans did not go out of their way to instruct the newcomers; they simply went about their business. Replacements, watching and listening, learned how to go about theirs. Most of the recent arrivals began to see themselves as part of the K Company family. They were becoming integrated with the others, "socialized"—though nobody in Lindern gave much thought to the process. They had more pressing concerns.

Before dawn that Monday the pattern was established. Two platoons on line, two in Lindern's cellars. Switch every twenty-four to forty-eight hours—always in the dark. The weapons platoon now functioned primarily as another rifle platoon, so there was no need for a more complicated rotation.

The cellars were the posh part. There wasn't a hell of a lot left that wasn't cellar. As Amici said, "That was the most destroyed town I've ever seen. Just the shells of houses." And the holes were the edge of the known world.

To get to the holes the men ran a gauntlet—*literally* ran: They crossed a bridge over the railway cut, then fanned out to left and right. Platoon exchanges always occurred at night; Jerry machine guns laid down enough interdicting fire on the bridge and the railroad cut itself to keep the men honest. Once beyond the bridge, in addition to worrying about the Germans, the men had to learn to cope with life in the two-man holes.

The *Soldier's Handbook,* likening Army and family life, noted that family members "shared the same dining room, the same bathroom, and the same amusements. . . . [All] were largely dependent upon each other for comforts, pleasures, and a living." But the book hadn't prepared men for Lindern's holes, where dining room and bathroom were one and the same, and comforts and pleasures were few and far between. So the men on line threw the book away and began writing their own, a book on how to deal with daily routines in a life lived under extreme conditions, and how to get along with foxhole buddies—and with the Germans.

Like Lindern's houses, the holes were German-built. The L-shaped one Jim Sterner and his buddy shared was typical: "Over one end the Germans had put trees across and a big mound of dirt on top. It could have taken a direct hit from a 120mm mortar." Tom Miller and George Lucht christened their similar deluxe hole the Hotel Astor. At night the men used entrenching tools to make improvements. Pop Mothershead, over six feet tall, and Frenchy Lariviere, under five feet eight, were the long and short of it in one hole. Mothershead had to dig considerably further for cover and comfort. Frenchy found that Mothershead was "a terrific guy, but he got kind of peeved at me because I had to do so much less digging than he did."

New men were placed in holes with old so that experience could be shared. Stewart saw the importance of these pairings: "In a situation like Lindern, the only thing you've got to keep you going is this guy with you. And then you go through this bit: 'After the war certainly we'll meet, etc., etc.' I suspect that's part of the dynamic of the Old Boys' Club. People obviously don't recognize it at the time, but at that stage the major link is survival."

Some pairings, however, did not survive round-the-clock proximity. The fellow Richard Heuer had been buddied with was nervous, and in the middle of the night had the habit of cracking gum so that it "sounded like all hell was breaking loose." He also repeatedly told Heuer that he wished he were home with his wife eating apple pie and drinking milk. This annoyed Heuer: "I told him I wished I was home, too, going out with the girls."

The heavy rain aggravated Heuer's problem: "The sides of our hole started caving in. The door on top came on in and pinned my buddy's legs. He let out a scream and kept screaming. Finally I said to him, 'If you don't shut up I'll shoot you instead of the Germans.' Then I crawled out and found another hole for myself."

When the platoon went back into town Heuer asked for a new partner. "My first one was making me a nervous wreck," he says. "That's when they assigned me to Walter Roman. He was a small guy who seemed to have no fear. He'd been in the Air Force, but I guess he didn't feel he was doing an adequate job. He wanted to get into the fighting end of it. When I found that out I told him he was nuttier than a fruitcake. He could be back in a nice fart sack, taking it easy in the Air Force. Instead he chose to be with the infantry. Roman and I hit it off real good. He and I had a relationship that was just like Bill Mauldin's characters, Willie and Joe."

Outdoor dining in the holes was no picnic. Tom Miller and George Lucht's Hotel Astor overlooked a field of cabbages—all rotting. To this day Tom can't eat cabbage: "I told George about it at the time. He said, 'Make believe they're watermelons.' I told him, 'If they're so good why don't you get a few watermelons for yourself?'"

The diet was K rations. A historian with the Quartermaster Corps praised this product as "the most nearly perfect combat ration ever developed for mobile troops." And the GI in Europe was "not only the best-fed soldier in World War II but the best-fed soldier of all times." Breakfast, dinner, and supper, each had its own double carton the size of a large box of Cracker Jack. The outer box was covered with water-resistant glue; the inner, dipped in wax that withstood temperatures up to 145 degrees. Each meal's entree—egg, cheese, or meat—came in a small can. Chewing gum, cigarettes, and dry biscuits (first cousins to the hard-tack of the Spanish-American War) were in all three meals, but the clip of ten matches came only in the dinner carton. Halazone tablets for water purification and OD toilet paper were only in the breakfast ration. Amici critiques the menu at Lindern's holes: "The cheese and crackers—pretty good. The coffee wasn't too bad. Scrambled eggs and chopped ham—after a while it tasted pretty good. That was for a couple of weeks, though, a long span."

Days got shorter, nights colder. Rain fell on twelve of our seventeen days there. More mud. The GI's *Handbook*, like a protective mother, said wet clothing should be changed "as soon as possible. Sitting around in wet clothes or with wet feet is almost certain to give you a cold or other serious illness." But in a wet hole, with your entire wardrobe on your back, a quick change into warm, dry clothes is a daydream.

Division tried to lessen the likelihood of trench foot by ordering dry socks to be brought up with the rations. In his study of cold injury in the 84th Division, however, Michael DeBakey, a physician who would later go on to a less pedestrian specialty, wrote, "In practice this arrangement worked out somewhat less satisfactorily than it sounds."

Though the men in the holes couldn't possibly keep dry (Sterner to Stauffer: "Hey, get me out of this bathtub!"), they worked on it. They bailed out, scraped mud from uniforms, changed wet socks, and made insoles from the waterproofed cardboard cartons that packaged the K rations.

Those chores didn't fill the hours. At times life was just plain dull. Chalmers Davis and the man who shared his foxhole considered starting some excitement by tossing a few grenades. Reluctantly they decided against it.

In the daytime quiet, Amici began a new routine. "It was the first time in my life I ever read the Bible," he recalls. "Sitting out there in the foxhole in Lindern, they'd shell us every damn day, and all you could do was take out the little pocket Bible and just read. My wife knows the Bible inside out, but hell, I don't know one passage from another. But I read it at the time."

Activity was even more limited at night. To sneak a smoke, men would duck down to conceal the lighted butt. With two in the hole, they took turns on watch; one of them could try to doze off for an hour or two. Stewart tried this early on in Lindern. Since he had a grenade in his right pocket, to be safe he stretched out on his left side. Morning came and Ed checked himself out; then he found he'd had a grenade in his left pocket as well.

He rested better than most, though. "I guess I was a pragmatist in many ways," Stewart says. "I found that almost no matter what happened I could sleep. So in Lindern I used to go into the foxhole with someone who couldn't sleep. I figured as long as I could sleep and this guy couldn't, that was the way to do it."

Daybreak didn't appreciably change the pattern. After dawn empty K-ration boxes fueled concealed fires warming canteen cups of water for soluble coffee. Other empties became portable toilets. With diarrhea commonplace, though, the skill and accuracy required for this use of the little cartons could not always be brought into play. On his first day out in the hole Heuer got dysentery. "I didn't want to crap in my helmet," he says. "So I decided I'd crawl outside at night." Since he wore two pairs of long johns beneath his wool pants, "it was a real chore getting down to the point where I could do my duty. And as I was doing my duty I heard some noises behind me. I thought they were Germans. I jumped into the hole without pulling my drawers up. That really startled my foxhole buddy. I had crapped in the first pair of drawers, so I had to stand there in the middle of the foxhole and cut it out. This wasn't easy, because I had to do the cutting with my bayonet. My buddy complained of the stench all the time after that."

Life wasn't much better back inside the town, but it was different. The men in the holes saw the town as rear-echelon. (John Bratten shared that view: "I privately reflected how lucky I was to be in a sort of rear-echelon position in company headquarters.") Once they were back in town, however, the men relearned the fact that "rear echelon" is a relative thing. The rearmost cellar for the resting platoons was only two hundred yards from the foxholes. The hulks of houses offered cover, but daylight movement was still risky business. Even in the town, we lived at or below ground level.

Food and mail came up after dark. The CO made sure it was *hot* food—or else. Nobody in the kitchen crew was anxious to exchange ladle or cleaver for an M1. We read mail and wrote letters by light from improvised lamps—rag wicks and gasoline in wine bottles. With a side effect, says Sterner: "You blew your nose and blew carbon out."

We talked endlessly of home, food, and girls. We cleaned our weapons and attempted—never with complete success—to clean ourselves. The cellars weren't as muddy as the holes, but they didn't have running water. A few men washed in a pond behind a house next to the railroad cut. Mike DeBello relied on his steel helmet: "We cooked in our helmets, did everything in our helmets. I shaved in mine in cold water. And from that day on I've always shaved in cold water. I use regular soap and shave once a week."

By the end of the company's stay in Lindern, something more than a helmet was needed. An aid-station notation: "We all feel pretty dirty as we have not had our clothes off in weeks." Temporary relief came when the battalion, on a brief pullback, took over the showers at a Dutch mine. The men soaked until the mud of Germany dissolved.

The *Handbook* advised regular bowel movements, "once each day at as nearly the same time as possible. Always go to the toilet to urinate, or when your bowels move. Using the ground for this purpose is a source of great danger to everyone." But German shelling was more regular than the men's bowels. Toilet facilities were better in the buildings than in the holes, but still they were not the Ritz. Flat-trajectory fire cut off the third platoon's CP from the outhouse. So Doc Mellon knocked the seat from a cane-bottomed chair and put the chair over the family butter churn for an indoor toilet.

In the first platoon they worked out a similar solution with a tall vase in a closet. "And when that was inconvenient, "Amici says," there were the drawers of a little dresser in the bedroom."

George Pope complained that higher headquarters got into the act: "To tell you the goddam truth, when we got into Germany I never took a crap outside. I don't believe anybody else did either. We were in the cellars, and we'd shit on the floor upstairs—in the parlor. As we got further into

Germany, division HQ moved up, and they were finally where we had been in the combat zone. But now it was quiet back there—no need for them to be in the cellars. They could sit in the living room. So they put out a written order, 'There'll be no more shitting in the houses, goddamm it. Use the latrine.'"

For much of the time Germans remained in the distance. Their presence was one of the conditions—like the weather, like the foxholes—to which we had to adjust. Events that left men shaken during the first few days became accepted by most as routine hazards.

Men in the holes learned to interpret the sounds of battle. At first, every time he heard a shell, Pop Mothershead would say, "Oh, oh, that's coming in." By early December, though, his buddy Frenchy Lariviere had fine-tuned his hearing: "I'd listen and tell Pop, 'Don't worry about that one.' You kind of get an ear for when a shell is going to be close or not."

The German Nebelwerfers were harder to get used to. Heuer had never heard of those multibarreled recoilless weapons that the GIs called "screaming meemies." When he heard them during his first night in Lindern, he was "so scared I automatically dug the foxhole two feet deeper."

They impressed Amici, too, who thought "the words 'screaming meemies' are just as accurate as you could say it." To him they sounded like "fifteen or twenty rockets going off, one after another. Each one was a loud screech, a sound you could hear for miles. It sounded like it was just across the street, just one after the other. Not knowing where they were going to land—it sent shivers up your spine."

Near Jim Sterner and Erv Koehler's hole another sound brought other problems. It was Sterner's turn on watch, while "Koehler was under his raincoat, which was a way to keep warm." Sterner heard movement behind him, and he could tell Koehler was scared. "Hell, let's face it, we were *both* scared to death. I had a BAR, and the last thing I wanted to do was fire an automatic weapon on the front line. And I looked around and here's a cow looking at me. I couldn't believe it."

Cows *did* wander around. One first platoon rifleman said: "You'd be told, 'Be sure to watch them,' because there were stories of Germans walking behind the cows. You'd look to see if there were any legs besides the four legs of the cows."

During the third platoon's first night on line, the sounds didn't come from cows. Repeated calls of "*Kommen Sie hier!*" brought four GIs from their holes. They in turn called for the Germans to come out. Shots were exchanged, and then the GIs turned back. Seeing a man on the ground, they hit the deck and challenged him. No answer—dead. He'd been there a week. Later that night James Teets, looking out to the front, saw someone and challenged him. Then he saw another and the shadow of a third. Teets fired, slightly wounding two. The third gladly gave up. Bill Reynolds and Douglas Naehring took the prisoners to the CP and on to the

PW enclosure to the rear. By then it was close to dawn, not enough time to walk the several miles back to Lindern in the dark. So the two of them took an unguarded jeep, drove it to Lindern, and reached their foxholes just before dawn.

In the second platoon, worried about the lack of sound on the left, Campbell and a squad leader slipped out to check the flank. They passed K Company's last hole, crossed a deep ditch, and warily walked a curve across open ground. *Nobody* there—American or German—until the two neared the railroad station. Challenged, they gave the sign and listened for the countersign. Instead came, "Nope, that's yesterday's." (It's the middle of a winter night nearly forty years later. Campbell awakens, finds two words on his mind: *coffin* and *varnish,* no clear link between them. Then he comes up with the one possible association. Maybe they were sign and countersign for that night back in '44.)

German guns had houses and holes zeroed in. Shepherd learned this near dawn after the first night. He was pulling guard at the top of the steps to the fourth platoon's basement headquarters. "I was just sitting there and heard this noise," he says, "and there was a damned German shell that come in." It was fortunate that it was a dud. "It come over the house, lit on the roof of another house, bounced off a wall, and landed right there about ten foot off me. But it didn't go off. I looked at that damned thing. It must have been a 240. That big. If it had went off it would have blew the whole damn building in."

Jerry artillery and mortar fire became the regular order of business. The battalion log noted, "Usual morning mortar fire." But Tuesday morning, December 5, was an exception. Naturally that was the morning the regimental commander came up to visit battalion headquarters in Lindern. Before heading back, the colonel radioed that Lindern was "peaceful and not as hot as they say it to be."

In late afternoon, Jerry got back on schedule. The log entry at 4:05 P.M. reported, "Heavy concentration of German Arty on Lindern and our positions." Then at 4:30 enemy tanks and infantry headed toward the battalion's right flank. Mortar, machine-gun, and artillery fire forced the enemy to withdraw; but ten minutes later the Germans resumed the attack.

By 5:10 P.M., battalion's S-3 radioed regiment, "Receiving concentration, heaviest yet." A minute later, "Three enemy tanks advancing on town firing direct fire into town." Division artillery then scored a direct hit, set a tank on fire, and stopped the foray.

Comments such as "usual morning mortar fire" and "heavy concentration of German Arty on Lindern" are bland enough on paper. But sit in a hole and wait for the shells to come in. Even the experienced can have trouble coping. A blast blew George Lucht out of the Hotel Astor. For a while after that he couldn't stay in his hole, but he figured out a way to push aside his fears. He spent time in the open, tracing down and repairing breaks in communication lines, checking the wires between positions and splicing the broken ones.

In a nearby barn tower, Lucht's foxhole buddy, Tom Miller, had been taking his turn observing the field in front of the platoon. A shell caught the barn, trapping Tom for several hours. That time in the tower left an imprint. "It bothers me now when I can't see daylight," he says. "I have to leave the draperies open at night. I always sit on the aisle when I'm in a plane—I need open space."

Not everyone learned to handle the shelling. Sterner helped one replacement who couldn't cope: "While he was up there he went blind. It must have been mental." Sterner led him back from the foxholes: "There were a couple of German riflemen popping at us, but I got him back to the aid station and never saw him again. He hadn't been hit, but he couldn't see a thing. I wouldn't know who he was—he'd only been up a couple of days."

Some, especially those who had successfully come through the company's first bout with German artillery, fought back on their own. Chalmers Davis wondered what the damp was doing to the ammunition for the company's heaviest armament, its three 60mm mortars. No rounds had been fired since the men had carried their apron loads in the mud and rain around the Würm River. So Davis figured now was the time to check some out.

He found an observation post at the top of a wrecked house; in the courtyard below they set up the little tube with its bipod and baseplate. Sterner and Stauffer dropped in a couple of rounds. Nothing happened—duds. Then Davis called down, "Hey, come up here and look at this." A haystack was gradually moving across the open field. Davis was contacting the CP to tell them about this camouflaged tank when a Jerry soldier got out of one foxhole and ran to another. Grinning, Davis suggested using a couple of rounds to have some fun. "He never should have been out in the daytime; he made a mistake." Damned if they didn't drop the third round right in the foxhole. They saw its little puff. It hardly mattered that when the artillery fired for effect they knocked out the haystack.

When German shelling let up that Tuesday night, the second and third platoons took their shift in the holes, first and fourth headed for their cellar break. Stauffer scouted out a safe haven. "We were going to get a nice rest in the basement," he says, "so I went into this one beautiful cellar." Then he looked for Sterner to share it.

But Sterner wasn't up to a move: "I was in this rickety old place, and Don came over and said, 'Hey, I've found a really great cellar, let's go.' I liked to be near Don because he was the only guy in the platoon that carried a blanket. But I said, 'Don, I'm so goddam tired I'm not going to move. I don't care if I get killed.' So he said, 'Okay, I'll stay here.' And he stayed with me. Then they brought in canned meat from Arbogast and

Bastian of Allentown, Pennsylvania—old Bastian was a relative of mine; my grandma Moyer's name was Bastian. And we sat there and ate these little hot dogs."

In another basement someone opened up a box of ten-in-one rations, the kind that included jam and hard candy. Keith Lance had heated water for a cup of coffee and was settling down when Bert Christensen, the platoon sergeant, came to him and said, "We're going to have to find another basement. Too many men in this one."

Keith, his shoes off, was rubbing his feet. He planned to switch his wet socks with the pair he'd been drying between his shirt and undershirt. He did that whenever he could. "I'd made up my mind I wasn't going to get trench foot," he says. "That's why I had my shoes off." But now Bert said they needed another basement, and Keith said, "Okay."

The two went across the street and found a basement—the "beautiful cellar" that Don Stauffer had abandoned to stay with Jim Sterner. Keith looked it over: "It wasn't very big, but we figured we could take about eight or nine in there. That would relieve that many."

Then Keith and Bert went back to ask for volunteers. "You know how many we got," Keith says. "We didn't get any. So Bert asked me, 'You pick out some.' I just pulled them off the top of my head. Unfortunately when you do this you always get the people you know best. I always figured I picked these guys to go to their death."

With Bert and the "volunteers," Keith moved to the other basement, then stretched out. "I can tell you I was exhausted. I like candy, but I never even did take a bite of mine. I thought, I'll do that tomorrow. I'm pretty tired now. We lay down just along the wall. Remember how we used to lay like a bunch of hogs? Bert was in the far end; I was in the other corner. Which was the only thing that saved my life. I went to sleep *right now*."

The shell hit it in early morning. "When it hit—man, it knocked the senses out of you for a while," says Keith. "And so much dust. You couldn't breathe, couldn't do anything. You first thought, Well, I've had it. The next thing I can remember was these guys breathing that stuff, trying to get air. They're buried there and trying to get air. The only thing that saved me was this beam. It fell over me, was protecting me from the other stuff.

"Bert said, 'Are you all right, Doughhead?' Everybody called me Doughhead. I said, 'Well, I guess. I don't think I'm hurt.' He said, 'I can see the light above you. I'm going to see if you can't get out.' So I gathered myself together and started trying to pull this crap out.

"I couldn't see Bert, but he could see me. He talked me out—he told me how to get out of there. Why didn't I wonder why *he* didn't get out? I never one time asked him, 'Are you coming?' I wonder why I didn't. I just listened to what he said. He said, 'You've got to get help.' So I worked myself out and started for company headquarters.

"When I got there and told them what happened, they said, 'Where's your shoes?' I was barefoot, but I never once thought of that. Then Dempsey asked me, 'Where is it?' I said, 'I'll go show you.' He said, 'But you don't have any shoes on.' I said, 'That doesn't make any difference; I'll show you anyway.'"

The men in the CP headed out: Bocarski, a runner between the fourth platoon and the CP, who had wanted to bunk with his fourth platoon buddies—"There was room for five or six guys under the stairs, and they were already there. There wasn't room for another body, so I went back to the CP and bunked in with that crowd." John B. Cole and Oliver Tandy, a replacement who'd been assigned to him—"Tandy had just been up a few days. They told him he would be my buddy. He said, 'I'll look after John.'" Behind Lavelle, Leinbaugh, Brewer, Dahlstrom, and the others was Bratten—"I guess I'm alive today because I was in my sleeping bag under a stairway for protection, and it took me a couple more seconds to get over to the fourth platoon."

One of the men in that basement was the platoon leader, Richard Meek, who'd come up at Geilenkirchen. He'd felt safe "because the cellar had an arched brick roof which looked quite sturdy." But then the shell hit the upper part of the house, exploded, blew in the wall, and collapsed the roof of the cellar. So rescuers faced the ultimate jackstraws problem—how to find and tease out the right timbers to get to the men.

Cole, Brewer, Leinbaugh, and Bratten tried to clear the basement steps; Lavelle and Tandy worked at another entry. Then another round came in. It lifted Cole's helmet right off his head. A beam came down and flattened Brewer's helmet—he couldn't get it back on.

Bratten saw that Brewer, though scratched, hadn't been seriously hurt. "He lost his glasses, and me, a watch from my wrist," Bratten says. "It didn't occur to Brewer or me to look for Lavelle or Tandy. We were looking for a way to the basement. We found the stairway down. Initially we could not see anyone or anything because of the dust, but finally we found one GI, and Sergeant Brewer and I carried him upstairs. This was Sergeant Christensen. He only complained to us of a hurt shoulder."

Cole helped Dahlstrom, one of the wounded rescuers: "Dahlstrom was banged up by the second shell. He wanted a cigarette, but he couldn't keep it in his mouth; he had no feeling there." Then Cole looked for his buddy Oliver Tandy: "After I came out of the cellar I realized Tandy wasn't around. I thought he might have gotten out, so I looked for him in the aid station. He wasn't there, so I went back to the cellar. It was dark in there, but a flashlight was still burning; I could see where the timbers had fallen. I called and called to Tandy. Finally I knew it was useless to call—he was lost."

Fragments from the second round caught another rescuer just outside the doorway and blasted him partially under an abandoned car. Johnny Radovitch, helping with bandages, remembers Leinbaugh telling the fellow he'd be okay, was lucky because he'd be home by Christmas. But moments later the wounded man's luck and life ran out.

They'd carried Bert Christensen to the aid station that was set up in the post-office building, but he was beyond help. No visible wounds—but massive internal injuries. "Bert just stayed long enough to get me out of there," said Keith. "But I didn't recognize anything in his voice that made me think he was excited or hurt. He was just talking to me like we're talking, and he talked me out of there."

Later, some went to see the cave-in, but others couldn't force themselves to look. Graves Registration people came up to finish the job of digging out.

In the CP, Brewer sat holding his helmet, wondering why his head wasn't crushed—looking for all the world, Leinbaugh told him, like Aristotle contemplating the bust of Homer. The next day, aware that his sister had probably read news reports that the division was in combat, Brewer wrote: "I suppose you'll be concerned, but I hope you won't worry too much. There is real satisfaction—& must be for all of you too—in knowing that we're really doing the tough stuff. I need no longer worry about a guilty conscience after the war—as I surely would have done had I been forced to remain in the rear. Besides, I am *incredibly* lucky."

The cellar ended up strictly a company affair. Battalion's S-3 journal for December 6, 1944, noted the "usual morning mortar fire." Its only other entry for that date: "Balance of the day quiet except for intermittent mortar fire." For us, six men killed: Bert Christensen, from Fairview, Utah; Ab Copeland, Cross Roads, Arkansas; Erv Koehler, Gatesville, Texas; John Lavelle, Fargo, North Dakota; Oliver Tandy, Anderson, Missouri; and Paul Zupen, Grove City, Pennsylvania. At least eight others wounded.

The men of Company K would share many another cellar before the war ended, but "the cellar" would always be that one in Lindern.

9

AFTER THE CELLAR

We had five more days on the line before the Second Battalion took over
Third Battalion positions and we moved into reserve. On December 11,
K Company would walk out of Lindern, through mud, of course—another night march, illuminated by the usual German flares. We would
pass by artillery, silent guns in soggy emplacements beneath sodden camouflage nets. We'd also exchange glances, but few words, with another
rifle company heading up front.

But the K Company heading back that night was yet again a different
outfit. We had lost more men, not all to shelling. Replacements blended
in with the old originals. That feeling that we were on our own in Lindern, us against the world, had made a company man of almost everyone.
After a week on line—and after the cellar—ours was a quiet, thoughtful
crew, with more skills and fewer illusions.

We'd marched up to Lindern with five officers and marched back with
five. But even here there'd been a change. Captain Bradford was gone,
and Lage, the leader of the third platoon, was now a lieutenant. Mario
spent one day away from Lindern. Ninth Army HQ typed up the papers
giving Mario an honorable discharge—he was a civilian for a moment.
Then a second set of papers gave him a battlefield commission. He took a
shower, put on new ODs, and pinned the gold bar and crossed rifles of an
infantry second lieutenant to his collar tabs.

Mario was a natural for a commission. He looked good to Joe Namey,
the third platoon's runner: "He was tall, a little older than the rest; we

knew he was experienced. Handsome—the Hollywood type. And he was a survivor."

Ed Stewart, who himself had been given more leadership responsibilities than he'd anticipated, also liked Lage and studied him closely. "He was a free spirit, he really was," says Stewart. "Lage found out I was born in Brazil. 'Ah, ha,' he said, 'my ambition has been to go to Brazil and open a gambling casino in Rio.' I answered, 'I'll go back sometime and see you there.' 'Please do, but bring a lot of money with you.'"

Stewart admired Lage because he always kept his cool and because he enforced some useful rules. For example: "Never draw unless you're going to fire. Don't play around with your weapon. When you're using it, use it. When you're not using it, stop using it. It's all or none."

Stewart had even singled Mario out as a kind of personal talisman: "One of the things I was trying to do—it worked for a while—you needed some kind of positive magnet there, positive attraction, and I began generating it on Lage. I still remember thinking, 'If Lage is all right, you're all right. Don't worry.'"

Before Mario came back, Paul Dulin, newly moved to platoon sergeant, lectured the men. "No longer 'Lucky Lage,'" he said. "You guys remember he's an officer now." Still, Lage was lucky that Dulin and the others didn't see an item that turned up in the *Shreveport Journal*. After a report on Mario's battlefield promotion came this: "Known over here as a volunteer for night patrols, his buddies call him 'Killer Lage.'" Even Mario would have had a tough time living down the taunts that would have triggered off.

The day Lage got his commission, Captain Bradford got hit. He'd been with the company ten days. At night he made the rounds of the holes to check on the men. The way he did it, some thought, was the problem. "Captain Bradford came up one night and I almost shot him," Richard Heuer says. "All of a sudden this guy emerges at the top of the foxhole. I grabbed the BAR and was ready to let him have it until he spoke. 'How you guys doing?' He had snuck up on us like an Indian and then after talking with us he went on."

How it happened isn't clear, but sometime before dawn on Friday, December 8, he was hit. The morning report says, "Bradford, James M. Inf. Capt. slightly wounded in action near Lindern, Germany on 8 Dec 44." Stewart mentions that Bradford "insisted on personally making a round of the foxholes each night," and then reports the rumor that went through the company. While Bradford toured the line in darkness, "one of the men challenged him near the bridge but became scared and without waiting for a proper answer threw a grenade (so the story went) which wounded the captain in the leg."

Leinbaugh again took over the company. And soon he had to make a command decision—about a dog. On K Company's first day in Lindern men on the right flank had noticed it. It wasn't easy to see, this German shepherd; its coloring blended with the drab landscape. Still the men saw it navigate the fields between Lindern and Brachelen. When the dog repeated these trips, the men began to worry; maybe it was smuggling messages between the towns. This dog had to go.

The men in the holes came close to mutiny. They wouldn't shoot a dog. Finally a marksman agreed to take a shot. Doc Mellon, watching, thought that whoever fired did a good job. "One round killed him; that dog didn't even whimper. Later when they took the collar off to look for messages they didn't find a thing."

Shelling and more shelling. Battalion continued to log the "usual morning mortar fire," though the predictable fire was not confined to morning hours. In the second platoon they called it Dr Pepper, echoing ads recommending that drink at ten, two, and four o'clock.

A few more were wounded. We had another SIW. And a couple of exhaustion cases appeared on the morning report. These were not considered battle injuries, but they, too, may in a way have been casualties of the cellar. One of the men who went to the exhaustion center was a first-rate NCO who'd tried his damnedest, but couldn't stay up; he'd be back to try again. Another who went back for a rest wasn't held in such high esteem. The difference between the two was a matter of will: One wanted to be with the company, and the other didn't.

Late on the night of December 11 we headed out of Lindern toward Gereonsweiler. From there a blacked-out truck convoy carried us to Frelenberg, another beat-up village southwest of Lindern.

In Frelenberg, as in the other towns taken thus far, civilians had headed east before the fighting began. The only German presence was Bed-Check Charlie, a patrol plane that routinely flew over the area about nine each night.

When the company pulled in after midnight, Al Oyler and John Sabia were waiting with others returning from hospital. They'd come up from the Eighteenth Replacement Battalion and had catching up to do.

In North Africa, GIs had parodied an old song, "Wedding Bells are Breaking Up that Old Gang of Mine"; they dropped the first two words and sang instead, "Eighty-eights . . ." Now 88s and other Jerry weapons were breaking up the K Company gang. The men back from hospital asked their questions: Who'd made it so far? Who hadn't? They looked for old buddies. Oyler rejoined his light-machine-gun section, and in the second platoon Sabia and Campbell got together. Campbell, still feeling a little inexperienced, had learned enough to know that the sergeant who'd temporarily taken Sabia's place had to go. So he was especially glad to see Sabia come back.

Keith Lance, back from a pass to Paris, also rejoined the company. Keith had earned the trip; he'd been ready for it. But now he was home again. "That three-day pass was as good as three years, just getting off the line," says Lance. "Clean clothes, clean beds. And oh boy, they had such good food. I couldn't believe you could walk off the front line and into a hotel like that. The festive attitude of the people stationed back there in Paris did bother me, though. Of course, they wouldn't know what it was like up front. Neither would we if we hadn't been up there.

"Somebody had us talk with two congressmen—senators, I think. I was kind of put out by them. They had no feeling for what a war was like. They asked us questions; but they were concerned about appropriations, wanted to know about supplies, how much ammunition we had—things like that. It just didn't feel like infantry. Here they were, acting like kings, and it kind of burned me up. But you know I had that basement in Lindern on my mind."

Our three days back in Frelenberg weren't just break time. The companies in the battalion were scheduled for a training exercise, attacking a fortification. K Company took its turn. Sabia gave it mixed reviews: "Some bright colonel got the idea to give us training in taking a pillbox. You can just picture what we thought about the idea after learning the hard way. So a day was spent taking a pillbox using every weapon we had. That gave the new boys a chance to fire the bazooka, and the mortar section had some experience also."

Before leaving the line at Lindern, Dempsey Keller went on sick call. At the aid station they started the first sergeant to the rear for an operation. He'd be lost to hospital until the end of January. Franklin Brewer took over the key NCO slot in company headquarters: Brewer, the slender, slightly balding, thirty-seven-year-old, was fifteen years older than Leinbaugh. It was understandable that some of the replacements thought that the fatherly older man was the CO.

Ninth Army headquarters was having a good war. They had made arrangements to fly generals and colonels back to England for a three-day break, and the assistant special service officer had recently returned from a conference in Paris—preparation for VE Day. Plans were also afoot for the more immediate future: Christmas. In mid-November the assistant exchange officer for the Ninth Army had picked up 661,000 Christmas cards in Paris. The distribution didn't make it out to K Company's holes. Then in early December the scope of Ninth Army holiday activities widened. The army chaplain, assistant special service officer, and a local troop-entertainment committee held meetings: "A Dutch tableau, carols, trees, decorations in mess halls and dances for officers and enlisted men during the holidays were planned." The special service people put out a bulletin reporting entertainment scheduled in local theaters and show units available for booking. And "two (2) enlisted men American Red Cross Doughnut Dugouts were established using four (4) girls." At the Maastricht Dugout they proudly reported serving 6,000 doughnuts and 5,000 cups of coffee per day; in Heerlen, 10,800 doughnuts and 7,000 coffees daily.

No one in K Company knew about any of this. If we had, somebody would have said, "Army gets the doughnuts; we get the holes." But in Frelenberg we weren't complaining much, even though it was still raining and we were still in cellars.

Liquor rations arrived. The Army's caste system said officers only, but that went by the boards in line outfits. Christmas spirits flowed in the fourth platoon that night. "There were maybe ten of us in a room," Sterner recalls. "And this lieutenant came in and said, 'Hey, I just got a liquor ration. Would you guys like it?' There were three bottles of booze—one scotch, one rye, and one gin. And we passed the bottles around. We were in our sleeping bags, and we didn't know one bottle from the other, and we all got bombed out."

The sun came out on Wednesday, December 13. For most of the day the temperature was comfortably above freezing. People left cellars, inhaled crisp fresh air, visited buddies in other platoons. We had it made.

Battalion had a church call with a chaplain's service and carols, followed by a movie in the same building. Stewart rated the short sermon woefully inadequate from a soldier's viewpoint; Sabia complained that the power failed so many times during the first reel of the film that they called it off. Still the annoyances we had to grouse about were minor.

Bill Parsons, the company's musician, gave an impromptu recital that was the high point of the relief for Richard Heuer: "One of the first songs he played was 'Sunny Side of the Street.' Today when I hear that song I always think of him and the rest of the outfit. Every place we were where there was a piano, Parsons would play it."

For many in the company, though, Parsons's song was "White Christmas." He had as much of a lock on the tune as Bing Crosby did. That's the song in Bill's own mind when he turns to that day in December. "Curly Hoffman, Van Houten, Hector Musgrave, and half a dozen other guys—all the old guys were there," Parsons says. "A couple of guys come screaming over to me, 'We've got one! We've got one!' 'You've got what?' 'We've got a piano!' They had gotten a piano out of a house, carried it down the steps, put it in the middle of the street. And somebody says, 'Goddammit, play "White Christmas."'"

"So I played 'White Christmas.' And we're crying like a bunch of idiots. Funniest—but one of the greatest experiences, you know—'Dammit, play "White Christmas."' They brought the thing down a set of steps from the second floor. They carefully carried this upright piano—it must have weighed a ton. And they set it in the middle of the road, and they said, 'Play "White Christmas."' Of course I did, and we just laughed and cried. . . . Yeah—all the old guys were there."

Thursday afternoon, regiment alerted battalion for a return to the line. Back in Lindern the sound of an American swing band greeted us, coming from the Germans across the way. Then from Jerry loudspeakers came what seemed to be President Roosevelt's voice, though its distance from our lines made the speech unintelligible.

The break had done us good. Morale was up. We still had a healthy respect for the machine gun that covered the overpass, but it was now as much a nuisance as a threat. Maybe that learning to live with uncertainty, savoring whatever good came our way, is what distinguished our second stay in Lindern from the first. Stewart could tell he'd changed. "During the first period at Lindern," he says, "I had come to what I thought was close to cracking, but now these were things of the past." But there was some backing and filling as life went along.

When Mario took the third platoon out to the holes he knew that just sitting for a day or two at a time wasn't good—better to move around some. About dawn on their first morning back he and his men climbed out and began to stretch their legs. A single shot from the right flank clipped Naehring. Back in the hole, Naehring's buddy bandaged the wound. Then Johnny Bowe, who'd been lying in wait for German outpost guards, used his telescopic Springfield '03 to do some sniping himself— claimed he got the man with the third or fourth round. From then on the men rarely moved from the holes in the day and left them at night only when it was necessary.

Things soon began stirring. An hour before noon Friday, company commanders met at battalion for a briefing on Operation Dagger. Plans for the assault toward the Roer called for the 2nd Armored to pass through 84th Division positions and head northeast toward the river-banks. An armored column would move through Lindern. Then, follow-ing the rail line, they would launch an assault on Brachelen.

Later in the day a colonel who would lead the tanks turned up in K Company's area to scout out the terrain. He and Leinbaugh climbed to the top of the building housing company headquarters. While the colonel considered approach routes, Leinbaugh pointed out K Company's posi-tions, paying particular attention to those of the light machine guns and mortars. Then he offered the colonel the full support of our three 60mm mortars and two .30 caliber LMGs. The colonel's binoculars didn't waver. "The best thing your men can do is get down in their holes and keep out of our way."

In midafternoon 84th Division's G-3 came into town with some Air Corps officers to size up the situation. Information about who and what the division was up against was in short supply. So Lage caught a night-patrol assignment to ambush a prisoner for interrogation. In the company CP they discussed options. George Pope had a suggestion. Earlier that day, from his first platoon OP on a Lindern rooftop, he'd scanned the land that flanked the railroad cut leading off toward Brachelen. "Looking way out there I don't see nothing moving," Pope says. "Then something catches my eye. You know how movement will catch your eye. I look down—two Krauts were digging like sons of bitches. Holes this deep already. How the hell they got there I don't know to this day. You can see the shoveling and the dirt flying. I say, 'Get the M1.' The kid brings me up the M1 and we lay there. Pow, and we're kicking the dirt.

"That night I told Lage, 'Look, those two jokers are only a little ways out there. If you go down the railroad tracks and climb up where I told you, you can crawl to them only fifty yards from there.' But they wouldn't listen. And I didn't want to open my mouth again, for they'd say, 'If you know where they are, you do it.'"

Lage did lead the patrol. He, Jerry Dunne, and two others formed up along the railway cut that headed northeast, Dunne on the north side of the cut, Lage on the south. It was dark, but the railroad provided a well-defined route. Since plenty of enemy fire had been coming from the vicinity of the next overpass to the northeast, Lage had settled on that as a destination. Then if he and Dunne each held the end of a line, they could keep abreast of one another without unnecessary noise.

"We had the line between us," Dunne remembers. "We knew we might run into some poles along the way. So we were supposed to go to the poles and then pass the line around so we could continue. I don't know how far we went, but we went quite a ways. I'd estimate about 200 to 250 yards. Then all hell broke loose.

"There was another bridge down there, and they had a machine gun around it. We figured there'd be somebody down on the railroad tracks. And we heard a railroad car. Then I pulled the line to Lage. There was nothing there. The line came loose. That was after the machine gun went off."

When Dunne found no one on the other end of the line, he had no notion of what had happened. He waited and wondered. Then he heard someone speaking German up on the bridge, and he knew it wasn't Lage. Thinking Mario had gone to the rear, Jerry himself headed back and found Lage. "But," Dunne continues, "the guy who'd been with me—I didn't know who it was—wasn't back there. So I went out and brought him back. He was okay, just scared. He froze when the machine gun went off.

"They needed prisoners bad," Dunne says, "because the following night they sent us the other way. Down to the left, toward the railroad depot. But they had other patrols out. Which I didn't know. And they took prisoners that night."

It began to appear that the push to the northeast might face stiff opposition. Reports came in about a Panzer buildup intended to counter the planned American drive. Then before dawn Sunday, December 17, regiment's operations section called battalion with the news that fifty enemy planes were heading toward Lindern. Next at 5:50 A.M. battalion recorded a message from regiment in the log: "We can expect planes to drop paratroopers—to precede larger attack."

After dawn two P47s skimmed over Brachelen, but no Jerry ack-ack responded. Lindern remained calm. After sunset, however, enemy planes dropped flares and bombs. At 7:15 P.M. battalion passed on a report that paratroops had dropped behind Beeck; a half hour later regiment informed battalion that the report of a paratroop drop was false. Back to more routine fears. And the men in the holes remained blissfully unaware of the fact that at 5:00 A.M., December 16, a juggernaut rumbled west out of the fog, night, and snow, and struck deep into the Ardennes. The Germans had begun the Battle of the Bulge.

Midnight Sunday marked a second week on the defensive. Jim Grafmiller, in the rear with the rest of the 333rd's company clerks, entered two of the day's happenings in the morning report: One man lost to the hospital (Dennis Poling, a bloody head wound from machine-gun fire during a night patrol), another back from hospital (R. J. Bell, wounded on November 24). Then he corrected an old entry: For a man listed as MIA November 23, Grafmiller changed the report to "slightly wounded, gunshot, accidental." To the best of his knowledge, that brought the company's books up to date.

The morning of the 18th, division also began clearing its books of unfinished business. A mile and a half west of Lindern, twelve battalions of artillery, three cannon companies, a 4.2 chemical mortar company, and two 81mm mortar platoons shelled the living daylights out of Würm. In Lindern men took comfort from the distant din; it was ours. An hour after the softening up, two companies of the 334th Infantry had taken the town. The after-action report notes, "Opposition was generally light." The division had had a month of on-the-job training since the 333rd Infantry first moved out in a bloody push toward Würm.

Lindern took light shelling that day. But it was enough to snuff out another life. The outgoing mail well to our left may have lulled some of us into a false sense of security. Or perhaps after the fourth platoon's cave-in, cellars had lost their appeal. In the husk of a building a third platoon squad relaxed on the ground floor. They heard a low whiffle, then the explosion of an incoming mortar round. The men ducked for cover, but it was too late. Warner fell to the floor, the stool on which he'd been sitting overturned beside him. His cry, "I'm hit!" meant Warner was still conscious.

Ed Stewart, the squad leader, sent all but Johnny Bowe and Jim Teague to the basement. Teague dashed for the aidman. Stewart propped Warner against his knees. Bowe worked at the OD trousers to get at one wound. Ed tried to stop the flow of blood that covered Warner's neck and left shoulder. He thought the wound was in the neck, "but there was so much blood that it took a few seconds to find the hole above his heart."

Doc came rushing up and bandaged the wound while Stewart talked to Warner and tried to comfort him: "But he could no longer hear me," Stewart says. "His breathing was heavy and faint, his eyes were turning glassy, and his body was already getting limp, with his head falling on his shoulder. In a few minutes a jeep drove up. The aidmen put him on a stretcher and took him to the aid station. I walked outside with Doc and asked, 'How is he, Doc?' He didn't say anything, just shook his head."

Stewart and Bowe went back to the basement and rejoined the others in the squad. The men looked at one another with long faces. Then someone from the CP came in with recently arrived letters and packages. In each of his two large Christmas packages Stewart found several little ones, each individually wrapped and tied: "I opened them one at a time and passed them to Johnny, who then passed them to the others. Johnny and I were making cracks about so many little packages and outlandishly guessing what would be in the next one. The others mechanically passed them on, not cracking a smile. Finally Pop said something funny. The ice was broken, and in a few minutes everyone was normal again."

At twilight Stewart took the contents of one of the small packages—a pair of dice—to the CP. These were for Mario Lage, a gift honoring his promotion to lieutenant. That's when Mario told Ed that Warner had died just after reaching the aid station. Perhaps that moment signaled Stewart's realization that having Mario as a personal talisman posed a problem. When Ed first thought, "If Mario makes it, I'll make it," he hadn't considered the converse: "If Mario doesn't come through, I won't either." Lage as talisman had succeeded so well for Stewart that the thought now surfaced, "My God, what happens if he's killed?"

That night marked the company's last in Lindern. While we'd defended the town, illness, injury, and death had whittled away at our numbers. We'd come up from Prummern with a strength of 175, and some had come back from the clearing station and hospital since then. But when we marched to Gereonsweiler at 10:00 on the night of the 18th, we now totaled just over 150. We didn't know it, but our chances of getting up to full strength in the days ahead were slim. By mid-December, Ninth Army had run critically short of "combat replacement stockage." K Company would get no more replacements until the end of the year.

From Gereonsweiler, a truck ride to Palenberg, a comfortable seven miles southwest of Lindern. There after midnight we bivouacked with the rest of the battalion. Palenberg felt safe, even though an order came for officers to check dog tags and other identification because there was an alert for enemy troops in our lines.

When the sun finally came out on the 19th the town came alive. Men roamed the streets. Volunteer cooks prepared hot meals from GI rations and scrounged supplies. The second platoon medic put his surgical skills to peeling potatoes, then Don Phelps combined these with onions, beans, K-ration meat, and bouillon powder to make a stew. Dinner was served on genuine dishes borrowed from local cupboards.

Chick brought up the mail, huge stacks of letters and packages. In a letter home, Campbell listed the contents of his first Christmas package— knife, can opener, fruitcake in a tin, socks, homemade fudge, cheese spread, and RyKrisp, all cushioned for travel by loose popcorn filler. Then he commented on the resemblance between RyKrisp and the K-ration biscuits "which have been my more or less constant diet recently." Sabia's packages had the best Italian sausage, which he shared with the platoon. Brewer's packages, naturally, were more exotic. In a letter thanking his sister Rosemary and her husband he commented, "The caviar I wolfed solo. And where *did* you find the chocolat meunière?"

Hot baths again, this time in QM outdoor showers, then clean ODs. And promotions: Keith Lance moved up to tech sergeant, Ed Stewart to staff. Jerry Dunne became the first replacement to make buck sergeant, along with three of the ASTP boys, Johnny Moore, Bill Parsons, and Jim Sterner.

With so many good things happening, Sabia decided it was time for celebration: "I found myself a top hat and cane and went visiting different platoons, only to find that I wasn't the only one directly out of *Esquire*. Men all around had Homburg hats, spats, and vests, all trying to break the monotony of fear."

Then Mike DeBello came up with the tree. He hacked it down with his entrenching tool and set it up near the CP. Others helped with decorations. Brewer saw it and caught Leinbaugh: "Lieutenant, you have to see this." Then Brewer lectured, pointing out the symbolism in the improvised ornaments—military and civilian—that covered the little pine. The tree still stood in Palenberg when, a day later, the company pulled out in a rush to the Ardennes. But the green boughs stayed with us across the miles and the years.

A month after Christmas the tree turned up in a note Campbell sent from Paris back to Illinois: "Before we left Germany, a few days before Christmas, we had a Christmas tree. It was a little tree in a little town, decorated half in earnest, half self-kidding. Salvaged bits of colored cloth plus the tinsel substitute of long rolls of that white paper served as the major ornaments. Underneath the tree were the presents—a broken doll buggy, a toy gun, K rations."

In May 1946, it hit the pages of Stewart's notebook: "Up by the kitchen someone decorated a pine tree with toilet paper, our Xmas tree."

Sabia, in 1948, jotted down a recollection of the tree. "We rigged up a Christmas tree, for Christmas was only a week or so away. Not having the fine tinsel and all, the tree was dressed with bandoliers of ammo and hand grenades and the silver strips the Air Corps drops to deflect radar."

Thirty-five years after the occasion Leinbaugh reminded Campbell of this "scroungy little pine" and recalled that the topmost ornament was a flaxen-haired, teddy-bear-sized doll—wearing Mike DeBello's gas mask.

And in December 1980, the tree was still green for Mike himself: "Everything I could find I put on that Christmas tree. I put boots on it, socks, an old frying pan, tinsel. Them guys say to me, 'Hey, Mike, you're crazy.' But I said, 'We've got to have Christmas.' Everybody's got to have Christmas."

*   *   *

Before daylight on December 16, the vanguard of nearly half a million Germans in three armies plunged without warning out of mist and snow into the rugged Ardennes region of Belgium and Luxembourg. Along a sixty-mile front from the German town of Monschau in the north to the medieval Luxembourg town of Echternach in the south, the assault struck thinly manned American positions. Despite overwhelming German strength, American GIs fought stubbornly, but within forty-eight hours German armor penetrated the thin lines at several points and headed swiftly for the Meuse River. The objective was Antwerp. The goal was to isolate American, British, and Canadian armies in the north from Allied forces in the south. This was the beginning of the Battle of the Bulge, one of the great decisive battles fought by the U.S. Army in World War II.

The giant offensive was the idea of Adolf Hitler himself. It was a last desperate gamble to stave off certain defeat for Nazi Germany. When Hitler revealed his plan to his generals on September 16, 1944, at the daily Führer Conference in the Wolf's Lair in East Prussia, the 84th Division's GIs were still in Camp Kilmer, New Jersey. Their only concern was wangling last-minute passes to New York City before embarking for Europe. It would have been impossible for anybody in K Company or the division to have guessed that in less than a hundred days they would be involved in what Churchill described as "the greatest American battle of the war."

By the battle's end in January 1945, twenty-nine U.S. divisions had been involved, more than were committed by the United States in the entire Pacific war. Almost 300,000 American infantrymen saw action; K Company was just one of seven hundred participating rifle companies. American battle casualties during the battle totaled 81,000 killed, wounded, and captured. German manpower losses were even greater—at least 100,000 men.

10

CHRISTMAS IN VERDENNE

K Company's first three days in Belgium were peaceful—so quiet, in fact, that Doughhead Lance started a rumor the army was going to knock off our combat pay, the extra five bucks a month we got for fighting Germans.

Our Third Battalion was in reserve, no one in K Company saw a German, no one fired a shot. During the afternoon of December 21, after a long, cold, and rainy ride from Palenberg, near Geilenkirchen, we unloaded from our trucks in Serinchamps. This Belgian hamlet of several dozen houses was hidden away in a woods five miles west of Marche, a major road junction which was our division's assembly point. We chose the mayor's comfortable stone house for the CP, and wiremen strung an aerial to the roof to extend the range of the SCR 300 and ran sound-powered phone lines to the platoons.

Brewer was our contact man with the first civilians we had seen since Heerlen in Holland. In his persuasive French he assured the apprehensive mayor and the village's elderly priest the Americans had come to stay; we were going to stop the Germans' counteroffensive and they shouldn't worry. The mayor was skeptical. This was 1940 all over again; he seemed sure of it. He seemed to take perverse pride in explaining that Field Marshal Erwin Rommel had personally led the Panzers through the region en route to the Meuse four years earlier. The mayor asked about tanks, clearly hoping the Americans had something more substantial than K Company's M1s to stop the German armor. The local phones were working, he told Brewer, and he'd received calls an hour earlier reporting Panzer reconnaissance forces rolling through villages ten miles away.

The mayor seemed upset that Brewer and the company officers dismissed his reports so casually. Because we had been fighting Germans in the Siegfried Line, the prospect of doing battle with them in the open seemed more an opportunity than cause for panic. Germans ten miles away? That was beyond our scope of imagination.

Seeing no need to waste the night digging foxholes, we established three-man guard posts along the two roads into town and in front of the CP. The rest of the company settled down in warm houses and barns, but the extraordinary stillness and comfortable quarters somehow made sleep difficult.

K Company's sojourn in Serinchamps lasted but six hours. Before midnight a battalion messenger brought orders for the company to move to Baillonville to provide security for division headquarters. As we lined up, an agitated priest and mayor confronted Brewer, who did his best to calm them. The battalion was not retreating, he said, just moving to new defensive positions.

We cursed the weather and the Army as we plodded through freezing rain and slippery mud. Why couldn't headquarters make up its mind? Why all the uncertainty? What the hell was going on?

Our soggy GI overcoats soaked up pounds of added weight from the rain, and we were already burdened down with full packs and extra ammunition. The weather turned colder—cold enough for small dripping icicles to form around the brims of helmets and on the butts of rifles. Before we covered the seven miles to Baillonville, several men had collapsed from fatigue. The headquarters troops were lined up for hot chow at the edge of Baillonville, but we wearily set to work digging holes in the mud.

Rifle companies didn't warrant intelligence briefings, but we picked up scraps of information and plenty of rumors from men in division headquarters. Reports were coming into division about German paratroopers dropping in rear areas and infiltrators in GI uniforms driving captured vehicles behind our front lines.

New messages verifying the murder of GIs by the SS at Malmédy had come in. According to wounded survivors, SS troops had lined up at least seventy American prisoners at the Baugnez road junction outside Malmédy and proceeded to mow them down. The killers were tankers from SS Kampfgruppe Peiper, last reported in the vicinity of Stoumont, thirty miles northeast of us.

If K Company's reaction to the atrocity was typical, the Germans had committed their worst mistake of the war on the Western Front. We had fought by rules of a sort. In the heat of battle, prisoners were sometimes killed. We knew that. But this was mass murder, and the SS was going to have to pay and pay heavily.

Clayton Shepherd wanted revenge. "When Leinbaugh told us about

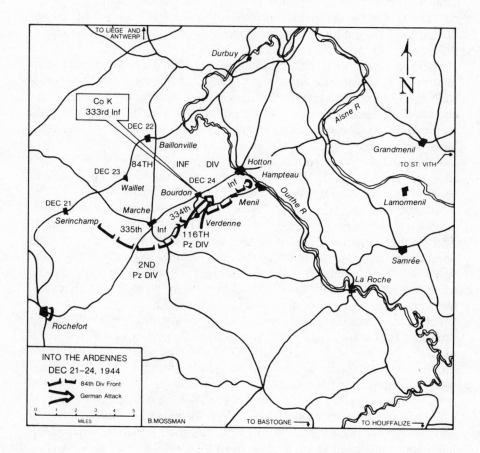

Co K
333rd Inf

INTO THE ARDENNES
DEC 21–24, 1944

84th Div Front

German Attack

0 1 2 3 4 5
MILES

B. MOSSMAN

the massacre, everybody got pissed off. I just wanted to get down to Belgium and start killing Germans."

On the 22nd, the division front, if it could be called that, was fluid. The 84th had received orders to hold a defensive line between Marche and Hotton, six miles to the northeast, "at all costs." The first regiment in the division's convoy, the 334th, had outposted Marche and established roadblocks at intersections, bridges, and neighboring villages. The 335th occupied ground south and west of Marche and sent one battalion more than ten miles beyond Marche, to Rochefort and nearby villages. Our own regiment's First Battalion probed fourteen miles west of Marche looking for Germans. Small jeep patrols were sent out along our entire front to try to find the enemy's line of advance. The lucky ones returned to our lines, some with dead and wounded. Other patrols simply disappeared.

Guards at roadblocks waved down officers in their jeeps, demanding that they identify the capital of Washington state or Betty Grable's husband. The security checks became a farce, for few of the officers knew answers to the questions and they became belligerent and angry at guards holding M1s in their faces. A bright fellow in headquarters finally figured it would be simpler to ask transients their shirt size, on the assumption that Germans accustomed to the metric system would have trouble remembering a 14½-32 shirt wouldn't fit a hefty six-footer.

Rumor had it that the division's flanks were wide open but that the 2nd Armored Division was coming down within the next twenty-four hours to fill in on our right. In our book, they were the best, real professionals. It was the only good rumor of the day.

No sooner were our holes finished than new orders came to move again and defend a country crossroads on the highway running north from Marche. "One more stupid move, one more hole," said Sabia, "and I'm going to lose interest in their whole goddam war." But we wiped our shovels, knocked the mud from our boots, lined up, and marched off again. We were told we could expect German armor from any direction, so we laid out our defensive positions in a closed circle with the CP at the center.

Mario Lage, our recently commissioned third platoon leader, keeled over while digging and promptly diagnosed his own illness—a recurrence of malaria picked up on Guadalcanal. One of the small handful of company indispensables, his departure was a serious loss.

The cloud cover that had blanketed the Ardennes since the first day of the massive German attack finally broke during the morning of the 23rd. Hundreds of planes, German and American, but mostly American as far as we could tell, crisscrossed the sky, leaving long contrails from horizon to horizon. The dogfights were fascinating. Near noontime five smoking planes went down simultaneously. Flight after flight of low-flying Thunderbolts, Mustangs, and Lightnings roared overhead heading toward German lines. The planes gave a big boost to our morale. As J. A. Craft put it, "They were like geese in the sky. Those first formations were a beautiful sight, I'm telling you."

On the 24th, the company made another seemingly aimless move to the nearby village of Waillet. No one in higher headquarters bothered to tell us why they were moving us again, so the grousing and complaining increased. Still, we appreciated our good fortune in pulling nothing more rigorous than rear-area guard duty and looked forward to a peaceful Christmas dinner.

Most men had fallen into an exhausted sleep when a battalion jeep screeched to a halt at our guard post. It was 9:00 P.M. A truck convoy was on its way. K Company was to lead off in a night attack to retake a town overrun a few hours earlier by German armor. That was all they told us. That was all we knew.

When we unloaded from our two-and-a-halfs, the battalion operations officer was waiting. He told us we were in Bourdon, a couple of miles east of Marche.

The platoons formed up along the village's main road while the officers and platoon sergeants crowded into the battalion CP in a school building for orders. The meeting was short, lasting less than five minutes. The only available map of the area was a badly printed, smudged black-and-white copy with roads and trails barely distinguishable.

The sky was clear, but the feel of snow was in the air, the ground lightly frozen and covered with frost. To us, the night was ominously quiet, the only sound the distant mutterings of heavy artillery. The sergeants were briefing their squads when the colonel hurried out of the CP and told us to get moving—the attack was already behind schedule. Seeking somes means of identifying each other in the dark, we tried tying handkerchiefs around our right arms, but their olive-drab color blended too closely with the dark brown overcoats to be of help.

We'd learned this much in the briefing. The 334th's Third Battalion had been defending a series of villages and strongpoints to the east of Marche, and some hours earlier German tanks had overrun the lightly held village of Verdenne. Heavily outnumbered, the GIs pulled back in good order, setting up new defensive positions along a woods line between Verdenne and Bourdon.

A sergeant from the 334th came down to lead K Company up the hill and point us toward the objective. According to the last radio message, four or five tanks were with the riflemen in the woods. They were to follow behind us in the attack, but details would have to be coordinated on the spot with the tank commander. Our battalion staff lacked precise information, but they thought at least a company of German infantry and several tanks were defending Verdenne. The tanks were our big concern. The colonel told Leinbaugh our regiment's attached artillery battalion would lay down a barrage on Verdenne just before the final assault, which was to begin at midnight. L Company, in reserve, was to follow behind K and help consolidate.

As the company moved out, Brewer was setting up a CP in the village. He called a quiet greeting to Phelps. "Merry Christmas, Don. Take care of yourself."

"Don't worry," Phelps replied, but he had a feeling that it was his turn, that he was going to get hit that night.

The company column crossed twin railroad tracks to begin a gradual ascent toward the ridgeline, then stopped as the road forked. Which road? The main road to the left, or the secondary road, a half-right? Our guide from the 334th hesitated, then pointed to the left. Pulling the map from his field jacket, Leinbaugh, shielded by a raincoat, struck several matches, but he was unable to pinpoint the road junction in the brief flares of light.

"What's the name of that goddam town?"

"Verdenne," Campbell answered. "I'm pretty sure that's it, about a mile, I'd guess."

"Yeah . . . . Well, as long as we're going up we're okay."

Heading left and uphill, the company moved on, traversed a horseshoe curve—the direction seemed right—and after a hundred yards entered a dense forest.

Just ahead a tank loomed out of the darkness, its huge bulk nearly filling the narrow road, branches pressing in on either side brushing its steel plates. The men at the front of the column stopped several feet away and passed back word to hold up.

The ground mist had thickened after entering the woods, so it was impossible to see more than a few yards. The time was exactly midnight.

As the column halted, Leinbaugh turned to Phelps. "Tell the tankers to follow the tail end of the company through the woods. We'll work out details for the attack on the far side."

Phelps felt his way slowly along the side of the tank and called out, but there was no answer. Pounding on the side of the hull with the butt of his M1, he yelled louder: "Hey, you guys, open up!" He pounded again.

The hatch opened slowly, a creak of metal, and the head and shoulders of a man appeared. "*Was ist los?*" the man demanded. Again, peering over the side of the turret, "*Was ist los?*"

It took awhile, more seconds than necessary—but suddenly as we hit the ditches we realized K Company's first full-fledged night attack was getting off to a bad start.

Compiled shortly after the war, the 84th Division's history noted that "the enemy's salient beyond Verdenne was discovered in a curious way."

The first man in the company to grasp what was happening, Phelps stepped back two steps and fired a single shot at the dark form in the

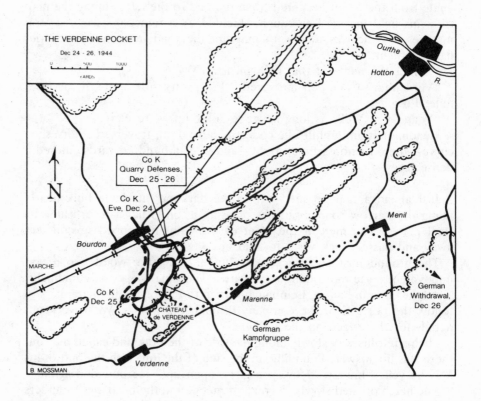

THE VERDENNE POCKET

Dec 24 - 26, 1944

0   500   1000
YARDS

Ourthe

Hotton

R.

Co K
Quarry Defenses,
Dec 25 - 26

Co K
Eve, Dec 24

Menil

Bourdon

MARCHE

Co K
Dec 25

German
Withdrawal,
Dec 26

CHÂTEAU
de VERDENNE

Marenne

German
Kampfgruppe

Verdenne

B. MOSSMAN

turret. The man screamed and collapsed from view. Seconds later the tank's hatch clanged shut.

Phelps yelled, "They're Germans! Get down!" And almost as an echo German voices from the woods screamed warnings. *"Amis! Amis!"*

When Leinbaugh heard the shot, he thought Phelps had made a terrible mistake and yelled at him to stop shooting. Only after hearing the German voices did he realize the company was in trouble.

Men at the head of the company column fired blindly toward the woods and hit the ditches. Machine guns on the German tanks opened up. Then everything began to happen at once.

Streams of tracers lit up the road, giving enough light for Bratten, the radioman, to see the large black cross on the front of the first tank. J. B. Cole, standing next to the tank on the left of the road, ran several steps and hit the ground. "I ended up right in the midst of a group of German infantry—foot soldiers who'd dug in to protect the tanks." Pope's platoon had been near the middle of the company column. "We heard this German yell, and then those stupid jerks start firing down the middle of the road. We parted just like that." The tanks revved up their engines, but remained in place, making no attempt to move forward.

Phelps yelled for a bazooka man, grabbed his rocket launcher—the man gladly gave it up—and ran forward along the edge of the road. He fired one round, which hit the second vehicle, an armored personnel carrier, or APC. It exploded, and Phelps reloaded and fired again, but his second round bounced harmlessly off the side of the APC. As he stepped back in the woods to check the bazooka, there was a sudden blast, and fragments from a German shell hit him in his hands and arms and ricocheted off the bazooka tube.

More German machine guns opened up, and the lead tank fired its big gun, aiming round after round of 75mm high-explosive shells down the road. Tanks farther back in the German column angled fire into the woods and bounced machine-gun rounds off the thick steel of the first tank to prevent us from closing in with bazookas or grenades.

As the firing increased, Leinbaugh grabbed the handset of the SCR 300 from Bratten in time to hear the battalion commander asking what in the hell was going on. Pressing the talk switch, he yelled over the noise, "Colonel, we've run into German tanks and have one hell of a firefight on our hands." The colonel was unimpressed. "Clear those Krauts off the road and get moving." The muzzle blast on the Panther tank's long 75mm spewed flame fifteen feet behind the men at the front of the company column.

Holding the talk switch open, Leinbaugh raised the handset a few inches over his helmet in order to give the colonel the full effect of the cannon's blast. Tossing the handset to Bratten, he yelled to the men around him: "Get the hell out of here."

Less than a minute had passed since Phelps had set off the little battle, but half a dozen men in K Company were wounded in that first exchange. Men began inching their way back along the shallow ditches.

Every man along that forest road between Bourdon and Verdenne on Christmas Eve brought back his own story. It was a night of vivid memories and the night K Company came of age.

After Sabia and an aidman bandaged Phelps's arm, he crawled toward the rear until it was safe to stand. Cradling his wounded hands to his chest, he took off at a slow run toward the aid station at the bottom of the hill, calling out, "Merry Christmas!" as he headed back.

Bill Parsons and his squad were no more than thirty feet from the German tank when the firing commenced. "They would have blown our brains out except they couldn't depress their gun enough. Thank God there was a depression angle on those babies."

Parsons had several new replacements in his squad. "I rolled over and yelled to those new kids, 'Get down! Get down!' As I turned around, whammo! It was one of those blue concussion grenades, about the size of a lemon." Parsons was hit in the face. "It was a small fragment, and came across and zapped out my eye." As Parsons told it later, "If it had been a fragmentation grenade I would have had my head blown off."

Parsons called to his platoon leader, Lieutenant Zadnick, telling him he couldn't see and had to leave. "Curly Hoffman, a real good man, came up to take over. Then I crawled down the ditch talking to the fellows as I felt my way along, wishing everybody Merry Christmas."

On his way down the hill Parsons ran into Ybarra. "He was hit in the elbow, and another guy got hit in the heel. I said, 'I can't see.' So there are the three of us—the crippled leading the blind." Ybarra led Parsons farther down the hill. "We got near L Company and I heard one of the platoon sergeants tell his machine gunners to half-load." Parsons recognized the voice—"a guy named Rhodes who liked to listen to me play the piano. I said, 'Rhodes, it's me, Parsons.'"

Rhodes told his machine gunners to hold their fire. On Christmas morning Parsons was in a field hospital, where surgeons removed his eye. "I can't say enough about the medical care—those doctors were splendid."

Back in the woods while the rest of the company was inching toward the rear, Cole remained trapped in the midst of the German infantry. He stayed flat on the ground playing dead, less than fifteen feet from the first Panther. "By this time the rest of the company had pulled back a considerable distance, but then I heard Leinbaugh's voice very plain over a radio. He was asking for aidmen and talking about company casualties. The Germans had apparently tuned in on our frequency."

Artillery started falling, but with the tree bursts Cole couldn't tell if it was German or American. "I stayed up there next to the tank most of the night. Just before daylight I crawled across the road on my belly and worked my way back to the edge of the hill and then down to the railroad." Men from another company challenged Cole, looked at his identification, asked him the names of the company and battalion commanders, and then led him to the battalion CP, where officers questioned him about what he'd seen and showed him the house serving as the K Company CP. "I walked in and Sergeant Brewer looked up at me and said, 'Oh my God, Cole, we thought you were dead.'

"Leinbaugh kidded me about my hair turning white that night. I allowed as how I did pick up a few white hairs that Christmas Eve."

Since Campbell's second platoon was to have led the attack on Verdenne, he and Leinbaugh were across the road from each other, talking in low voices, working out details for the assault, when the fracas started. Campbell found it impossible to get a clue as to what the company was facing. "From the tracers we began to make out a number of tanks and personnel carriers, but things happened so fast everything was a blur." Like his men—he learned later—nobody "had time to think about fear— our only concern was figuring how to resolve our predicament."

Incongruously, during the firefight Campbell remembered some doggerel on a tombstone in a fake cemetery at the Infantry School in Ft. Benning, Georgia.

> Here lie the bones of Lt. Jones,
> A graduate of this institution.
> He died on the night of his very first fight,
> While using the school solution.

Harvey Augustin and the company machine gunners were near the rear of the company column when the Germans opened up. "We all hit the ground and everyone was prone, but the guy right behind me got a bullet in the head. That's how low the bullets were coming down the road."

Clayton Shepherd dived into a ditch close to Augustin. "With those tracers lighting things up I could see two German tanks shooting machine guns at us. The bullets were whining off a big steel electric tower right next to me." The platoon sergeant yelled for Clayton to get bazooka ammunition. "The machine-gun bullets were coming so close you could feel the heat coming from the tracers. When I got back up with the ammo some shells came in. They knocked holes in the bazooka tubes so we couldn't use them." Shepherd didn't stop to question the order. "Somebody wanted those bazooka shells and there was nothing I could do—I just went and got them. I wasn't worried about getting hit, but I was scared that night, scared as anybody could be."

When the word came for the company to start pulling back down the hill, Topel and men in the first platoon spotted Germans behind them. "We saw this three-man Kraut patrol off to our flank and behind us. So Lieutenant Zadnick—he was a big fellow with a blond mustache—he stands up like the Lone Ranger and blasts away with his .45." Lying nearby, Sergeant Pope yelled, "Lieutenant, put that goddam popgun away and get down before you get killed!"

When the tanks opened fire, Mel Cline's squad broke from the road and into the woods. They found themselves in the middle of a German defensive position. "The fellow next to me had his helmet knocked off when he bumped into the flash hider on a German gun, and my helmet was blown off by a grenade. The Germans started to scatter, and we fired, hitting two who tried to run." Before joining the exodus down the hill, Cline and the other men made sure all the German foxholes were empty. "One hole had a small German mortar in it with a lot of potato-masher grenades next to it."

An officer sent Amici's squad into the woods to protect the company's rear in case of an encircling move by the Germans. "We found a hollow in this wooded area and we weren't there for more than three minutes when we saw a German patrol trying to get to our rear."

Years later Amici remembers every detail of the encounter. "I can still see them coming toward us, practically crouching, trying to sneak around like you'd see in cowboy-and-Indian movies. They were trying to be quiet and come around our flanks. We could see five or six, maybe more, before we opened fire." The squad held its fire until the Germans were within forty or fifty feet. "Well, it was like shooting ducks. We were sitting there waiting and everyone drew a bead on whoever they wanted." Amici had no idea how long the fight lasted. "Maybe five or ten minutes, maybe a lot less. We banged them pretty good and they didn't try again." Although the men had no idea how many Germans they killed, they were proud of themselves. "We took care of the incident and protected our flank. That was real."

George Lucht's squad also thought they had done a good job that night. Tom Miller remembers they were receiving machine-gun fire from higher up on the hill. "George got ahold of the map and we figured the fire was coming from an angle from behind some trees. So George and I found a bazooka and worked our way up the hill and fired one round. We got an explosion; we think we got a tank. Both of us felt pretty good about that."

K Company's engagement with the German tanks lasted less than half an hour. Pulling back slowly along the ditches and the sides of the road, the company captured a dozen Germans and killed or wounded as many more.

Moving down below the bend in the road, the company prepared defensive positions centered in a rock quarry in the side of an escarpment—less than two hundred yards from the German tanks. The nearest houses in Bourdon were only forty yards below the company's position and the main east-west highway between Marche and Hotton only another hundred yards away. That was the road that was to be held open at all costs.

As K Company withdrew, battalion and regiment reacted with uncharacteristic swiftness. While K Company dug in to block the road into Bourdon, L Company, which had been behind K, moved up the secondary road on the right, the one K Company should have taken, and was given the mission to take Verdenne. Locating the American tanks, L Company joined forces with K Company of the 334th, which by that time was down to forty men. Following close behind a heavy barrage, the GIs rushed the village. A grim house-to-house fight ensued with heavy losses on both sides.

With daylight, fighting around the village intensified. Tankers from the 84th's attached 771st Tank Battalion knocked out nine counterattacking Panthers, and the rifle companies in Verdenne, although heavily outnumbered, hauled in between three hundred and four hundred German prisoners. It was one of the outstanding performances in the Railsplitters' combat history.

In referring to the Christmas Eve encounter between K Company and the German armored column, the 84th Division's history estimated the so-called Verdenne pocket held five German tanks and two infantry companies. But those numbers were far from reality.

Twenty-five years after the battle, Campbell and Leinbaugh met the commander of the German tanks, Colonel Gerhard Tebbe. How many German tanks? they asked. Tebbe pondered for a moment and counted. "Maybe forty . . . forty tanks." In addition to Tebbe's tanks, Kampfgruppe Bayer contained an infantry regiment and supporting artillery and engineers.

If the counterattack to retake Verdenne had proceeded as planned—if K Company had gone to the right instead of the left—the Panzer Kampfgruppe concealed along the forest road might well have rolled forward unopposed on Christmas morning, cut the vital Marche-Hotton road, and entered the open country leading to the Meuse. American reserves would surely have intervened, but K Company helped change at least one short paragraph in the story of the battle.

The U.S. Army's official history of the Ardennes battle referred to K Company's encounter with the German tanks as a "lucky fluke" which revealed the German threat to the all-important Marche-Hotton highway. The volume also revealed that General der Panzertruppen Hasso-Eccard von Manteuffel personally set out by automobile on Christmas Eve to give his 116th Panzers "a little ginger" in preparation for the attack to break the highway at Bourdon.

Manteuffel obviously erred in failing to anticipate K Company's crucial role in the battle. Anybody in K Company could have told him that the company was bound to get lost in the woods and thwart his well-laid plans.

Before daylight Christmas morning, the company completed its defensive perimeter around the rock quarry. It was a near-perfect position with stone nooks and crannies and provided complete protection from flat-trajectory fire. Any German tank approaching across the open field from the forest road faced the danger of crashing over an almost vertical thirty-foot cliff. The company established listening posts and sent out patrols to keep an eye on the German force in the woods. One squad returned to the horseshoe bend beyond the top of the hill to string antitank mines across the road.

Early Christmas morning, around 3:00, the CO received orders to go to the division's forward CP in Marche to report on K Company's encounter with the German armor. Sabia rode shotgun. At the command post in a large brick schoolhouse, the two were carefully questioned by MPs before being guided to the map room, where a general and several staff officers were studying a large wall map. From the disapproving glances, Sabia suspected he and Leinbaugh were the smelliest, dirtiest pair ever to gain entrance to the inner sanctum.

The general wanted to know the exact location of the tanks and an estimate of the size of the German force. He marked the location of the enemy armor on the acetate overlay, and motioning across the wooded area on the map, said the answer was to load doughs on the backs of tanks and sweep the Germans out of the pocket.

The idea was unworkable—tanks couldn't move ten feet through the forest—but nobody said a word. Leinbaugh made several attempts to explain that K Company had the perfect position for tank destroyers to move into hull defilade and work over the Germans in safety, but the suggestions were ignored. After checking with the general, a major told Leinbaugh he'd better get back to his company.

By the time the two returned to Bourdon, the bad news was already waiting. Tanks were on the way, and K Company had been alerted to load up and clear the woods of Germans.

Lucht went down to the highway to meet the Shermans and lead them forward in the darkness. Two platoons, the first and third, climbed aboard the tanks and began the ride up the hill while the rest of the company prepared to attack on foot across the field beyond the lip of the quarry. Crawling slowly up the hill, the tanks reached the horseshoe bend, and Miller and Lucht climbed down to pull the daisy chain of mines into a ditch.

Lucht looked down the road where they'd encountered the Germans at midnight. "Their tanks had pulled forward, and even in the dark I could see the 88s tracking us. They were that close." Lucht yelled to warn the tanker. "He didn't hear me or just ignored me, and said to get back on the tanks, and we started to move." Tom Miller watched as the German tank gun broke its camouflage and began tracking them. Miller yelled, "Right flank!" At that moment the German tank fired, scoring a direct hit on the leading Sherman. Everybody in the tank was killed except the tank commander. Lucht, Miller, and the rest of the squad were shaken and bruised when they jumped off the rear deck, but nobody was seriously hurt. The men deployed behind the tank for cover.

Just beyond the road inside the woods, Miller saw a German helmet poke out of a pit. "I yelled, '*Kommen Sie heraus.*' Two Germans came out, one an officer." Miller felt sure there were others, "so we hit the ground and I started to toss a grenade. Then another officer and two more men came out and surrendered."

With the lead Sherman knocked out, the second and third tanks in line shifted quickly to reverse. The second tank backed right over Johnny Bowe, who had been thrown backward on the road. Doc Mellon, who had been next to Johnny on the tank's deck, thought, "My God, he's ground up." But the tank's treads straddled Bowe and he emerged shaken and bruised, but otherwise unhurt.

Meanwhile the third tank, backing around the bend, ran over K Company's daisy chain in the ditch, losing a tread when the mines exploded.

Cline was on the second tank. "When the first tank was hit, we went flying off like popcorn. Our tank backed up and I was pinned against a tree. A few more inches and I would have been crushed." Cline yelled at the tank commander, "Pull your tank up, or I'll blow your head off."

As Lucht's squad began herding its prisoners to the rear, one of the tankers suddenly took out his .45 and shot two of the Germans. Lucht found it "horrible to watch." The men grabbed the tanker before he could fire again, but Lucht understood the man's rage. "Those tankers had just lost most of their friends."

Pope lit into the tankers. "You dumb sons of bitches," he told their lieutenant. "Now we're going to get some of our guys killed going out and trying to get more prisoners."

With the loss of the tanks and the road blocked, Leinbaugh halted the two platoons moving forward on foot and waved the men back to their holes around the quarry. "I radioed battalion and told them as far as I was concerned that was the end of the counterattack."

As Christmas Day broke, we heard firing from the direction of Verdenne, but K Company's perimeter remained quiet, only random mortar shells interrupting our rest. Two German soldiers came stumbling toward our positions in the half-light, hands held high, yelling, "Don't shoot, don't shoot." We discovered they understood little or no German, and they finally made us understand they were Ukrainians, drafted into the German army. After questioning the two were sent to the rear.

The enemy's positions beyond the hill's crest were close enough so we could hear them shouting orders. They were a talkative bunch, hollering in our direction, "Fuck the Americans," "Roosevelt eats crap," or worse, "Fuck Eleanor." Several men not overly fond of the president yelled back agreeing with the Germans' comments. Our responses must have dumb-founded our adversaries—the dialogue quickly ended.

After bringing up the mail, Ciccotello spent Christmas morning with Brewer in the company CP. He helped care for men with minor wounds and after the fighting died down found a Catholic church in the village. "We had a new boy in the CP with frozen feet. He wasn't Catholic, but when I told him I was going to Mass he asked to come along." The church could hold only a small group of parishioners, and the GIs felt conspicuous. "We were the only two soldiers there and weren't sure what to do with our rifles, but decided to take them to our pew. We heard shelling all through the Mass, some of it close by. This young guy told me it felt good to be in church, but it made him awfully homesick."

During the church services, German gunners near the edge of the escarpment poked their long 75s out of the woods line and took potshots at jeeps passing along the highway through Bourdon. We yelled encouragement downhill to the drivers who were bracketed on the road, the unhappy victims of a cat-and-mouse game. As the shells exploded, the drivers would come to a screeching halt, quickly accelerate and stop again as the German tankers tried to anticipate their next move. Side bets were made on the outcome, but word soon spread that the highway was unsafe, and the game ended—fortunately without casualties.

Fred Butler, who had joined the company at the château near Geilenkirchen, poked his head over a boulder at the edge of the quarry to get a better look at the German positions. As he raised partially erect, a sniper's rifle cracked from the high ground across the field. The round hit Butler in the middle of his forehead, killing him instantly, the company's first fatality in the Battle of the Bulge.

We lost our appetites for lunch when orders came to move around to the far side of the woods, locate the rear of the German tank column, and attack. At the best our M1s could irritate the German Panzers, nothing more. Although nobody was able to arouse much enthusiasm for the new assault, we headed out, the platoon leaders doing their best to hide their misgivings. A section of tank destroyers near Verdenne was to provide fire support.

As the company swung around the back of the woods and guided on a trail in approach march formation, Leinbaugh saw the rear of a vehicle in a clump of trees and thought it was one of our tank destroyers. When he waved his map and called, a German jumped from the turret and ran. Leinbaugh yelled for the company to pull to the left across a firebreak and build up a firing line. As the men crossed the open space, German machine gunners opened fire. No more than a dozen men got the word; the rest of the company continued straight ahead into the woods. Heavy firing broke out.

In the confusion, Dunn found himself alone. When he heard someone charging through the heavy underbrush straight ahead of him, he dropped to his knee and waited. "Suddenly a German officer in a long coat burst into the small clearing twenty-five feet in front of me." The two saw each other at the same time. "I raised my rifle, he raised his pistol. We got buck fever at the same time, and both hit the ground for cover. That was the end of the encounter."

Minutes later Dunn and his friend Mellon ended up next to each other and "almost barged right into this German tank hidden in those fir trees. We were within twenty feet of it—so close the Krauts couldn't lower that gun barrel enough to hit us. But they sure as hell tried. Old Dunn and Doc crawled through those woods so fast you couldn't believe it."

Campbell for a moment thought he'd picked up a Purple Heart. "It was embarrassing. A potato masher looped in next to me, exploded, and I felt a sharp pain as a fragment got me in the left hip pocket." Gingerly exploring the situation, Campbell found the fragment had broken his pocket comb and driven the teeth of the comb into his rear end. "Earlier I had told Leinbaugh the correct name for the Germans' grenade was *die Stielhandgranate*. The only sympathy I got now was his asking if it felt any better because I knew how to pronounce it."

One of the first platoon's squad leaders, Max Sobel, spoke some German. "Both sides were yelling back and forth, and the lieutenant wanted someone to holler to the Germans to put down their weapons and come out with their hands up." Although Max felt his German was a bit rusty, he gave it a try. "I started yelling for them to surrender, but a lot of good it did. After they picked up my Jewish accent they redoubled their fire."

Amici found visibility the big problem. "In those woods, you couldn't see six feet in front of you, just heavy pines and underbrush." Amici and his partner were spotted by the Germans. "I could see the leaves and trees whipping back and forth, with the bullets going past three feet in front of us. We hit the ground just as someone threw a potato masher." The concussion made Amici's nose and forehead bleed, and he took fragments in his calf and foot. "I emptied my rifle where I saw the leaves moving, and then we got up and hightailed it out of there. My foot started swelling real bad, and by the time I got to the bottom of the hill I could barely make it."

A second platoon sergeant, Quent Nelson, took a machine-gun bullet in his leg. One of his men gave him a hand, but before going a dozen yards the man helping Nelson was wounded by shrapnel. The two eventually struggled down the hill together to safety.

Paul Dulin, a tall, lean North Carolinian, had taken over as third platoon leader after Lage suffered his malaria attack. Dulin found that "control was the big problem in those woods Christmas Day. Trying to keep a squad in control or even in sight was difficult—a platoon was a hell of a problem, almost impossible." Dulin nearly ran into a camouflaged German tank. "It was partially dug in and the gun started traversing not twenty feet away. The Germans were talking right in front of me, but I wasn't spotted, and backed out crawling."

A BAR man in the first platoon, Richard Heuer, became separated from the rest of the men. "I got too far out in front and caught some Germans on a road, twenty-five or thirty of them, backing into the woods. I emptied a full BAR clip at them and had time to reload and empty a second clip." So surprised were the Germans that they did not fire a round. Running back, Heuer found other men from his platoon. "I crouched down in a ravine, and that's when I got hit by shrapnel from a tank round. I was hit on the left side of my jaw near my ear and a piece went through the roof of my mouth and on into my head. My throat was ripped open and my shoulder was almost severed in half."

An aidman turned Heuer on his back and sat on his chest to work on him. "I think this was his first face wound. He was really nervous and I think I was more calm than he was." While being bandaged Heuer was hit again—this time by small-arms fire. "It ripped my pack and overcoat to ribbons. I couldn't talk but pointed to my right shoulder."

Two men from the platoon somehow found a stretcher and carried Heuer out of the woods and down the hill to the aid station. At the evacuation hospital he saw Parsons on an adjoining stretcher. "This was one of the few times that K Company wounded were even briefly together in the hospital chain."

At last recognizing the futility of sending riflemen against the massed machine guns and cannon of the Panzers, battalion in midafternoon radioed to break contact and regroup. K Company withdrew several hundred yards and found cover in a line of old foxholes.

After dark men went downhill in small groups to get Christmas turkey at the CP in Bourdon. Baptie waited until the men in his squad returned to their positions and headed alone down a dark trail to get his meal. Hearing a vehicle moving slowly behind him, he moved to the edge of the trail, ran along behind the truck, tossed his rifle to a soldier, and swung onto the tailgate. "I turned around—the truck was packed full of Germans. I jumped back on the road and yelled for the guy holding my rifle to throw it to me, and he did." Baptie later realized that without thinking, he'd yelled to the man in German. It was dark and Baptie would never know whether he had hitched a ride with a truckload of German reinforcements or with a load of prisoners being taken to the rear from a neighboring battalion. Taking another trail, he continued downhill for his cold Christmas dinner.

Bratten, the radioman, went with the company commander to the battalion CP. As Bratten remembers, "There was an argument. The colonel said K Company was going to have to attack again through those woods, but Leinbaugh told him he didn't have enough men left in the company for another attack."

At midnight we learned from headquarters that A and B companies were to mount a night attack against the armor holed up in the woods. As the two companies walked slowly up the hill, we watched them march by silently, eyes on the ground. We knew what they were going up against but thought, "Better them than us." The men disappeared into the forest. M1s against Panthers again. We listened to the battle begin, watched the tracers float overhead and die out, and heard the German tanks open fire.

Afterward, survivors of the two companies straggled out of the forest helping their wounded. They were silent still, eyes on the ground.

Moving back to the rock quarry, K Company manned its holes with half the men on line, half in the houses at the foot of the hill in Bourdon. As Sterner recalls, "For the first time we had the new C rations at lunch, hot dogs and baked beans, a big improvement over the Ks." As Sterner, Stauffer, and three others started up the hill, a mortar round exploded in the road a few yards in front of them. Sterner was hit in the leg; nobody else was scratched. "I sat down and pulled my pants leg out of my combat boot and Stauffer came up to help and a medic ran out of the closest house." Stauffer and the medic were kneeling over Sterner when a second round came in. "It knocked Stauffer in the ditch and killed the medic—he fell dead over my legs."

Stauffer was momentarily stunned. "The blast was so close it was deafening. It blew most of the medic's head off. And there was another medic, following the first one, who was badly wounded by that second shell. He wasn't killed on the spot, but he died a short while later."

The second round hit Sterner in the thigh and buttocks. "I had some good-sized holes. That second round did a lot more damage than the first one." Sterner didn't know the medics who ran up to help him. "They were with battalion aid, not attached to K Company. I don't think I wanted to know their names or who they were."

The sixth sense every front-line soldier develops told Sterner that those two rounds had come from American mortars. He was being loaded on a jeep when "the mortar lieutenant who had been directing the fire came running up. Don't worry, he said, it isn't going to happen again." The lieutenant told Sterner he hadn't seen the first round hit and called in a second one. Then he realized they were falling way short.

At the quarry, Leslie Carson and Leach had dug their foxhole on the left flank of the company. Carson remembers, "Leinbaugh came over and told us to keep watch on a barn out in front where he thought a couple of snipers were holed up." As the CO turned and started back, a German shell exploded at the edge of the men's foxhole. "That one got both Leach and me. The explosion broke both my eardrums and I was wounded in the stomach, upper thigh, and foot. One big piece of shrapnel lopped a third of my left foot right off."

Carson spent thirteen months in army hospitals recovering from his wounds, yet the company morning report carried him as "slightly wounded in action."

The next morning artillery observers convinced division they could shell the large pocket of German armor in the forest without endangering our troops. Leinbaugh was patched through to the artillery fire direction center and gave them map coordinates for the head of the German column.

The artillery officer at battalion radioed that one battery would be firing to range in on the German positions, and he would be needing accurate adjustments. Beginning his countdown, he warned, "On the way!" Four shells whistled in close over K Company's position and exploded in the trees two hundred yards beyond the lip of the quarry. Incredibly, against all conceivable odds, the four rounds were precisely on target. They blew up the tank at the head of the German column. The tank's exploding fuel and ammunition merged into a fireball that boiled high above the treetops.

The artillery officer said he would be firing "time on target," not only 105s but the big guns, 8-inchers and 155s. He said it would take a while; each battery, spread out over a number of miles, would make calculations based on the first salvo and then begin the firing sequence. The more distant cannon would fire first, so that all the shells would land on the German positions within seconds of each other. The idea was to deny the Germans time to disperse and take cover. "King Six," he radioed Leinbaugh, "tell your guys to crawl in the deepest holes they can find, and for God's sake keep your heads down."

We heard the distant heavy rumble of the 8-inchers and the 155s, and finally battalion after battalion of 105s, much closer behind us. The shells landed simultaneously on the line of German armor in the forest.

Twelve-year-old Jean-Jacques Lesceux was in the cellar of his family home in Marche, three miles distant. He heard the bombardment commence. He wanted to run upstairs to the second floor to watch, but his parents refused his pleas. From the sounds of the shelling, the family knew the fighting was centered near Grandfather Lesceux's farm outside Verdenne. Even the boy realized the battle was reaching a climax.

The shells continued falling on the German force in the pocket. Conventional explosive rounds were mixed with white phosphorus and fuse delays. How long it lasted, we could only guess—probably no more than five minutes, but it seemed endless. Whole trees were tossed into the air, and the forest disappeared in clouds of white-and-gray smoke, ripped apart by red explosions which merged into a continuous roar. Rocks and clods of frozen earth pelted K Company's perimeter. A few shells from the 105s fell short, exploding between our holes, but only two men received minor wounds.

It was the heaviest, most devastating bombardment we had ever witnessed.

When the fire stopped, the cries for help from wounded and dying

Germans carried clearly to our lines. We admitted to ourselves that we were sorry for the poor bastards up there in the pocket.

Before midnight, an order came to send a strong patrol to check out a German assembly area beyond Verdenne. It was the weapons platoon's turn, and Oyler got the assignment. Since the fourth platoon had no BAR men, Paul Cote from the third platoon joined Oyler's group.

Oyler went to the CP for a briefing and a look at the map. "One of the battalion officers was there. Apparently they were worried about security, because we piled our wallets on a table in the CP, got rid of old letters, and even removed our dog tags. Somebody was taking this one seriously—we figured they knew something they weren't telling us."

As the patrol was forming up, Ciccotello told Cote he had received a couple of food packages from home. "I slung my BAR and took a package in each hand. They were addressed to Paul Cote, Company K, 333rd Infantry, APO 84, N.Y., N.Y. We'd gone down this road at least a mile when Alfred O. waved us to a stop." Oyler told Cote that "if anything happened the addresses on those packages would really screw up our security." Cote felt it much more likely that Oyler was getting hungry, but he agreed. "I opened the packages, and we sat there in a little circle in the snow in the dark and ate all my Christmas cookies."

As the patrol continued, Oyler put his friend Flattop on the point. "We were guiding on a small road in the woods, and he gave the high sign to hold up. I walked up and we could see a lot of bodies; I estimated twenty or thirty dead Germans, stretched out in the road and ditches." Oyler whispered to Flattop to check the bodies to make sure all were dead. "I didn't want any of those guys playing possum and shooting us in the back. We moved ahead very slowly, very cautiously, expecting to be ambushed any second." As the patrol came to a clearing, Oyler saw Flattop had fixed his bayonet to his M1 and was prodding a German body with the point. "I asked him what he was doing. 'Oyler,' Flattop whispered back, 'if they're dead, it won't hurt them. If they're pretending, I want to be the first guy to know.'"

The patrol found its objective but saw nary a soul. "We climbed a rocky bluff to check our location and figured we had to be in the right place. We didn't spot any tanks; no trucks—nothing."

Oyler admitted to bad feelings about the patrol. "Somehow I thought none of us was going to make it home that night." Coming back he worried about the trail the patrol left in the new snow. "But nothing happened and we got to the CP at daylight. Brewer was waiting for us. He had a hot pan of coffee on the wood stove—the best cup of coffee I ever drank."

Battles raged throughout December 26 in the vicinity of Verdenne, Marenne, Menil, and Hampteau, four small villages strung along a secondary road east of K Company's positions. Snow fell during much of the day, and the cold intensified. Here, as elsewhere in the Ardennes, the villages controlled the roads and dominated tactical considerations. On the 26th all four villages were in American hands, but each was under pressure from probing attacks by company-size German units, infantry and tanks.

Defended by our battalion's Item and Mike companies, Menil was the site of the next crucial engagement. During the evening of the 26th a strong enemy armored force coming up the road from Marenne entered the outskirts of Menil. The lead tank swiveled in a wide arc and ran over a pile of antitank mines that had been roped together as a daisy chain. The giant explosion knocked the tank on its side and tore a hole in its underbelly.

Blocked by the knocked-out Panther, the rest of the German column left the road, swung into a pasture, and found themselves in the middle of a minefield. The GIs defending Menil called for heavy concentrations of artillery and swept the German force with nonstop machine-gun and rifle fire. German tanks and armored personnel carriers were soon burning in the fields, and scores of German infantrymen were killed or captured.

While the battle was still in progress, K Company was hurriedly rushed in trucks to bolster the defenders, but our luck was changing; by the time we arrived the fighting was over. German tanks and APCs were still burning, and medics were ministering to the German wounded. The Germans lost twenty-six vehicles, including six tanks, to mines, bazooka fire, and artillery.

As Leinbaugh and Campbell learned years later from the German tank commander, Colonel Tebbe, the German force entering Menil from Marenne was the same embattled Kampfgruppe which had held K Company at bay in the woods between Bourdon and Verdenne.

When the battle commenced at midnight Christmas Eve, Major Tebbe was in his command tank studying his maps. Over the radio came the sounds of bells ringing in Christmas at the cathedral in Cologne. He heard rifle shots at the front of his tank column and slammed closed the hatch of his tank.

The mission of Kampfgruppe Bayer was to pierce the Marche-Hotton highway and then proceed northwest and attack Ciney. Following the unexpected encounter with K Company, the German task force in the woods received new orders. "Hold position, defend against all sides and at all cost block the Hotton-Marche road."

An "after action" dispatch prepared by Panzer Regiment 16 reported shortages of infantry and ammunition and heavy enemy pressure from all sides on Christmas Day. On the 26th, the Kampfgruppe reported receiving severe artillery bombardment (three continuous drumfires, three times of three minutes' duration) and that the opposition attacked five times in battalion strength. Late in the afternoon of the 26th the German forces in the pocket were ordered to break out and withdraw south by way of Marenne and Menil. The German command reported their troops were suffering from exhaustion and were without water, food, and medical supplies.

After the battle K Company walked to the rear and went into reserve in Hotton along the Ourthe River. Within an hour the company was again alerted. G-2 reports indicated two German armored corps were advancing on Hotton, one on either side of the Ourthe. K Company, as the only ready reserve, was ordered to locate the best possible defensive positions, dig in, and delay the enemy force as long as possible. The colonel, for once, was completely forthright. "It's impossible to stop them; just do the best you can, fellows," he told us. Two hours later, word came that the initial intelligence message had been garbled. Nobody was coming. Forget it.

On the last day of the old year, the company walked back to Menil, dug new defensive positions on hills beyond the village, and established outposts a half mile to the front. German artillery fire all but ceased, but a steady procession of buzz bombs passed over us heading for Liége. Puttering along at two or three hundred miles an hour at an altitude of a few hundred feet, the black cigar-shaped rockets with short stubby wings offered a tempting target for M1 practice. Word was passed not to shoot at them. The destructive effect of an aborted buzz bomb in the company area would be disastrous.

At midnight on New Year's Eve, American artillery let loose a mighty salvo on German positions all along the front. Thirty seconds later German artillery replied in kind. The only damage to Menil was broken windows.

On New Year's Day we were relieved by British troops of the 53rd Division, who had sat out the fighting behind the Meuse. In contrast to our bedraggled appearance, the Brits were rested and close-shaven and wore clean uniforms. Their officers seemed surprised by our lack of saluting and our casual attitude toward rank. Pope's comment to their captain—"Where the hell were you guys when we needed you?"—left them a bit nonplussed; their relationship with senior sergeants, we gathered, was much more formal. They didn't entirely approve of our defensive positions and put crews to work enlarging our foxholes and covering them with logs and earth, German-style. Men in the CP joined the Englishmen for a warm and friendly farewell toast of red British rum and the company headed for Hotton to pick up trucks for our next move.

The first week of fighting in the Ardennes cost K Company forty casualties, but a dozen replacements and hospital returnees bolstered our ranks. Like the other rifle companies in the 84th, we were considerably understrength.

Rumors floated down from division that we would be going over to the attack. We didn't know it, but the first half of the Battle of the Bulge was over.

11

FROM GRANDMENIL TO SAMRÉE

January 3, 1945, was D-Day for the Allied counteroffensive to seal off the German bulge. H-Hour was 8:30 A.M. The second half of the Battle of the Ardennes began during the worst winter weather in memory.

The First Army's VII Corps was to attack due south toward Houffalize while Patton's Third Army would move north from Bastogne to meet it. Simultaneously the tip of the bulge would be forced eastward by the British XXX Corps. The American VII Corps was made up of two battle-tested tank-infantry teams—the 84th Infantry and the 2nd Armored divisions on the right, and the 83rd Infantry and the 3rd Armored divisions on the left. The American armies on the north and the south were separated by twenty-five miles of rugged hills and gorges, frozen rivers, tortuous icy roads, snow-laden forests, and tens of thousands of battle-hardened German troops. For K Company the counteroffensive began in the small Belgian village of Grandmenil.

Grandmenil's location, near the juncture of several meandering forest roads, was its misfortune. During the final days of 1944, German and American forces waged a bitter battle for control of the village. Artillery duels and Allied fighter-bombers virtually leveled Grandmenil. When K Company arrived on January 3, the village was a shambles.

The stark stone walls and charred rubble were familiar sights. Grandmenil was a Belgian version of Prummern and Lindern, but German mud and rain had been replaced by Belgian snow and ice. We saw no civilians. The ruins of houses offering protection from the cold winds were jammed with troops; no shelter remained. K Company established its command post in the corner of an open pigsty occupied by two frozen hogs and a frozen German. Our initial objective, we discovered, was the village of Lamormenil, three miles to the south.

K Company's CO joined battalion staff officers for a quick reconnaissance of the line of departure. As the party's two jeeps crunched through the snow toward the assembly area, a group of GIs alongside the road waved them down. A distraught captain, obviously fresh from the States, said one of his squads had been ambushed while moving into a blocking position to protect our battalion's attack. He and his men were close-shaven, clear-eyed, and wearing clean uniforms. Bayonets were fixed to their M1s. They seemed totally out of place—an alien cast which had wandered onto the wrong stage.

The 325th's artillery observer and Leinbaugh climbed an embankment and crawled forward to a tree line to take a look. They were sickened. Twelve men in brown GI overcoats, an entire squad, lay sprawled in the snow like duckpins. Instead of working their way through the woods and flanking their objective, they had advanced straight across a field of deep snow toward a fieldstone hut. The Germans let them get in close, just the right distance, and then methodically mowed them down. Every one of the men was dead.

The artillery observer waved up his radioman and called for smoke. With two quick adjustments for overages, rounds for effect came in on top of the German gun positions—probably nothing more than a two- or three-man outpost. "We were as mad at the new outfit as we were at the Germans—maybe more so." Leinbaugh remembers. "The FO kept calling them dumb bastards. Twelve good men were dead. This sort of thing couldn't have happened to us; we knew better."

For the first time since going into action we realized we were veterans.

K Company's CO hiked the last mile through deep snow to Lamormenil, reaching the town shortly after 2nd Armored tankers rolled through the streets. A quick look around revealed only dead and wounded Germans. K Company could walk in and occupy its objective without a fight.

While waiting in Grandmenil, Lance had sent out a reconnaissance patrol. "The guys located a big porker weighing in close to two hundred pounds. Right afterward this pig met with a sudden accident, and Sergeant Davis had it cleaned out in no time. We found an old stove and a big skillet and had chops cooking when orders came to move out. We cut off the hindquarters and roped them to our packs. We weren't looking too military when we lined up."

On the road to Lamormenil our column came under long-range fire from German Nebelwerfers. Leaving smoky trails in the overcast, the screaming meemies were more sound than fury. In the entire Third Battalion they searched out a single target—Paul Coste, K Company's only Harvard-educated BAR man. "The Nebelwerfers came screaming in and

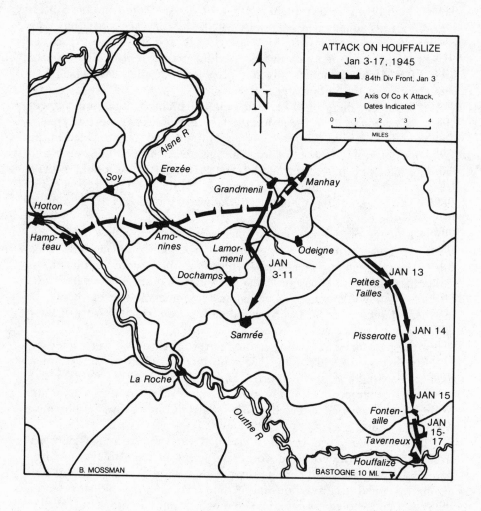

ATTACK ON HOUFFALIZE
Jan 3-17, 1945

84th Div Front, Jan 3

Axis Of Co K Attack,
Dates Indicated

0   1   2   3   4
MILES

Aisne R

Erezée

Soy

Grandmenil

Manhay

Hotton

Hamp-
teau

Amo-
nines

Lamor-
menil

Odeigne

JAN
3-11

Dochamps

Petites
Tailles

JAN 13

Samrée

Pisserotte

JAN 14

La Roche

JAN 15

Ourthe R

Fonten-
aille

JAN
15-
17

Taverneux

Houffalize

B. MOSSMAN

BASTOGNE 10 MI.

one landed at my feet and I was knocked down. No pain; just great surprise. I was getting my act together when someone told me I had been hit. I didn't think so until I saw a little blood and a tear in my field jacket." A piece of shrapnel had lodged in Coste's left top rib. "No damage to the muscles, no pain, no infection—the million-dollar wound."

While Doc Mellon bandaged the hole, Coste cheerfully emptied his field pack and pockets, passing out chocolate bars, tea bags, gum, and tins of cheese and Spam he'd hoarded from his K rations. Paul was given a tall glass of cognac at the aid station and quickly evacuated to a hospital in Liége.

It was almost dark when the company settled into Lamormenil, set up a CP, and decided on locations for the holes. Sabia, Campbell, and Leinbaugh were marking the second platoon's sector on the overlay showing the artillery concentrations. They were standing on the broad limestone steps of a two-story house. It was rapidly becoming dark.

Sabia suggested going inside to get a better look at the map with a flashlight. "I pushed open the door for the two lieutenants." The men stepped inside the front room. "I had just closed the door, my hand was on the knob, when a mortar shell hit, a big one. It blew the door off its hinges and knocked me to the floor." The explosion filled the room with plaster dust and flying glass from shattered windows. For a minute Sabia couldn't see. The three patted themselves down for wounds and peered outside. The shell had landed squarely on the wide stone steps, demolishing them. Later John thought about his timing. "That round had to be at the top of its trajectory when I mentioned going inside. Somebody's guardian angel was sure as hell working overtime that night."

The fourth platoon was digging in beyond the wall of a ruined house when Harvey Augustin took a breather sitting on a dead German. The machine gunners knew the man had been killed recently; the body was soft enough to be comfortable. After completing their emplacement, the gunners walked to a house and finished the food left on the table by German soldiers. Two very young dead Germans were stuffed in a woodbox on the porch of the house. The next morning Clayton Shepherd noticed one of the dead youngsters had a gold ring on his finger. An hour later someone had cut off the youngster's finger. The ring was missing. Shepherd shook his head; he couldn't believe it. "I told the guys with me, 'Now ain't this a damn thing.'"

Even the company veterans, inured to scenes of mayhem, were disquieted by unusual forms of death. Max Sobel can't forget the appearance of the dead German at the entrance to the village. "He must have been run over by a dozen tanks—he was a yard wide, at least; but in the subfreezing cold his outline was still intact—you could tell that bloody mass had been a man."

Doc Mellon, who had treated almost every kind of battlefield victim, encountered a new and perplexing one in Lamormenil. "Dunn and I found this dark-complected man, a civilian, hanging from a fruit tree in back of a house. He looked like an Arab and was frozen stiff. We found another dead civilian in a barn in back of the same house. We couldn't figure it; who were these people? Why would the Germans bother to hang a man instead of just shooting him?"

By the time K Company completed digging in and siting its weapons, a message came through from battalion. The same old story, a new mission. A company of infantry from the 2nd Armored was in trouble in the forest on the hills to the right of town. The orders were to search the hills, find the armored division men, and help hold the ground they'd taken. It was the worst kind of hit-or-miss operation; no one knew where these men were located.

The company headed into the hills through snow more than a foot deep, cursing and swearing as we fought our way through the tangle of fir trees and underbrush. Every few minutes we stopped, listened, and, hearing no firing or activity, pushed forward again. After two hours of floundering, we gave up the search, hunkered down on the side of a big heavily forested ridge, and got through to battalion on the radio. Sit tight, they told us, while regiment checked with 2nd Armored.

We waited and waited. By midnight it was treacherously cold. We were cold in a way we'd never been cold before. Most men, expecting a brief mission, had left their overcoats behind. Officers and sergeants moved through the company, making sure no one fell asleep. Wind whipped across the hillside, drifting snow to three-foot depths.

Finally Leinbaugh and Campbell decided they had to make one more effort to find the 2nd Armored men. They headed diagonally downhill, feeling their way through the dark, forcing their way through the drifts, stopping frequently to listen for sounds of nearby troops. "We paused," Campbell says, "and heard a rustling noise, very close. We dropped to a crouch alongside a narrow trail." A quick-moving line of shadows came toward them; a dozen men moving quietly through the forest. "They were Germans, and they weren't lost. They passed so close we could have reached out and tripped each man as he hurried by."

K Company spent the rest of the night shivering on the windblown ridge. Despite the risk of freezing, a few men dozed off.

The next morning, after the mission was scratched, we plowed through the drifts back to Lamormenil. The company jeeps brought up food and ammo. We hoped and prayed for a few hours of rest. After a cold pancake breakfast in the comfort of shell-battered houses, everybody dozed off—but not for long. The CO was called to battalion for new orders. The battalion had the job of sweeping a large forested area between Odeigne and Dochamps to secure the ridgeline overlooking Samrée. Samrée was a fair-sized town, another of those vital road junctions headquarters worried about. After our battalion had taken the high ground, a tank-infantry team from the 84th and 2nd Armored would mount a frontal assault on Samrée from the west. The colonel saved the good news for the last. "Leinbaugh, K Company is going to lead off."

The maps showed several trails bisecting the forests, but no landmarks to guide on. The officers and sergeants were especially concerned about the firebreaks, open logged-off areas, perfect spots for ambush. We had no idea of the resistance we might encounter, but knew there were German outposts on the high ground directing artillery and mortar fire on Lamormenil. When we moved out we saw a 2nd Armored medium tank take a direct hit. The crew bailed out and ran for cover as the tank burned and then exploded.

The company verged on total exhaustion, but that was nothing new. We climbed the sloping ridge to the forest's edge. It was still snowing; more than a foot of powder made slow going. Item Company followed, echeloned to the right. L Company was backstopping the advance. Our line of skirmishers made a tempting target, but the sergeants kept their squads widely dispersed. Despite a combination of German artillery and mortar fire, the edge of the woods was reached without casualties. The company halted and regrouped.

The three rifle company commanders held a quick conference before K Company entered the woods. Everybody realized this was going to be a rough one. The fir trees grew together solidly and were heavily weighted with snow. The rough ground was laced by small ravines and broken by steep embankments. To cover the area, all four platoons would necessarily be on line, leaving no reserve when we hit trouble. The platoon leaders and sergeants talked it over. We decided to go two hundred paces, stop, straighten the line, and do another two hundred. The platoons would guide on the company headquarters group in the center of the line. Captain Mitchell from I Company said he would drop off squads to protect our right flank as we attacked.

After five minutes we were in deep trouble—far worse than feared. The firs had grown together in impassable clumps. The branches were weighted down with snow that cascaded on us, worked inside clothes, melted, and froze. It was impossible to maintain a steady pace of advance. One squad would be climbing an icy embankment while another was sliding down a ravine. Maintaining direction was next to impossible. Once in a while a tall tree provided a check on our compass bearings, but mostly it was a case of listening to the sound of the men on either side and trying to maintain some semblance of a straight line.

This was Fred Olson's first actual combat mission. An eighteen-year-old Iowan, "Junior" Olson joined the company on New Year's Eve. "Not one person offered advice or information on what I could expect going into combat. It was as if there was no way to explain it, or that I would find out for myself in due time." Olson sensed the men wanted to be alone with their thoughts. "Pop Teebagy offered the only words of comfort I was ever to receive in K Company. He said everything would be all right. The fact he was an old man—thirty-five years—helped give his words some credence."

Now, several days later, Fred was still very much on his own. "You couldn't see in those woods. I tripped right into a foxhole with a dead Kraut. He was just lying there sprawled out." The body had begun to decompose. "I fell flat and started pulling myself up and there he was. We were not under fire, I just fell in. He didn't have a weapon, but he was in uniform with a cartridge belt and his helmet. That was my first experience with death. I don't know if he was young or old, I couldn't look at his face. I was not aware of wounds—he was just there."

At the first firebreak the company stopped. The scouts who ventured forward to take a look were spattered with machine-gun fire; intermittent short bursts, twenty or thirty rounds at a time. Through the snow-laden underbrush and tangle of fallen timbers we spotted the location of the machine guns poking out of log-covered bunkers. We were close, well dispersed, and we poured heavy rifle fire into the openings, the men rising to their feet, emptying a clip, dropping to the ground, moving, and firing again. It had to be M1s; mortars were useless in the woods.

Walter Anderson, who had just made squad leader, was the morning's first casualty. A tall Kentuckian, an ex-policeman who had joined the company in Geilenkirchen, Walter was hit in the forearm by two machine-gun bullets, the holes so close together they looked like a single wound. An aidman wrapped a tight bandage and fixed a quick sling, and Anderson headed back alone through the woods to the CP in Lamormenil.

The firing stopped and the company reorganized. Sabia was given a map and told to keep on an old cart path with the company guiding on him. "So we push out meeting nothing, but we sure can hear a lot going on all around us. Up behind us comes Captain Mitchell of I Company with his runner." Mitchell and Sabia stopped to check their maps. "About a hundred yards up the path all hell breaks loose. Tice grabs me by the arm and pulls me into the woods. Captain Mitchell and his runner are hit and hit bad. Those Kraut machine gunners must have burned out a dozen barrels. A squad from the platoon comes over and I tell Tice to take these men and guard our flank and when I give the word to move up where the fire is coming from."

Johnny Moore crawled up with rifle grenades and fired several rounds which didn't go off. Sabia called to Tice to open up and give him covering fire. "I was going to try to pull in the guys who were hit. I scoot out and grab the closest one. It sure was tough pulling, because of the snow, and I could hear and see the shots the Krauts fired at me. They were hitting a tree inches over my head."

Sabia was hit. "I feel a burning pain in my leg, so I crawl back in. After three or four minutes—it seems like an hour—I start out again. Moore comes up with his grenade launcher and we toss a few more in, but no dice." Sabia and Moore crawled as close as possible to the wounded men. "Moore says, 'No, Johnny, you've got a wife,' and he pushes out. Then he got it. I saw his head fall forward. I pulled him back through the snow and then I saw the hole through his neck."

Sabia yelled for an aidman. "At first he wouldn't crawl all the way out to us; it was open space, no cover. So I took out my pistol and told him to crawl up and look at Moore. He came. If he had refused I believe I would have shot him. There was nothing we could do for Moore. He was dead. Then I started crying."

The Germans called in mortar fire. "The shells snapped me out of it," Sabia says. "They fell mostly behind us, right in the middle of I Company. It was hell; you could hear screaming all over the place. After things settled down they bandaged my leg as tight as possible, and the CO asked if I could make it back to town by myself because the company couldn't spare a man. I told him, 'Hell, yes, I can do it.'"

A limb was cut for Sabia to lean on, and he headed back to the rear hopping awkwardly in the snow on his good leg. He stopped after ten yards, turned around, waved his makeshift crutch in a gesture of defiance and exuberance. He bellowed, "Hey, you bastards! Clean sheets! Clean sheets!" And as a friendly reminder, someone yelled after him, "Take care of all them nurses for us, Big John."

It was close, but Sabia made it back to Lamormenil. Brewer wrapped John in blankets and Barnes rushed him to battalion aid. The surgeon found five machine-gun bullets in Sabia's right thigh.

Back on the slope, heavy German fire continued sweeping the fire lane, and several men from I and K companies, dead or wounded, were trapped in the open.

According to Harvey Augustin, this was one of the few times he remembers getting a direct order in the middle of a firefight. "Leinbaugh came plowing through the snow over to the machine gunners, yelling for us to follow him. We hurried over to the right flank. He was firing tracers to show us the Germans' location, and yelling, 'Target at three o'clock.'" The gunners fired several belts as quick as they could load, raking the area in front of them. The rest of the men fired their M1s and carbines as fast as they could shove in new clips.

The firing stopped only after we were sure we had silenced the last German. A squad edged across the clearing and found two machine-gun positions, dugouts with firing slits covered with logs. The Germans inside were dead. Three more bodies were found nearby. The men looked around for tracks to make sure none had escaped. Nobody was particularly anxious to take any prisoners.

Captain Mitchell and his runner had been killed instantly; both had been hit several times in the chest. Mitchell, as always, was wearing his green officer's trench coat. He had the hood fastened over his head under his helmet. We used to tell him that damn coat would get him killed someday. In K Company the officers wore the regulation brown GI overcoat without insignia of any kind. The CO and platoon leaders carried M1s, a reasonable bit of insurance, as they saw it.

Sergeant Moore had crawled within ten feet of Mitchell before he was killed. His helmet had been knocked off by a bullet; his black hair ruffled in the wind. A sergeant from Item came up. He was crying. He said he'd get a detail to carry the captain and the others back down the hill.

Kneeling in the snow, Leinbaugh pressed the talk switch on the radio. "Mitch is dead, over." There was no answer from battalion. He repeated, "Captain Mitchell's dead."

Finally the colonel answered. "Are you sure, Leinbaugh?"

"Yes, he's here next to me. A machine gun got him and three others."

The colonel could barely talk. "I'm sorry. I'm real sorry about that." After a long pause, he said, "That's real bad, real bad. Get him back down the hill right away."

"Yes, sir. We need litters, colonel. Four of them."

"Okay. Tell that new lieutenant, whatever his name is, to take over Mitch's company."

K Company began to form up. The men from I Company waiting next to the bodies were still wiping tears from their eyes and swearing. These men had been trained by Mitchell; he had brought them overseas, cared for them, and led them bravely in battle. His men felt far more than the normal respect for a competent commander—they worshiped Mitchell.

"When we moved out again, the line stopped," Olson remembers. "I was standing there right by Johnny Moore. The wind was blowing and the snow was beginning to drift up over him. That was a strange thing. It never bothered me with a dead German. But a GI, I never got used to it, I could never be comfortable with that."

The snow, the wind, the cold increased. Army weathermen reported blizzard conditions in the area with forty to fifty feet visibility.

Sergeant Corkill tried to find a spot where he could see across a fire lane. He pushed between two trees and parted the branches to take a look. A German was directly in front of him, carefully separating the branches between the same two trees—so close their hands brushed. Corkill came plowing backward, meeting the CO and J. B. Cole. He was in a state of near shock but laughing so hard he could barely stand. The two men had stood staring at each other a couple of seconds, looking at each other's helmet and face. The awful truth struck them both at the same time, a full-fledged double take. Each spun around and took off.

Howard Broderick remembers that a small group of replacements joined the company a few days before the attack. "One of them ended up in the third platoon. He was a real braggart, tough-acting, who kept saying, 'Boy, let me at 'em.' Dulin, our platoon leader, told me to keep a close eye on the fellow." The new man's combat career lasted less than a day. "After we sweated a couple of shellings and ran into the machine-gun fire at the first firebreak, the guy broke down completely. He couldn't cope. He was worse than useless and we had to send him back."

Fred Olson's squad on the company's extreme right was told to keep contact with I Company. "But we'd lost sight of them early on. Next we discovered we'd become separated from the rest of our own platoon on the left. Paul Zerbel was the only sergeant with us; there was Hoffman the New Yorker, George Thompson, Crookshank, one or two more." The squad stopped to figure out what to do. "I was crouched down looking out over this firebreak, and Zerbel said we've got to find the rest of the company. Then all of a sudden he says, 'Here they come,' and across the firebreak we see these German helmets heading our way, so we opened up."

According to Thompson, the firing was really bad for a while. "Then one German somehow got through back of us. We were all lying down prone in the snow. He got right behind me, just a few feet away." The two men saw each other at the same time. "This sergeant with us rolled over on his back and got the German with one shot. He killed him. It was just the matter of a second. Then he said let's get the hell out of here, and we all jumped up and ran."

The cold gave Fred Olson an appetite. "I was eating one of those damn chocolate bars out of the K ration, but I wouldn't have been munching if I'd known that Kraut was right behind us. That German was within five or ten feet—I didn't even hear him. Zerbel beat him to the draw. Then he said to haul ass."

Zerbel led, with Olson the last one out. "We were going single-file down through the trees, and I tripped." When Olson fell a burp gun went off, chopping limbs off right above his head.

"You won't believe it; you know, it was the only time this ever happened to me. They talk about when you have death staring you in the face, how this motion picture, this projection reel, is going in the back of your mind. For me it was past-life kind of things; it didn't last long, just a matter of seconds. I still know in my own mind that if I hadn't tripped I'd have been killed."

The German fire was close enough to rip an epaulet from Hoffman's overcoat, but none of the men in the squad was injured. They found a trail and followed it downhill toward another firebreak. By now they were throughly lost. They worked their way cautiously along the edge of the break and almost bumped into a platoon of Germans gathered around five tanks.

Zerbel's leadership impressed Olson. "He was in charge, and he did a hell of a nice job. He moved forward and checked out the Germans, and then he told us, 'There's one thing we ain't going to do, guys, and that's disturb that bunch.' They didn't see us, so we didn't bother them."

The rest of the company heard the firing, and two men went to investigate. They found footprints, a lot of spent cartridges, and Zerbel's dead German, but no sign of the squad. In the confusion it was not possible to get a nose count to determine who was missing. The company reformed in a line of skirmishers and moved forward. We tried maintaining direction by having the squad leaders fire off two rounds every few minutes.

At nightfall Zerbel's small force spotted a section of American tanks from the 2nd Armored. The tankers showed them a map and oriented them, and the cold and hungry men headed off through the snow. Thompson remembers it took most of the night, but eventually they found the K Company foxholes. Leinbaugh was relieved and surprised to see them. "I had given up hope. I was sure the entire squad had been killed or captured."

When Zerbel and his squad reached the company, Olson too was greatly relieved, but for private reasons of his own. "I was told it was past midnight and January 7th had been my birthday. For some strange reason I had persuaded myself that if I could live through my nineteenth birthday, I could make it all the rest of the way through the war; that somehow everything was going to be all right. Here it was, January 8th, and I'd made it."

By dusk the company had encountered two more German delaying squads, and three more men from the company were wounded in the firefights. One of the wounded, Lieutenant Meek, the fourth platoon leader, had been with the company six weeks. His left arm was badly shattered by machine-gun fire. Several men, including a new lieutenant, were sent back with frozen feet. We dug in before dark in a large semicircle, our flanks pulled back for all-round protection. Being on high ground, Cole was able to keep in touch with battalion on the SCR 300. But without landmarks in the woods, it was impossible to give them accurate coordinates of our location.

A forward observer from the 325th came up with his more powerful radio. With time, patience, and a good ear, he brought in defensive artillery concentrations so 105 rounds were exploding less than a hundred yards in front of our foxholes. That made us feel a lot more secure and let us fix our location.

This particular artillery FO was a good officer. We always asked for him on an attack. It was standard operating procedure for forward observers to head back to their batteries at dark. They didn't have to stay with rifle companies. But this chap and his radioman dug a hole and spent the night with us. Later we heard their colonel awarded them both Silver Stars for remaining overnight in our perimeter. The FO was embarrassed. On his next assignment with K Company he apologized for the medal. He felt it was unfair as hell. The CO told him not to sweat it. The company had desperately needed their help. No one begrudged the observers their medals a damn bit.

Jess Canchola, Cole recalled, had been complaining all day about his side hurting. "Leinbaugh thought he was goldbricking and made him help dig his foxhole and share it with him that night. The lieutenant fell asleep, and he was real unhappy when he woke and found Canchola gone. He had taken off during the night." Later when the company returned to Lamormenil, Brewer told Cole that Canchola had come to the CP doubled up with pain and half frozen. Brewer suspected appendicitis. "Sure enough, we heard from the aid station they'd diagnosed him as having an acute attack. Leinbaugh felt like a damn fool when he found out Canchola was bad off. Jess was a tough, spunky little fellow. He would never take off unless he was sick as a dog."

Frenchy Lariviere missed only one night away from the third platoon during the entire war. "It was that first night on the hill outside of Lamormenil. I had to go back and spend the night in the CP. I had walking pneumonia and was shaking and trembling so bad I couldn't hold on to my rifle." Brewer gave Frenchy hot broth and wrapped him in blankets. By the next morning Frenchy felt much better. "I loaded up with bandoliers and headed back up the hill and found the company by guiding on the sounds of rifle fire. You sweat it out being alone in the woods."

Lariviere's big fear during combat was getting captured. "That to me was a lot worse than getting killed or wounded. I made up my mind right from the first day I'd never get taken prisoner. I was sure of that."

Wiley Herrell, who had been a Stateside civilian six months earlier and a member of K Company for only four days, was clued in by a couple of old-timers before the attack started. His briefing was short, to the point, and easy to remember: "When we duck, you duck."

Herrell spent his first night in a foxhole with Doyl Hill. "Some Germans slipped up to our hole and tossed a grenade. The explosion knocked me backward and I lost the watch I was holding in my hand. It was one my sister gave me. The Germans must have seen the radium on the watch dial and that's how they found out where we were."

In the dense forests of the Ardennes, patrolling was an unpleasant and downright dangerous chore. George Lucht and other senior sergeants took turns heading the patrols. "We dreaded those patrols, every one of them. It was that first night out of Lamormenil that the CO told me we had to check a road junction. We marked a route on the map and he told me to take a good man with me."

Lucht accepted the assignment philosophically. "I don't remember anyone arguing about orders—we knew what had to be done and just accepted the fact." Lucht had trouble finding a partner. "I asked a couple of fellows in my squad to volunteer, but didn't get any response. After a while Leinbaugh came over, a bit pissed, and asked, 'You still here?' Then a new guy, I hadn't even asked him, said he'd go with me. His name was Jones, a real heller."

The two fired their M1s to be sure they weren't frozen and borrowed extra grenades. "We took off, it seemed an awful distance, and then we looked around and saw movement behind us. We were being followed. Three or four indistinct forms were behind us, stalking us Indian-fashion." Lucht and Jones would stop every so often, lie down in the snow and watch, and then get up and move. "We stopped, and they would stop. We never did get a good look at them—the woods were too thick. I can't even be certain they were Germans; they must have been, but then they could have been GIs from another outfit thinking we were Germans." The two went ahead, found their objective, spotted a group of Germans next to a halftrack, and came back and reported. Looking at the map afterward Lucht estimated they had been two or three miles into German territory. "I was mighty happy to get back inside that little friendly circle of K Company holes. It was home as far as I was concerned."

We gave battalion map coordinates for George's halftrack, and within minutes heard the muffled echoing explosions of rounds from the 325th's howitzers. Our gunners were awfully good—with a little luck, good enough to hit a vehicle at better than five thousand yards.

According to the book, one Halazone tablet will purify one canteen of water. Just before dawn, Campbell and two men from his platoon hoisted five-gallon GI cans and headed to a little stream for water. No one had a bottle of Halazone tablets, so to be prudent, Campbell took his last two little pills and dropped them ten feet upstream from where the cans were filled. The lieutenant and his water detail picked up a fair amount of criticism when it became light. A frozen German, obviously of ancient vintage, was spotted half immersed in the stream.

In the morning it was Rex Scott's turn to go patrolling. "I got orders to take out a couple of men and try to locate a trail that showed up on the map. We'd only gone a hundred yards or so when we were fired on at almost point-blank range by a machine gun. I was carrying a cocked .45 and fired back instinctively, hitting both gunners. It took a bit of luck to get two Germans with a .45, but they were so close I could hardly miss."

When Don Okenfuss joined the company on New Year's Day he was assigned to the third squad, third platoon. "Sergeant Stewart was my squad leader. He was very disciplined and intelligent, and had very good judgment." Johnny Bowe, Stewart's assistant, took Don under his wing. "Bowe was easier going than Stewart, a very gentle person. Those two had the greatest respect for each other, and I felt lucky to be in their squad. Though we'd been under shelling before, the attack through the woods, the 7th and 8th of January, was my first real combat experience."

On the second morning of the attack, Okenfuss ended up next to Carl Bauer, the last man on the company's left flank. "We were pushing our way through the snow and came close to a cut-over area. I look across this open space and there, going exactly the opposite direction, is a whole line of guys. It must have been a company, doing the same thing we were doing, sweeping the woods in a skirmish line." Don noticed what they were wearing. "I say to Carl, 'Hey, look at the long overcoats.' Carl turns, takes one quick look, and says, 'Oh, my God, those are Germans!'" The two men froze in a crouch. "I whisper, 'What do we do now?' And Carl, he was an old-timer, says to me, 'Don, we don't do nothing, we just keep going.'

"They passed us, we passed them. I think both Bauer and I were scared stiff. I know I was. We kept this to ourselves, we never told anyone."

Erickson was the next man to get involved in a sortie beyond the company's lines. "We kept getting separated, one squad or a platoon would get in a firefight and be held up—there was no way to keep the skirmish line together." One of the platoons got too far forward, and Erickson and another sergeant were sent to locate them. "We go out a ways and clear a rise and come face to face with half a dozen Germans. We saw them and heard their voices at the same time. We were hardly ten feet apart." The Germans were dressed in white camouflage suits and were almost invisible in the snow. The two patrols fired at the same moment. "One shot from a burp gun hit my submachine gun and kicked it out of my grip. The shot jammed my barrel, and when I pulled the trigger again nothing happened. I considered the situation very briefly and decided it was a good time to leave. We duck back over this crest and they gave us several long bursts, but somehow they missed us."

The company moved down a slope with a small stream at the bottom. A German lay prone in the snow on the far bank. Two men covered him and called for him to surrender. He was absolutely immobile, dressed in a camouflage tunic and a soft garrison hat. The men jumped the stream and approached him carefully. His eyes were half-open, watching—he seemed to be playing dead. The men nudged the body, rolling it face up. They thought sure he was breathing ever so slightly. They watched for at least a minute before deciding the man was actually dead. The body was fresh, not frozen, and there was not a mark on him. We couldn't figure what killed him.

The stream was our best reference point of the day. On our map it was labeled Rau de Jouistet. The company was less than a mile from its objective, the high ground due north of Samrée. The ridge had an odd place name, La Lu.

Our map, a May 1944 edition, had been printed only four weeks earlier, "10/Dec 44/654th Engrs," according to the legend. The ten-meter contour intervals were printed in black, with the streams and marshy areas marked in a light blue. In poor light it was impossible to tell a winding logging trail from a winding stream or a contour line, which added to our considerable navigational problems. The men plodded slowly ahead through the deep snow, eating K rations on the move. We had to reach our objective before dark.

Dulin sweated out each new firebreak. "The Germans had zeroed in on most of them with their mortars. We'd fire across the clearing first and shove across a few men at a time. I know it's impossible, but I saw one mortar round coming in. We were moving forward and I glanced up and saw this round heading right for me. It exploded ten or fifteen feet away. I got nicked by shrapnel fragments, but no damage. I picked a few little splinters out of my face and neck. My coat absorbed the rest."

Topel noticed that all the new men in the company seemed to end up with a BAR or a bazooka. "Nobody wanted to lug the goddam things— they were too cumbersome." Topel carried a bazooka. "I don't remember which firebreak, but I tried to fire the thing and nothing happened. The damn round was frozen solid inside the tube. I banged it against a tree, but couldn't get the shell out. I finally decided to hell with it and buried the damn thing in a snowbank, and then I got an M1 from one of the wounded guys."

Down a firebreak, the ground sloped sharply past snow-covered fields and clumps of fir forests and we could see a distant village in the valley below us. The little town seemed peaceful and appeared undamaged. Smoke rose from the chimneys. Shepherd, who was half-frozen, remembers suggesting to the CO that they go down there and take the place. "Leinbaugh told me, 'I'll make a deal, Shepherd. You go take it. The rest of us will follow you.'"

Shepherd was glad the company reached its objective before dark. "They said dig in, so we dug some holes. I walked down to get me pine-tree limbs to make me a bed in the bottom of it. I had no more than got those broken branches off that tree when three or four shells come in right after each other. A big piece of shrapnel almost got me—it could have blown my damn head off."

As Shepherd ran for his hole, he heard calls for a medic. "It was Bell, my foxhole buddy. He had a big wound in his chest. Besides Bell, Harvey Augustin and another man were wounded bad. Cirilo and some other guys carried Bell out, but they came right back and said Bell had died. The next day we were moving back. I remember seeing Bell next to the trail, all frozen."

Shepherd and Bell had talked on the way to the ridgeline. "Bell told me, 'When this war is over I'm going to stay over here.' He told me he liked Belgium and was going to stay. He did. He must have had an idea he was going to die or something. I don't know."

Bell was killed by the same shell that wounded Harvey Augustin. "It was our own artillery. I was hit in the back, but I didn't know I was hit until I felt warm blood running down my back." When he realized he was hit, Harvey was happy. "I'd had it. That past week I hadn't had more than forty-five minutes' sleep. I had a strong religious background and prayed for something to get me out of the fighting. When I was hit I felt the Lord had answered my prayer."

Mellon and the other aidmen went to work on the wounded. "Working in that snow at night was hard. You had to rip through six layers of clothing to find the hole. You just felt around for the blood. Then I'd sprinkle on sulfa and pack the wound." A sergeant held a flashlight under a raincoat so Doc could see. "My hands were filthy dirty, but I guess it was so cotton-picking cold the germs didn't have a chance. It got down to zero in those hills, and when a guy was hit he'd go into shock real fast."

The temperature plummeted during the night. The terrible cold was Doc Mellon's chief concern. "One of our Spanish-American boys, a real good man, fell asleep in his hole that night. When we got him out in the morning, both his hands and feet were frozen. His boots had split, there was ice between his toes, and the skin on his hands was burst open."

George Thompson was digging in at the base of a tree when a shell came in. "I had my rifle right beside me, and a shell hit it and blew it apart. All I could find was the stock and the barrel; the trigger housing was gone, the rifle was just split apart. And this was just an arm's length away. The shell ripped my cartridge belt and split my canteen open, but it never really hurt me; I was just numb for a while."

Paul Cote was evacuated during the night with frozen feet. "I also was nicked by shrapnel—not bad, but I bled like crazy and then the wound froze over. I checked with Leinbaugh, and he ordered me out, making another guy take my BAR. My feet were swollen like balloons when they got my boots off at the aid station. When they finally got me back to Paris, the medical captain told me I was in the early stages of gangrene."

The shells that killed Bell and seriously wounded Harvey Augustin and two other men came from our rear. After the first four rounds came over and exploded in the trees, showering shrapnel on the company, the CO frantically radioed battalion to lift the fire. Battalion said to wait while the guns were checked and relaid, then another volley would be coming over. Twelve rounds passed above the company and exploded on Samrée. Four more hit the treetops and exploded on top of us.

Again we radioed to stop the barrage. This time the battalion commander said it had to be German artillery hitting our positions. We told him we damn well knew the difference between incoming and outgoing. A man came running over to the radio with a big piece of shell casing that had "Rock Island" visible on its base. We told the colonel if this was German artillery, they sure as hell were using shells made in the Rock Island Arsenal.

By firing the batteries individually, the culprit was finally identified. Somebody had miscalculated the height of the trees on the top of our hill. At last we were able to doze fitfully in our frigid holes while the 105s sighed reassuringly overhead en route to Samrée.

At 9:00 P.M. Lance made his rounds, checking on the machine-gun positions where they tied in with L Company to our rear. Earlier the gunners had heard activity, so Lance took a man to investigate. L Company's foxholes were empty. We got battalion on the radio. Several hours later a message came back that the L Company CO had decided his men were in no shape to make it through the night and had pulled them out. After a protracted and heated argument at battalion, L Company, accompanied by the battalion operations officer, returned to its positions.

At first light, Able Company joined K Company on the ridgeline. Both outfits were in bad shape; most of the men's weapons were frozen. Our battalion commander arrived with orders from regiment for the two companies to advance another half mile to support the main effort on Samrée. Captain Prophet, Able's CO, and Leinbaugh both flatly refused to move their companies.

Leinbaugh finally gave in to the colonel's threats and agreed to try it, but only after the battalion adjutant said he and Lieutenant Braley from M Company would take a patrol and check out the objective. Prophet stuck to his guns. Later we heard papers for his court-martial were being drawn up. When the colonel told Prophet he was going to have him court-martialed for refusing a direct order, Prophet said, "Colonel, there's nothing I'd like more right now than a nice warm court-martial."

There comes a point when men have already accomplished the impossible and can no longer function. Neither of the company commanders was challenging the Army's authority; they were just arguing the facts.

The colonel refused to believe our weapons were inoperable. Luckily the M1s and the BARs tested for his benefit were frozen solid. After firing, moisture condensed on the rifles and ice formed in the trigger mechanism or fouled the gas operating cylinders on the M1s. Disassembly or thawing the piece over a fire usually corrected the problem.

During his brief visit the colonel was highly critical of the company's appearance. He said it looked as if nobody had shaved for a week. Leinbaugh said the lack of hot water was the real problem, not any lack of interest in our personal appearance. The colonel, who prided himself on being a product of the old National Guard, let us in on an old remedy. "Now if you men would save some of your morning coffee it could be used for shaving." Leinbaugh stepped over to a snowbank, picked up the five-gallon GI coffee can brought up that morning, and shook it in the colonel's face. The frozen coffee produced a satisfying thunk. He shook it again. "That's enough," said the colonel. "Goddammit, I can hear."

Morris Dunn was more interested in mail than coffee. "They brought mail up that morning, the first time in a week, along with the frozen coffee. But none of us replacements got letters, just the old boys. I left the States in October and hadn't gotten a single letter from back home. My morale couldn't have gotten any worse; I hit bottom that day."

George Thompson could tell the colonel was in a foul mood. "When the colonel came up he and Leinbaugh had some sort of an argument, it got pretty heated, a lot of swearing back and forth. Finally the colonel took Leinbaugh aside so the men in the company couldn't hear what they were talking about."

Okenfuss later heard the CO had refused a direct order to attack. "He said he would take a court-martial before moving out. He told the colonel that our weapons were frozen and with the company at less than half strength, it was in no condition to go on."

Latherial Barnes had a rough week. "It was tough to get food and ammo up to the men and to keep the jeep running. The antifreeze had the consistency of sherbet." Barnes left the kitchen area about four o'clock each morning with breakfast. "It got awfully cold driving through those hills; it was worse than walking. You couldn't drive along and keep a cigarette going, so I chewed tobacco." Barnes tried to get as close to the company's position as possible, heading up old logging trails in the dark. "For a couple of days I lurched over this big pile of timbers and finally decided to get out the ax and clear the trail. I chopped out the logs and underneath the pile I found this frozen Kraut. I hauled him over to the ditch so we wouldn't be running over him anymore."

Charlie Sullivan   John Hargesheimer *(left)* and Sullivan *(right)*

John Radovich, Leinbaugh, and Morris Dunn

Jerry Dunne

Riley Martin

Clayton Shepherd

John Bratten

Bruce Baptie

Alfred O. Oyler

Harvey Augustin

George Lucht

Leslie Carson

John B. Cole

Walter Anderson

Louis Ciccotello

John B. Dolan

Joe Namey

Ray Bocarski

John Corkill, KIA

12

$\triangledown$

THE ROAD TO HOUFFALIZE

"Co. moved by truck and foot at 0400 to Petites Tailles, Belgium, and jumped off in attack at 1015. Majority of men exhausted and scarcely fit for combat. Co-Ord VP 599857 Map of Belgium and NE France sheet (1/50,000) #91."

This "record of events" appeared on K Company's morning report filed January 13, 1945.

The editorializing naturally came from Franklin Brewer, acting first sergeant, who had spent the previous twenty-four hours making sure the men in the company had hot food, dry socks, and ammo waiting when they came off the line. Brewer was frustrated and angry. He kept up a running argument with the company commander. "There is not one man in the company fit to walk another mile, much less fight." Brewer, as usual, was right.

The previous day's morning report noted K Company had moved back to Grandmenil, Belgium, for rest and reorganization. But there was more to the story. The company had trudged back through blizzardlike weather from the hills above Samrée, arriving in Grandmenil at dusk. The brutal cold hovered near zero. Grandmenil's ruins were still jammed with GIs, so again the company took what cover was available and "rested and reorganized." Translated to English from Army lingo, this meant finding the ruins of a house to break the wind, huddling down in a frozen overcoat, and falling into an exhausted sleep in the open.

At 3:30 A.M. K Company lined up for tepid coffee and Spam-and-cheese sandwiches. Then we walked east of town to meet the two-and-a-halfs, which hauled us, skidding and sliding in blowing snow, three miles through the dark, down a forest road toward Petites Tailles. Since we had rested and reorganized, our battalion had been picked to lead off in the next attack—a seven-mile trek toward Houffalize to meet up with George Patton's Third Army coming up from the south.

Petites Tailles had been captured after a night-long battle by our regiment's First Battalion. Casualties had been heavy. Moving on foot the last miles through thick woods toward the hamlet, we passed burned-out tanks and trucks from both armies. Hands and boots of German dead protruded through the drifting snow.

Near the village crossroads we passed through Able Company's positions. An old sergeant told us what we'd already guessed. It had been a hard battle, "rough as a cob," as the sergeant described it. First Battalion had taken more than seventy prisoners, mostly non-German conscripts who said they'd been abandoned by their officers and noncoms as the battle turned against them. The conscripts then surrendered at the first chance.

The sergeant gave us the bad news. Captain Prophet, Able Company's CO, had been killed during the fighting. This put an end to his threatened court-martial. Later it was learned that Prophet had been posthumously awarded the Silver Star for heroic action during the battle.

At 10:15 A.M., on the numbing cold morning of January 13, the attack began. The infantry led, the tanks from the 2nd Armored came behind us. K Company was down to nearly half strength. Across the road, Item Company was in much the same situation with two new officers and a handful of sergeants in charge. Lumped together, Item and King added up to one tired, very cold rifle company. But at higher headquarters, staff officers assigned objectives based on unit symbols, not strength figures.

The order to attack was received with a general lack of enthusiasm. The CO said we might as well get on with it—and off we went in the infantryman's traditional half-crouch.

Machine gunner Danny Cirilo remembers wading through the snow with Sergeant Davis singing behind him, "Some people likes it in the summertime, but I likes it in the snow in the wintertime." "He would sing this damn song when we were all freezing to death and then laugh up a storm. Then he would ask me, 'What's the matter, darkmeat, are you cold?'"

Davis had pulled double duty in the company since the fighting near Geilenkirchen. One of the mortarmen called Orville had proved less than aggressive in battle. He was an amiable, likable fellow who argued with considerable conviction and logic with anybody who would listen that he was a lot more scared of Germans than anybody else in the company. He hung back whenever possible. To solve the problem, Leinbaugh placed Orville under Sergeant Davis's full-time care.

"The arrangement worked just fine," the CO remembers. "Orville's orders were to stick to Davis like a shadow, and he did. He was a lot more afraid of Davis than the Germans." Davis was tough and tireless. He was the strongest man in the company, with biceps bigger than most men's thighs. If one of his crewmen faltered, Davis shouldered the extra load and kept on singing and kept on going.

Providentially, K Company met little resistance on the 13th. Our orders were to clear the woods of Germans a quarter of a mile from the road. Enemy foxholes were found where we knew they'd be, covering the first open field along the road. Our dirty brown overcoats made splendid targets against the snowy background; but the Germans had pulled back deeper into the woods. We followed their tracks cautiously and tried to guess when and where they would hunker down for an ambush. A German tank fired occasional tree bursts in our direction, and one man was slightly wounded by shrapnel. During the day half a dozen German laggards were ferreted from concealed emplacements, and in the late afternoon we stopped to begin the nightly ritual of digging in. The ground was deeply frozen. The next hours were spent hacking away with entrenching shovels to sink our holes to a safe depth.

A critical message was received after dark. Battalion, regiment, and division—and as far as we knew corps and army—were all unhappy with our progress. The company had advanced about a mile and a half.

Men in the first platoon brought a needed smidgen of humor to our day. The company had stopped in a clearing labeled Pisserotte on the map. The men weren't all that sure how to pronounce it, but they could, and did, spell out our location by pissing with great care and deliberation into a snowbank alongside the road. Crossing the double t's proved the hard part.

We were grateful for a relatively uneventful day. But ironically the 84th Division made headlines back home on the 13th. Because of the time difference between the Belgian battlefield and the States, afternoon papers carried a detailed report on the progress of the counteroffensive.

Fred Flanagan's parents in Louisiana filed away an extra copy of the *Shreveport Journal*. The one-inch double headline for the 13th read, "General U.S. Offensive Opened Against North Flank of Bulge." The secondary lead reported that First Army soldiers advanced more than a mile, fighting to within eleven miles of Third Army troops beating up from the south. According to the news account, "The 2nd Armored and 84th Infantry fought through snow-crusted woods, and the remnants of the German army were pulling back at top speed. With the premier emphasis on the foot soldier a heavy burden fell upon two things—officer leadership in the field and youthful stamina."

But then something happened. The correspondent must have taken a break while a solicitous colonel poured him a double shot of bourbon. He went back to his portable, pulled up closer to the fire, and started a new paragraph. "With their men," he wrote, "officers engaged in hand-to-hand combat with the enemy under the most difficult battle conditions.

American officers, such as full colonels and lieutenant colonels, who usually are in command posts, took positions in the front line with their troops and personally led and spurred them on."

The CO wasted half the night looking for battalion headquarters so he could pick up the next day's attack order. After looking over the maps and jotting down the code names for the artillery concentrations, he got a special bawling out from the colonel for permitting the company to drag ass during the day.

He caught a ride back to Pisserotte in the kitchen jeep. It was black as pitch, and Barnes had his hands full threading his way around tree trunks and past lines of tanks parked along the road. Leinbaugh, totally spent and suffering from lack of sleep, suspected he was on the verge of passing out from fatigue. The jeep reached the company at first light, but a heavy hallucinatory fog had blanketed the area. Unable to spot a single helmet above the line of foxholes, the CO, too tired to react rationally, was convinced K Company had been wiped out to a man.

"I stood in the jeep looking at our line of holes and couldn't see a soul, not a sign of life. I was afraid to find out what had happened." He was halfway across the clearing before he spotted a helmet sticking out of a foxhole. Mel Cline from the first platoon was the only man in the company still on his feet. He reported everything was quiet. The entire company had collapsed from exhaustion.

After we had breakfasted on cold pancakes the fog lifted and K Company was on the move again, staying just within the line of trees along the road. Advancing under occasional rifle and mortar fire, everybody was in the same groggy, drained-out condition.

The next half hour established that two of the company's best sergeants, Baptie and Dunne, had lost all of the experienced rifleman's normal perception of danger. Baptie describes what happened. "Up through the trees we could make out several buildings. We stopped and the company commander waved two of us over. He thought maybe a patrol could con the Germans out of those houses and talk them into surrendering."

The three men spread-eagled in the snow watched the houses through field glasses and discussed the odds. Baptie said this one was his. "I checked my grease gun, and Jerry Dunne and I headed out in a kind of a stupor. It wasn't a rational act. We were both bloody tired. The difference between doing something and being a coward is not very much after all."

Dunne worked his way through the woods to the left and got to the rear of the houses where the Germans were holed up. "Two of them tried to sneak out the back, and I gave them a couple of rounds. Baptie was in front of the buildings and yelled at them in German to come out and surrender." The Germans asked for time, and after more talk one of the Germans waved a white flag. "Baptie and I lined them up. About that time the rest of the company came up. I think we took about twenty of them and one officer."

Dunne walked the batch of prisoners back down the road to battalion. "A war correspondent was there and he wanted to know all about how we captured them. I was barely able to speak; I'd lost my voice." The correspondent wanted to know how many Germans Dunne had killed. "That's when I got pissed. I just pointed to my throat, indicating I couldn't talk, and headed back to the company."

Baptie and Dunne received Bronze Stars for "courage, initiative, and resourcefulness," and Dunne a next-day promotion to staff sergeant. The immediate effect of their action was to give the company new confidence. Baptie and Dunne had tried a risky coup—and pulled it off. Our luck seemed to be changing. After seeing Dunne and Baptie's dejected prisoners we began to realize the Germans were every bit as cold and exhausted as we were—maybe more so.

The next encounter with the enemy's rear guard further boosted morale. The lead squad came under fire from the now familiar log-covered emplacements. The Germans made the understandable mistake of opening fire too quickly, permitting our men to pull back and take cover without casualties. We estimated we were facing a German platoon—in the neighborhood of twenty-five or thirty men.

There was a quick solution for this problem. Within minutes of calling for artillery, more than a hundred rounds of 105 shells whistled low overhead, pulverizing the woods to our front. The artillerymen thoughtfully included fuse delays and white phosphorus in the mix. As the barrage lifted, the company moved forward quickly and built up a firing line within forty yards of the German positions. The small-arms exchange lasted only a few minutes before a white rag on the end of a rifle was waved frantically from a hole. The Germans—eight or ten of them—crawled out of their holes, stretching their arms as high as possible as they trudged apprehensively toward us through the snow. Baptie and Bocarski quizzed them. With M1s pressed in their midsections, the prisoners told us more than we wanted to know. They said they'd left several wounded and dead in their old positions. The rest of their outfit and the tank that had been pestering us all day had pulled back.

We advanced cautiously toward their positions, climbing over felled trees and forcing our way through a network of fallen branches. A dozen dead and wounded Germans sprawled on the ground. The artillery had done a thorough job, a case of overkill. The snow was blackened by huge chunks of frozen earth; several German gun emplacements had received direct hits. White phosphorus fragments smoldered and hissed in the snow. The stench of cordite and clouds of smoke hung over the hollow.

Walking forward, we saw a German officer propped against the base of a pine tree. His folded cap was next to him in the snow. He wore a clean camouflage jacket and was holding a cigarette awkwardly in his left hand. His right arm hung limply at his side. He was blond-haired and blue-eyed, with classic Teutonic features. His face was ashen-white, devoid of color. We took the man for a captain or maybe a major.

The German's right leg had been cut off at midthigh with near-surgical precision. The severed leg, bent at the knee, was wedged behind his shoulders, pinned between his neck and the tree trunk. The polished black boot on the severed leg lay across his chest. The stump wasn't bleeding, apparently cauterized by shrapnel or the intense cold. Recognizing the K Company CO as an officer, the German said quietly and in good English, "Please shoot me."

Leinbaugh couldn't take his eyes from the man's face. He said nothing. He kept on walking.

Farther on, one of the company's veteran sergeants fell in beside the CO and asked if he'd seen the guy with his leg blown off.

"Yeah, he asked me to shoot him."

"Yeah, he asked me, too," the sergeant said.

"Did you?"

"Hell, you know I couldn't walk off and leave the poor son of a bitch to die like that."

The advance continued south toward Houffalize and the Third Army. The 2nd Armored's tanks were following to our rear on the highway. The weather cleared, and a spotter plane appeared overhead flying slow loops in the cold sky over the front of the column. Twice we halted when the tankers relayed word from the plane to hold up while artillery was directed on German armor. We passed several vehicles and a tank knocked out by fire from the plane-artillery team.

That afternoon Shepherd was carrying one of the light .30s. "The Germans had mined the trees along the road. They'd wrapped dynamite around the trunks, but most of them weren't blown. We followed a German tank all that day. He'd go up hill and dale, and periodically he would shoot at us with that big gun of his."

Several men felt the shock waves of the tank's heavy, armor-piercing rounds—four or five pounds of hardened steel—traveling faster than a rifle bullet. Bill Masters's helmet was nearly lifted from his head when a round passed inches from his ear. A few of the newer men, not knowing when to be intimidated, played a cat-and-mouse game with the German gunner, offering a moving target by bounding across to I Company's side of the road.

That evening K Company held target practice. We'd hoped to be in houses by nightfall, but found ourselves at the foot of a long, snowswept slope with only the stone foundation of a single fire-gutted house for cover. While hacking away at the frozen ground one of the men spotted four Germans several hundred yards to our left. They had foolishly decided to break from the cover of the woods, and were heading through deep snow for a haystack in the open field. A dozen men opened up with their M1s, and Johnny Bowe ran over with his sniper's rifle, an '03 with scope. He fired several rounds; two Germans were hit. It was as much fun as a shooting gallery—everybody cheering when a German went down.

Lance decided his mortarmen could use a little practice. Sergeant Davis set up the 60s. It took three rounds to get on target—catcalls from the audience—but the last three smacked into the haystack, tossing up an impressive pall of smoke and dust. The mortarmen modestly accepted cheers from the riflemen.

But now the Germans on high ground a mile to our front decided it was their turn. They were looking down our throats and zeroed in quickly with their 120s. They poured hundreds of shells into the battalion area. L Company in the woods to our rear received the brunt of the barrage, taking numerous casualties.

"It wasn't too bad for K Company," Shepherd remembers, "until a tank came in—one of them peewee light tanks—and pulled in behind the house. The Germans started throwing fireworks and knocked the track off." Two men got out of the tank, and then a third man came crawling out and fell to the ground. "He was wounded in the head and one eye was hanging out of the socket. I grabbed him and put him in a hole with a medic, but I don't think he made it."

Shepherd watched as Kelley, a recent replacement, was involved in a bizarre accident. "A damned AP round came in and cut the top off a big pine and clipped this guy next to me behind the collar. It passed between his shirt and overcoat and pinned him to the ground, just like a spear. It took three of us to pull that jagged treetop out of the ground so the guy could move. He wasn't hurt too bad—just scraped up pretty good."

Shepherd picked up the light .30 caliber. "I went into this wrecked building and took the machine gun and the company commander decided we should set it up inside the door so we could cover the slope out front. The Germans were shooting at the house, and there was a mule tied to the well out there in front, bucking and half-crazy from all those shells."

Shepherd waited for the shelling to die down so he could turn the mule loose. "It seemed to me the Germans were just deliberately shooting at that mule. Finally I said I gotta go, and . . . phew, just like that. That's when the war ended for me. I was standing up beside the door looking at that mule and a tank shell hit right next to me."

Shepherd told Leinbaugh he was hit and had to go back. "The CO got me a medic and asked me how bad it was and did I need someone to go back with me. I said, no, I'd be able to get back alone." The medic cut away Shepherd's jacket. "I had on so many clothes they didn't have enough for the rest of the United States Army. I had them all. Finally the medic got down to my skin and looked at me. 'Clayton,' he said, 'what's the matter with you, are you cold or scared?' And I said, 'I'm both.'"

The medic gave Shepherd a shot of morphine and started him back to the rear through the woods. "I was lucky and met one of the cooks. Man, I scared him good. He thought I got it in the head because I was covered all over with blood, and I told him, no, I was hit pretty good in the shoulder, a big hole, and in my arm."

The shelling lasted more than an hour, taking a heavy toll. Dick Stagg, a second platoon BAR man from DeWitt, Arkansas, was killed instantly by a mortar shell while digging his foxhole. A married man and father, Stagg had come into the company at Geilenkirchen. A strong, rugged fellow with a sense of humor, he had fitted in immediately.

During shellings Stagg always called out the impact point of the German rounds as if he were at the center of a target on the rifle range. The Army used the clock system superimposed with numbered rings for scoring targets. If a round was high and close to the center of the target the call would be a three or four at twelve o'clock. If off a distance to the left, the call could be a one or two at nine o'clock. The black center circle was a bull's-eye, and a complete miss was a Maggie's drawers. When the German mortars were way off target, Stagg would bellow gleefully, "Maggie's drawers, you bastards."

Stagg had a good ear, but the round that killed him was exactly on target. One of the men hauling him out realized the unfairness of it all. "Hell, he didn't even have time to yell 'Bull's-eye!'"

In addition to Shepherd, who was listed on company records as slightly wounded in action, with the notation "(Pen W, rt upper arm sv, shell)," other men were wounded, including Kelley, who had been pinned by the treetop. Ralph Ciullo from Brooklyn received a massive, near-fatal chest wound; Alfred Swanson was evacuated with a scalp wound; Jess Canchola was sent back with a puncture wound in his thigh; Willard Taylor was slightly wounded, but not evacuated. Five more men were evacuated as nonbattle casualties. Our losses were offset during the night by an equal number of men returning to duty after temporary hospitalization.

With our depleted ranks, the officers and sergeants became obsessed with numbers. Pope worried when his platoon dropped down to squad level. "I was a firm believer in numbers. I was never happier than when I saw ten guys come into my platoon. That brings your odds right back up, right? You get stories about guys getting pissed off, talking about shooting a platoon leader or somebody in the attack. It's a figure of speech, it's bullshit, a bunch of crap, because we were all looking for that extra number."

13

TAVERNEUX

Late during the night of the 14th, toward midnight when the shelling had eased off to an occasional round, the CO headed for the meeting of company commanders. Lance volunteered to go along for the exercise. Twice a German night fighter, the only one we encountered during the Bulge, forced the two into ditches. The plane's red and green tracers ricocheted off the asphalt and bounced off a line of tanks parked alongside the road. It was nearly 3:00 A.M. before they found battalion headquarters. The colonel was irate and wanted answers to a question. "Where," he demanded, "is that goddam new lieutenant from I Company?"

It had been four days since Captain Mitchell's death. A tall, quiet-spoken Kentuckian, and the battalion's senior rifle company commander, he had been awarded two Silver Stars for bravery during his brief combat career. His replacement, an older lieutenant with less than a month on line, had been forced into the impossible task of taking Mitchell's place. Now he was missing.

After the last firefight in the afternoon, a tech sergeant from I Company had ducked across the road and told Leinbaugh their CO was missing. No one knew what had happened to him. The sergeant took over command, and the two companies operated as a unit until they reached their objective. The colonel decided Lieutenant Schumacher from M Company should take command of Item until matters could be straightened out.

At the meeting a captain from the 2nd Armored lodged a complaint against K Company. The previous night shadowy figures had climbed the rear deck of three tanks and made off with four cases of ten-in-ones—cardboard boxes each packed with enough food for ten men for one day. They were considered a particular delicacy by foot soldiers, who subsisted largely on K rations. The CO, who had shared the loot, stoutly denied any complicity on the part of K Company.

As the final item of business, K Company got orders to send an officer-led patrol at dawn to scout out the long ridgeline overlooking their present location. The job by default went to Campbell's second platoon. He was the only officer left in the company besides the CO. But a problem existed. His platoon, with a PFC as second in command, was down to a dozen men and lacked the firepower for the strong combat patrol envisioned by battalion. Nothing could be gained, however, by arguing the matter.

Lance prayed he'd get back to the company in time to sit down for thirty minutes' rest before another long day—"but believe me that didn't happen." Lance wondered why battalion didn't move closer to the rifle companies, "but for five dollars a month combat pay, I figured I wasn't being paid to think too clearly."

The runner discovered that Campbell and Rex Scott had the best sack in the company. They'd found an old mattress, slit open its end, and crawled in. Awakened from a comfortable sleep, Campbell went to the CP, but couldn't get much sense out of Leinbaugh, who kept nodding off. Finally the CO roused and pulled out a map. Before the combat team renewed the attack, Campbell was to take his platoon and check the ridge.

Campbell worked out a dogleg route for the patrol: about eight hundred yards across an open field, and then into the trees for another eight hundred yards. The objective was a farmhouse in a small clearing just past the crest of the hill.

On the way to the woods the new men in the platoon could practice what they'd been taught in basic. Two scouts out front and a pair of flankers. Campbell was behind the scouts, followed by a burly replacement carrying the SCR 300. Then the rest of the patrol strung out in a staggered open column with Rex Scott, the acting platoon sergeant, at the end of the line.

Len Bowditch, behind the radio operator, had few illusions about his role—"a rifleman is a rifleman." Coming to the company after Thanksgiving, Bowditch was now a member of the family and feeling good about it. "I really felt I belonged to K Company after we moved down to Belgium. That's when you found out that everybody was your brother."

Wiley Herrell had a couple of weeks of experience. "I learned about shells, whether they were coming in or going out, and I knew by the crack of bullets whether they were near or not." But this was his first patrol, and he was worried. He told himself, "I've been taught this, but I don't know what to expect."

It was safe to expect the unexpected; something was bound to go wrong. When the patrol entered the edge of the woods and tried to contact the company, the radio failed. The SCR 300 could receive, faintly, but transmission was gone. Nobody knew how to fix it, but a new battery might help. George Thompson was sent back alone to get a new one; the patrol could not spare a second man. George had been out a couple of weeks with a badly sprained ankle and had returned to the company New Year's Day. "I was glad to be back. That's where I belonged. We all were in it together. Each one's life depended on what the other one did. With the group there we were trying to stick together for our own survival."

Moving farther into the woods, Campbell took over the point. A frame hut was spotted on the right flank. The patrol halted, and the lieutenant crept to the door, .45 drawn and ready. He burst in. The hut was empty. The men went another fifty yards. A farmhouse became visible, and the patrol halted. Leaving seven men behind with Scott, Campbell picked George Bond and Walter Roman to cross the clearing with him and check the place out—George, the slender six-foot ASTPboy just back from the hospital; Walter, the serious little fellow from the Bronx, whose issue overcoat ended well below the tops of his combat boots.

The three men studied the farmhouse. No tracks in the snow-covered clearing, no smoke from the chimney, no movement around the house or the neighboring trees. They headed out, Campbell in the lead. Their combined firepower: two M1s, one pistol, and half a dozen grenades.

Bowditch remembers his first inkling that the enemy was waiting. "Three pine trees alongside the house started to move and we heard a grinding, rumbling noise."

Olson at first didn't comprehend what was happening. "I was leaning against a tree, scraping frost off the trunk, when I heard the engine start on the tank. It didn't register—it just didn't register."

Wiley Herrell was equally surprised. "We were about forty yards back in the woods when Campbell, Bond, and Roman headed out. That was one of the worst experiences of my life. I've had a lot of nightmares from it. That German tank seemed to come from nowhere."

The sound of the rotating turret stopped the three in the snow-covered meadow. It didn't require Campbell's "Go back!" to turn them. Each step was an effort. The tank held its fire. The three made it halfway to the woods before the tank fired. This was one time Campbell wasn't afraid. He figured it was too late for that. As he zigzagged toward the woods, he said to himself, "What a stupid way to die."

When the German gunner fired the first high-explosive round, Bond was hit and went down. The other two men moved toward him. His wounds were massive; Bond was dead. The next round, seconds later, dismissed any thought of carrying Bond back. Roman and Campbell were both hit. A shell fragment ripped a hole in Walter's throat. He was bleeding heavily and unable to speak. Campbell took hits in his neck, arm, shoulder, and back. Both arms were immobilized.

Olson watched as the shells exploded. "Bond was down, and Campbell and Roman stopped to check. Campbell's suspender straps on his cartridge belt had been torn loose by shrapnel. Then back in the woods we took a tree burst. We didn't know where that tank was coming from or if it was coming after us, and we weren't going to stick around and find out. We got the hell out of there."

In the confusion of the shelling, the two groups lost contact. Scott tried to get the rest of the patrol out of the line of fire and under cover. When the firing stopped, Scott led his little group down the hill, but couldn't find the company. He headed for battalion and gave a report on the tank encounter to be passed along to artillery.

Roman and Campbell made it to the woods line and were trying to return to the company when Thompson spotted them. He had no idea what had happened to the rest of the patrol.

"After picking up a new battery I followed the same trail we'd taken earlier. I got almost to the woods when I met Campbell and Roman coming out, going very slow." Thompson thought Campbell was going to fall. "His head was drooped and he was standing like a man in a daze. Roman was bleeding through a cut in his throat. I knew I had to get Campbell back, because he would have never made it, I'm afraid. That's what I thought at the time. If he fell in that snow he might have frozen to death in a matter of minutes."

Thompson dropped the heavy battery and slung his M1 over his shoulder. "I got both men under my arms. I knew we'd never make it if we took the long way around, so I brought them straight down the ridge through the open fields. How we made it without getting shot, I don't know." It was hard going, with snow up to the men's knees. "We just plodded along with no protection at all."

Thompson and his two charges arrived back at the bottom of the hill, where Captain Wooten from battalion met them. He had an aerial photo of the ridge, and Campbell pinpointed the tank's location. Then Roman and the lieutenant were bundled into a jeep and started back through the evacuation chain.

At the aid station, a medic made a note in the log. "A soldier was wounded with hole through larynx and unable to talk unless he had his finger over the hole. Rather amusing."

At the foot of the ridge we had watched the patrol's progress through field glasses until the last man disappeared over the crest. Then we heard the tank fire. The patrol was in trouble, but we couldn't reach them on the radio. Higher headquarters decided not to wait for the patrol report and ordered K Company to advance to the top of the ridge. Following the second platoon's route in the snow, we headed slowly up the long hill.

Halfway to our goal, battalion radioed for us to hold fast. Two huge self-propelled 155s from the 2nd Armored pulled out beyond the trees into the open field below us. The gunners dropped the tail spades and commenced firing at the ridge. The huge shells exploded in a clump of pines near the road. We were halfway between the guns and their target, left of their line of sight, and half a mile from the point of impact. Even at our distance, we felt giant shock waves from every round. The big orange-red explosions made our friendly 105 concentrations seem puny in comparison.

Pope came to his feet cheering the gunners in pure Brooklynese. When the noise stopped, we radioed battalion. "Where's our patrol? That stuff could be falling right on our guys." Battalion told the CO everything was under control and to hurry up and get K Company moving. Leinbaugh radioed back that K Company was not taking another step until we found out about Campbell and the second platoon. Then the entire company plopped down in the snow. We sat and refused to budge.

The gambit worked. In a few minutes battalion radioed that Campbell and another man had been wounded, but had been able to walk out. The battalion adjutant said the 2nd Armored's general had come up and ordered the 155s to pull out from the woods and blast the top of the ridge. He assured us the wounded men were okay and being evacuated.

Satisfied now, the company moved on to the top of the hill, where we found tracks in the snow left by the patrol. We poured heavy fire across the clearing, but received only silence in return. With a covering squad leading the way, we advanced cautiously toward the farmhouse.

George Bond was sprawled dead in the open field, facedown in the snow. We stuck his M1 upright next to his body and went on. The 155 shells had knocked a tread from the Panther; its gun was depressed, the flash hider almost touching the ground. The tank was empty. The only body we found was that of a wizened old man—a civilian—in a frayed overcoat. The corpse was cold. A stained black leather cap was tied to his head, and his small wire glasses were in place over wide-open eyes. A puddle of blood stained the rough cobblestones.

A sergeant covered the body with a strip of canvas. We'd grown used to bodies, we'd seen scores of dead soldiers; but this pathetic old fellow's death bothered us—obviously he had been killed by our artillery.

Sandbagged Shermans, a battalion at least, headed up the hill behind us. They were out of the forest, at last in the open, and had maneuver room in the frozen fields. As the long line of armor rolled toward us, Pope watched delightedly. "Look at those babies come! That's the most beautiful sight I've ever seen."

The Shermans' big guns aimed reassuringly over our heads provided the extra measure of confidence we needed to make it the last mile.

Fontenaille, a hamlet five hundred yards to the left of the Houffalize road, was the next stop. With friendly 75s in the neighborhood, we were no longer concerned about small-arms fire. The company reached the first houses without difficulty. The squads quickly fanned out, covering each other, sticking close to the walls of buildings, running from doorway to doorway, M1s and grenades ready.

A new man who'd been with the company two weeks heard a noise in a cellar. He called, "*Heraus!*"—but panicked when there was no reply. He pulled the pin and rolled a grenade down the steps. The cellar was jammed with civilians. After the wounded were carried from the basement, Mellon and our other aidmen opened their kits and started to work. The rest of the men walked away, unable to watch.

The Third Battalion aid station, which moved into Fontenaille shortly after K Company completed its sweep, reported in its log, "Suffering among civilians in the village is very severe, and many are without shelter and warm clothing." The medic's report contained a final entry. "Treated one family injured by hand grenade. Mother had penetrating and sucking wound of the chest. Ten-month-old baby had nose blown off. Grandmother had penetrating wound of the abdomen with protrusion of intestines. Sister had compound fracture of rt. arm."

The company returned to the highway and advanced the final half mile toward the intersecting highway, the First Army's final phase line. We were on high ground only a mile from Houffalize. With a cold sun breaking the clouds, with the tanks from "Hell on Wheels" spread along the ridgeline, and with fighter-bombers patrolling the skies to the east, it had suddenly become a lovely war. But not for long. After we had dug new and elaborate holes and lined them with straw, word arrived to continue the attack.

The new objective was Taverneux, half the distance to Houffalize. Again we were assured this town was the final objective. Curly Hoffman took a jaundiced view of battalion's promises. "K Company takes Berlin. Then they tell us, 'Hey, you guys, one more town—Tokyo.'"

Fortunately, the route to Taverneux was all downhill. Climbing one more ridge would have been out of the question. A platoon of light tanks followed behind the company, firing continuous strings of tracers overhead. Halfway to the village we opened up with marching fire, which made a lot of noise and boosted our spirits. We climbed over three barbed-wire fences and moved into the first houses. Our job was to clear the right half of the village, while Item Company, taking a more circuitous route, was to swing through a woods and clear the other half.

At the center of Taverneux we were greeted by civilians who guided us to the cellars where the Germans were hiding. The company collected thirty prisoners, who seemed anxious to surrender. Guards escorted them up the hill to battalion. Belgian housewives waved wine bottles and bread from the doorways. A celebration of our bloodless victory had just commenced when a teenager came running up to report more German soldiers were hiding in cellars across the street in Item's half of town. After a brief conference next to the village fountain, we decided to hell with it. Those Germans weren't our problem. They would have to wait for I Company. We returned to our wine-drinking.

K Company was absolutely, totally spent, used up. Everybody was groggy and numbed from lack of sleep, sunken-eyed and unable to function in any normal sense. Several men slumped to the ground, leaned against the fountain, and promptly fell asleep. That last struggle through the snow had required every particle of energy. Only a few more details remained.

Lance located a house at the edge of town for his platoon CP. "The old Belgian couple were awfully nervous. Something was wrong, so we checked in back and found six or seven Germans hiding in the barn. The guy in charge was a big blond good-looking fellow. He wanted to be friendly and kept trying to shake hands. I told him they could all go to hell."

After digging holes, Lucht and his squad guided two tank destroyers into covered positions inside courtyards. "After dark I went up to the company CP. Brewer was talking to a Belgian lady who had sneaked a German map from their headquarters just before they left, and a Belgian nurse who had come by looking for medical supplies. Leinbaugh was on the radio with battalion. Barnes had brought up hot food, our first in days. Corkill, Pope, and Flanagan had started eating.

"There was big explosion outside. The CO, Corkill, and Flanagan ran out to check. In a minute Corky came running back inside the house and said, 'I'm hit.' Pope grabbed for him just as he collapsed to the floor.

"The Belgian nurse knelt over Corkill, searching for a pulse. She took a mirror from her bag, held it in front of his mouth. She looked at Brewer and told him in French he was dead. She was crying. Hardly any of us could move. Brewer asked a couple of us to get a blanket and move Corky over by the door. I couldn't touch him. I just couldn't do it.

"I walked outside in the snow to get some cold air. That was my worst time of the whole war."

Pope and Corkill had been eating in the CP. "The rounds came in. Corky started to head out, he was worried about his squad, and I told him, 'Hey, man, they'll take care of themselves. They can find a hole.' But he went out anyway and a minute later he comes running in yelling my name and collapsed right there on the floor."

The men in the room stripped Corkill, trying to find a wound. Pope noticed a small mark. "It was just like somebody took an indelible pencil and drew a little jagged line on his abdomen. There was no blood. I remember that Belgian nurse holding this mirror to his face to see if it would fog up. But he had no life. You know, Corky and I were pretty close. I liked him. He was a little older than we were, and I made him squad leader. It really hit me hard when he got it."

Minutes earlier, Sergeant Bocarski and three men had walked up the road past the church and the cemetery to the CP to see if chow had arrived. "One round came in close—a big one, I'd say a 120." All four men were knocked to the ground. "The guys with me were hurt badly. One of them screamed for the medics. I got up to help them, but then another round came in and hit in the same place. It was a narrow cobblestone road with walls on both sides that confined the explosion and made it worse. That's when I got hit. I was lucky, just a little leg wound."

Until that night in Taverneux, Flanagan was persuaded that getting wounded happened to other people. "Sergeant Corkill, the Lieutenant, and I ran out of the CP when we heard the explosion and someone yelling for the medics. We were within a few feet of the wounded men when the second round hit. It seemed right on top of us. It was like getting slugged with a baseball bat, and I went down. I had no idea how badly I was hit; it was in the thigh, but I had no sense of penetration, none."

"I remember the red cone of flame, and then while falling having everything switch to slow motion," Leinbaugh said. "I was knocked out, but only briefly. I got to my knees and fingered a warm piece of shrapnel that ended up in the lining of my field jacket, but decided I wasn't hurt."

One of the wounded men had lost a leg. It was completely severed, lying three feet from his body. In the dark Leinbaugh couldn't tell who he was. The other wounded man, Marusich, a big fellow from Wisconsin, fumbled for his aid packet. "Moose was conscious, but his leg was badly shredded. The third man was dead." After the wounded were taken to a house, Leinbaugh went back and checked the dead man's dog tags. "He was one of the replacements—Bill Termin. I didn't know him."

Mellon, asleep in a house down the street, heard the screams for help. "I went running up with a couple of guys. We got the wounded men inside the closest house. Sergeant Sobczynski had lost both legs—high up, close to the crotch. We got belts and tried to put tourniquets around the stumps. I was working on one, the CO was trying to get a belt around the other one, but it kept slipping off." Sobczynski, a burly replacement sergeant from Chicago, remained conscious. He asked Mellon for a cigarette. "I lit one and put it in his mouth. He forced himself up on both elbows and looked down. He could see both legs were gone. He said, 'Bad, ain't it, doc?' He died real quick."

Another aidman came to assist, and Mellon, seeing Leinbaugh was getting ill, sent him outside for air. "We went to work on Marusich. He got a lot of shrapnel and one leg was in bad shape. I didn't figure it could be saved, but we worked as best we could and fixed up a splint to hold him till we could get him back to the aid station. Bocarski and Flanagan had been hit too, but not too bad."

Flanagan was put on a stretcher. "They laid me on the back of the jeep, parked right in the roadway where the shells came in. Someone told me the aidmen were working on Moose. I couldn't move. I was petrified, absolutely petrified, lying out there alone waiting for that next round to come in."

Bocarski was helped into the front seat. "Just before we left for the aid station, Brewer gave me a German map that this Belgian lady had stolen in the German CP. Brewer told me it was important, showing the Germans' escape route, and I should make sure it was given directly to Captain Wooten at battalion headquarters."

When Leinbaugh walked back to the CP, Brewer broke the news: Corkill was dead. "That was one of the worst moments of the war. Of all the fellows in the company who were killed, Corky's death hit me hardest. The fighting was over—that made it all the harder to accept his loss."

Pope, Brewer, and the Belgian nurse stood in the light of the Coleman lantern looking at the body. The nurse was crying. Pope, white-faced and with tears in his eyes, was swearing softly. He finally picked up his rifle and looked at Brewer and Leinbaugh, shaking his head. "I gotta get the hell out of here."

AFTER ACTION

The Battle of the Bulge ended for us on January 16, 1945. Patrols from the American First and Third armies met in our sector near Houffalize and we were promised a long rest—the first in nearly a month.

Again it was time to tot up our losses. GIs from veteran outfits such as the Twenty-ninth who had been on line since D-Day claimed membership in three divisions: one on line, one in the hospital, and one in the ground. By the end of the Bulge, K Company had reached that point—we had more men in hospitals and cemeteries than present for duty. In the final twenty-four hours of battle five men—Stagg, Bond, Sobczynski, Termin, and Corkill—had been killed. Our casualties in the Ardennes totaled eight men killed, over forty wounded, and forty nonbattle casualties. But we had fared far better than our sister rifle companies. Item had twenty-five men killed during the Bulge, L Company eighteen. Our battalion was worn down near the level reached following the fighting around Geilenkirchen.

The Germans we fought against also suffered heavily. The commander of the 116th Panzers, Lieutenant General von Waldenberg, whose headquarters in Taverneux were taken over by K Company, reported that by January 15 it was no longer possible for his battle-weary division to hold positions in the vicinity of Houffalize. "The division was ordered to withdraw to the east, leaving weak security detachments at Taverneux." The Germans moved their CP from the village just hours before K Company's attack. "The division," according to von Waldenberg, "was tired out and used up to the utmost. Its former value was gone forever."

On our first morning in Taverneux, Chick brought up an official letter addressed to the Commanding Officer, Company K, 333rd Inf., APO 84, New York, N.Y.

The letter was from a colonel, the Post Supply Officer at Camp Claiborne, Louisiana. After the 84th's departure for overseas, an audit found K Company short one M1 rifle, which had been issued to a private who had been AWOL a number of times and sentenced to seven years at hard labor. As the accountable officer, K Company's CO was instructed to forward his personal check in the amount of $69.00 to reimburse the army for the missing rifle.

For once during the war Brewer lost his composure. He was enraged. He sat down at the company portable and banged out a two-finger reply swearing after every sentence. During the past twenty-four hours, he wrote, five men in the company had been killed and a dozen more wounded, so fortunately for the colonel we had a number of extra M1s on hand. He said we were most sympathetic with the colonel's problem, and suggested he drop by for a visit so he could make a personal choice of our surplus rifles. In his closing paragraph Brewer mentioned our fond memories of Camp Claiborne and Louisiana, and noted the men in the company were delighted to have the opportunity of contributing to the nation's war effort by helping balance the camp's property books. Brewer watched the mail for weeks but he never got a reply to his letter.

Then Brewer became involved with a woman. Our division's newspaper carried an account of what happened, and his story later appeared in newspapers throughout the States. "Our company had taken Taverneux and the CP was set up in a large farmhouse. That night we were caught in a terrific artillery barrage, which wrecked a great many of the houses. It was rather a surprise the next morning when I saw this woman crossing the debris-cluttered courtyard of the farmhouse to our office. She was wearing a beautiful fur coat and picked her way through the clutter from the shelling with the nonchalance and poise of a lady crossing a drawing room. There was no escaping it, she was charming.

"She explained the Germans had used the same house for their CP. During dinner the Germans received the news of the sudden American advance which threatened the town. In the Germans' hurry to get packed, the woman noticed a map on the table marked with the German escape route. She was able to slip the map under her coat. The German colonel started yelling, 'Where is my map?' Pretending to be helpful, she swept all the maps on the table in one pile and said, 'Here they are, colonel. Let me help you pack them.'"

K Company's visitor did not identify herself, or explain what she was doing in Taverneux. She did say she had escaped from prison camp earlier in the war after the Germans had imprisoned her for espionage, and showed Sergeant Brewer a forged German passport, which made it possible for her to travel in German-occupied territory. Then our visitor left— we never saw or heard from her again. She could have been a member of the Belgian underground or the resistance, but that was only speculation. The purloined map was sent back to division intelligence.

We ran several patrols out of Taverneux and occupied a large stone house on the ridge overlooking Houffalize where we could observe the center of the town. Battalion reported the 2nd Armored General wanted K Company to move in and protect the bridges over the Ourthe if they were still intact. Lance and a patrol spent the afternoon watching the town. "I couldn't tell for sure if the bridges were destroyed or not, but sent back reports they were blown so the company wouldn't have to make another attack." Then came the message we'd been waiting for. The regiment was to be relieved: the 2nd Armored was assuming responsibility for our sector.

The next afternoon the company trudged through the heavy snow up the ridge behind Taverneux and entrucked for Palange forty miles away. We passed Fontenaille, drove past the ridge with the knocked-out German tank, through the woods and the clearing at Pisserotte, and at Petites Tailles bore left toward Grandmenil. The attack south from Petites Tailles to Houffalize had lasted four days. It took fifteen minutes for our trucks to cover the same distance back north. Armored bulldozers had cleared the road of fallen trees and new snow covered the signs of the battle.

From our new billets, Pope wrote Erickson in the hospital to let him know about his friend Corkill.

Somewhere?
Hello Stud,
Just a few lines to let you know I am still with the outfit. You know I'm not much on this writing so don't expect too much. There is not much change in the platoon. They did put me in for a commission, how about that shit?
    Sobel took over your job after Corky left. I guess Curly [Hoffman] told you about Corky. It sure was tough losing him, you couldn't ask for a better man. What hurts me most about Corky, it happened the night before we got a big rest.
    Well kid that's about all. I wish you luck,
                                                     Your Buddy, Pope

Our rest period lasted only three days. On the 21st we moved again, and spent a night in the snow in the woods in regimental reserve while the 84th attacked toward Beho. We displaced forward to Cierreux, but did not get involved in any fighting and received only light artillery fire. During this time the company received replacements, including three new second lieutenants, and Lieutenant Bill Masters from M Company requested a transfer to K Company. "Moving over to a rifle company is not a move that anyone in his right mind would make. Who would want to be in the situation where the only person in front of you was an unhappy German? Most of the time since I was in actual combat I was with K Company, and I considered them to be the best of the best. It seemed to me that the government had an investment in me and if they were going to get a profit out of me, I should be in a rifle company where I could contribute more."

In Cierreux a German paratrooper lay frozen in front of our CP and one of the new replacements who had worked in a mortuary cut off his finger to get a gold ring. J. B. Cole tracked down the culprit and our new

man was warned that he would be court-martialed or shot if he ever
pulled another stunt like that. Later the CO got a call that Cole's brother
in a neighboring division had been killed in action. Cole took one look at
the CO's face. "It's my brother, isn't it?" he asked. Then J.B. took a long
solitary walk through the forests.

From Cierreux the company moved to Nonceveux, miles to the rear,
and remained in reserve with the rest of the 84th from January 24 until
February 2. After resting for a couple of days we became restless and
began patrol activity again—this time behind our own lines. The company needed more firepower and more vehicles. A patrol from the weapons platoon stole a big 4.2 mortar and ammunition from a chemical
battalion, and another patrol found a ton-and-a-half truck that belonged
to division headquarters. The next night we stole the regimental commander's jeep but had to give it back when rain washed our whitewashed
K Company insignia off the bumpers. We escaped with a chewing out—
no one in higher headquarters could devise a punishment sufficient to
intimidate a rifle company.

Near the end of the month Captain Gieszl rejoined the company and
Leinbaugh became the executive officer. Gieszl's wounds were still both-
ering him, but the hospital doctors got tired of arguing with the obstrep-
erous captain and certified him fit for duty. He showed up at the CP
without advance warning, his helmet at its usual rakish angle, pale and
thin, but insisting he was feeling fine and glad to be home. Then he sat
down and Brewer and Leinbaugh went down the casualty list: Christensen, Corkill, R. J. Bell, Warner, Captain Mitchell, Johnnie Moore,
Captain Prophet and all the others.

More than a quarter of a century after the battle in the Ardennes,
Campbell and Leinbaugh, touring the area in a rented Mercedes, discovered the distances between villages much less than remembered, and
that the height of hills and ridges had shrunk dramatically. They met
Pierre and Elizabeth de Radzitsky at the Château Verdenne and realized
the fields and woods where they had battled one Christmastime were no
longer German or American but were private property and belonged to
people. The former K Company lieutenants toured Château Verdenne—
locked up since the war. They saw the family portraits punctured by
strings of machine-gun bullets, the walls pierced by three-inch-shell holes,
the wine cellar where Elizabeth and neighborhood children had sought
cover while the building above was held first by GIs from the 84th and
then by grenadiers from the Panzer battle group. They had long talks
with their former adversary, Colonel Gerhard Tebbe, pored over old battle maps, and exchanged divisional insignia.

14

CLEAN SHEETS

More than 120 K Company men made the ambulance trip back beyond the aid station during our month of action in the Bulge. Over eighty—old-timers and replacements, privates and NCOs, and six of seven lieutenants—went on to hospitals. Over half of those hospitalized had been wounded—more by shell fragments than by machine-gun and rifle bullets. One in four sent to hospitals was a victim of the weather; the morning report listed it as "cold injury, ground type, feet," and mentioned gangrene with a handful of these. Some men even went back for more "civilian" complaints: arthritis, angina, possible scarlet fever, epilepsy—and one muscle strain from "carrying five gallons of coffee." More mundane than battle wounds, yet men hospitalized for such reasons as these were just as lost to the company as those who were victims of enemy action.

For the casualties the field and evacuation hospitals in crowded tents and buildings behind the lines were outposts of civilization—with hot chow, American nurses, and white sheets. But, as Ed Stewart noticed, the change from the front came abruptly. When litter bearers carried him into what once was a schoolhouse, the place disturbed him. "They made a deadly mistake," he says. "They put white sheets on. You looked at those white sheets. You got off on those white sheets. The white innocence of the sheets was more than you could bear."

Stewart and the others were now in the hospital pipeline and would be there for a while. Only one in eight of our hospital evacuees came back up before the company's war was over. Men might go back through different channels, their treatments and lengths of convalescence would vary, and they might never see another K Company man during the time away from the line. Still, one man's experiences would resemble those of another, though individual reactions might differ.

By the time they reached the evac hospitals, most casualties were re-signed to leaving the line, maybe even glad to be out of it. Quite a few shared the perspective of George Thompson, a post-Thanksgiving re-placement, who went back with lobar pneumonia at the end of the Bulge. "You can't go on being lucky, you know," he said. And besides, "by that time most all the old fellows I'd been with were gone."

Here Thompson and others differed from George Gieszl—or Gieszl differed from them. Going back along the evacuation route in November, he'd been just as strong-willed in the hospital as he had been with the battalion. "I talked with a chaplain," Gieszl says, "tried to tell him how I wanted to get back. It was this loyalty thing, *esprit de corps.* I thought they needed me. He didn't understand. He was trying to give me a dose of that bullshit. I was telling him, 'I got more important things to do. I got to get back.'

"I lost a lot of respect for the religious types in those situations," Gieszl asserts. "They didn't understand the inaneness of attempting to sell that to somebody who wasn't interested. I even used to wonder why those damn guys were there. It might be just me; maybe other guys were strengthened or comforted. I didn't get bitter. I was just cynical. It took a day or two to penetrate that I was going to be out for a while."

The company Gieszl had trained and led into combat was still up there, so he had to get back. For him it was as simple as that. For other casu-alties, though, other factors complicated their feelings. In the early hours, sometimes even serious wounds weren't all that painful. Shock, morphine syrettes, fatigue, or possibly something else may have taken care of that. Then, too, the care lavished by doctors and nurses did a lot to boost spirits. So contentment or even a little euphoria was common. Yet at the same time some had twinges of regret, even guilt, about leaving the line—part of the price of the million-dollar wound. And there was that line marking the boundary between "them" and "us," the people who'd been there.

This invisible boundary distinguished between combat troops and oth-ers, but ties with the company also entered in. There was always the hope that other K Company people would turn up. Most of the time, however, our wounded saw no other casualties from the company. Bill Parsons and Richard Heuer were an exception. In the evac hospital their stretchers were side by side, but conversation was limited. They'd removed Par-sons's grenade-shattered right eye, and Heuer had a jaw so damaged he couldn't talk. But Heuer needed to make contact with a buddy. "I got a pencil and paper," he says, "and wrote down some questions to ask Parsons. While I was there a priest came along and administered me the last rites. I thought this was it, that I was going. But obviously I made it.

"They had a tag on me that showed I was from St. Louis," Heuer continues. "I remember one good-looking nurse who trained at St. Louis Jewish Hospital saying, 'I'm going to take good care of you.'" Heuer *needed* good care, because he had a bad cold at the time and was gagging, too. Surgeons would remove shrapnel from his head and wire his jaws shut. "They applied suction through the wound to take the stuff out that was gagging me," Heuer says. "Then they operated on me with a local anesthetic. They trimmed the bone down. They said, 'You won't feel it because it's in the bone,' but I did."

Heuer's encounter with surgeons may have been more traumatic than most. But for the wounded, surgery itself was a common experience. In the company, men had been pretty much interchangeable parts. In the hospital they remained interchangeable parts, but now they needed repair. For many this repair began on the operating table in the evac hospital. The first step meant getting down to bare essentials. John Campbell wrote Nelle Laughlin, at college, about what that entailed for him: "They cut off two wool undershirts, two sweaters, a shirt, field jacket, overcoat. I'm glad your sweater hadn't reached me yet." After they'd peeled away outer layers it was clear he'd lost weight, down maybe to under 120 pounds. The nurse who prepped him for surgery added insult to injury by commenting, "Lord, you're a skinny kid." Surprised he wasn't more indignant, Campbell realized he was glad to be out of the line. Hospital time. Relax and enjoy it.

Liége, Belgium, some thirty miles north of the division's Ardennes front, was a main link in the evacuation chain. In this provincial capital astride the Meuse, factories, schoolhouses, forts, and even hospitals served as hospitals. Here aids to ease and comfort showed up, and men began to relax.

One midnight, surgeons operated on Jim Sterner in a Liége schoolhouse. The next thing he remembered was "waking up with a nurse standing over me, taking my pulse, and asking if I was all right. Right behind her was a Red Cross girl who said, 'What do you have?' I said, 'A wool knit cap and a pipe.' And she said, 'Do you need a toothbrush? Toothpaste? A comb?' I've given to the Red Cross every year since. She was right there."

John Sabia benefited from a more personal touch. He'd gone back through 2nd Armored Division evac channels and in Liége wound up in a room with a Canadian and an Australian—and a setup he owed to his sister, an Army nurse in Alaska. "They washed me down and laid me on a bed. That's the first comfortable feeling I had since I was hit. Then when they came with a stretcher to take me out, this nurse says, 'Are you related to Agnes Sabia?' I said, 'Yes, she's my sister.' And she says, 'Oh, your birthday's next week, too, isn't it? I got a letter from her about a month ago.' She says, 'You have nothing to worry about, we'll take care of you.'

"After I got operated on and was awake this nurse came in. 'What can I get for you?' I had a couple of drinks, whiskey, cognac, birthday cake. We had a good time, me and the Canadian and this Aussie. Every nurse that came by would bring something. For a week I lived like a king—no, better."

But the easy life in Liége had its limits. Adrian Wheeler, the company's first casualty, found that out in late November. A doctor opened Wheeler's left eye, the one with the severed optic nerve, and had some doubts. Then he bent Wheeler's fingernail down to see if blood would return to it. Apparently he wondered whether Wheeler was gone. The right eye had a bandage covering it, and the tracheotomy made talk impossible, so Wheeler hurriedly moved his hands and arms to let the doctor know he was still alive.

Germans also threw up obstacles to relaxation there—buzz bombs, V-1s. These pilotless, winged bombs putt-putted along like toys, but several seconds after the motor stopped you knew different. They had been hitting Liége for months; back in November a buzz bomb slammed into the hospital where Gieszl had gone. "There was a lot of smoke and debris," Gieszl said. "I was real unsteady on my feet. I got out of bed to see what the hell was going on. Those buzz bombs seemed innocent as hell."

Innocent-seeming or not, they put already wounded men in double jeopardy. Paul Coste thought he had it made when he reached Liége. "The wound was nothing," he claims. The shrapnel in his rib had done no major damage. He had what many infantrymen dreamed of, "the million-dollar wound." His main discomfort came from eating too much of the chocolate that he had in his pockets when he was hit. "But I nearly got another hit at the hospital in Liége," he says. "A buzz bomb landed in the courtyard of the hospital half an hour after I got there."

Don Phelps hadn't expected that first V-1 blast after his trip to Liége. The ambulance left him at a factory: "Steel windows, lots of wire. They had blankets hung across the glass for two purposes—blackout and buzz bombs." Supper hour had ended, but Phelps hadn't eaten, and he needed someone to feed him because he couldn't use his hands. "In the middle of supper a buzz bomb hit the surgical wing," he says. "Fortunately it didn't get anybody. The glass behind me just came showering down. Whoever was feeding me said, 'You'd better not eat that pineapple, there might be glass in it.' I just said, 'I'll strain it through my teeth.'"

If you weren't ambulatory and couldn't take cover, you couldn't do much to cope with the V-1s. No wonder Sterner thought of Liége as "the most buzz-bombed city in the world. You'd lie there and hear the buzz bomb cut off and just wait until it exploded." V-1s came in whether the men were coming or going. After Liége, Tom Miller was headed for a general hospital farther to the rear. First, however, he had to make it to the train: "The medics would bring the stretchers down from the receiving hospital by the railroad station. If buzz bombs came in, the medics would drop our stretchers. They got behind sandbags where they were safe, but we were sitting—or lying—ducks." It was enough to make a soldier want to go back to the company—or to Paris.

GI casualties from all over the Western Front filled the litters on hospital trains. Then steam locomotives cut loose with soprano whistles and puffed off toward Paris. Sterner, one of the first of K Company's Bulge wounded to make the stop-and-go trip that took one to three days, thought it was one of the worst experiences of his life. "My canvas cot on the bottom tier was like concrete," he says. "I was hurting bad. It took a half hour to move from my back to my side. And by the time I did it my shoulder was so raw I'd want to go back on my back. Two guys had legs off and had tension on the stumps. Every time the car bumped they would scream in agony."

A month earlier Wheeler had taken the train to Paris. His head swathed in bandages and a tracheotomy tube in his neck, he lay on a litter a few inches above the floor of the car. Doctors and nurses on board helped him rest easy. Wheeler took in their efforts with detached amusement. "They had to change my tube every so often because it would fill with phlegm," he says, "and I was on the bottom tier. Evidently there was a fat doctor, and when he'd bend down he couldn't bend far enough to work on me. It tickled me to death. Finally this nurse said get up and get out, and she got him away and changed it. It was quite a deal all the way to Paris."

Paris was the magnet that had drawn Allied and Axis soldiers alike. First the Germans had come. Then in late August the Allies took their turn when the German military governor of Paris surrendered to the commander of the 2nd Free French Armored Division. And soon Paris became an American city.

A week before Christmas the rumor circulated that we would get a bulk issue of passes to Paris. Visions of the Eiffel Tower, the Louvre, the Folies Bergère, Place Pigalle—and hundreds of Parisiennes on cork-platform shoes—had danced in our heads. But for Paris-bound casualties, post-Christmas reality was different. Instead of the Louvre and the Eiffel Tower there were hospitals; in place of the Folies, the operating theater; rather than Parisiennes there were GI medics wearing clean ODs, creased trousers, and ties. And there were still Germans. During the occupation the Wehrmacht had taken over the Paris hospitals. When the city changed hands in August, German medics, now PWs, stayed on to carry litters and do the dirty work on the wards.

Still, the hospitals were in Paris, and a batch of K Company men would spend time there. Time for treatment, time to adjust to hospital life, and time to write the folks back home.

That first letter home had special importance. Men knew telegrams would head out to next of kin but didn't know when they'd be sent or when they'd arrive. Some tried to soften the impact of the wire by beating the Army to the draw. They fired off a V-mail, or if they had an envelope and a six-cent airmail stamp, they sent a full-fledged letter, with the hope it would get to the States before the official "regret-to-inform-you" telegram.

Jim Sterner's Paris V-mail reached his wife Sis at college. "I got a letter from Jim before the telegram came," she recalls. "It said he was wounded, but not seriously wounded. It helped a lot hearing from Jim first." The official telegram to Sis went to her parents' home in Wilmington. When the man delivering it learned that Sis was off at college, he didn't want to give the message to her parents. Finally they convinced him that they knew all about it, that they'd heard from Jim: "So the man was greatly relieved. He came in the house, and they had a couple of drinks together. Had a nice party, and everybody was happy."

Campbell's initial letter home was anticlimatic. First Nelle Laughlin, at college, called John's parents: "There's a rumor here that he's been wounded." Then a neighbor telephoned John's father: "Have you seen the *Chicago Tribune* today?" When the answer was no, she ended the conversation. Then the *Tribune* came, and John's parents read an account of the second platoon's mid-January patrol. Next, the telegram arrived. Finally came John's first letter from Paris with the optimistic message: "I'll soon be back with the company."

The Army handled notification of next of kin with care. Telegrams reporting men wounded, missing, or killed followed stock formats. For families of men in the hospital, postcards, with blanks appropriately filled in, gave progress reports in the weeks after the telegram. Sometimes, however, there were snafus. When Tom Miller was wounded, the wire to Tom's parents said that he was missing in action. So his mother and father were grateful when later on they learned that Tom was in good American hands.

Paris hospital life had its compensations. The wards were at least as good as Army barracks, and the duty was easy. At nine in the morning, radios brought the news. Even better than the news was the music on the Armed Forces Network. "Dance with a Dolly," a tune the men had last heard just before leaving the States, continued to be popular. And a new one, "Don't Fence Me In," got a lot of play from early December on. The "Kriegies," the GI PWs in Germany, liked to hear this song when they tuned in radio sets they'd secretly assembled. The men within the barbed-wire fences surrounding the compounds thought the words had been written specifically for them.

Red Cross workers brought paperback books and writing materials to the wards. Live entertainers made the rounds. Ambulatory patients saw movies fresh from the States. Tom Miller went to a hospital concert by the Glenn Miller orchestra. This was the first performance since their leader had been lost over the Channel, so Tom could understand why members of the band had broken down.

Even during treatment one could meet entertainers. Once Richard Heuer, with his wired-up jaw, had a long wait for the dentist. Heuer's patience was rewarded when he met the person who had preceded him— Marlene Dietrich. Heuer deserved whatever reward he could get from the dentist. His jaw would be wired shut for nearly a year, except for two-week intervals when they were reconstructing it. And he'd live on a liquid diet—milk shakes, beer, and the like.

"As bad as I was hit, I could always find someone else who was worse," Heuer says. "There was a big guy who'd been hit by a burp gun, and he was completely cased up in a body cast. There was another guy in a body cast who'd come up with a dose of clap. The doctor came around and wondered how in the hell did you get this. Finally the fellow in the body cast told him. He said he talked broken French and when one of the French ward girls came up, he propositioned her. She put a screen around his bed and then she climbed up on him."

Since Paris was rear-echelon, officers were segregated from enlisted men. Though infantry predominated on his ward, Campbell found a wounded chaplain and a few tanker officers. A 2nd Armored captain in the next bed had a daily routine. Each morning he went to surgery for repairs. An hour later orderlies wheeled the still anesthetized captain back to the ward. Soon he'd begin to wake up, always with a beautiful sodium pentothal jag. The captain had one noisy refrain until he sobered up: "Miss Egbert, I love you." This he repeated over and over again to a blushing little Lieutenant Egbert, the nurse in charge.

Such minor events broke the routine. So Campbell was content to enjoy his "vacation." A week after his arrival in Paris, surgeons doing patchwork on him hadn't yet let him sit up, but his letters persisted in saying he'd soon get back to the company.

For many, however, Paris ward life was no vacation. It certainly didn't start out as one for Len Erickson. He had too much on his mind. In the field hospital they looked at his frozen feet and told him, "You're going to lose your right foot and maybe your left, too." So the future looked bleak. "My first reaction was, you lose one foot, that's not too bad," he says. "But God, if you lose them both, that's another story."

In the Paris hospital he lay in bed with his feet exposed to the cool air. "There was a lot of pain for a while, but that was while they were thawing out." Then his feet began to get better. "I lucked out on a change in the Army's medical policy," Erickson says. "The policy had been to amputate to minimize the spread of gangrene. But the hospital-ward gossip in Paris was that that had been changed. There was no cure for trench foot, but penicillin could check the spread of gangrene."

From Paris Erickson would fly to the States, but he wouldn't be ambulatory for a month and a half. "A captain there in Colorado Springs said he didn't understand why I didn't get gangrene."

Where K Company men went after Paris depended on surgeons' decisions. Those who would require more than 120 days in the hospital were ZI'ed—scheduled for shipment to the Zone of the Interior, the States. Some on release from hospital went to limited-duty assignments. Others were marked "duty" and returned to the company. And quite a few ended up in the UK—the United Kingdom, Britain.

Adrian Wheeler had headed for the UK while the company was still in Germany. He reached England on Sunday, December 3. That evening a doctor took the tracheotomy tube out. With a Band-Aid over the hole, Wheeler could breathe naturally now. Soon the hole had closed up enough for him to talk a little. That was the good news. The bad news came along more slowly.

After he'd been hit Wheeler had felt the wound in his neck and thought it must be a bad one, but he didn't even know about the wound in his temple until the Paris X rays and operation. Even then the surgeon didn't mention the extent of the injury. In England when they finally told him that his eyes were badly damaged they still did not say that sight in the left eye was completely gone. Wheeler supposes they wanted him to get his body built up more before they gave him the word.

While he was at the 136th Station Hospital near Manchester the hemorrhaging in his right eye began to clear up, and Adrian could make out hazy images of large objects. Then later he could distinguish some colors. But the sight he now had was as good as it ever would be. Shrapnel had severed the optic nerve in his left eye; it was completely gone.

There at the 136th, Lieutenant Tommy Thompson, a nurse from Boston, became Wheeler's guardian angel. She put him in an orthopedic bed, bought extra rations, and made sure the nurses gave them to him at 9:00 P.M. "She'd get food for me at the officers' mess, and she said to me, 'Wheeler, you'll never be able to commit suicide. Most people either cut their throat or shoot themselves through the temple. You've had both and it didn't kill you.'"

The casual way the surgeon made the decision to ship him to Britain surprised Don Phelps. "I was laying there, half dozing," he says. "My right hand was just leaning over the end of the bed with the wrist relaxed. Then the inspecting surgeon came along and picked up my chart. He read the description of the injury, saw this hand hanging there, and knew they wanted to get that tendon before the wrist locked. So he said, 'Air evac, England, dropped wrist.'

"They loaded us on a plane," Phelps continues. "Twenty-four or so, on stretchers, three in a stack. I was asleep for the takeoff. It was only a short hop over the Channel; I woke up when the plane touched down in England. My first plane ride, and I slept through the whole damn trip."

On New Year's Day, Phelps arrived at a hospital near Liverpool. "The reception was nice," he says. "But nobody was feeling very good—the staff had had a party the night before. Nobody got their back rubbed for three weeks because they couldn't replenish the medicinal alcohol that had been drunk."

Bill Parsons, who'd lost an eye Christmas Eve, also went on to England. Here he'd have more surgery and then begin the convalescence and rehabilitation that would end months later back in the States. "I spent from New Years to mid-March in England having repair work done under marvelous conditions," he recalls. "I met some fine people while I was there. It was a special set of circumstances; one couldn't repeat the kinds of contacts one would make there. There weren't the emotional pressures that normally exist—where we build up our protection, our facades. People are more open under those special circumstances. They're more honest, more inclined to say 'Hey, this is the way it really is.'"

In England Parsons began to adapt to the loss of the eye: "I played Ping-Pong. That's what they told me to do, play Ping-Pong. And of course one of the other things I started doing right away was play the piano."

When Sabia joined the parade to England, he was determined to rehabilitate himself and do it his own way, as usual: "A doctor in Belgium said to me, 'You'll never walk.' I said to myself, 'You're full of shit, doc.' Today there's very few people know I limp—these are guys have known me for years. But I bust my ass to walk straight up, head up, eyes up; oh yeah, I do. I don't care how it hurts.

"When they sent me to England," Sabia says, "I had a cast from here down on my leg, but they had this part open so they could work on it. I was determined to walk, that was the only thing in my mind—to walk. After I found out I could stand up, I'd steal clothes, cut the pants for the cast, put them on, and go to town. Most of the time I was hobbling with crutches. The MPs picked me up about six times. Then when I could walk, we began taking these marches, each one a little longer. Finally the last ended up like a three-mile march. Well, I did it. I cried all the way, but man, I did it."

After three weeks Campbell also headed for England. On the way to the train station the ambulance driver gave the men on the litters a guided tour of Paris, calling out sights that none of his passengers could see: "Notre Dame"—pronounced like the university in South Bend, Indiana; "Conquered Place"—his translation of Place de la Concorde. From England John's letters repeated a familiar theme. The third week of February he again wrote, "It won't be long before I go back to duty."

After the Bulge had wound down, some of the company's early casualties came home to King Company. When George Gieszl had persuaded the doctors that he was ready, he and John Dolan, his radio operator, came back on January 25. On February 8, Dempsey Keller and some others returned. But Mario Lage, who'd been sent to the hospital just after the company's move to Belgium, didn't make it back.

For Lage, naturally, things were different. He must have been the only soldier in the ETO who in the depth of winter was hospitalized with malaria. In England he shook the symptoms, and the doctors were giving him a quick examination before sending him back. "Wait a minute, Lieutenant, let's take another look at those hands." They diagnosed it as Raynaud's syndrome. The label drew a blank with Lage, but the clinical description fit: "pallor, cyanosis, engorgement and pain of the extremities, especially the digits. Attacks may be brought on by cold."

So Lage went back to the States and an assignment that was tailor-made for him. He ended up on a team making the rounds of war plants, selling war bonds and boosting morale. Mario Lage, veteran of the fighting in the Pacific and Europe, wearing Class A uniforms and the right fruit salad on his chest, and as lean and darkly handsome as ever. He really had it made.

15

ON THE ROER

For seven days and nights K Company remained on relief in Nonceveux beyond reach of German artillery for the first time since November. Our billets—brick houses, store buildings, and schoolrooms—were heated with wood-burning stoves. We did our best to relax, but certain habits were deeply ingrained. M1s were kept within hand's reach, and most men wore helmets indoors. And despite the lack of shelling, no one used the upstairs bedrooms.

We ate better than we had for weeks, standing in chow lines for three hot meals a day, with warm apple pies for dessert. An exchange rate had been worked out with the Belgian housewives: one pie, without sugar, for one pack of cigarettes.

On the morning of February 2, Wiley Herrell's Belgian landlady told him the company would be leaving that night at six to return to Germany. Wiley questioned several sergeants, and none knew of departure plans, but he was not surprised when the CO called in the NCOs at four and "sure enough we left at six. You could always learn more from the civilians than from headquarters."

Before the division headed north, back to our Ninth Army sector near Geilenkirchen, orders came from regiment to rip off our shoulder patches and paint over the Railsplitter insignia and company designations on the bumpers of our jeeps and trailers. The 84th had been placed on a special top-secret list and our move was to be made after dark under strict security regulations. No one, not even the 102nd Division troops our battalion was relieving, was to be told our identity.

The secrecy gave us a feeling of importance as we unloaded from trucks and toiled along the rutted muddy road from Gereonsweiler to Linnich. Guides from the 102nd, waiting at the edge of town, led us down back alleys, past the ruins of gutted houses and out to the line of foxholes facing the Roer River. By the light of the Germans' familiar green parachute flares we sized up our new home. Linnich had been shelled and bombed so long and so often it was hard to imagine it had ever been anything but a battlefield. Bomb craters, shattered tree trunks, shallow communication trenches, rolls of barbed wire, and the mud—the place could have been left over from World War I.

With daylight we could see the Roer, a swollen fifty-yard-wide torrent separating us from the enemy. Weeks earlier, German engineers had partially destroyed the upper Roer dams, transforming the normally placid stream into a formidable barrier to gain time against the inevitable Allied crossing. The Germans knew Linnich was a strategic location for an American bridgehead; they shelled the town regularly.

And in spite of our attempts at secrecy the Germans definitely knew who we were. The day after moving into our holes they greeted us with a barrage of propaganda leaflets, welcoming the 84th back to Germany.

"You will be the first victims," the pamphlets read. "We have made our preparations. . . . You will find out what surprises we've got in store for you. . . . In front of you, between us, is the Roer River, with lots of water—maybe too much for your taste." So much for security.

Since our cover was blown, we dug out needle and thread and laboriously sewed our red-and-white Railsplitter patches back on our field jackets and repainted the "K Co., 333rd Inf." logo on our jeeps.

The next day our psych-warfare folks prepared a reply. Stuffed in canister shells, the 84th's pamphlet was addressed to the officers and men of the 183rd and 59th Volksgrenadier divisions. It listed the German divisions battered by the 84th at Geilenkirchen and in the Ardennes and was signed, "The Railsplitters." Curiously, inexplicably, the leaflets were printed in English.

Another batch of green safe-conduct passes, in both English and German, offered food, medical attention, and immediate removal from the danger zone to Germans wanting to surrender. The hard-nosed German infantry across the river undoubtedly used the leaflets the same way we used theirs—for toilet paper.

We settled into our secondhand foxholes for what looked like a long siege. Our battalion manned the river line while the rest of the division's battalions practiced river-crossing techniques near the Dutch border. For once we thought we had the best possible deal—paddling across the Roer in a rowboat in the face of German machine-gun fire was an experience we'd just as soon avoid. We knew nothing about assault boats or river crossings, but after Lindern and the Bulge, the company had learned to make the best of life in a foxhole.

Most of the Linnich holes, though soggy and muddy, had thick roofs,

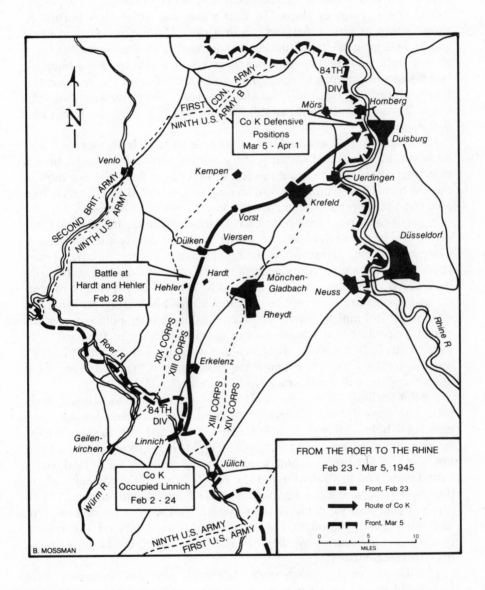

FROM THE ROER TO THE RHINE
Feb 23 - Mar 5, 1945

Front, Feb 23

Route of Co K

Front, Mar 5

0   5   10
MILES

B. MOSSMAN

and some were big enough to hold several men. One occupied by a new man, Goodwin, along with three old-timers Gordon, Okenfuss and Howard, seemed almost palatial. It had a sturdy log-and-dirt cover and a kitchen of sorts, a small gasoline stove with a short stovepipe.

Close by in a conventional two-man hole Morris Dunn and his partner operated on two-hour shifts. To heat water for coffee they burned K-ration boxes or mixed dirt and gas in a can. The mixture burned like a candle and gave off too little light to be visible to the Germans. Dunn shared stale cookies that he received in his first package from home. It had taken four months to reach him, and he still hadn't received a single letter. Dunn was especially anxious for news, since his wife had been expecting in October, and he still had no idea if he was the father of a boy or a girl.

Dunn occasionally crawled out of his hole to stretch his legs, but once he made the mistake of standing still a minute too long. A bullet hit not three feet away, and he spent the rest of that day in his hole. For most of the old hands like Dunn, random sniping was accepted as a familiar hazard, but the newer replacements still had to get used to it.

A small-town boy from Nebraska, Clarence Menke, the eleventh offspring in a family of thirteen, joined the company shortly after Christmas. Clarence was only eighteen. As the first platoon's runner, he carried messages out to listening posts near the riverbank and made regular trips back and forth to the company CP, and he seemed to get caught in mortar and rocket fire on every trip. Clarence quickly learned to avoid the main street in Linnich, where "the Germans had a huge pillbox across the river that could fire machine-gun fire down the center of the road." He worked out back routes through buildings and alleys and found "the trick was not to think too much about the risks—if you brooded about what might happen, you could crack up in a hurry."

Lieutenant Ray Jarvis, who took over as the third platoon leader after the Bulge, gave Johnny Radovich a brand-new replacement for his three-man BAR hole. "He was a kid from New York, and boy he was shaky—he wouldn't even get out of our hole at night to get food or take a leak. For a while we brought him food from the platoon CP." Radovich's ammo man tried to straighten out the new fellow. "He'd go back and get this guy's food and eat both portions, but finally I had to complain to Jarvis. I told him we couldn't trust the guy and we got rid of him, sent him out." Johnny thought the medics must have labeled the man a psycho. "I don't know how they handled those cases, but he never came back to the company."

The layout of the company's defensive positions surprised Paul Leimkuehler, one of the new platoon leaders. "Some foxholes were 150 feet apart, so it was pretty thin as far as I was concerned—not like they taught us at Officers Candidate School at Fort Benning. If somebody decided to cross the river and come through I couldn't see how there was going to be much resistance."

But most men felt reasonably secure. The German barrages, heavy at times, never approached the intensity of the shellings beyond Geilenkirchen or in Lindern, and with the Roer in front of us we could ignore the threat of Panther and Tiger tanks.

K Company's front extended along the river for three quarters of a mile, from the center of Linnich north to the edge of Brachelen, where we tied in with Item Company. Located in a whitewashed brick-vaulted cellar, the company CP was tied to the platoons with sound-power phones and to battalion by both wire and radio. Daily schedules were arranged so that men in the foxholes spent every second or third day in cellars behind the line.

In a wire-service story carried in the States, a war correspondent described his visit to K Company's CP in "downtown" Linnich. "Down the hazardous steps through the doorway covered by a blanket, you enter a long arched cellar that looks like an underground Nissen hut. . . . The eerie, flickering light of a gasoline-filled wine bottle with a rag wick fills the room. Through the yellow haze you see Tech. Sgt. Franklin Brewer hovering over a typewriter, beating out the morning report. At the switchboard PFC Van Houten checks the lines with battalion. Corporal Louis Ciccotello and PFC Dolan warm their hands at the stove. They have a reliable shell warning system. Every time there is a rush and a clatter upstairs they know the guards are running for cover and Sgt. Brewer puts the cover on his precious typewriter and everyone moves to the side of the cellar."

Days and nights along the muddy river settled into a routine. Fifty pairs of eyes constantly scrutinized the Germans' defenses across the river. The enemy's daily activities closely mirrored K Company's. From an OP we could watch them forming up for chow, and occasionally glimpsed lone riflemen scurrying between ruins or briefly silhouetted in front of smoldering fires. Every night our artillery plastered them, and in return they swept our area with long bursts of tracers. All night long the Germans fired parachute flares, which painted strange shadows that moved eerily as the parachutes sank slowly to earth. The enemy, knowing the precise location of our emplacements, walked mortar rounds back and forth along our line of holes, making enough noise to keep us from sleeping.

K Company suffered only a few casualties from enemy mortars. Schu mines were a greater threat. Before pulling out of Linnich and retreating across the Roer, the Germans had buried hundreds of these wicked little devices in the mud. The Schu mine was simple enough—a quarter-pound of TNT, which looked and felt like Fels Naphtha laundry soap, in a wooden container the size of a box of kitchen matches. Pressure on the box lid forced a nail into a detonator, setting off a sizable explosion. Scores of these mines had been exposed by heavy rains, and we tried to blow them up with rifle fire.

One morning Robert D. Martin from Arkansas was loading a bazooka round in a small trench. "We were trying to run some Germans out of their foxholes down by the river. The ground was beginning to thaw, and I must have stepped right on the trigger of a Schu mine. I thought a mortar shell had hit between my feet."

The explosion blew Martin clear out of his shallow trench, broke both his legs, and might have blown off one foot if he hadn't been wearing shoe pacs with thick rubber soles and heavy felt liners which had been issued to the company a day earlier. By the next day Martin had reached a hospital in Holland. "My one leg swelled to twice its normal size and turned green—but I didn't lose it."

After Martin was evacuated, the company asked for help in clearing the area. White engineer's tape stretched out by battalion's antitank platoon soon marked the paths connecting the platoons. We had no more casualties from Schu mines.

Doc Smith and two volunteers brought Martin in after he was wounded, but for the aidmen the first couple of weeks on the Roer were quieter than usual. Doc Mellon patched up John DiMaio, wounded during a mortar barrage, checked for trench foot, diagnosed a couple of cases of bronchitis, and poured big swigs of paregoric. But one brisk sunny morning a change occurred in his daily routine.

Several men had reported hearing a GI yelling for help during the night. At daylight they finally spotted him lying helpless near the riverbank. Battalion told us a patrol from a cavalry unit had lost a man, and we decided to send out a stretcher team at nightfall to rescue him.

Mellon thought the man needed help right away. He didn't check with any of the company officers; he knew they would veto his rescue scheme. Pulling on his Red Cross bib, Doc stood in the open to make sure the Germans spotted him. He then walked slowly toward the river. He worked his way through a roll of concertina wire and crossed a small creek. Mellon reached the wounded man and found he had been shot through the ankle; the bones were shattered. The fellow was conscious, but suffering from shock and unable to move. Realizing he would be unable to carry his patient a quarter of a mile to the safety of our positions, Doc bandaged the wound, squeezed a morphine syrette into the man's side, and returned slowly to the company area.

Doc remembered seeing a vehicle in a ruined shed that might solve his problem. He looked it over and headed again for the river. "It was an old beat-up wheelbarrow with a wooden body, no sides, and with a metal-rimmed wheel. It was heavy and bulky, and I had one hell of a time getting it through that concertina wire." Doc ripped his hands on the wire, but finally wrestled his wheelbarrow over the obstacle and through the creek. He checked the wounded man's bandage and loaded him on the wheelbarrow.

By that time the word had spread up and down the line, and every man in K Company was watching apprehensively. Men yelled across the river to the Germans, "Okay, hold it, hold it," and the Germans hollered back, "Okay," but when Doc began his trip toward safety, one German fired. It was impossible to tell if the shot was aimed at Doc, but word was passed not to return the fire. The worst that could happen was for Doc and his patient to be caught in a crossfire.

The rescue proceeded in agonizingly slow motion. Balancing the man on the wheelbarrow, Doc pushed it slowly across the muddy ground to the little creek. He stopped, carried the man across on his shoulder, set him down, and went back for the wheelbarrow. To get through the belt of concertina wire, Mellon repeated the process.

"All the way back," Doc remembers, "some crazy German bastard kept shooting at us. It was rifle fire, and some of it was mighty close. I told the guy to try and hold on, but he kept falling off the wheelbarrow and I'd have to lift him back on. He was hurting pretty bad. I'd swear at him and tell him to hold on tighter."

When Doc and his cargo were within a hundred yards of safety, a German machine gunner opened fire, digging up spurts of mud only a few feet from the pair, but Doc plodded along deliberately, making no effort to hurry or take cover. As he finally pushed the wheelbarrow into an alley behind a ruined house at the edge of Linnich, a cheer went up from every man in K Company.

After his patient had been evacuated to battalion aid, Doc came to the CP. Soaked to the crotch, covered with mud, one hand bandaged, Doc pulled out a cigarette and took a deep drag. "That settles it," he announced. "I've just decided. No more house calls."

Had the Germans been trying to hit Doc? We had no way to know, but a protocol of sorts had been established between K Company and the German infantrymen on the opposite bank of the river. Several times during our weeks in Lindern, German aidmen had picked up casualties between the lines, and we made it clear to our replacements that nobody was to interfere with such rescue efforts. Special rules of conduct did apply for the wounded.

One rainy afternoon Pope spotted wisps of smoke from a new German position. From his OP in the ruins of a factory, he zeroed in on the emplacement with a bazooka, scoring a direct hit with his third round. An hour later he noticed a big Red Cross flag planted in the ground next to the demolished dugout. Pope with his runner headed for a building at the water's edge and looked out a window. "Christ, I could spit on them. German aidmen with big red crosses on their chests and backs were carrying this sucker out on a stretcher. I yelled, 'Hey, you Kraut sons of bitches, this is your last day on earth,' and pointed my M1 at them. They started hollering, 'Nicht shoot, Red Cross,' and after letting them sweat a bit, I said all right, and let them go. But it was fun."

Several days later the mortar crews decided to pull an ambush. From their OP on the top floor of the waterworks north of town they had been watching the Germans line up for morning chow. The enemy became increasingly careless, and finally the mortarmen decided the time was ripe. John Hargesheimer, a big fellow who'd been a Texas rancher before joining the company on New Year's Day, helped zero in the mortars ahead of time. "We waited till these Germans were all lined up with their mess kits and then walked a dozen fast rounds right down the column. With our final round we made a direct hit on the chow truck, messing things up pretty good." Lance had the mortar squads relocate their tubes. "It was sure good thinking, because that night," Hargesheimer remembers, "the Germans blasted the hell out of the old emplacements we'd been using."

During our first week on the Roer, the Germans unveiled a new weapon. Around midnight they would fire two or three huge rockets into Linnich. The explosions were powerful enough to destroy an entire house. After a near miss, Leimkuehler left his CP to take a look. "The size of that hole was unbelievable. It was big enough to hold a davenport."

The big rockets left a long trail of smoke and flame but had a relatively short range. We figured the launcher was mounted on a truck or half-track so the Germans could bring it into defilade position, fire two or three rounds, and get out.

We tried to pinpoint the location of the firing site, without much luck until Max Sobel and Curly Hoffman decided to use elementary mathematics. If they could get reasonably accurate azimuths from our extreme left and right flanks, they knew they could get a good fix on the launching site. After the inevitable midnight barrage, Max and Curly plotted the intersection on the map in the CP. It was apparent the Germans were bringing the launcher into a dead-end spur behind a railroad embankment four hundred yards behind their lines.

The next day, with help from the 325th Artillery observer, we fired artillery rounds on positions across the river. During this period of random shelling, we adjusted several critical rounds on the suspected firing location. That night the artillerymen loaded their guns and waited for word to shoot. The moment the rocket ignited, we yelled "Fire!" over the open phone line and the gunners pulled their lanyards. The first four artillery rounds landed on the German launching site before the slow-moving rocket exploded in Linnich. Then our batteries fired for effect, slamming round after round across the Roer. With every salvo Sobel and Hoffman from their observation post yelled, "Beautiful, just beautiful." That was the last night the big rockets kept us awake.

We realized the Germans had targets far more important than Linnich. One of the main launching sites for the V-2 rocket, the first ballistic space weapon, was located due east from our positions, obviously some distance beyond the Rhine. We occasionally glimpsed the red trails of the V-2s as they lifted slowly from the horizon and curved out of sight in the night sky, headed for London or Antwerp.

The noisy low-flying black plane which sped along the Roer was an enigma. The sergeant who first spotted it swore that it did not—and he repeated "did not"—have propellers. He added, "It's the fastest son of a bitch I ever saw." He also swore he was stone cold sober. The plane, of course, was a jet, the first we'd ever seen or heard about. It was undoubtedly flying photo-recon missions, surely not interested in K Company, but in the massive preparations for the river crossing. We banged away at it with rifles and borrowed the .50 caliber machine gun from the kitchen truck, but our tracers never came close. The overflights of the twin-engine mystery plane—battalion eventually passed down a classified report identifying it as a jet—were actually a welcome diversion during the long, cold, and dreary days.

The lieutenant, sprawled on a dirty mattress in the corner of the room, was dead—no doubt about it. Leinbaugh lifted the candle and took a closer look. The big .45 was still clutched in the man's hand. The heavy bullet had blown a big hole in the top of his head, then ripped through his helmet. The body was still warm.

For several days the officer had commanded a rifle company during the Bulge. One afternoon during an advance he had simply disappeared. The next day he was found wandering down a road behind the front lines and was placed under company arrest and charged with desertion in face of the enemy.

The charge was serious. Wartime desertion carried a death penalty or a lengthy prison sentence at hard labor. Since the lieutenant had disappeared when his unit was attacking next to K Company, Leinbaugh was familiar with the circumstances. He was to testify at the court-martial and had been delegated to bring the prisoner to Holland for trial.

The lieutenant was being held in a front-line house. A young Spanish-American GI standing guard inside the doorway told Leinbaugh the lieutenant was in the back room. After finding the body, Leinbaugh returned to the entrance and asked the guard if he knew the lieutenant was dead. The guard said, "Yes sir." Leinbaugh asked him when it happened, and the guard told him, "Just before you got here." Then he asked him, "Why in the hell didn't you tell me the lieutenant shot himself?" The guard hesitated only a moment. "Sir, you didn't ask me."

Leinbaugh walked up the street to the company CP and called battalion to let them know the court-martial was off. The battalion adjutant, Captain Wooten, drove over from battalion, and after discussing the situation the two officers agreed the man had been killed in line of duty, which was duly noted on the morning report.

* * *

At Linnich, we had time on our hands and money in our pockets. On Valentine's Day, Ciccotello took orders for long-stemmed roses to be sent, via the Red Cross, to mothers, wives, and sweethearts back home. They cost six bucks a dozen, but what the hell? We didn't have anywhere else to spend our occupation marks. Altogether the Railsplitters wired more than sixteen thousand dollars in flower orders back to the States.

Soon we had another reminder of home. Following the nightly food and mail run, Barnes and Chick proudly deposited three wooden cases of Coca-Cola on the middle of the map table in the CP. The division had received an allocation from a plant in France. The familiar-shaped bottles were handled as if they held a rare prize vintage. Once Keller determined the allocations, messengers made a special Coke run to the platoons. Our quota came to half a bottle per man. And then the final touch to add to our homesickness—we had to return the empties.

"Boredom," as Keller saw it, "was one of the big problems in Linnich." He'd just rejoined the company after a hospital bout with kidney stones, and he immediately sensed the men's restlessness. They were too cooped up. He watched Mike DeBello, sporting a top hat, pedal around town on an old bicycle, with no tires, just rims. Mike's buddy, Flattop Gonzales, had been trying to pinpoint a German position in a house across the river and had persuaded Mike to pedal along the river dike to try to draw their fire, but the Germans kept their heads down.

As the days passed, restlessness changed to recklessness. George Lucht, one of the most levelheaded men in the company, was persuaded to go exploring. "Things were quiet that day, and like a damn fool I let Curly Hoffman talk me into checking out the sports plaza down by the river." The two sergeants reached the small arena without difficulty.

"A sniper spotted us. His first round hit between Curly and me. His second bullet drilled two neat little holes an inch apart in my pants leg at the knee joint. I was swearing a blue streak and warning Hoffman this was the last damn time I'd ever take a walk with him. At the CP I was looking for sympathy, but didn't get any. Gieszl and Leinbaugh sided with Hoffman and thought our little escapade was pretty funny and accused me of bucking for a million-dollar wound. I almost had one, too."

Other members of the company spent hours trying to blast open a locked safe in the ruins of a bank building on Linnich's main street. When rifle grenades didn't work, they got the help of an engineer and wedged a satchel charge and a couple of Teller mines under the safe's corner. Kaboom! The impressive blast hurled bricks and debris in all directions, but failed to budge the safe's door. Jarvis, the platoon lieutenant, called a halt to the safecracking operation before someone got blown up.

Occasional visitors helped break the monotony at Linnich. With the Roer as a buffer, rear-echelon types who normally stayed away from the line paid us a call. First we had the correspondent, and then two colonels from XIII Corps headquarters showed up at the CP to take a look at the crossing area. A runner escorted them to the first platoon OP, where Pope did his best to play the accommodating host. "They were middle-aged guys in their thirties. I took them up to the second floor of a building that offered a good view up and down the river."

The officers, Pope noticed, wore neckties and had the chin straps buckled on their helmets. "A couple of rounds come in, little stuff, not particularly close, and these sons of bitches hit the goddam floor. You wouldn't believe it. They were scared shitless. They said, 'Let's get out of here.' I almost broke up, but I didn't say one damn word. For once I kept my big mouth shut."

Our steadiest, most rewarding diversion was the search for booze. Months earlier, as British and American divisions neared the German border, the unhappy burghers of Linnich had been evacuated to relocation areas behind the Rhine, carrying with them only clothing and small personal belongings. Other valuables had to be left behind. While it was sad to discover personal family possessions buried in gardens or concealed in cellar walls, it was elating to uncover caches of bottles. Wine, cognac, champagne, exotic liqueurs—the company GIs didn't always know what they were drinking, but they drank it anyhow. Nobody considered the search for these hoards as looting. We saw it more as a race against time, an attempt to salvage as much liquor as possible before it was destroyed in the German shellings.

As D-Day approached, the engineers stepped up preparations for the crossing. The assault across the Roer had been originally set for February 10, but the operation was postponed indefinitely after the Germans flooded the river. The delay gave division, corps, and army staffs much-needed time to refine plans for the crossing and the drive to the Rhine. Regiment's I and R platoon sent patrols in small rubber boats across the Roer to locate minefields and gun emplacements and to capture prisoners. Each night engineer teams passed through our lines to inspect the crossing sites and check the flood level. A week before the crossing, assault boats and bridging equipment were trucked to the outskirts of Linnich and hidden under camouflage netting.

Three infantry footbridges were to be thrown across the river directly in front of K Company. The engineers hoped to have one footbridge operational within forty-five minutes after the first wave of boats hit the far side of the river. Within five hours, an infantry support bridge capable of carrying two-and-a-half-ton trucks was supposed to be in place. A floating treadway—a big bridge heavy enough to support tanks—was to be sited just downstream.

K Company's D-Day role was modest. Our three 60mm mortars, placed in a courtyard with the rest of the regiment's 60s, were given the job of saturating the east bank of the Roer between the edge of the river and the line of enemy foxholes. The object was to destroy the Schu mines scattered along the muddy riverbank.

Hargesheimer counted the rounds piled next to the K Company mortars. Each squad had 546 shells to fire off between H-Hour minus fifteen minutes and touchdown time for the first boat wave.

Everything came together on the night of February 22. Scores of Sherman tanks rolled into Linnich. The tank commanders stood in the open turrets as guides from K Company motioned them forward with narrow-beamed flashlights, leading them to firing positions along our line of foxholes. It was a bit hairy—nobody could hear incoming rounds over the growl of the heavy engines. Other men from the company helped FOs from the artillery battalions string wire and set up observation posts in the upper floors of the buildings closest to the Roer.

Engineers lugged the four-hundred-pound assault boats through deep mud to forward assembly areas. The 557th triple A battalion brought its quad 50s and 40s into town to defend against Luftwaffe strikes on the bridges. GIs from the smoke-generator battalion opened the valves on their huge steel canisters, and vast gray clouds spread across the river. Huge trailer trucks with girders and pontoons for the heavy-duty bridges ground forward to final staging areas.

GIs from the 334th's Able, Baker, and Charlie companies slogged into Linnich and made their way down the slopes toward the river, where they crouched beside their boats. We felt special kinship with these riflemen as they waited in the mud for the order to jump off. The tankers were safe behind their armorplate, most of the support troops were in cellars or holes, but these poor bastards had no place to hide.

At 2:45 A.M. on February 23, the United States Army laid down one of the heaviest barrages ever mounted on the Western Front. The artillery, tanks, and antiaircraft crews opened up simultaneously, blasting the German positions across the Roer. K Company's mortar crews joined in, stuffing rounds in the tubes seconds apart. After a few minutes the base of the tubes began to glow dark red from the heat of the propellants. Then came a frantic message from the assault units to hold fire—the shells were falling short in the middle of the river. The red-hot tubes were igniting the powder increments in the mortar fins before the main propelling charge detonated, and rounds were falling way short. The gunners stopped to let the barrels cool; less than a third of the 60mm rounds allocated for the barrage were actually fired.

K Company sat out the rest of the night. We'd held the line for three weeks; for the next few hours we had nothing to do but watch. While we had seen artillery in action before, we'd never witnessed a barrage on such a massive scale.

In the middle of it all, a lone German machine gunner decided he'd had enough. He fired a long burst of tracers at his tormentors. It was his last mistake. Every tank, every antiaircraft gun, every machine gunner within range returned the fire. Waves of tracers and flat-trajectory rounds swept toward the hole, engulfing it in a single continuous explosion. We cheered lustily, and Gieszl commented, "Now that's an awfully dead German."

At 3:30 A.M., Able and Charlie companies of the 334th climbed into thirty-five boats and paddled for the east bank of the Roer. A Company made it across without casualties, but two boats from C Company were swept downstream and several men were killed. The second wave of boats, carrying Baker and Dog companies, followed close behind, and by 4:00 A.M. the entire First Battalion was on the far bank. The men dropped their life preservers, ran for the protection of a railroad embankment, regrouped, and headed for Korrenzig a mile to the north. The artillery lifted its barrage to enemy positions beyond the railroad.

In the dark it was impossible to gauge the progress of the attack from our lines. Smoke from the generators and from the 4.2's white phosphorus shells hid most of the river, but in the glare of shell bursts we glimpsed boats being furiously paddled across the river and watched the engineers struggling to anchor pontoons in place. The stench of cordite and acrid smoke was overpowering. Tankers climbed out of their turrets gasping and vomiting from powder fumes.

In the morning, flight after flight of medium bombers roared overhead, dumping explosives on German positions well beyond the river. One B-25 hit the ground, exploding in a giant fireball. The dull thump of the big bombs carried clearly over the nearby din of artillery. From the company's OPs, with field glasses glued to our eyes, we tried to follow the 334th's advance. Finally at 9:30 A.M., through the clouds of smoke still clinging to the low ground, we glimpsed our troops filing through Korrenzig.

The outcome of the Roer crossing was never in doubt. Our strength was overwhelming, but tactical considerations played an important role in the success of the initial attack. Instead of crossing the river and heading due east for the Rhine, the entire Ninth Army wheeled north and northeast, doubling the distance to be traveled. As a result, German positions were rolled up on their flanks rather than frontally. From the beginning, division, corps, and army hoped to achieve a quick breakthrough. The attack orders read, "Pursue the enemy relentlessly to the limit of every man's endurance."

As it grew lighter we could see the engineers were having problems. The first footbridge across the river could not be anchored due to enemy small-arms fire. Footbridge number two was completed well before dawn, but was knocked out by drifting boats and pontoons from the 102nd's crossing area on our right. The third footbridge was destroyed by a direct hit from German artillery. Not until noon on the 23rd was a footbridge completed and firmly anchored in position. By dusk the larger infantry support bridge was also in operation. It was noon on the next day, the 24th, before the heavy treadway bridge was finished, allowing tanks and tank destroyers to join up with the infantry across the river.

Since we'd held the river line our battalion was now placed in corps reserve. While every other unit in the Army was headed east, we waited for orders to pull back for our promised rest. At 8:00 A.M. the next morning we marched five miles to the rear, reaching Leiffarth at noon. After twenty days in muddy holes we were a filthy crew, unshaven, fatigued, and wanting showers and clean clothing more than anything on earth. But three hours later we were alerted to hike back to Linnich and cross the river. With K Company leading, the battalion returned to the crossing site, which was now receiving heavy long-range German artillery fire and bombing attacks.

Navigating a narrow, swaying footbridge in the dark while lugging thirty or forty pounds of combat gear is no simple task. Half the duckboards were under swift-flowing water, and only a single strand of cable provided a handhold. The Germans had the range, and their shells exploding in the river doused the struggling line of GIs with water and mud.

Lucht remembers his dash across the bridge. "The Germans had regrouped and their artillery was falling on both sides of the river, and I was thinking, Boy, this is just like Hollywood." Lucht hit the far bank and dove under a tank. "A major was already under there. He asked me what I was doing. I said, 'Resting.' He said, 'Your rest time is over, get going.' I crawled out and took off, but I noticed he stayed there."

16

THE BATTLE FOR HARDT

For forty years, George Pope carried guilt for what happened to K Company on the last day of February 1945. "Who remembers a date? I remember that goddam date—I've always blamed myself for the 28th of February, I've lived that son of a bitch.

"We were going to attack this town of Hardt, right? And they're going to attack with one company behind the other. And then Gieszl was going to attack with one platoon behind the other, and the first platoon is going to lead. He's giving me this attack order as we're walking down the road. We're going to cross the line of departure about eight in the morning, so we get there just about eight. And the line of departure was the First Battalion. So we finally find some guys from A Company, that was my old outfit, and I asked a sergeant, 'What's happening here?' He said, 'Pope, I don't really know. My platoon is here. Where the other platoons are, I don't know. What are you going to do?' And I said we're going to attack the town, this village out front here. And he says, 'Well, man, there's a lot of Krauts out there.'"

The Able Company sergeant was better informed than division, corps, or army intelligence officers—a lot of Germans were out there. During the night, First Battalion's rifle companies had their hands full. They overran a field artillery battery between Beeck and Hardt, capturing more than one hundred men; then at midnight they skirmished with three German tanks and fifty infantrymen. When they reached the vicinity of Hardt and Hehler at 4:30 A.M., the companies were widely scattered. When K Company arrived on the scene the situation remained confused.

Our platoons, spread out in fields along a secondary road, waited while Gieszl and the company officers tried to sort out the situation. In the distance through barren trees we glimpsed tile roofs of houses in Hardt and Hehler. The enemy, wherever he was, remained quiet.

The battle began on the fifth morning after the Ninth Army crossed the Roer at Linnich. Spearheaded by its attached tank battalion, the 84th Division had advanced nine miles on February 27, overrunning fifty-four villages and towns and capturing more than a thousand prisoners. This was a new and different kind of war for the Railsplitters. In the Siegfried Line and during the Bulge offensive, day-long advances were measured in hundreds of yards. Now lead rifle companies, hanging on to the backs of tanks, sometimes covered several miles in a single hour. K Company, in reserve and on foot, was hard pressed to keep pace.

The Associated Press, the *New York Times,* and *Stars and Stripes* carried lead stories on the Railsplitters' breakthrough across the Rhine plain, with the AP commenting that the German lines "fell apart." Back home, Betty Gieszl pasted a clipping in her scrapbook from the Phoenix paper. It reported that the 84th Division, racing forward, "encountered virtually no opposition in more than ten miles and captured German officers and men in a state of great confusion."

The 84th had outrun the divisions on its left and its right, which pleased everybody, particularly our generals. Both flanks were wide open, and though we were vulnerable to counterattack, it was considered vital to maintain the drive's momentum. Gieszl was not surprised when he was told our battalion was to pass through the First Battalion on the morning of the 28th and continue the attack. The main effort was to be concentrated in a two-mile-wide corridor.

K Company's sector was on the division's extreme right boundary. Item Company on our left had an insane-asylum complex at St. Josefsheim as its objective, and L Company was in reserve. Tanks would provide close support. The flanking divisions were miles to our rear—nothing was on our right but thin air and Germans.

K Company spent the night of the 27th in Beeck, a few miles south of Hardt and Hehler. Melvin Goodwin had never been so tired of walking and waiting in all his life. "My feet were worn down to stubs." He'd heard the rumors that Germans shot American prisoners with German equipment, and as an eighteen-year-old from a small town in Arkansas, he was inclined to believe the stories. "I realized I must not be captured because I had this German blanket—if there was a possibility of being captured I would fight till the end."

Morris Dunn, by now an old veteran, was in bad shape following the forced marches of the past three days. "Everybody was still wearing the winter Shoe-pacs issued at Linnich. They weren't designed for walking because they didn't have arch supports. Our feet swelled and developed painful blisters, and it got so serious we had to wait for trucks to bring up our combat boots. Most of us couldn't even lace our boots because of the swelling."

Dunn lost track of the days and nights but remembers stopping at a small château on the 27th. Completely exhausted, he quickly fell asleep. During the night he heard a commotion. "I heard someone calling out my name asking if I was in the room. It was Sergeant Jerry Dunne, who had received a message from the Red Cross intended for me. It read: 'Son born, October 10, normal birth, both fine, family writing.'"

Chief Hair and Fred Olson talked the night before the attack. The Chief, a big Cherokee from Oklahoma, was not given to small talk; he seldom spoke of his wife, Eliza, or his family. But that night while oiling his M1, the Chief told Olson he regretted not writing his mother. He didn't know why he hadn't written her for the past several weeks; he just hadn't done it, and he felt bad. He told Fred he was going to write her the next day for sure. Then the two rolled up in their blankets and went to sleep.

After a hurried breakfast in the dark streets of Beeck the battalion was on the move an hour before dawn. The ground was covered with heavy frost; the light snow flurries had ceased, and with the coming of first light, we found the landscape had changed. We passed houses with glass in the windows, and smoke eddied from chimneys. Somebody was home, but the civilians remained out of sight.

Keller pulled aside a man who was having trouble keeping up the pace. Becoming suspicious of the size of the fellow's pack, he took a look inside and found it stuffed with silver flatware. Keller was furious. "Dump it, every last piece of it." The loot was tossed in the ditch, and Keller shoved the man back in line.

Moving toward Hardt, Wiley Herrell felt a lot more sure of himself than he had when he first joined the company. But every time the company headed for an attack, Herrell lost his appetite. "For me it was a sickening feeling knowing that someone else would get wounded, others killed. That morning as we got near Hardt, Chief Hair told me he wasn't going to make it. He asked me, 'Wiley, what do you do if you feel this isn't going to be your lucky day?' I told him I'd be tempted to hang back, but the Chief said, 'No, it wouldn't be fair. I'm staying up with my buddies.'"

Near the Hehler road a heavy shell roared low overhead so close it sucked the air from our lungs. It exploded at the base of a large brick house forty feet away, collapsing the building in a huge explosion. Nobody in the company was hurt, but the civilians in the house could not have survived the tremendous blast. It was our own artillery, an 8-incher or a 240, too big for close-in infantry support. "For God's sakes," Gieszl radioed, "stop that fire. Tell those bastards they're hitting right on top of us."

Gieszl was not his usual self that morning. He was exhausted before the battle began. The company had marched twenty-five miles since Linnich, and Gieszl, with his nightly battalion meetings, had had only a few hours of sleep during the past four days. His old wounds were acting up, he kept shifting his carbine and rubbing his right arm. He looked tired. Brewer and Leinbaugh asked him if he was feeling okay. "Thank you very much," he said, with the old vigor in his voice, "but I'm fine, just splendid."

Pope, determinedly independent and unimpressed by rank, had an exchange with the colonel. "We got delayed looking for A Company. And now eight o'clock has come and gone and Pope hasn't jumped off. And here comes Gieszl and the battalion commander, right? And the battalion CO says, 'For Christ sakes, Pope, it's after eight and you haven't . . .' And I stopped the colonel right there and said, 'What's the big fucking rush? Where the fuck you think you are at, Louisiana on maneuvers? This ain't maneuvers, this is real shit, and I'm going out there, not you.' That's what I told the colonel, right? I didn't give a crap about nothing."

Fred Olson felt reassured when men in his platoon heard the company was moving into a town that had been taken by another unit. The day could be an easy one, Fred thought—it had begun routinely enough. The platoons moved off the highway and crossed a field. "Then we saw the roofs of houses. The word came to form up as skirmishers and move out."

"Lord, I was tired that morning," Goodwin recalls. "We stopped and pulled off the road. Johnny Bowe, my squad leader, told me, 'Goodwin, get your rifle off your shoulder—we're getting near the Germans.'"

Olson remembers rifle shots cracking overhead as the company approached the houses in Hehler. "That's when we began receiving our first sporadic small-arms fire. And we began firing back through windows at no one in particular. We got to the first houses without too much trouble and were moving down the main street with houses on both sides and absolutely no sign of life. I was carrying a BAR, we had beefed up our firepower with two BARs to a squad, and I began firing along with everyone else, but there was something wrong with my weapon—it would only fire single shots, not fully automatic."

Although Pope's recommendation for a battlefield commission was pending at division headquarters, he was still a tech sergeant the day of the battle. "We had this new second lieutenant with us, Leimkuehler, and it was his first real engagement, his first attack, and Gieszl tells him, 'Stay close to Pope, he'll show you the ropes.'"

"I told our guys we're going to go across this field shooting. And we went across this goddam field, it was, oh, about five hundred yards, and pretty soon you see the goddam sheets, you see helmets on sticks—GI helmets. We're shooting the shit out of the rest of Able Company. A Company we find out had half of the town and the Krauts were in the other half, in the houses. And then we find a hole almost as big as a room. So down we went. We get below ground level, and there's about ten of A Company and fifteen or twenty Krauts. All night long our guys had those prisoners sitting there in this big-assed hole."

After the first platoon got in the houses, the rest of K Company moved up and the Germans started taking off. "You could see a whole shitpotful running, right?" Pope quickly sized up the situation. "I thought we had those sons of bitches, so I said, 'Come on, you guys, let's go.' We started across that next field. And those bastards waited for us. They waited till we got halfway across that field and then they cut down on us. That's the reason I blame myself for the 28th of February."

The first long stuttering bursts of machine-gun fire became a continuous stream of bullets as more guns joined in. The fields were crisscrossed with bursts of mud kicked up by interlocking bands of fire. In that first moment one man in K Company was killed—almost cut in half. More men were wounded, we didn't know how many. The platoons hit the ground. Sergeants yelled for their squads to return fire. Men scrambled to cover in the nearest houses, others hunkered down along a woods line on the company's right flank and built up a firing line.

"I've always blamed myself for letting those bastards ambush us," Pope says. "I thought we had 'em on the run, and that's when you have to keep pushing, keep on the pressure."

Early in the battle Gieszl's level of frustration began to match the level of his exhaustion. German machine guns, expertly positioned, created an almost impenetrable wall in front of the company. The captain couldn't call in artillery—the locations of all the friendly troops in the area were unknown. And the promised tanks, a platoon of Shermans which could have dealt with the German machine gunners, had not shown up. The captain sent word for the platoons to finish mopping up the houses along the Hehler road and to clean out the farm buildings on the company's flanks. While the platoons were consolidating, the first batch of company wounded and a dozen civilians found hiding in cellars were evacuated.

Lucht's squad took advantage of the brief lull. Checking out a large brick house, they discovered breakfast had just been prepared. Fresh eggs and ham and German bread were on the table. The squad had a decent meal with everybody taking turns looking out the window and firing an occasional round between bites.

The battalion commander radioed Gieszl every few minutes. Regiment and division were on his back—when was K going to continue the attack? Only after satisfying himself that Hehler was secure did Gieszl send word to the platoon leaders to move out.

The third platoon advanced from a wooded area across an open field toward two farmhouses. Morris Dunn saw bullets kicking up a line of dirt directly in front of him. He went down so hard that Willy Niese thought sure he'd been hit. Lieutenant Jarvis was in front of Dunn when a bullet creased him across the back. Dunn ran up to him. "I pulled up his shirt. The wound wasn't bad; it looked like a hot iron had branded him. I dusted sulfa powder down inside his shirt, and we went on and reached the houses."

As the platoon moved forward they were hit from both sides with machine-gun and rifle fire. The squads ran for cover behind sugar-beet mounds.

"Johnny Bowe told us to dig in," Goodwin recalled, "but I lost my shovel coming across the first field, so I started digging in the muddy ground with my steel helmet. Before we finished Johnny tells us we were going to attack the next farmhouse. We started running, and the Germans let loose with machine guns. I was praying and shooting and I suppose other soldiers were praying too.

"Horton hollered out and says, 'Goddammit, I'm hit.' Morris Dunn, Sergeant Waddle, and me were next to him. Horton was hit below his left shoulder. He was bleeding from the mouth, eyes, nose, and ears. We gave him a drink of water and helped him the best we could."

Dunn tried to stop the bleeding. "Horton asked for his Bible. Then we stuck his rifle in the ground next to him so the aidmen could find him. He was a new replacement, seriously wounded."

Billy Waddle's men took cover in a corner of a garden behind a row of fence posts. "We set up a firing line. The German machine-gun fire was so heavy it cut several of those posts right in two. The posts dangled there from the wire just inches above our heads."

Goodwin saw more men hit. "That's where Mutt Tomlinson got killed. Our squad kept advancing and took a farmhouse. We reorganized, and Johnny told me and Okenfuss to go upstairs in the adjoining building and knock holes in the tile roof and give cover while the rest of the squad advanced across the next field." Then they rejoined the rest of the men. German tanks opened up. "Those 88s urged me to run like hell. We went in another farmhouse and Jim Teague, he was Johnny's assistant squad leader, he and Maurice Michel went to check out the barn. An 88 got Teague right next to the barn. Apparently he died instantly."

Johnny Freeman's squad, down to half a dozen men, was running across the same open field. "Chief Hair was the man next to me on my right when he was hit by machine-gun fire. That's where they cut him down. Doc Smith came up and was bandaging him and then another burst hit the Chief, killing him. One of our new men cracked up after Frank Hair was killed. The fellow ran back crying. He said he had a new baby at home and shouldn't have been sent to a rifle company."

One of Olson's close friends was hit. "It was Morris Hoffman, our thirty-seven-year-old from New York. He picked himself off that field and headed toward the rear rejoicing that he had finally been hit—he had received that million-dollar wound and was getting the hell out. This in the face of continuing fire from those Kraut machine gunners. Every time we were in a firefight Morris refused to get down. He said he was too old to be getting up and down, that was for us young guys. I really liked Morris—I think he seemed to always watch over me."

George Cappiello remembers Hoffman had a clean hit. "The bullet passed right through his shoulder. Doc Smith bandaged him up, but Morris refused to be evacuated. He must have walked around for an hour, saying it was the best thing that ever happened, talking away and making sure he told all of his buddies goodbye before he went back."

While the company's rifle platoons were advancing by fire and movement, the mortar section set up the 60s near the edge of the woods and worked over a German machine-gun location. Hargesheimer remembers they knocked it out with the third round. Then two Germans who had been hiding in a foxhole made a break and ran inside a hen house to hide out. A mortar crewman tossed a grenade. The Germans, both slightly wounded, came out with their hands up, stunned, but able to walk. Moments later Hargesheimer was hit. "Shrapnel from an 88 got me in the foot, making a good-sized hole. I was carried back more than a mile to the aid station by two slave laborers we'd liberated. I was a heavy load and we were under fire most of the way, but they did it, they got me back."

Bocarski, who had returned to the company after being wounded at Taverneux, remembers the ammo problem. "We did a hell of a lot of preliminary firing with the machine guns until we finally ran out of belts. We had some new people with us and I kept telling them to stay down, but for some who hadn't been under fire it had become a game. We had our light .30s in position under some trees. A big branch was just a foot in front of me. All of a sudden it was gone—shot in two. I couldn't believe it."

According to Oyler, the machine gunners did a really good job. "The only problem was not having enough ammunition to draw on. Every time the guns opened up everybody would yell at us we were drawing fire. The typical replacements hadn't had enough experience with either the machine guns or mortars to be of much help, so it came down to a few old-timers to do the job."

Doc Mellon couldn't have used a wheelbarrow if he had one. Heavy German fire made it impossible to evacuate the seriously wounded from the flat fields beyond the Hehler road. Doc Smith and Mellon did the best they could—tied quick tourniquets to control bleeding, applied pressure bandages, gave wounded men a shot of morphine, made the man as comfortable as possible, and moved on to the next casualty.

Mike DeBello's luck finally ran out at Hardt. "It was bad. The Germans were in little groups of houses and barns. Some had thatched roofs. I kept shooting at the roofs with tracers, trying to set them on fire and burn the Germans out. We did a lot of damage.

"Then I got hit. A machine-gun bullet ripped right through the upper muscle of my right arm. Doc Mellon was the bravest kid I ever saw. He came running right through the machine-gun fire and put a tourniquet on my arm."

Johnny Radovich by this time in the war had decided Doc Mellon was invulnerable. "I don't know how he did it. He was all over the place bandaging up the wounded—a real cool guy. He never got excited."

While most of K Company was skewered to the ground, the company aidmen kept moving. Though the medics wore Red Cross armbands and helmets with a painted cross in a circle, the insignia was no protection during firefights. Only a few men realized Mellon himself was a casualty.

"The 88s were coming in heavy, and early on I got smashed into a hole by a blast right next to me." Doc's shoulder was pulled out of the socket. "I couldn't go back to the aid station; there were just too many wounded guys to work on, so I took some codeine and morphine. I couldn't raise my arm beyond my waist, so here I was trying to work on these wounded guys with one hand."

When his platoon moved out again, Olson found Graf to his immediate right. "Initially we were a good distance apart, I would imagine ten to fifteen yards. Graf was a very new person, and in a way I guess I felt some responsibility for him. As we moved into the open field we began to receive small-arms fire and I told Graf to hit the ground and take cover in a pair of German tank tracks, maybe six inches deep. He was in one track and I was in the other, directly across from one another. Graf was firing his M1 and I told him to cut it out. I sure as hell didn't see anything out there in the way of targets. I was just lying there facing him not knowing what action to take. Then I saw the bullet penetrate his armpit. His arm was outstretched holding his rifle. My eyes were riveted on the spot where the bullet made its entrance. I saw it hit and penetrate. When the bullet hit, Graf's body came up off the ground, it seemed a couple of feet, and he began to bleed profusely from the mouth—blood was just gushing out.

"I hollered to him to turn around and go back. He understood me. We crawled all the way back to the houses. He was swaying and weaving and losing blood fast. He didn't appear to need my help at the moment. We got back to where we had jumped off; others from the platoon were there. Graf died at that moment."

Pope and the first platoon were a short distance ahead of the rest of the company when they ran low on ammunition. "To show you how hot it was, this kid—Menke I think it was—the kid crawled up with the bandoliers, but he couldn't come out behind that slope and so he throws the bandoliers as close to the doorway of the house as possible. And then we tried to reach out with our weapons to drag the bandoliers inside."

"The platoon was down to its last few rounds," Menke recalls, when Leimkuehler and Pope sent him back for more. "I scrounged all I could get—some of the weapons platoon guys had extra bandoliers. Then I ran back across the field and up a ditch and threw the ammo across the road to the houses where the platoon was holed up.

"We found periscopes the Germans were using from their emplacements and burp guns with bent barrels for firing around corners. The area we were moving through was sprayed with automatic fire. That was the most intense fire I ever saw during combat. Our tanks, three of them, as I remember, got bogged down in the mud and didn't come up until late—we needed those tanks."

One at a time, men in the first platoon dashed across a road in their attempt to outflank German machine gunners holding out in cellars. As Mel Cline ran across, he spotted a machine gunner firing at him from a basement-level window. "He was leading me too much and I got across okay, but when I got inside one of the fellows noticed my shirt collar had a couple of holes. A bullet had passed through the front of the collar tabs and then cut the epaulet on my field jacket in two."

When the platoon got ready to continue the attack, Cline was in a room with Bill McMillan. "While we were waiting Bill broke down. He was crying and in bad shape. He told me he couldn't go on, he knew he was going to be killed. Two of us tried to calm him down and reason with him. He finally got hold of himself and moved out with the rest of us. We should have told Bill to stay behind. He was killed a few minutes later out in the middle of that next open field."

A second platoon squad took temporary refuge in the local tavern. Several men were already inside drinking beer. The beer taps were located in front of a big window facing the street. The only safe way to get a beer was to crawl across the room, reach up and flick the tap, and then maneuver the mug on the floor, catching the beer as it cascaded down. After a man filled his glass and crawled to a safe position, the next man would move up for a refill.

After having a beer, Olson crawled outside to a hedgerow where a firing line formed. "I stuck my BAR through the hedge, flash hider and front bipod, and was looking for something to shoot at. The Germans must have known we were there and began throwing mortars on us." Everyone started pulling back, but Olson couldn't free up the bipod on his BAR; it was caught in the hedge. "It was an interminable period of time before I found the combination and charged for the rear amidst the mortar shells."

One of the new platoon leaders insisted the men keep the bipods on their BARs. "I was perturbed about it. After this narrow escape I went back in one of the houses and the platoon leader was sitting there. I unscrewed the flash hider and bipod and heaved them across the room at a picture on the wall behind the platoon leader. Glass splattered all around. The fellow didn't say anything. He just sat there."

Later a sergeant sent Olson to an upstairs room that had a clear view down the street. "I grabbed a chair back from the window and was sitting there eating a piece of bread and jam I found in the room when five or six

Krauts appeared moving down the street in our direction. I began firing single shots from my BAR and had the feeling my shots did register. The rest of the Germans disappeared between two houses."

Jarvis sent Jerry Dunne's squad to check out several German school buildings. "Nobody was there, but there was a hell of a firefight off to the left—that was Item Company moving through. I had my squad line up as skirmishers. Johnny Bowe was on the left. The whole goddam company was on our right. We didn't know this machine gun was out there in front of us. Those Germans just waited until we began to get close and then opened up. I knew some guys were hit, but I didn't know right then Johnny Bowe had gotten killed."

Don Okenfuss had total confidence in his squad leader. "Jerry Dunne was an absolutely fearless soldier. He could get people up and get them to move when they didn't want to go. At times I thought, That man doesn't have a brain, he'll get us all killed. And at times I thought he was just too good a soldier. But he really had the ability to move us. We were working with some tanks, we were being shelled and we were all pinned down by fire. Jerry stood up and said, 'Come on, let's go,' and he started out. We followed him. If I'd been left there on my own, I would have stayed and got shot to pieces."

Dunne's squad rejoined the rest of the third platoon. "I found the lieutenant and pinpointed the gun location that was holding up our advance. I'd run completely out of ammo and no one would give me any because we were all low. I grabbed McClure's BAR and emptied a clip at the machine gun as fast as I could, and then I went up with the only thing I could get, a German concussion grenade. I went alone to the fence and walked to the entrance of the building and at the entrance two Germans jumped out of a hole. I heaved the grenade at them. They were the two that shot Johnny Bowe."

Several times during the day J. A. Craft felt the Germans were on the run. "But then they stopped. During the fight I saw two Germans sticking their heads up from a foxhole. I had a .45 caliber squirt gun, and I told the guys behind me to run up with me. I yelled, 'Heraus!' The Germans came out and we sent them back through our lines."

A barn behind the lead skirmishers began burning. Mel Goodwin ran back. "It was the barn where Teague was killed earlier. His body was just outside the door, so two of us ran back and moved him. We were afraid the walls would fall on him."

Mel Cline called on skills he'd not used since basic training. "We were flat, prone on our bellies in the field where both Zurga and McMillan were killed. This German machine gunner was directly to our front. That was the only time in combat that I fired aimed shots like we did on the range in training. We could see this German come up from his hole, fire, and duck down again. I adjusted my sights, got the range, and squeezed off several clips before I finally hit his gun and put him out of action.

When we reached his hole, I found the bullet had glanced off his machine gun and mangled his arm."

Bowditch was in a turnip patch when he was hit with shrapnel in the right knee and index finger. "They were getting ready to evacuate me, and Leinbaugh was talking to several of us who had been wounded. I told him I wanted him to have my scarf as a good-luck piece, so I gave it to him and he wrapped it around his neck. He told me it couldn't have been too lucky, since I had just been hit. I said it worked just fine for me since I had a million-dollar wound and was going home."

The battalion operations sergeant jotted brief notes in his S3 log as the battle unfolded. At 10:00 A.M. he reported that both I and K companies were receiving heavy shelling. At 10:30 the log showed K Company was taking machine-gun fire from the rear—from houses in Hardt outside of our zone. At 11:10, K came under direct tank fire. It was not until 1:30 P.M. that the log reported Captain Wooten, who had gone to locate the missing tanks, came back to the outskirts of Hehler guiding twelve mediums. Six tanks were assigned to support K Company. The others were sent to I Company.

Baptie, the second platoon sergeant, by now a qualified battlefield critic, admits he was impressed by the Germans' defensive positions. "They were well dug in and concealed, and some of their positions were real fortifications. They covered the fields continually with interlocking machine-gun fire. Our tanks finally came up, but got stuck in the middle of a muddy field. When the one tank finally advanced and threw several HE rounds into those buildings to our front, that made all the difference. If that tank hadn't finally made it up, I wouldn't be here."

One tank advanced through a plowed field followed by the first platoon; another moved up along a trail in the woods. An 88 hit directly in front of the tank in the field and then a second round just behind it. The crew bailed out and ran into the woods, leaving the first platoon exposed. "We had no alternative but to pull back too," Leimkuehler remembers. "Later we got the second tank to move to the edge of the woods and fire its 75 at a stone fence with Germans dug in behind it."

The battle finally took a turn for the better. The tank's machine guns and 75s knocked out half a dozen German positions. The lead tank ventured again into the open, but almost immediately got stuck in the mud. Both Leimkuehler and Leinbaugh talked to the driver, who insisted he was bogged down and unable to move. A half hour passed before the platoon commander's Sherman arrived and three tanks, moving forward in echelon, began blasting the company's objective, Hochfeld, with their 75s.

Leimkuehler and the first platoon again used the tanks for cover. "With the 75s blasting and the machine guns firing over our heads we were able to advance toward the objective. We had some wounded, and the first platoon captured eight or ten German soldiers and a couple of medics.

"I remember Lieutenant Masters leading that final charge. He killed a machine gunner and opened the way into that little town. He was leading, running down the main street like a madman, shooting up everything in his way."

It was Bill Masters that Bocarski remembers best from the long day near Hardt. "Masters—a brave man. He ran up and I was following him. We both had carbines. I was wondering what was going to happen, because I thought Masters had run out of ammunition. But he knelt, reloaded, and got both those machine gunners, one round for each one."

Pope remembers getting caught in the open with no cover anyplace. "We were all pinned down, and I see guys turning their heads, I felt like doing that myself. It was flat as a floor. There wasn't a blade of grass you could hide under. I'm yelling, 'Shoot, you sons of bitches!' That was a tough time."

And then Pope watched the tide change. "Talk about Masters, then you saw a guy with some cool head, man. I bet he said this to himself: 'If I'm going to get killed, goddammit, they're going to kill me on my feet.' And he jumped up and took off straight for those machine gunners with his runner behind him, that little kid, a tough little meatball from Chicago."

Bill Masters's account of the final assault was very matter-of-fact: "I was in the edge of woods with part of the fourth platoon. All three rifle platoons were pinned down in those flat fields, and the German machine-gun fire was awfully heavy and the casualties were increasing. I decided I had to get these guys moving or a lot more were going to get killed." Masters ran forward yelling and swearing at everybody to get on their feet and move ahead. "I got up as far as a sugar-beet mound that gave some cover, close enough to toss a grenade at the German machine gunners right in front of me. But I couldn't get the grenade out of my pocket—it was stuck." A German tossed a potato masher at Masters. "It landed right next to me but didn't explode. Then I got up and ran forward firing and was lucky enough to hit the Germans in their foxhole, and that cleared things out so I could get to cover behind the first building. I had this dead-end kid from Chicago I'd made my bodyguard. He came in close behind me, and then a number of men pulled up and we went from building to building cleaning out the place and captured a sizable batch of German paratroopers in those houses."

Frenchy Lariviere and Sergeant Smart took cover alongside a house. Frenchy came around a corner. "I almost ran into this German. After I captured him I found out he was a medic. We had a lot of wounded, so we put him to work patching up our guys. He was really helpful and did a good job. We kept him with us most of the night until we evacuated all our wounded."

Pope's platoon pulled in a number of prisoners. "We got into the little town, but we lost a lot of people outside, a hell of a lot were lying out there. We dug in and there was an ack-ack gun out there that we fired at, and the crew took off running. And then I look around and said, 'Where's Lieutenant Leimkuehler?' When I go inside to the CP there he was lying there with his leg almost blown off. And he asks me for a piece of chocolate. I'll never forget that. He says, 'Hey, Pope, you got a candy bar?' That was the last we saw of him."

After the town was captured, Captain Gieszl and Leimkuehler were talking with the field artillery observer. Paul recalls the details, "We were standing in a big archway leading to a courtyard. We heard a shell land and just about that time I felt something hit me. My leg felt real warm, and I realized I was bleeding. All I did was lie down, and the aidman took off my belt and put a tourniquet on me. The next thing I remembered was being in the animal stalls of the barn along with other wounded, and some captured German aidmen were helping our medics with the wounded.

"I'm sure they must have given me morphine to make me comfortable, but I was not in pain. People are often concerned about dying, but I don't think dying is difficult at all. Because I could have died right there in that stable. It's just like going to sleep, I would have never known the difference. As far as dying, it's not miserable when you die that way.

"When it got dark they put me on a door. Two German soldiers carried me, and one of our people went along as a guard. I kept telling them to loosen the tourniquet, because I knew that every fifteen or twenty minutes you were supposed to loosen it to keep the circulation. At the time I didn't know how serious my wound was. Then I was put on a jeep with four litters and taken to a field hospital. I woke up in a tent and looked down at my left leg. From the groin down it looked like a big sirloin steak, but the next time I looked it was sewed together. It got the main artery and the main nerve and also it got my middle finger, damaged the fourth finger and part of the fifth. The same shell did all the damage—I think it was the same piece. They debated about saving the other fingers and I had to argue with them about that."

The battle was almost over. Squads checked out cellars and poked through barns and outhouses looking for stray Germans. Gieszl's worry now was the tanks and 88s firing at the company from the Mackenstein road, a half mile beyond Hochfeld to the north. He went to the second floor of a building with the artillery observer to direct fire on the German positions.

Lance is sure the Germans spotted the two. "They knocked the stairway out from under them with an armor-piercing round and Gieszl came flying down out of the upstairs like a bird. Then we got inside a barn and the Germans kept shelling us with the APs [armor-piercing rounds]. They would take out walls and go all the way through a building."

The next German round struck the stone archway at the entrance to the barn. A huge hunk of masonary smashed down on Lance's shoulder and back. "One of the captured German medics looked at me and told Gieszl he thought my back was broken. George insisted on giving me morphine. I think he gave me three shots, and I was trying to fight them off mentally, because I was sure the Germans would counterattack."

Gieszl and the FO called for a TOT (Time on Target) on Mackenstein. "The direct fire from the 88s stopped after that." The captain was knocked out by the shell blast that sent him flying down from the upstairs room. "I was banged up pretty good," Gieszl recalls. "We got Lance on a stretcher on the hood of the jeep. Max Sobel had been slightly wounded; he and another man helped the two of us back. The doctors must have sedated me pretty heavily; I was out of it. The truth is I didn't know what was going on for the next three or four days."

Jerry Dunne received a final mission before dark. "This antiaircraft gun out to our left flank had been giving us trouble, and Leinbaugh sent me and a couple of guys to check it out. We found the Germans had left, but they had spiked the gun before they pulled out."

Frenchy and several men located a decent cellar. "That night one of the new replacements talked to me. He was in bad shape. He was frightened to death he'd shot one of our own men that afternoon. He was firing prone toward some houses and someone suddenly stood up out in front of him, right in his line of fire, then the guy went down. I talked to the fellow and tried to persuade him it was the German machine gunners who hit our man."

Six German paratroopers caught in the open while attempting to flee Hochfeld lay dead in a field fifty yards from the end house. A BAR man had cut down on them from an upstairs window. From the uniform he felt sure one was a German officer. We checked out the bodies. They were a young, tough-looking lot; one was a captain with a map case attached to his belt. Examining the case inside in the CP, we found six bullet holes through it. We were looking for the enemy headquarters and artillery locations, but when unfolded the map was so badly riddled it was impossible to tell if it had any markings of value.

At dusk, foxholes were dug beyond the buildings. We expected a counterattack after dark, so defensive artillery concentrations were fired and brought in as close to the perimeter as possible.

Craft was totally exhausted. "I got in the hole belonging to two Germans we'd captured earlier. When the sergeant got there I told him I was going to sleep that night. He said, 'You might wake up dead.' I told him, 'I'll just have to wake up dead.' I couldn't help it; I needed the sleep, and I got it, too. After that I got rid of the grease gun—it had no range. So when I go in the buildings I got myself another rifle from one of the wounded guys and kept it."

Pope, always the good sergeant, spent most of the night on the prowl.

"When I was making my rounds that night I found our dead-end guy trying to rape this German broad. The mother and father were right there in the goddam house. I was ready to shoot him right there on the spot."

Long afterward Lance talked about his evacuation from Hochfeld. He is shy on details, but remembered every rut the jeep hit on the road to the aid station. He thinks from battalion aid he was driven to division clearing or a field hospital; "All those places look the same when you are on a stretcher," he said.

Doughhead was in better shape than many of the wounded. He was stretched out on a cot when orderlies brought in Lieutenant Leimkuehler. "By the way the doctors and medics were hustling around, I knew he was in real bad shape. They were giving him blood and shots, and I heard the doctors saying they couldn't move him. Medics put a portable screen between our beds. I could hear every word. They were working four feet away from me, and I tried to block it out, but I couldn't. The doctors were uptight. I remember one was swearing all the time they were working on him.

"I'll tell you one thing, I didn't think the lieutenant had a chance in a thousand the way those doctors were talking, but I was moved out that night so I don't know what finally happened to him."

Mel Goodwin made a final head count before he fell asleep. "We had started out that morning with eleven men. The wounded and dead were lying in the beet field and the medics were doing their jobs. At last we got in a cellar; there was hardly any talking. Everyone's head was hung down. Finally Maurice Michel said, 'Goodwin, let's go see Johnny Bowe.' In my mind I say I can't help them now. It's best I remember Johnny, Teague, and the other buddies when they were alive."

After the battle was over, we learned the 8th Paratroop Division, among Marshal von Rundstedt's elite combat troops on the Western Front, used the 26th and 27th of February to create a strong, integrated defense line along that east-west road between Hardt and Waldniel. The defensive positions, supported by tanks and artillery, were located three miles south of Dülken, a fair-sized city which was the 84th's next objective. If anyone was aware German paratroopers were waiting for us, the intelligence never reached down to the rifle companies.

The 84th Infantry Division in the Battle of Germany, the Railsplitters' official history, carried a brief account of K Company's battle on February 28th.

"Company K had to cross about 400 yards of open ground to get to Hochfeld from a clump of woods. Hochfeld was held by 70 paratroopers, all armed with automatic weapons. In addition, heavier guns farther back were helping out. Two 75mm guns were shooting at Company K from Baumgeshof, as were two 88mm guns from Mackenstein and two self-propelled guns from the road between Baumgeshof and Mackenstein. The fire was hot and the company was flat on the ground.

"Lt. William D. Masters started running toward Hochfeld with a carbine in one hand and a radio in the other. A German machine gunner blocked his entrance into the town. They exchanged a series of shots, both missed, both ran out of ammunition at precisely the same time. Lt. Masters calmly stopped, knelt on one knee, reloaded. Again they looked up at the same time, but this time Lt. Masters fired first. He put a bullet between the machine gunner's eyes. When Lt. Masters took off his helmet, he found a bullet through it.

"While the carbine was fighting the machine gun, S. Sgt. Jeremiah H. Dunne was leading his squad of eight over to the right flank about 200 yards to a single farmhouse, held by six Germans, three of them armed with submachine guns. The squad rushed the house, killed two and captured the rest. These two blows seemed to break the back of the resistance in Hochfeld because the rest of the company was able to advance and take the town, killing about 20 and capturing the others."

A number of men picked up Purple Hearts after the battle. Bill Masters received the Silver Star, the only medal for heroism at Hardt. Masters deserved the Distinguished Service Cross at least or the Congressional Medal, but we didn't realize it at the time. Gieszl and Leinbaugh, Keller and Brewer should have seen to it that Jerry Dunne, Doc Mellon, Doc Smith, Pope, Leimkuehler, and a dozen others were awarded Silver or Bronze Stars, but nobody wanted to remember the battle; we did our best to put it out of our minds.

After the war Keller made a medal count. At least one hundred men in the company received Purple Hearts for wounds. Three men in addition to Bill Masters—Gieszl, Campbell, and Phelps—were awarded Silver Stars, and Klebofski and Moore got the medal posthumously. Fifteen men received Bronze Stars for valor, and one man a Belgian decoration. That was all the medals K Company picked up during the war.

The medal situation was better in the rear. The fifty-eight officers in our 84th Division Headquarters pulled in about four times as many medals as the men in K Company. Enlisted men in division headquarters received twice as many medals as we did. The MPs and quartermaster troops also outdid us in decorations. We know of several one-hour periods when K Company took more casualties, killed and wounded, than the total casualties sustained during the entire war by all of these rear-echelon outfits lumped together, but that was the way it was.

17

GETTING THE WORD

Like those who had gone before them, the men wounded at Hardt wrote letters home, hoping these would arrive before the Army's telegrams.

Mike DeBello needed help. A nonwriter, he'd had to ask friends to do all his letter-writing. After he was hit, Mike got a lieutenant to write to his girlfriend, Rose. She could handle the problem of telling Mike's mother the news. "I wanted the letter to get there first," he says. "It would ease it off—I didn't want the telegram to shock my mother." The letter to Rose won the race with the wire to Mike's mother. It worked out fine for Mike, including his marriage to Rose when he got out of an Army hospital in the States.

In Worcester, Massachusetts, the notification of next of kin went by the book. At St. John's High School they called sixteen-year-old Bob Bowe from class and told him to come to the administrative office. The principal didn't have anything specific to tell Bob, just asked him to go home right away. That was all. On the bus that would take him to Pleasant Street, Bob saw his mother's sister, and she was crying. Someone had called her to come home. Now Bob expected that the news about his brother Jack, K Company's Johnny Bowe, would really be bad. The war Department's telegram had just arrived:

BA51 31 GOVT-WASHINGTON DC 14 34 9A
MRS MARY H BOWE =
    1012 PLEASANT ST WORC =

THE SECRETARY OF WAR DESIRES ME TO EXPRESS HIS DEEP REGRET
THAT YOUR SON SGT JOHN A BOWE JR WAS KILLED IN ACTION IN
GERMANY FEB 28 1945 CONFIRMING LETTER FOLLOWS =
                              J A ULIO THE ADJUTANT GENERAL.

"In those days a little white-haired guy in uniform delivered the telegrams," Bob recalls. "When my mother saw him coming she had a feeling that it was going to turn out the worst. Every time after that when
she saw the man who delivered them my mother was reminded of that
morning.

"The family priest came soon after the telegram arrived," Bob says.
"My mother was pretty down. We all were. This was so close to the end
of the war, we wondered why did it have to happen then." When Bob
went into the Navy during the Korean War he intentionally named his
uncle, rather than his mother, as next of kin. "I didn't want her to go
through the same experience again that she did with Jack."

After the day of the telegram, Bob stayed out of school, and the family
had a funeral Mass. Then a letter came from Major General A. R. Boll-
ing, the 84th Division's commander: "Your son, a squad leader in the
third platoon, was leading his men in an attack against an enemy strongpoint in the vicinity of Hardt, Germany, on the day of his death. Heavy
small-arms fire was directed upon them and it was during this assault that
he was killed. His body was recovered immediately and prepared for burial in an American Military Cemetery in Holland.

"The cross above his grave," the letter concluded, "is permanently
marked with his name and army serial number. . . . Whatever personal
effects he may have had will be sent to the Effects Quartermaster, Kansas
City, Missouri, for shipment to you."

The regiment's Catholic chaplain also wrote: "Words seem feeble when
one tries to express sympathy to another over the loss they have suffered
in the death of a loved one. . . . A Mass will be said for John and I can
assure you that many of his buddies will attend and offer their Holy Com-
munion for him."

Jack Bowe, the St. John's graduate who'd been talked out of early
enlistment by his father (who had himself gone off to war when he was
sixteen), Jack, whose parents wanted him to become a doctor and who'd
already had a year of premed at Holy Cross, was dead. Every day
brought reminders of that fact. Packages and letters came back to the
Worcester post office. Bob, who worked there on a part-time basis,
stopped as many as he could. His parents, having a difficult enough time
as it was, didn't need these additional reminders. So he brought them
home and hid them in the cellar. Unfortunately, however, some months
later his father found them.

Bob also watched the arrival of a series of letters from the government.
"They said, in effect, 'Fill out these forms and we'll send you the final pay

due your son,'" Bob remembers. "My parents didn't accept this. It was kind of psychological, I think, but my parents ignored it."

The Veterans Administration sent off Insurance Form 1579, Notice of Settlement, National Service Life Insurance. With appropriate blanks filled in, it came to Johnny's mother: "You are hereby notified that, as beneficiary of insurance in the amount of $10,000.00 granted to John A. Bowe Jr. by the United States under the National Service Life Insurance Act of October 8, 1940, as amended, you are entitled to monthly payments of $50.80 beginning February 28, 1945, to continue for life, with 120 monthly installments certain. . . . All future communications with reference to this case must bear the File Number XC-3,882,549 and 28N-10,659,747."

Mail from a Dutch family was more personal. The Army had buried Johnny's body and those of other GIs killed in late February in Holland. There local people "adopted" the graves, took care of them, and contacted the American families. Letters and photographs—white crosses and raw earth mounds in a snowy field, a young man kneeling by Johnny's wintry grave—provided consolation. But it still wasn't over.

"Jack's death as a whole thing was a long-drawn-out affair," his brother says. "My folks were from the old school, so when Jack died we had a year of mourning." No weddings, no social engagements. Bob and his father both wore black ties throughout the year. "One day a guy said, 'Don't you have any other tie?' I had to explain to him what it was about.

"My dad had been having headaches before Jack's death, and these headaches continued and were intensified after this. My mother handled it better. Or at least she concealed it better. My father had been on the Worcester police force since 1924; he'd handled everything real well. But after Jack's death it was different. There were times when my father would be crying if he got into a situation he didn't know how to handle."

In late March when K Company was on the Rhine, Johnny's friend Ed Stewart returned from two months in the hospital. He checked in with the third platoon. "It was painfully clear that many men were missing," he wrote in his journal, "but no one mentioned them. Finally I asked Pop about Johnny. He shook his head. I left the squad and took a solitary walk through woods. I returned, but more settled than when I had left." After Johnny's death this thought stuck with Ed: "If you get too close to someone, it will kill him."

In March, family and friends began to hear from Keith Lance, who wrote from his hospital bed in Paris. His mother, in Twin Falls, Idaho, got the word about Keith's February 28 wounds on the same day that she received his first Purple Heart medal—for wounds from that cellar in

Lindern in December. And on Thursday, March 15, a letter from Keith reached Jeanette Tomlinson, the wife of Keith's friend Mutt.

After the company left Claiborne, Jeanette wrote her husband every day. That Thursday in March, the letters stopped. That morning Mutt's friends Beulah and Harold Standlee invited Jeanette to ride in to Twin Falls with them. Harold Standlee went to the Elks Club while Beulah and Jeanette shopped. "When Harold picked us up," says Jeanette, "he handed me a letter from Keith, sent to the Elks Club. Mutt had worked there when he was drafted. I can still remember parts of the letter: 'There's a pale moon shining over Paris tonight. Beautiful in itself, but shining down on some of the world's worst misery. I'm sorry that misery has touched you. I'm sorry about Mutt.'

"Keith was wounded on the same day Mutt was killed. Of course he couldn't give any details, so I didn't know if Mutt was wounded or killed until we returned to Gooding. Western Union had tried to deliver the telegram to me that morning, after we had left."

The standard phrases of the message on the Western Union form— "the Secretary of War desires . . ."; "deep regret . . ."; "confirming letter follows . . ."—changed fears to reality. Mutt had been killed on February 28. For several nights after the arrival of the telegram, Jeanette burned a candle in her bedroom window. "I don't know why I did that. Maybe hoping Mutt would see it or hoping none of it was true," she says. "Sounds immature now."

Friends and family gave comfort and protection. Her parents came from California, and Mutt's sister Lela provided practical help. "She knew how to go about the legal end, Social Security, veteran's pension, and Mutt's GI insurance," Jeanette says. "I was so dumb and shy—without a little push I doubt if I would've made any effort toward that end." Then Jeanette moved back to Twin Falls and, with help from friends, began to learn accounting. "They no doubt talked it over and decided I needed to be out on my own and start taking care of myself. I didn't realize how much my friends and family helped me. Not especially by being with me, but by *caring*.

"But I went a little crazy after being alone and on my own for a while. That part of my life I would like to do over—I can see now that I was wrapped up in my own misery. I couldn't accept my friends whose husbands or loved ones had come home from the war, and would go out of my way to keep from seeing them and telling them that I was happy for them. I wasn't happy for them; I bitterly resented their good fortune and kept asking, Why Mutt, why not their husbands, sons, or sweethearts? I had to stay busy and couldn't stay home after dark. I don't know how I held down a job—I never had enough sleep."

Keith wrote Jeanette regularly. "I think I lived for those letters and the thought of him coming home so he could tell me about Mutt."

*   *   *

Kay Leimkuehler in Cleveland, Ohio, was three months pregnant when her telegram came. She had received no mail for several weeks; it was the 16th of March when Kay learned that Paul had been wounded on February 28. "My uncle said, 'Well, there's one consolation. If he has lived through the first two weeks, usually a person will survive. If he'd died, you'd get the word immediately.'"

The first letter came from a chaplain. "He explained the extent of Paul's injuries—the telegram just said 'seriously wounded.'" That letter told of the amputation and mentioned that Paul had lost a couple of fingers and could not write. "Then I heard from the Red Cross, who would write for him," Kay said. "Eventually Paul himself was able to write."

That he would be a wartime casualty surely hadn't crossed anyone's mind when Paul and Kay met at an ice-skating race about eight years earlier. He was a first-rate skater, but bike racing was where he shone. In 1936 he'd won the Ohio State cycling championship. Kay, too, had done some bicycle racing. Shared interest in sport was the starting point for a friendship. Then they married, and life for the Leimkuehlers found a steady footing. Paul worked at Tinnerman Products, a Cleveland firm, as an experimental engineer—deferred because of defense work. Their future looked secure.

Even after he lost his deferment and was inducted in 1943, prospects looked good. Paul's employers figured they'd have him out in a few weeks. Basic training at Camp Edwards, then a cadre assignment for Paul, and a secretarial job there for Kay. Then a transfer to Fort Bliss, where the break came. The battalion commander told Paul he could choose between returning to his defense job or staying in the service. "It took me about fifteen minutes to decide I'd go back to my job," Paul says.

Six months later, though, he was again in the Army. Then Paul received his commission at Fort Benning's Infantry School on November 29, 1944—a week after K Company moved out on its first attack. Home leave, then a Christmas tree in a hotel room, and moments with Kay in New York. On New Year's Eve he boarded the *Queen Mary*.

Two months after he and Kay had said goodbye, Paul was hit. As he lay in a hospital bed in a Dutch schoolhouse he knew he had a badly damaged hand, but he was more concerned about the massive shrapnel wound in his left leg: "The service has regulations that you can't amputate for five or seven days—I forget what it was—with the idea that sometimes amputations are done too quickly. With a little time the human body does a lot of healing, might recover, and the amputation would have been unnecessary. But after five days the leg was so sore that if you'd run your finger across the flesh it felt like you were pulling adhesive tape and hair off the skin. I knew it wasn't going to get any better. So I told the surgeon, 'I think you ought to take it off.'"

The surgeons tried to amputate below the knee. But they found that if they stopped there the flesh would not heal. So they amputated through the knee joint.

A week later they carried Paul onto a C-47 for a flight to England. A glance brought both satisfaction and amusement. The trim on the plane's windows was secured with speed nuts—lightweight, spring-metal nuts designed for quick, vibration-proof fastening: "I'm lying there, and here, holding the frames on the windows, are these speed nuts which I had developed."

Paul reached England in mid-March, about the same time Kay received word that he'd been wounded. During his stay there they "revised" the stump, taking half the joint off the femur. Because of the pain he needed sleeping pills at night. And then there was the penicillin. "When you were on penicillin I don't think you ever caught cold, but you got it every three hours, twenty-four hours a day. So even when you did get to sleep, the nurse would come around and wake you up and give you this damn shot of penicillin."

Several weeks later they took him aboard a hospital ship scheduled for Charleston, South Carolina. While the ship steamed westward, VE Day arrived. "That was a happy occasion," Paul says. "I could finally sleep without any painkillers. Evidently things had healed enough."

They moved Paul on to McGuire General Hospital in Richmond, Virginia. Kay joined him as soon as she could. "Paul's mother and I stopped in Washington to change trains," Kay recalls. "There was a soldier there, an amputee, walking on crutches. I followed him around just to get myself braced up, because I didn't know what an amputee looked like. I had seen people, but had never really paid much attention to artificial legs or anything like that. So I followed this soldier around just to prepare myself for when I would see Paul."

How would Paul look? Well, he had a mustache, his very first. His weight had dropped from about 150 pounds to 125. ("Of course I'd lost the leg, so maybe that was fifteen of the pounds," Paul explains.) And the hospital pajamas that he wore had the empty left leg tied up, "so I guess it was a kind of shock to Kay when she saw me underweight, with a mustache, and a knot where my leg had been."

Kay agrees: "When we walked in, that's when I got the shock of him sitting there in the wheelchair and looking so thin. Then the next day his mother and I came to see him. I said to his mother, 'Gee, he looks so much better already, and we've only been here one day.' Well, the reason he looked so much better was because he'd shaved off the mustache."

The hospital was just setting up its limb and brace shop, so Paul began to speculate about a replacement limb. "I really didn't know what an artificial leg looked like," Paul says. "I'd seen pictures but didn't know too much about how they were held on, how they worked. I wanted to see the shop and so did Kay, so one evening she wheeled me to it. But we couldn't see in. So I conned her into standing on a ladder so she could look in the transom over the door and describe what she saw—an artificial foot over here, a part of a leg over there." Paul shakes his head. "That's how naive we were at that time."

Kay stayed at a rooming house near the hospital. Paul was restless, so she bought equipment for hooking rugs, and the two hooked by the hour. In another revision, surgeons took more bone from Paul's leg. Then in July, Paul and Kay went back to Cleveland.

His 1938 Hudson Terraplane was waiting. Company officials and employees at Tinnerman Products, where Paul had worked, solved a major problem for Paul: how to depress the clutch pedal. They used a steering-post clamp, a piece of brass, and a rod with a roller at the bottom and a handle at the top to make a gadget that let Paul push the clutch pedal out with his hand. "The day I came home I could drive," he says. "George Tinnerman and several of the workers came over, and they were so proud of that."

Paulette was born while Paul was still home on leave. He held his daughter for just five minutes and then had to return to the hospital in Virginia. Back at McGuire, Paul learned that the limb and brace shop had a two-month lag on the delivery of prostheses. To lend a hand and make time pass he asked to help out. The reply from the man in charge of the shop was a qualified okay: "He said, 'It takes eight years to become a fitter.' He didn't know if I could help. I said, 'I can file, and rivet, and hacksaw. I'm sure I can be of some help.' He agreed.

"I'd worked in this facility about two weeks," Paul continues, "and he realized I was being considerable help. So he said, 'Paul, how about us building your limb?' I said, 'Oh, that's great!' I helped him, and he fit me. When I got the limb I started walking on it and receiving gait training in the therapy department. But all of my spare time I still worked in the facility there."

Paul began to fit artificial limbs to the patients. "I had more time," he says, "and wasn't really working under supervision because I wasn't getting paid. So I rounded the corners and paid more attention to the little details. The officers on my ward found out and wanted me to fit them with limbs."

In time the doctor asked Paul to make the rounds with him to check the amputees with prostheses: "One day he asked me about this one gentleman who had the first limb delivered in the hospital. He'd had problems. I said, 'Well, if you take his limb off and stand him up and look at him, his stump goes to the outside, it doesn't go straight down. When you look down into the prosthesis, the socket doesn't go like his stump. I think the socket should be tipped out.' So he said, 'Go ahead.' I did. To my surprise and everyone else's, the patient was much more comfortable."

Paul spent Thanksgiving leave in Cleveland, and his wife invited guests over. Kay reconstructs the evening: "He had just received his leg a few weeks before that, and was walking with a cane, was very upright, very cautious. We had all our friends get together. They were very uncomfortable when they first saw Paul—not knowing what to say, seeing him this way.

"It was to be a potluck dinner," Kay continues. "One friend brought ice cream. She was so nervous about seeing Paul that she laid the ice cream on the floor next to her—she was sitting on the davenport. And the ice cream got softer and softer. That's how upset people were, apprehensive.

"Paul was very good about it," Kay says. Her eyes light up as she recalls how her husband handled the situation. "He said, 'You know, you guys have probably never seen an artificial leg.' So he unzipped his pants, took them off, and walked up and down in his shorts, showed them how the leg operated and how the ankle worked, how everything worked. After that, the whole group just sat back in their chairs and heaved a sigh of relief. Paul completely broke the ice. In fact, later on when he'd demonstrate his leg to nurses, he would drop his pants like that every now and then and show them the leg. I would tell him, 'Be sure you're wearing shorts that are ironed.'"

Adrian Wheeler started for the States on New Year's Eve—the day Paul Leimkuehler had sailed out of New York Harbor for Europe. Leaving England, Wheeler traveled light. For his uniform he wore a pair of hospital pajamas. His luggage was a blood-plasma box that they'd first tied to his chest after they'd cut off his clothes at the field hospital. His belongings: watch, knife, billfold, pocket New Testament, medical records, and a piece of gauze-wrapped shrapnel—"the only souvenir I got out of Germany."

Wheeler's train to the north reached Prestwick, Scotland, just after the hospital ship *Aquitania* headed out to sea. So they carried him aboard a plane bound for Andrews Air Force Base, near Washington, D.C. Ship or plane, it didn't matter to him—nothing for him to see in either case. The trip wasn't entirely routine. They made an emergency stop before the flight legs to the Azores and Bermuda. Supper in Bermuda. While they led Wheeler to the mess hall he formed his main impression of the island—it was warm and balmy. Next a snowstorm in the Washington area diverted them to La Guardia, where they landed twenty-three hours after leaving Scotland.

At Mitchell Field's hospital, a woman brought a portable telephone and helped him call his wife, Lib, and it didn't cost him a cent. But Wheeler hadn't known his next destination until just before the plane left. To keep Lib posted, he persuaded a sergeant to send a telegram: He would be going to Dibble General Hospital, Menlo Park, California—to a ward with forty other GIs, all but four totally blind.

"A doctor examined Ade's eyes soon after Ade got there," Lib says. "He told Ade that he couldn't do anything for him, he would never see again. A week or so later a psychiatrist had Ade come into his office. As soon as he got into the room the doctor said, 'Do you know you're blind and you'll never see again?' Ade said, 'I know it, and it's just by the grace of God that I'm alive.' Ade didn't have to go to the psychiatrist again."

Adrian thought the psychiatrist was testing him. But for this patient such testing was unnecessary. Lieutenant Tommy Thompson, that nurse in England, was right—Adrian would never commit suicide. He'd gone well beyond just facing up to his blindness. He wanted to get on with his life. And he especially wanted to get home to Lib and his son Tom.

In February, Wheeler caught a C-47 for a thirty-day furlough. He and another blind GI persuaded the crew to take along a Red Cross worker just back from Leyte. They figured they could help her out by claiming they needed her as an escort. In Utah the plane switched pilots and picked up B-29 parts. Just room for the cargo, so passengers had to debark. But Wheeler and his two companions stayed on. "The lieutenant who flew us in from San Francisco cussed out the captain taking over," he chuckles, "and persuaded him to take us along"—the only passengers, all the way to Chicago.

When his furlough ended, Adrian, Lib, and two-year-old Tom left for California. Another month and the Army transferred Wheeler to Old Farms Convalescent Hospital at Avon, Connecticut, for rehabilitation training.

"Old lady Whitney of Pratt and Whitney built Old Farms as a prep school for rich kids in the '20s," Adrian says. "It was built on a quadrangle style, like Oxford University. It had big wooden beams in the ceilings, the beds were built in the walls, and it had winding staircases like an old castle. It was a beautiful place. If you had to go to school you couldn't beat it—it was like being on vacation."

Old Farms was nearly fifteen miles from Hartford, where Lib and Tom stayed, and everything was expensive there. So after a week Adrian's wife and son went back to Indiana. When Lib managed to get back for a week around Adrian's birthday, June 8, she found that he had settled in for his last few months in the Army.

His companions were other servicemen who had also lost their sight—people like Raymond Rhodie, who'd been blinded by a mine. Wheeler reports a conversation when the CQ found Rhodie under his bed with a flashlight: "The CQ said, 'What are you doing there?' Rhodie said, 'I'm looking for my eyes.' 'What color?' 'Must be polka-dot, 'cause that's what I see.'"

At Old Farms, Wheeler, like Rhodie, gained a different perspective. And relying on old skills, he also acquired new ones. "I've always been fortunate with my memory," Wheeler points out. "I could name from memory the items on a shelter half. I'm sure glad, 'cause everything has to go that way now. I already knew touch typing. In '35 and '36 I'd learned on the new Royal that had glass keys, no letters on it. So I at least knew the feel. I did a lot of typing for guys in the dormitory.

"I took shop. That's what I knew at home. But they couldn't take care of me on anything advanced, so they sent me and two other fellows in to Hartford, to the high school. I operated lathes and automatic milling machines. That's why, when I came back to Indiana to go to work at the shop, I knew I could do it. But they wouldn't believe me. That hurt worse than anything. . . . That was a hard thing to face when we got home."

Gerhard Tebbe

Campbell and Leinbaugh

Bill Masters

Frank Gonzales

Paul Dulin

Fred Olson

Frenchy Lariviere

Mike DeBello

Max Sobel

Lathariel Barnes

Ervin Frankenberry

Howard Broderick

Don Okenfuss

Paul Leimkuehler

Fred Flanagan

James Huffstutter, Bill Reynolds, and J. A. Craft

Edward (Len) Erickson

Gene Amici

My Jesus have mercy on the soul of

Sgt. John A. Bowe Jr.
Born August 27, 1924
Killed In Action February 28, 1945

Greater love hath no man
than he give his life
for his country

John A. Bowe, Jr., KIA

Jim Sterner

Don Stauffer and Jim Sterner

Melvin Cline and Carl (Curly) Hoffman

One of our men returns to the Ardennes.

18

TO THE RHINE AND THE ELBE

During the Hehler-Hardt battle, nine men from K Company were killed, twenty-three wounded, and a half-dozen more evacuated with blast injuries or minor wounds. In Item Company four men were killed and eleven wounded; in the rest of the battalion four men were wounded. Our battalion's S3 journal claims the Third Battalion captured between three hundred and four hundred prisoners on February 28, surely an exaggeration. K Company's morning report for the 28th read: "Moved up on foot into the attack. Leaving 0800."

One of every four men who went into the attack that last day of February became a casualty—in less than six hours K Company lost the equivalent of a full platoon. The next morning we walked the fields—the bodies of twenty-five German paratroopers lay sprawled on the muddy ground or slumped in foxholes. More had been wounded and evacuated through our aid station. K Company sent at least fifty prisoners to PW cages.

If the tanks had arrived on time, if a spotter plane had been overhead, if our flanks had been secured, if Gieszl could have called in artillery at the outset of the attack—the battle might have been decided more quickly and at far less cost; but we had no time for useless speculation.

The morning after the battle the Third Battalion passed into regimental reserve, and as Goodwin recalls, "What was left of our company got in open squad columns and started advancing. When we started out I saw a

German civilian lying in a beet field. It looked like someone had taken a saw and sawed the top of his head right off."

K Company walked from Hochfeld to Mackenstein, past dead German soldiers and burned-out tanks and trucks, then headed across flat open fields toward Dülken. The Second Battalion was leading the attack half a mile to our front; at dawn the town had been heavily shelled. Tanks with loudspeakers moved past us. "*Achtung! Achtung!*" carried for miles. Then came the ultimatum. "You have one hour to surrender the city. Hang white flags from your windows. If American troops are fired on, artillery will level the city and Dülken will be attacked with overwhelming strength." Bedsheets began fluttering from upstairs windows, but German troops in the town ignored the ultimatum and at 11:00 the artillery again blasted away. As we watched, Second Battalion skirmishers eased cautiously into houses at the edge of town and down the streets. Within thirty minutes Easy Company was busy mopping up—resistance was negligible.

We moved forward, and again the artillery opened fire, shelling truck convoys retreating to the north. Beyond Dülken's rooftops we saw puffs of steam from a locomotive. As the train pulled out the German engineer sounded a mournful blast of the whistle—a strangely incongruous, civilized intrusion in the midst of battle. The familiar sound echoing across the plain made us homesick.

K Company walked into Dülken and moved into a block of substantial concrete buildings. Minutes later we heard a loud explosion and cries for medics. The building, housing a squad from the second platoon, was a smoldering ruin. Rex Scott and James Suggs were seriously wounded. Kermit Hagy, crumpled in the corner of the room under a pile of bricks and timbers, had been killed instantly. Nick Scalzi and Guy McWreath were less seriously hurt. A German soldier, bypassed in the mop-up, must have fired a Panzerfaust through the window. We searched the area but found no one. Hagy, from Abingdon, Virginia, was one of the new men, a replacement who had been with K Company for five weeks.

After moving into Bistard beyond Dülken that night, we were awakened at 1:00 A.M. and told we had to make a forced march to seize a concrete bridge, strong enough to support tanks, over the Niers Canal. The orders contained the familiar appendage—the bridge must be taken "at all costs"—but by this time in the war we ignored such verbiage. Heading out in the black, we blundered our way through hedgerows, across fences, through streams and fields, staying off the main highways. We heard German convoys moving along nearby roads, but nothing more menacing than curious Holsteins delayed our advance. With the first streaks of light we reached the canal and found the bridge intact. The lead platoon double-timed across and ran through the small town of

Vorst. The town was undefended; frightened civilians peered at us from behind blackout curtains as we lined up in the streets for breakfast.

The local burgermeister came to the CP to explain the town had one small factory, a machine shop. "It is vital to the village's economy," he told Leinbaugh, "that the factory keep operating." Bocarski, serving as translator, asked several questions, then laughed. The machine shop made nose-cone assemblies for 88 shells.

We pushed forward another five miles to Unterweiden near Krefeld and ran clear off our maps.

Although the breakthrough had become a rout, K Company was involved in a firefight with a small German force after nightfall. Five Germans on bicycles followed by fifteen infantrymen barged into the middle of the company column. A point-blank exchange of rifle fire and grenades lasted several minutes. Four men, including Lieutenant Masters, were slightly wounded by grenade fragments. Several Germans were shot; the rest surrendered. We were lost. We weren't sure where we were, and weren't sure where we were going. The problem was solved by persuading a captured German sergeant to guide us to our objective, where he helped talk a small batch of German paratroopers into surrendering.

The brief engagement's postmortem involved checking Bill Masters's field jacket, which was ripped open and oozing red. Unbuttoning the jacket revealed shrapnel had ripped open a can of C-ration stew Bill had stashed between his shirt and his jacket.

On March 3 the company walked four miles to Krefeld, a city of 160,000 where we found billets—our most luxurious quarters of the entire war. We moved into an undamaged high-rise apartment, waved the owners to the streets, and discovered electricity, hot water, working toilets, and telephones with dial tones.

We had time for hot baths—the first good soaking since our visit to the mine showers in Holland in November. We found a cache of black cigars and bottles of cognac. Bocarski lit up, sat down in an easy chair, got a befuddled German operator on the phone, and bullied his way through to a military headquarters in Berlin. He told the German officer he could expect K Company within the week.

By nightfall on the 5th of March, the 84th Division had cleared the west bank of the Rhine and held a sector between Rheinhausen and Homburg across the river from Duisburg. In ten days the Railsplitters, attacking almost due north, had advanced forty-five miles between the Roer and the Rhine and captured more than five thousand Germans. Hundreds more were killed and wounded. The Ninth Army's drive involved ten divisions; together they took more than thirty thousand German prisoners and captured or destroyed quantities of tanks, trucks, and artillery.

During our first days along the river, white sheets hung from the windows of houses on the far bank, and we knew the Rhine could have been crossed in our area practically without opposition. Two days later seizure of the bridge at Remagen gave the American First Army the honor of establishing the first bridgehead across the Rhine; we were quite content to sit out the hard fighting on the far bank.

By every sensible measure the war was over. The Russians were on the Oder concentrating forces for the drive on Berlin. The German armies in the west were shattered beyond repair, the major cities in the Third Reich were in ruins, the Luftwaffe had all but disappeared. We expected the Germans to sue for peace any day, but like everybody else we underestimated Hitler's fanatical grip on the German nation. So we sat and waited on the west bank of the Rhine for nearly a month and the war went on.

We wrote letters home, slept in undamaged houses, went to movies, and to Paris, Brussels, and rest areas in Holland on leave. For the first time during the war we were occupying a heavily inhabited area—nonfraternization rules were stringently enforced. While Hitler had called on civilians to prey on Allied troops, we found the Germans in our area docile and outwardly cooperative.

Army regulations permitted mailing Nazi souvenirs home—flags, daggers, and uniform items bearing swastika emblems—but mailing loot— nonmilitary items such as cameras, jewelry, and other small valuables— was strictly prohibited. Ciccotello and company lieutenants inspected outgoing parcels, and a certifying officer's signature was required before any packages could be mailed.

We practiced firing captured German Panzerfausts, the German antitank weapon, a more efficient and powerful weapon than our bazooka, and battalion even issued a training schedule, which we totally ignored. We received a few random artillery rounds every day, but lived in comparative luxury. The company's OP, providing a clear view across the Rhine, was a sofa behind an unbroken picture window.

During our weeks on the Rhine, K Company's mess sergeant was the sole casualty. He was wounded by a stray shell while bringing up food in a jeep. We figured his departure could only improve the quality of our daily meals, and Lance's reaction, "Now there's a German gunner who's really on our side," was typical.

Our weapons platoon was upstaged when artillerymen emplaced a big 8-incher between two ruined buildings in the company area. Mel Cline fired a round at the Krupp works in Essen, but decided he preferred his M1: "The recoil, the cloud of smoke and dust and the concussion were unbelievable." Our visitors, in addition to the artillerymen, included Red Cross girls driving doughnut trucks, and Lily Pons and her husband, André Kostelanetz, who entertained the Railsplitters at a concert and fired a captured 88 across the river.

It was a toss-up whether the German civilians or the visiting colonels were the biggest nuisance. Since the giant levees bordering the river offered immunity from small-arms fire, and German artillery was practically nonexistent, the brass decided it would be a good time to inspect the rifle companies. We tried to be sociable and offered tours along the top of the embankment where we kept our outposts, but found most visitors lacking in curiosity. Jarvis, Broderick, Dunn, and Crookshank got special training in boat handling for a patrol across the river, but to their relief the trip was canceled at the last moment.

On Friday night, the 23rd of March, we listened to the massive artillery bombardment to the north where Montgomery's Twenty-first Army Group and two U.S. Ninth Army divisions crossed the Rhine near Wesel. George Gehrman, a K Company cook, had experience handling small boats on the Chesapeake; he volunteered as a crewman and helped ferry U.S. assault troops across the river.

On April 1 our division was motorized and rode in 264 two-and-a-halfs to Wesel. We drove past seagoing Landing Craft Infantry, and saw our first sailors since crossing the Channel. In recognition of their cooperation at the crossing site, we yelled, "Fuck the Navy," as we drove past.

A traffic jam in the west-bank assembly area was caused by three-wheeled German vehicles which had been commandeered during the drive from the Roer to the Rhine. The three-wheelers couldn't navigate the two-track treadways and were reluctantly abandoned by their new owners on the west bank, filling a three-acre parking lot. At dusk when our convoy edged slowly across the three-hundred-yard river on pontoons, the crossing area was lit by giant floodlights so engineers could work around the clock on permanent bridges. We were amazed that the engineers no longer considered the German air force a threat.

Front-line troops had pushed ahead nearly thirty-five miles beyond the Rhine by the time the 84th assembled on the east bank. Our column, headed by the 5th Armored, was followed by the 84th, with the 102nd, our sister division, bringing up the rear.

As our miles-long convoy passed a line of hills, several rifle shots cracked overhead and we saw puffs of smoke from positions near a hilltop. Our trucks braked to a quick stop and a thousand M1s returned the fire. In a minute, a white handkerchief waved vigorously from a foxhole, and two bedraggled Germans, hands in the air, came stumbling and running down the hill to appreciative cheers. We drove on, leaving the two standing forlornly in a ditch.

We passed groups of displaced persons and watched as they squatted along the autobahn feasting on butchered German army horses; we tossed them K rations and cigarettes. Our route skirted the north side of the Ruhr valley just south of Münster. Our battalion did not see action until we reached Bielefeld on April 4 and skirmished briefly with German delaying forces on the town's outskirts. Then we were involved in squelching a riot involving hundreds of displaced persons rampaging through a flour mill and food stores. When K Company arrived, most of the rioters were roaring drunk. The division then attacked toward Hannover, the twelfth-largest German city. The city fell on April 10, and the *New York Times* rewarded the Railsplitters with front-page headlines.

On April 6, K Company was ordered to take over guard duty at division headquarters and three men from the company were picked in the division's first Stateside rotation. Captain Gieszl, Johnny Radovich, and Orville McClure were the lucky ones. "I was standing guard duty," Radovich remembers, "when Sergeant Smart came up and told me to get my gear together, that I was heading home on rotation that night. I didn't believe him, of course, but it was true. I couldn't believe it." When Gieszl left, Leinbaugh again took over as CO, but several days later he was assigned to liaison duty with XIII Corps headquarters, and Lieutenant Masters became company commander.

George Pope and Keith Lance received their battlefield commissions, and Baptie and Lucht were accepted for the ETO's Officers Candidate School at Fontainebleau. After twelve weeks' absence they would return to the regiment with second lieutenant's bars and be assigned as platoon leaders in our regiment's First Battalion.

After several days of headquarters guard duty, Masters checked with the sergeant who ran the division mess to see if he could wangle hot food for the company. We had been living on K and C rations, while headquarters personnel received their usual three hot meals a day. Within an hour the headquarters commandant ordered the division cooks out of bed and gave them an hour to prepare a hot meal for the K Company men. For the rest of the tour the company got hot food. Masters remembers one company rifleman being requested to recite the General Orders by the division's chief of staff. Knowledge of the eleven orders—to take charge of this post and all government property in view, to walk my post in a military manner, etc. etc.—was somewhat less pertinent than knowledge of the Ten Commandments, but typical of rear-echelon hazards encountered by the company.

A few days before the war was over, Brewer unburdened himself in a letter home which was printed in the *Philadelphia Bulletin*. "I do believe that these Germans are touched with the madness of militarism. I think it was Clemenceau who said one could do one of two things with a mad dog—shoot him, or lock him up—and since we aren't sufficiently barbaric to liquidate the race, what else remains? . . . It is horrible, a real Götterdämmerung, and it will take everything the world has, and then some, to set us to rights again. And we must use intelligence, not emotion. Pity is as destructive as hatred, and far more insidious, and if we aren't careful it will sink us after the war is over . . . One sees the Hitler Jugend who have no conception of any other standard than force and war (one of them, twelve years old, wounded one of our officers the other day). . . . I am convinced, of course, that education is the only hope; but it is a very long-term project, and meanwhile we must be firm with present generations, for I think there is no hope of doing anything with the Germans, en masse, above probably ten years of age. You people at home must remember that; you must refuse to be sucked in on reducing the severity or the duration of the life sentence which this nation must receive. This has nothing to do with revenge. It is, I am convinced, a purely realistic policy and our only feasible alternative."

While on liaison duty with XIII Corps headquarters, Leinbaugh heard of atrocities at Gardelegen and drove to the town, which had been captured hours earlier. Retreating SS troops had herded more than six hundred prisoners, mostly Russians and Poles, into a large tile barn and set fire to hay in the barn with Very pistols. That night Leinbaugh ate with a French commando, a naval officer who had parachuted into occupied France before D-Day as a saboteur. In a letter he explained, "He was the only survivor and pretty much of a wreck—he knows the only solution is practically annihilation of the Krauts. They've degenerated into a state lower than animals. . . . I never knew what hate was till I saw what remains of those poor devils." The French survivor had crawled to the door to breathe and piled bodies over himself to escape the flames. The dead men were little more than skeletons, but some had clawed holes with bare hands through the tile walls of the barn and thrust their heads through the holes. Each skull bore a single bullet hole. Inside the barn GIs pressed wet handkerchiefs to their faces—the stench of burning flesh was overwhelming. The 84th and other divisions sent truckloads of men to see the bodies, and German civilians within walking distance were herded gagging and vomiting through the barn.

During the three-week 250-mile drive to the Elbe, the 84th gathered in more than sixty thousand prisoners—the equivalent of half a dozen combat divisions. Many PWs were merely waved to the rear along the autobahn without escort. Others were collected in huge wire enclosures several acres in size, and in an ingenious scheme to save time, our engineers drove around the PWs dropping off barbed wire and posts and then supervised while the prisoners fenced themselves into their own enclosures.

For recreation we ran contests to see how many PWs could be packed into a two-and-a-half-ton truck. The trick was to fill the truck, have the driver quickly accelerate and throw on the brakes, and then shove more prisoners over the tailgate. As best we remember the all-time record was seventy PWs in a single truck.

And while diehard bands of Germans continued the fight, even at the Elbe, K Company escaped further casualties. We spent the last days of the war waiting to meet the Russians.

19

WHEN THE WAR WAS OVER

May 8, 1945, was VE Day, but for the men in K Company the war had ended a month earlier when we were assigned guard duty at division headquarters. When the Germans formally surrendered we were in Salz-wedel near the Elbe, seventy-five miles from Berlin.

We had survived, and we knew the importance of writing letters home so families and girlfriends would receive letters postmarked after VE Day. The transition to peace took time—it was a week before we drove our jeeps at night with headlights and remembered we no longer needed blackout curtains covering the windows of our billets.

Al Oyler had a double reason to celebrate, since May 8 was his twenty-fourth birthday: "It was a good excuse to try and drink enough schnapps for both celebrations." And Dunn was wondering, "Are they going to send us back to the States for leave and then on to the Pacific, or are we going to stay over here and pull occupation duty?"

News of the unconditional surrender first came to us over the German radio at Flensburg. After the Allied High command confirmed the surrender details, we listened to Churchill and the newscasters and then left our radios and went out in the streets of Salzwedel to celebrate. "For a while it was like the Fourth of July," Keller says. "Everybody was firing their weapons but matters began to get out of hand, and orders came down to cut out the shooting." And the first sergeant almost became K Company's last casualty. He was walking around the back of a building when someone threw a grenade out a window. "I heard the handle snap, but there was no explosion."

Olson remembers twin .50s on the two-and-a-halfs firing "V for Victory" tracers in the sky, but division quickly ordered a halt, and company officers were sent to the platoon areas to stop the celebrations. The platoon sergeants, Augustin remembers, ordered everybody to clean his weapon "in a hell of a hurry" so if battalion or regiment checked, "they couldn't prove we'd been firing."

The company had been allocated 117 bottles of wine from a storehouse in Krefeld—most everybody got either drunk or sick. But there wasn't much we could do to celebrate. No flags, no church bells, no pretty girls to kiss. We had guard duty to pull and sent out jeep and foot patrols to bring in German army stragglers and enforce curfew regulations for German civilians and displaced persons.

The *Stars and Stripes* Victory Extra on Tuesday, May 8, 1945, headlined, "Nazis Quit!" and quoted orders from Doenitz for the German armed forces to lay down their arms. Later, when magazines from the States arrived, we were irked by the photographs of GIs celebrating in Times Square—guys playing heroes who'd never been closer to the front than Camp Kilmer, New Jersey.

On May 2, a patrol from our regiment's Second Battalion had met a Soviet reconnaisance troop on the east side of the Elbe. Later that evening our commanding general met with senior Russian officers and made arrangements for a formal ceremony the next day to celebrate the historic juncture. Several thousand German soldiers, hoping to cross the Elbe and become American prisoners, witnessed the meeting.

During the next few days, senior Russian officers from Cossack and Russian Guard divisions held meetings with our division staff and exchanged medals and gifts. Our regimental commander presented his Russian counterpart with a newly painted American jeep and in return received a handsome Russian cavalry stallion.

K Company, in uniforms hurriedly dry-cleaned in gasoline, lined up in the background and watched the ceremonies and the exchange of medals. It never occurred to us that the men who actually had done the fighting should be receiving the decorations. We exchanged cigarettes with Russian soldiers, fired each other's weapons, and communicated with the help of men in the company who knew a smattering of Russian. Our only argument dealt with the Russians' jeeps, which we insisted had been built in Detroit. They argued the jeeps had been built in Russia, in factories behind the Urals.

Olson remembers a high-ranking Russian officer who visited our division headquarters with a bloody bandage on one arm. He had obviously been severely wounded, but we were told the Russians did not evacuate their casualties unless they were unable to function in combat. And we were surprised to see a number of burly Russian women in uniform accompanying the headquarters troops.

In Salzwedel we visited a small-arms munitions factory, a so-called work camp, operated by three thousand women slave laborers. Though malnourished and living in filthy barracks, these women considered themselves privileged prisoners compared with those working in the extermination camps. Their barracks, surrounded by barbed wire, were burned and the women transferred to a former German air force barracks, where division medics placed them on carefully controlled diets.

Several weeks later when Russian troops moved into Salzwedel we had our first look at our combat counterparts, Russian infantry and tankers. The first Russian tank that rolled into our area was pulling four German farm wagons loaded with loot—chests of drawers, kitchen equipment, and box springs and mattresses. The Russian GIs were a tough, hard-looking lot, and the German civilians were terrified when they drove into Salzwedel. Hundreds of frightened German women and old men who tried to flee toward the British and American zones were turned around at roadblocks and ordered back to their homes.

After being relieved by Russian troops in our sector, which was to become part of the permanent Russian occupation zone, we left Salzwedel and moved back near Hannover before our trip to southern Germany, where we would become part of the occupation forces.

On VE Day, men from K Company were scattered from the Elbe to California. George Gieszl was at Ft. Hood, Texas. Jim Sterner was in Le Havre on his way back to the company from a hospital in England. Bob Martin was also in Le Havre, but heading west, back to the States. Don Phelps, after his discharge from a hospital in England, was placed on limited service and spent VE Day in the railway marshaling yards outside Paris. John Campbell was in London's Piccadilly Circus, and Mario Lage was at the Waldorf in New York. Bruce Morrell was in Marseilles with an Italian prisoner of war construction crew. Sabia was undergoing rehabilitation therapy in England, and more men were in general hospitals in both Paris and England.

Claudie Daniell, Charlie Sullivan, Bob Schiedel, Clayton Shepherd, Ed Erickson, Adrian Wheeler, Bill Parsons, Richard Heuer, Rex Scott, and a dozen more were in hospitals in the States.

At Ft. Hood, an officers' reenlistment board tried to persuade George Gieszl to sign on for another three years in the Army, but with the Okinawa campaign in full swing and knowing the chronic shortage of rifle company commanders, George decided it would make a lot more sense to get back to college.

In London, Campbell joined the mob at Piccadilly Circus and watched while the crowd at Buckingham Palace chanted "We want the King!" That night London crowds burned giant bonfires in the parks, British bombers lit up the night with flares, and the blackout ended.

In New York, Mario Lage was at the Waldorf after traveling along the East Coast with other bemedaled officers on a bond drive. Mario headed out of his hotel with an airline stewardess for something to eat and became part of the celebration. "Hey, I kissed all the broads on the street."

Jim Sterner remembers the excitement at the cigarette camps on the hills around Le Havre. "The Frenchmen went wild, blowing horns and ringing bells," Sterner says, "but then rumors spread that everybody in the reinforcement depots would be shipped off to Japan, which dampened our enthusiasm in a hurry."

Don Phelps and the men in his replacement pool broke into a boxcar loaded with wine casks and held their own VE Day celebration among the 40-and-8s.

Bob Martin, who had been a prisoner of war for five months, was freed by advancing Russians from the prison camp in Neubrandenburg north of Berlin early in April. By mid-June he was back home in California, minus his front teeth and thirty pounds.

"Two nights before we were liberated," he recalls, "British planes parachuted food into the prison camp, and by the next day the guards were gone. The Russians approached during the night, and though Neubrandenburg had been declared an open city, a few diehard Germans, twelve-year-olds and old men, decided to defend the city. The Russians just lined up their rocket guns and leveled the damned place, absolutely leveled it."

When Martin went into the city the next day, "I didn't even recognize the place. There were tons of dead people." Neubrandenburg was a hospital center. "The Germans were trying to get these wounded out on trains and there was just piles of bodies along the railroad like you're waiting for a train, except they were all dead."

The Russians moved the prisoners to a nearby school, "pretty brick buildings with hot water, and we got Red Cross parcels that the Germans had withheld from us." Martin was with the Russians for nearly a month. "They couldn't do enough for us. Then a British jeep and truck came through bringing food and clothes and got everybody's names. The Russians took us to the British lines, but before they turned us over they had this elaborate banquet set up, tables out in the open underneath the trees with all the vodka you wanted to drink." The British processed the prisoners and flew them to Camp Lucky Strike at Le Havre, where they spent VE Day.

When Martin had been captured and wounded in Würm he was carried on a stretcher to the rear under guard. "It really pissed me off; they had a bunch of guards that looked like they were twelve-year-olds. And a funny thing, for two or three years in the Army I'd always been carrying a gun, and now all of a sudden I wasn't carrying a gun. That was the thing I remember."

Martin was first taken to a prisoner camp near Cologne and then sent to a Gestapo camp near Bremen. He was interrogated there by a German colonel who had lived across the street from him when the German had been an exchange student at Stanford in Palo Alto. "We knew the same people. He asked me about the American family he'd been living with. I told him the boys in the family were flying bombers over Germany, but I actually had no idea what they were really doing."

Martin's interrogation proved routine. "They just told us we'd stay in isolation until we told everything we knew. The interrogators knew all about the 84th, when we left the States, the names of our ships, everything about us." After giving up on the questioning, the Germans sent Martin and a group of prisoners to Neubrandenburg. "I got sent out to work on farms, five or ten of us under guard, in what they called commandos. We'd volunteer for these work details, because that's how you got something to eat, the same food the farmers ate. The farmers knew the war was going to be over soon and didn't treat us badly; we even rode first-class on the trains back and forth to the farms. The thing that scared us more than anything was getting caught in one of our own bombings."

Late in the war, after Martin's family received word he was missing in action, his family began receiving anonymous hate mail with swastikas from New Jersey and New York. "These letters said your son is a prisoner and is over there in Germany for no reason, that sort of crap."

From Le Havre Martin sailed to Norfolk and called his mother in California. "But I was so anxious to get home that I didn't tell anybody I was coming and just walked up to my house at nine o'clock at night and rang the doorbell. I weighed about 129 pounds, had no front teeth, and a bandage around my head. I scared the hell out of my family."

After reaching our first occupation area in Dossenheim, north of Heidelberg, Oyler, Brewer, and the CO paid a courtesy call on the local office of military government. "We walked upstairs in this large government building," Oyler recalls, "and went into the burgermeister's office. A pompous heavyset German fellow was sitting at the main desk obviously in charge, and a young American first lieutenant and his sergeant assistant were at little desks off in the corner behind him. We had that office reorganized in two minutes flat—the American officer at the front desk running things, and the German very much subdued, back in the corner."

Postwar discipline—keeping two hundred healthy young GIs with time on their hands out of trouble—proved a major headache. K Company maintained a training program of sorts, and the Army set up trade schools and university classes, formed divisional baseball and football teams, and instituted liberal leave programs. But getting drunk, and brawling with civilians or rear-echelon types, remained a problem for all the companies in the division. KP duty and restriction to the company area for a week were punishment handed out for minor infractions. Digging a hole six feet square and six feet deep and then refilling it, together with forfeiture of pay, was reserved for more serious infractions.

Maintaining permanent guard posts, including one at the VD hospital in Weinheim, was part of K Company's occupation responsibilities. "We got a little lax and didn't check the guards like we should have," Lance remembers, "so Bocarski and I decided to check, and the first stop we made was where this fellow Mike was supposed to be on guard. I got out of the jeep, and of course, he's supposed to challenge me. I just kept getting closer, and finally I said, 'Now Mike, if you don't challenge me, I'm going to bust you up the side of the head with this rifle,' and this guy says, '*Nicht verstehe.*'"

Bocarski questioned the man in German. "He was the younger brother of Mike's girlfriend, and Mike had given him his rifle, helmet, and field jacket, and had him standing guard while Mike was in bed with the guy's sister." Lance and Bocarski rousted Mike out of bed and found his excuse reasonably forthright—"Well, we whipped 'em, and should be able to do anything with them we want to." Rather than a court-martial, Mike received a heavy dose of company punishment.

After VE Day when Fred Olson was promoted to buck sergeant he went to Lieutenant Lance for advice. "I don't know anything about being a sergeant—what am I supposed to do?" Lance had the answer: "Just don't tell anyone you don't know, and you'll get along just fine." But shortly afterward, when inspecting the second platoon, Fred encountered his first disciplinary problem in the person of Private L. D. Edwards, a rawboned soldier from Texas. "I looked at his boots, which were partially laced and dirty. I told Edwards this, and he looked me straight in the eye. 'Sergeant Olson,' he says, 'if you want my goddam boots shined you'll have to shine them yourself.'"

Daily training sessions were held on a pleasant hillside east of our billets in Weinheim, in the shadow of an ancient Roman watchtower positioned on the line of long hills behind the town. The training area had been carefully selected to provide good observation, and guard posts were established to warn of the approach of battalion or regimental officers. We spent most of our time writing letters, reading, and sunbathing, and followed a serious training schedule only when we saw visitors approaching.

An hour every morning was spent in physical training, and Lieutenant Masters and Lieutenant Lance introduced the new men to the intricacies of handling the company's 60mm mortars and .30 caliber lights. Additional time was devoted to basic military tactics, and hours were spent lecturing on rules and regulations governing relationships with the Germans, displaced persons, and the role of military government.

*   *   *

The Army's postwar nonfraternization policies were first relaxed on July 20, according to an announcement in our division newspaper. The new policy allowed GIs to speak with German adults and children on streets and in public places, but the article noted, "You CANNOT shake hands with Germans, visit with them in their homes, attend dances or social events, drink with them, or engage in games or sports with Germans." At the next company meeting the new edict was discussed in some detail. General agreement was reached that you didn't have to shake hands, dance, or drink with a German girl to have a good time.

When we received a supply of athletic equipment, the local burgermeister was told the company was starting an athletic program for children at the local sportzplatz. At eight the next morning the burgermeister reported at our CP leading a column of village youngsters lined in marching order by height. The regimentation was too much for the first sergeant. Keller dispersed the ranks of children and after berating the confused burgermeister had Brewer explain that the kids could wander down to the sportzplatz anytime they pleased—but no more schedules, no more marching, no more orders.

In August, following the Potsdam Conference, President Harry Truman, whose nephew was the Railsplitters' chief of staff, reviewed the 84th in Weinheim and lunched at the commanding general's villa. Accompanied by Secretary of State Byrnes, Eisenhower, and other high-ranking officials, Truman drove between miles of Railsplitters lining the roads and reviewed a special honor guard of Missourians, including Alfred O. Oyler, who met and shook hands with the new president.

On Wednesday, August 15, Bill Masters came running into the mess hall with the announcement of the Japanese surrender. Our newspaper, *The Railsplitter*, anticipating the announcement, quickly distributed a Peace Extra with six-and-a-half-inch headline proclaiming, "It's Over!" *Stars and Stripes*, the official daily newspaper of U.S. Armed Forces in the European Theater, carried the headline "Peace" and reported, "The greatest war in the history of mankind came to an end at 1 A.M. this morning (ETO time) when the United States, the Soviet Union, China and Great Britain officially announced that Japan had surrendered unconditionally."

Following VJ Day, everybody's concern was to get back to the States as soon as possible and make up for the time we felt we had wasted in the Army. Eighty-five points were needed to get on a boat for home. The point system, based on time in the service, overseas time, time in combat, and number of children, was as fair as the Army could make it. Each child counted twelve points, campaigns and medals counted five points, and longevity and overseas service were worth a point a month. The system proved reasonably fair, but contained inequities; a Purple Heart was worth the same five points whether for a shrapnel cut on the arm or a bullet wound through the chest.

When John Sabia got back to the company in Weinheim after being discharged from the hospital in England, he reported to the CP and found with his 135 points he could leave the very next day for home.

John went first-class. "Man, what a trip I had coming home. First we flew to North Africa, where the pilot found a problem with his engine so we could stay a couple of days. Then we flew to Buenos Aires, where the engine trouble lasted for a week." When Sabia landed in Miami he had three hundred dollars left from the three thousand he started with. "But I sure as hell had a good two weeks."

Don Phelps worked his way home from Le Havre. "After I left the hospital I was carried on limited duty and was assigned to a headquarters company doing administrative work at the cigarette camps in Le Havre. I heard they needed men for a detail that would get me home, so I volunteered." Four hundred general prisoners who had been convicted of serious crimes in the ETO had to be escorted under heavy guard to prisons back in the States. After requalifying with a .45, Don became a guard on the Liberty ship returning the prisoners to New York.

Men leaving the company on points were reassigned to other units ready for the trip home and ended up spending ten or twelve days on slow Liberty ships. Replacements who had come to the company after the Bulge generally had low point scores and were reassigned to outfits which would be remaining in Europe on occupation duty.

Joe Conner, twice wounded and a father, returned to the States with an artillery unit and was sent to the separation center at Indiantown Gap. When the corporal filling out his discharge forms typed that Conner was with the artillery, Joe raised hell. "You put down there that I was with K Company, 333rd Infantry," he ordered the man. "And he did."

A lot of men in the Army learned a trade, becoming pilots, skilled mechanics, medical orderlies, supply experts, and administrators; but when a rifleman left the service his skills were difficult to transfer to civilian life. We joked we were going to become hit men for the mob, but we actually considered the matter a serious handicap for the future.

Twelve men from K Company formed into a special drill team won battalion, regimental, and divisional competition and were rewarded with a trip to Paris, where they performed the manual of arms to music on stage. Others signed up for special education courses. Mel Cline and Max Sobel went to school in Biarritz, and Morris Dunn signed up for an Army diesel school in England. Paris was the ETO's number-one tourist attraction, but many men, like Bocarski, were bothered by "the rear-echelon guys in Paris with nine-to-five jobs. It would have been better to keep them separated and keep us combat guys together."

Franklin Brewer was the only man in the company with old friends to visit in Paris. In a letter to his sister he commented on "a wonderful vacation. I never dreamed the Army could achieve anything like this, and truth to tell, I doubt if it would be possible except for a few men who, although in uniform, aren't Army." He added his own postwar commentary: "I'm not certain that I've any faith left in anything (don't talk to me about atheists and foxholes!) but if I do, I think it is in the possibilities of human experience and achievement." Continuing, he commented on how devastating it is "for some to realize the idea of God is entirely man-made and it is surely a relief, as Huxley says, to drop the idea altogether and with it the agonizing question of why God permits war." After his return to Weinheim from France, Brewer mentioned his long Paris conversations with his old friend Gertrude Stein, who was to borrow his name for a title role in her book *Brewsie and Willie*.

One of the final commentaries on K Company's stewardship in the Army of Occupation arrived in the form of a letter to the commanding officer from the regimental commander. Forwarded through the commanding officer, Third Battalion, it read in part:

1. Your organization had two cases of gonorrhea during the week of July 22–31. This high venereal rate is among the highest in the regiment, and a majority of other companies have had no cases at all.
2. Your attention is directed to Memorandum No. 60, Headquarters 84th Infantry Division, 23 July 1945, entitled "Venereal Disease Control," and in particular to paragraphs (1), (3), and f, g, h, i, j, k and 3, 5, 7, 8 and 9.
3. Medical authorities are convinced that even in the case of exposure to gonorrhea by sexual contact that the use of a condom and the taking of a prophylaxis by self-administration is practically one hundred percent protection. . . .
4. You personally, and your officers, will give this matter your personal and constant attention. . . .

Two company alumni were married in Europe before returning home. Lieutenant George Lucht and an Army dietitian were married in Heidelberg, and much later Doc Mellon married a German girl in Mannheim after fraternization rules were relaxed.

During the Christmas holidays in 1945, the 84th Division began its trip home. By this time the division and K Company served primarily as carriers for men from throughout the ETO with the same number of points. Only two officers who had served with K Company in combat, Masters and Lance, returned to the States with the company. Oyler was the first sergeant, though three other first sergeants came back with the company. Only a handful of originals returned with the company: Bocarski, Freeman, Musgrave, Smart, Pablo Luera, Curly Hoffman, Max Sobel, and

Lafreniere. Barnes, the jeep driver, Tice, Augustin, and Sterner were also on the return trip, but most of the men were strangers.

K Company traveled home aboard the *Waterbury Victory* and landed in New York, where tugboats hailed the veterans with the traditional water-fountain salutes from fire hoses. The company went to Camp Kilmer, where the division was demobilized during the first days of January 1946, and the men then traveled individually to Army camps near their homes for discharge.

20

HOME AGAIN

The end of the war meant homecoming and the picking up of traces—returning to families and to jobs, or for the younger ones, finding that first "real" job. All who came home would go their separate ways and get on with the business of living.

For most of the ASTP boys, homecoming included getting back to college, more education before careers began. Bruce Baptie couldn't wait to get back to New Haven and Yale. "The war was an interlude," he says. "We were shafted out of four pretty good years. Kids go through a lot of good social experiences between the ages of eighteen and twenty-two. But three or four years out of a life can be a hindrance." Bruce returned less motivated, not as willing to knuckle down unwittingly to authority. "I took a more practical, cynical approach to the fenced-in world of academia. Still, the army was a lark in some ways. It compares with today's kids taking off a year or two; it was a maturing experience for me."

Louis Alicandri, whose family had brought him from Italy to America in 1929, began his postwar career with a change in nationality. He'd earned his U.S. citizenship in combat; the Army gave him his papers when they discharged him.

For Gene Amici, discharge led to a change in career plans. His trade, diamond cutting and polishing, was a good one, "but after the war I just could not ride the subway every day, sit on the same stool and do the same thing day in and day out. After two and one-half years of being on the move, I was restless." So he went to Miami and signed up on the GI

Bill for a trainee job with a tile company, with the government picking up part of his salary.

Back on his father's farm in Mississippi, J. A. Craft found that he was restless. "We'd always been on the move in the Army," he says. "So when I got back home I wanted to ramble. I'd hear a train whistle blow and want to go." But then he married Doris. Craft had gone to school with her. "She was just a friend then; I was going with another girl. But I got a 'Dear John' letter while I was overseas. It didn't bother me. If someone doesn't want me around, I don't want to be around them. I started writing to Doris, and we fell in love and got married."

Clayton Shepherd, returning to civilian life, would have to find a job he could handle even though a portion of a shoulder was missing. At the Army separation center they asked him if he wanted a pension. "I said it don't make no difference to me," Shepherd says. "They started giving me one anyway. Started giving me sixty-nine dollars a month—60 percent. Then they cut it back to 37 percent." Bad shoulder or not, he found work as a laborer, installing drywall plasterboard. It wasn't easy, but he was getting started.

Getting started again didn't mean a clean break with the past. For Ed Stewart, whose friend Johnny Bowe had been killed at Hardt, the past intruded even while he slept. "I dreamed that I was walking over undulating green meadows," he wrote in his journal. "Suddenly I came upon a cemetery with twenty or twenty-five tombstones. I knocked one stone awry, and straightened it, before I was conscious of where I was. I knew the place and had the impression that I had been looking for it. I examined the tombstones until I found a particular one, and I knew that it was my purpose to find it. I was no longer in the sunlight, but in semi-darkness. I was no longer surrounded by tombstones in an open cemetery, but by vaults in a great room of a cathedral . . . looking at the memorial of Johnny Bowe. . . . At the bottom was a Medal of Honor, which was what I intended to find out. I seemed to be satisfied, as if someone had finally done what I had always thought was proper."

The wartime past also unexpectedly returned to Leinbaugh, Lucht, and Campbell after they had gone back to college campuses. Late in 1946 a long-distance call came to Campbell, a graduate student at Harvard. On the line was a man whose son had been killed in the Ardennes. Some "spiritualist adviser" had said that the boy still lived and, though gravely wounded, was being nursed back to health in a monastery somewhere in Europe. The father wanted to believe this story, but must have seen how unlikely it was. So he'd called, hoping for some reason to continue to hope. John had to tell the father that the boy was dead.

The father also called George Lucht at Lawrence College. "I have no idea how the family got my name," George says. "Someone had gotten in touch and said that their son was still alive. If they would give him X number of dollars he would put them in touch with their son. I was infuri- ated that some shyster would do this. I wonder if this guy didn't realize that this was a fairly wealthy family. And he must have said to himself, 'Here's a live one. I can collect something here.'"

The family lived near Knox College. So Leinbaugh had an unexpected visitor. From a swing on the Teke House porch he watched a tall, well- dressed man approach. The stranger asked for Mr. Harold Leinbaugh. Bud, in dungarees and sweater, identified himself. Then, uncomfortable in his casual clothes, he said he couldn't talk now. Could they get to- gether for dinner? In a suit and tie he thought he could deal with the father on a more equal footing. He too confirmed the boy was dead.

The Army gave Adrian Wheeler an artificial left eye and a spare before he left the hospital. When he first got back to his wife, Lib, and son, Tom, in Shirley, Indiana, he had enough vision in his right eye to distin- guish large objects; when his daughter, Susie, was born in 1946 he could "see" her as a lump. Then even that level of vision failed.

Adrian had hoped to go back to the Chrysler plant where he'd worked before the Army, but the people there temporized for a year. So he talked with a man from Washington about the problem. Walter Winchell even became interested, thought he could make a "trial case" of this. Finally Chrysler agreed to rehire him, so Adrian worked there just long enough to prove to himself that he could handle the job. By that time, however, he had contracted to buy the dairy farm.

Though he had a little problem persuading Lib, when he bought that eighty-acre farm Adrian was happy, and with help from the family he could manage. His father pitched in for a while, and then by the mid-'50s young Tom was old enough to feed the cattle. But the dairy inspectors were afraid that Adrian's blindness would prevent his keeping the equip- ment clean. Adrian sold the farm and went to work assembling light- dimming switches in Delco Remy's Anderson plant. Then his church, as well as his family, became a consuming interest, and he began teaching an adult Bible class.

Since Bill Parsons had "only" lost one eye, he decided he'd get on with his education. He returned to Penn State, where he met his wife, Polly. With a couple of bachelor's and master's degrees and a doctorate he went on to college teaching.

The grenade that cost Parsons an eye on Christmas Eve is simply part of the past. "I came away awfully, awfully lucky," he says. "Sure, I lost an eye. Cosmetically, though, it didn't do a terrible amount of damage. I didn't have to walk around with a broken face like a lot of my friends."

He doesn't bear any mental scars about losing an eye. "If I'd lost my right *arm* I might feel very differently. But I miss my friends. That outfit, the men there, with very, very few exceptions, are some of the finest people I've ever met. Sure, there were guys that did some things I didn't like. That's always going to happen. You get a guy that shoots himself in the foot to get out—I don't have any sympathy with a guy like that. I just don't. If I gotta sweat he oughta sweat.

"There is no traumatic thing relative to the war that really tears me up or breaks me out in a sweat," Bill says. "Sometimes, if I hear a sound like a machine gun, it does bother me. Sure." Bill coped with that problem by beginning to fire a rifle again. "Target rifle—I'm not talking about shooting animals, because I don't believe in that. But I taught myself to fire that stupid target rifle left-handed and then coached the rifle team for several years. The kids liked it, and I never mentioned why I fired left-handed." Bill also enjoyed it because of the challenge: to ask himself, "Hey, can you still pick this thing up, can you still hold it steady? Was that such a terrible experience that you can't do that?" And to be able to answer, "I can do it all."

Paul Leimkuehler worked in the limb and brace shop at McGuire General Hospital until the Army gave him his discharge. Then he went back to Cleveland, to his wife, Kay, and their baby daughter, Paulette—and to the skating and bicycle-racing trophies from his athletic past, a past that must have seemed hopelessly remote. He picked up his old job, experimental engineering and research, at Tinnerman Products. Soon he began to work in prosthetics, initially on a part-time basis.

"A friend of mine, whom I knew through a local amputee organization, was interested in getting into the business," Paul says. "We bought a company that had been well established, and started out with two good fitters, but no orders." His partner worked full-time, and Paul, evenings and Saturdays. Then Paul bought his partner out and went into the prosthetics business full-time.

"At that time people got their leads to amputees through a clipping service," says Paul. "Anything that had to do with an amputation they'd clip out and mail to us once a month. It was sort of like ambulance chasing. When you would go to amputees there would be four or five other companies that had contacted them too. Some of them were pretty spectacular: The person they were talking to maybe had a hip disarticulation amputation, and maybe the salesman had a leg off below the knee, and he would run up and down stairs and jump over chairs for demonstration."

Paul began to realize that the new amputee had to start someplace, and that was with the doctor. "So I started to write letters to the doctors when I delivered the limb and told them what I had done for the patient, what I thought he should do, what he could check, and so forth. Then doctors started to refer patients to me after the amputation. Sometimes they would call and consult with me. So I didn't need the clipping service anymore. Really what I was doing was becoming more professional—in my ignorance, I guess. Paul sums up those early years by saying, "I took advantage of my disadvantage. That changed my life. When I look back I don't know how I would have worked out without becoming an amputee."

Most K Company men faced lesser hurdles in their transition to civilian life, but their combat past still changed their perspectives. Lucht had been quarterback and captain of the Lawrence College football team before the war. In those days, he says, he was a "hard-nosed guy." But when he returned to Lawrence, he tried to avoid confrontations. "I began to play first-team football again. About halfway through the season, however, I lost all interest in aggressive behavior. I thought, the hell with it. It wasn't that important to me."

Jim Sterner came back to Wilmington and settled in easily. "The biggest thing in my life next to marriage was combat," he says. "I don't think it changed me any, though. I came home, and my parents and my wife were disappointed that I adjusted immediately. I was an altogether different person in combat than I was before or after, just like a different human being. I can't hunt, can't kill a deer. I can't kill a rabbit. And I had trouble killing a rat when I had to. Yet I know I've killed a human being and it doesn't bother me."

For those who could not so easily forget the war, talking about combat might have seemed a reasonable way to cope with the experience. Soon after Ed Stewart came back, people began to ask him about his war. The first time they asked, he tried to talk about it, but they interrupted and cut him off. "So the second time I was asked how it was," he says, "I cut myself off after a couple of words. It was clear that people didn't believe me, or even if they believed me they really were not interested in the raw experience. They wanted the embellishments, the glory, the success, the survival—but not the raw experience. People don't want that."

The difficulty of communicating the nature of that experience may be part of the problem. "You have to go through it yourself," George Thompson thought. "Nobody else knows exactly what it is—the cold, the terror, and destruction. And you just can't tell 'em how it is. Of course, war has been like that all down the ages. Still is—Korea, Vietnam, and it's hard to tell what's going to happen now."

Clayton Shepherd also found that when he came home he couldn't discuss his experiences casually. "You can't tell nobody about that," he says. "You got to keep that sort of stuff to yourself." He has worked out a compromise solution, however, and just talks about those days with his wife, who says, "I've listened to the K Company story of World War II. For all these years this has been my life. I've lived through it."

When Fred Olson came home he just didn't feel the need to talk about it. "Maybe that's a kink in my nature," he says, "but it's so foreign, so unlike, so abnormal for people. But I spend a lot of time recounting little things to myself—just thinking about them. Why they pop into my mind I don't know, but they do."

*   *   *

Since talking about it wasn't easy, some attempted to deal with the past by getting it down on paper. Ed Stewart, taking college courses while still serving in Germany, poured recollections and feelings onto pages of his course notebooks. John Sabia filled a 1948 desk calendar with reconstructions of his days on the line. A year or so after the war John Bratten and Raymond Bocarski also wrote about their combat experiences. Back in college for a creative writing course, Leinbaugh began a wartime "novel" paralleling the company's first weeks of action. And for a sociology term paper, Campbell focused on "Some Social Aspects of the Small Combat Infantry Unit."

The one we thought most likely to write the K Company story was Franklin Brewer. But Brewer, the company's intellectual in residence, published nothing after the war. His libretto for *The Masterpiece*—a comic opera favorably reviewed in 1941 by both *Time* and *Newsweek*— and a handful of letters are all that remain.

For Keith Lance, the starting over began at the separation center at Ft. Douglas. He had been in three campaigns and had been awarded the Bronze Star, the Purple Heart with oak leaf cluster, and the big blue Combat Infantry Badge. Now they issued him the standard discharge emblem, the golden-eagle lapel button that the vets called the "ruptured duck."

Before he'd joined the Army as a twenty-year-old private, Keith had been a sales clerk at Jack's Drive-Inn. In the service he'd earned a battlefield commission and a different job, combat platoon leader. Two days out of the Army he was back at work, running the bar at the Bank Club, a bottle club in Jerome, Idaho. There wasn't much call for civilian platoon leaders in Idaho.

Something more important to Keith than a job also required his immediate attention. He needed to get in touch with Jeanette Tomlinson. At Howze and Claiborne he had enjoyed being with Mutt and Jeanette. But on the day Keith had been wounded for the second time, Mutt had been killed. The reunion with his widow might not be easy. Jeanette's friends the Standlees smoothed the way with a bottle of scotch.

"About the scotch," Jeanette says, "Harold Standlee had bought it for Mutt's homecoming and had given it to me for Keith after we knew Mutt wouldn't be coming home. Keith got home early in February of 1946. The first time we got together he came to the apartment and we drank scotch while he told me what had happened to the boys I knew.

"One night we went to an Elks dance with Mutt's sister and her husband and the Standlees. Keith was so open with them, telling them what they wanted to know about Mutt's death and answering all their questions.

"Keith was always so cheerful. We had such fun together and were such good friends. He didn't give me a chance to feel lonesome or left out. We talked about everything and anything. His stories helped me tremendously, and I'm sure that telling them helped him overcome his tragic experiences. He made me realize that I could start over and there was something to live for.

"Everyone loved Keith—all my friends thought he was the greatest thing that could happen to me. I think most of our friends had us married long before it occurred to either of us."

After their marriage Keith bought out the owner of the Bank Club and obtained the first legal liquor license in Idaho. Jeanette continued her bookkeeping but took an extended break from that when their son Kent was born. Kent grew up with K Company bedtime stories told by his father. So when Kent met George Gieszl, Frank Gonzales, J. B. Cole, and Dempsey Keller he thought it was just like meeting Robin Hood and his merry men.

Before the war receded into that bedtime-story past, though, there were sometimes problems. For Wiley Herrell there were the dreams. "I had nightmares of shelling," he says. "I'd wake up and find I'd stuck my head under the pillow." He doesn't sweat it now, though. "Just once in a great while I'll have a reaction of that sort." And for a while Johnny Freeman's problem was booze. "I had a good job, assistant manager at the A&P," he says, "but adjustment to civilian life was rough. To be honest with you, I turned alcoholic and was pretty drunk for two years. Why they didn't fire me for my drinking I don't know. Then I went cold turkey—sick, sober, and sorry."

Morris Dunn and his wife Dorothy had to struggle with the war for several years. "I was very nervous," he says. "I'd suddenly break out in heavy sweats. If I was in a meeting I'd just have to get up and walk outside. Once my wife and I were driving downtown late in the evening and suddenly I heard a shrill, piercing noise which to me was an artillery shell coming in. I hit the brakes, slammed them on, and she bumped her head on the windshield. That was just one incident."

Dorothy found that her husband couldn't sleep. "I would awaken and find his side of the bed empty, the car gone. Sometimes he would break out in a sweat and he would say, 'I have a thousand needles sticking in my body.' Then he'd excuse himself, go out and not come back. Once he even told me he couldn't live with me anymore. He came home to this baby and me, and he loved us dearly, but he couldn't even live with himself."

Their doctor worked with them, even suggested that buying a home ("which we couldn't afford, but we managed") might help. "The doctor told me," says Dorothy, "it wouldn't be today, it wouldn't be tomorrow, it wouldn't be a year from now, but give him five years. He improved, but he had a bad time, a bad time. When our son went in the service I relived all those hours."

Looking back, Dunn says, "If it were to happen all over again, I believe I would be one of those who would go to Canada. We were lucky that we didn't really know what we were going into. But other than that I recuperated pretty good. It took five years, and then everything worked itself out."

The war's imprint showed most clearly in the early years. Yet even today, in minor but persistent ways, its effects appear in the shadows. Ed Stewart commented that he had "never known a combat soldier who did not show a residue of war," and he remembered a man "who had puzzled me until I learned of his combat experience, then his behavior fell into a mold." Stewart himself wasn't immune. A few months after he came back to the States, his mother told him that he "left Europe but never arrived home." And for Ed the little habits linger. "To this day I habitually cover my face with the inside of my right arm before sleeping, and I prefer to sit with my back to a wall, rather than toward open space."

When George Thompson came home, the sounds of war came with him. "As long as someone's in the house with me it makes a big difference," he says. "But when I'm home by myself, at nighttime, it all comes back. I'll hear the noise, the shells exploding. I stay awake thinking about it. And I can see it as plain as if it happened yesterday. I guess it comes from being in a foxhole—the long hours of nighttime by yourself—and everybody's wondering whether they can make it."

Several of the men who hunted before the war haven't gone since. "I just don't have any use for guns," says Fred Olson. "I suppose I could have shot a deer afterwards, but I had no need for it. Pheasant season and all—I just eliminated them." And Tom Miller's war comes back on a winding road in the Wisconsin countryside. "To this day," he says, "I can look out and be reminded of the woods that we had taken when we were fighting. I examine the area for cover, for concealment, for defilade. Once in a while I mention this to my wife Marylou and she says to me, 'Hey, what's happening, forget about the war.'"

The war, though, isn't easily forgotten. Some, however, do manage to put much of the wartime past aside. "There have been other things in my life—my family, my friends, my business—that I've concentrated on since the war," Raymond Bocarski says. He has gone to no reunions, has kept up with none of the men. "I look at the old K Company crowd in an abstract way. I never followed through with those people after the war. We were in an artificial atmosphere there. Once the war was over we went back to our old ways.

"We were such a small part of such a big picture. It's surprising all those little Company Ks had that much effect. To this day I wonder, was it worth while to be out there? But I've not really thought about it. I've just gone on to other things. I've put a lot of K Company behind me.

"I do still have an old Eisenhower jacket that dates from the war years. One of my kids told me that back when they were in high school they used to wear the ribbons that had been on that jacket. They wore them on their sweaters. I guess it was the style then."

21

▽

LOOKING BACK

It could be Atlanta, Las Vegas, Boise, or even Springfield, Illinois—the hometown of Abe Lincoln, who, like the men in the division, was known as the Railsplitter. Every year since 1946 the Railsplitters Society has held reunions. The group has met in thirty-two cities and twenty-four states so far—a reflection of the geographic diversity of the men in the division. For the last decade or so well over five hundred have attended annually.

The reunions are well orchestrated. Look for the Railsplitter banner at the hotel entrance. Get your nametag at the registration desk—if you're a first-timer your tag will have a blue dot on it. Purchase tickets for the annual banquet; sign up for special events—there are always the golf and bowling tournaments. Consider one of the tours—Lake Tahoe (Reno), Pennsylvania Dutch country (Harrisburg), Biltmore (Asheville). And look for the sign "K Company CP" to locate the men whom Dempsey Keller, the old first sergeant, calls "Gieszl's Go-Getters." Thirty or forty from the company show up. ("Does that include wives?" a spouse at her first reunion asks another who has been to many. "Oh, no, dear," comes the reply. "Wives don't count.")

Attendance began picking up in the early '70s, and for a number of years K Company's turnout has topped that of other Railsplitter components. Keller can take a lot of credit for that. He hadn't gone to any reunions until 1968. He didn't need any reminders of the war. But company clerk Jim Grafmiller did some arm twisting. Keller began attending, later served a term as Railsplitters president, became the society's executive secretary, and made locating old K Company men his prime effort.

Some men are reunion regulars. Others appear only if the reunion site is near home. And some never put in an appearance. One nonattender remains bitter: When the medics sent him back to the hospital, someone appropriated the "souvenirs" that he had scrounged and stashed away to take home. Some, not disaffected, but more involved in other things, simply have put the past aside. But there are still others: the small number of American Indians, and the Hispanics, singled out on the morning report in those days as "race, Mexican." Does that say something about the Army's, or our own, failure to bring them into the band of brothers? And the SIWs—self-inflicted wounds—are also absent. Are feelings about that particular past still too strong—for them, and for us?

Count on seeing Keith and Jeanette Lance. They hosted the reunion at Boise and haven't missed one for years. He's a past president of the Railsplitters Society. John Sabia and Leo Topel, both from near Philly, will be there with their wives. Perhaps the two men are wearing their identical sport coats. As usual, John will have a can of beer in his fist, and someone from the second platoon will suggest he could use a little less beer and a little more exercise.

Keller may be setting out a large bowl for contributions to the kitty to defray the CP expenses, and he may issue a reminder: "Call it a reunion, not a convention. *Convention* gives the wrong idea." And be sure to add your name to the others on the note that will go out to the K Company people who didn't come this year. Don Phelps, the florist from Rochester, usually brings red carnations. For munching in the CP, Frank and Mary Gonzales provide apricots and pecans grown on their ranch. Other items appear that are not routine: Thirty-one dozen cookies for the company turned up at Reno, baked by Morris Dunn's wife, Dotty; at Hot Springs, Robert Martin brought a watermelon—it weighed in at 109 pounds.

Although Keller, Grafmiller, and Lance have been largely responsible for K Company's recent turnouts, some of the credit belong to time itself. The passing years have softened some of the edges of war. The stock expression comes up every year: I wouldn't do it again for a million dollars, but I wouldn't take any amount for the experience. Now men go to the reunions to be once again with the K Company family.

Beyond doubt those who attend *do* see it as a family. "I have a real feeling of kinship," says Fred Olson. "What is amazing is that this feeling that had its genesis in just a few months has persisted all these years. It isn't that I owe anyone anything or that together we had a hand in preserving democracy. It's just the plain fact that I shared this brief and extremely dangerous time with a group of men." Olson and Sabia shared just one week of combat; they next met in 1974. "I was unable to place the face," says Olson. "But the very moment he spoke I remembered the voice. It was the one appealing for volunteers—Sabia storming back and forth on his knees after he was hit, wanting volunteers to go after Captain Mitchell. It's a fact that I have no memory of Sabia prior to that time."

Strong feelings persist, but at the same time we can look back at those days with a more distant, detached perspective when we share that past with others who were there. Tales are told, events embellished, and sometimes even the depth of feelings about those days is revealed. As a rule, though, the tales in the company CP are the familiar ones—often amusing, sometimes poignant, occasionally accurate. For us our shared past has become family history—or even folklore.

Three men stand at the bar in the K Company CP—George Gieszl, the noncom-turned-officer who shaped the company; George Pope, whom Gieszl had made a platoon sergeant and who later earned a battlefield commission; and Ed Stewart, an ASTPboy who became a sergeant soon after combat began. But this CP is far from '44 and '45. It is 1983, the reunion at Harrisburg. Gieszl is a recently retired school administrator from Arizona, Pope works in a Connecticut silverware factory, and Stewart, a cross-cultural psychologist, will soon be on his way to a university post in Japan.

Pope is telling about his abortive patrol from Taverneux into Houffalize—just before the Ardennes Bulge was closed. Gieszl and Stewart had both been in the hospital then, and they're hearing the story for the first time. Pope gets to the part where he and his patrol fall asleep in the town and fail to radio in every hour. "The whole goddam place was asleep," he continues in his Brooklyn baritone. "And the goddam light is starting to come in. It felt so nice, so warm, layin' on that floor. So I said, what am I going to tell them sons of bitches? I said, fix that radio, I told the kid, bust the tube. And the son of a bitch did."

Gieszl, his eyes fixed on Pope, cracks up. Stewart, listening to Pope, but watching Gieszl, also explodes in laughter—enjoying both the humor of the story and Gieszl's reaction. Still an ironic observer of the company, Stewart sums it up: "The reunion taps the tear ducts, but also has its humorous side. There is an image of courageous soldiers with a distinguished string of victories, but the celebrants turn out to be a group of harmless old men."

Pope, like the rest of us at that reunion, was a civilian, but he'd gone back into the Army to fight in Korea and spent many more years in the Army. Still he always remained partial to his own first war. "I say those guys in World War II were better soldiers than they are today," he tells us. "I don't care what Benning or anybody says. If the kids today had to go through Belgium the way we did, if they lost their equipment they wouldn't survive. Give you a for instance. First time I slept in a sleeping bag here in the States I thought it was the greatest thing that ever happened. Ten, twelve, fourteen years later I'm in Ft. Ord, California. Beautiful, right? Christ, you could sleep under the stars, really, out on bivouac. We're out there a week and these sergeants say, 'Jesus Christ, it was cold last night.' And we're in California and got this beautiful sleeping bag."

The rest of us are also partial to our war. After all, it was the only war we had. There is, however, the special case of Vietnam. We are glad that wasn't our war. Should our country have been there? The spectrum of views in the company are those of the nation itself. But the question is not a major issue for debate. Given our age, what matters most about Vietnam is our sons. Jerry Dunne, who didn't claim his Purple Heart until he found the award would add the points needed for discharge, was surprised and proud when his son enlisted and served over there in the Navy. Bill Masters, who voluntarily moved from heavy weapons "safety" to a rifle company, so the Army could collect on its investment, was initially disgruntled when his son went to Vietnam. But Masters decided he wouldn't ask for any favors—"I might as well let him take his chances too." Jim Grafmiller's son served as a helicopter pilot there and was wounded. Walter Anderson, who took machine-gun bullets in his arm during the Bulge, lost his only son in Vietnam.

Still, if Vietnam crops up in conversation, it does so only obliquely, when someone refers to the terrible waste of war. "There sure as hell isn't anything romantic about it," says Gieszl. "I have no animosity toward the Germans or toward the service. My animosity is directed toward *war*." Jim Sterner says, "Vietnam was an immoral war." He goes on to add, "Hell, we fought a *moral* war, if there is such a thing. But they're all immoral."

For some, though, it may be more complicated than that. Mario Lage looks back and unhesitatingly says, "War is an awful waste." But he continues, "The excitement of war overshadowed everything else—it's the supreme sport. In a bullfight the poor bull doesn't have a chance. But combat is more even, more fair, because at least the other guy's got a shot at you." Mario enjoyed the sport. "That's a hell of a way of putting it," he says, "but that's the way I approached it. Being in a roller coaster bothers me, but getting shot at doesn't. It was exhilarating."

Lage struggles to put his feelings into words: "The human reaction to a situation—all those emotions combined—plus the desire to survive—and it's all so compressed in time. It's such an unusual, such a strong, such a dramatic thing. You can go through a thousand lifetimes running the usual gamut of emotions and never have the opportunity to see something like that. It's almost a shame that people who haven't been in it—people who pride themselves in having seen the elephant and heard the owl—they will never know."

For some, combat could be exhilarating, but it had brought other feelings, such as loneliness, as well. Why loneliness, with comrades all around? "In the final analysis it was the imminence of dying that created this," says Olson. "Dying was a personal matter, something that was going to happen to *me* at a particular instant—all alone and to no one else." So in those days he heard little talk of loneliness or death. "We avoided the topic as if it didn't exist. Still I learned that I was not afraid of dying and was concerned only about the sadness it would bring to others. That very thing brought me through those times when I just wanted to die—just to hell with it. And you know, those times did exist."

The sense of isolation, which could touch anyone, can remain vivid. "The terrible thing about that experience is the utter, complete aloneness," says Gieszl. "There isn't anything else—just you. Someone can be just two feet from you, but there's nothing there. It's like you're shot into space and there you are. When things started happening we switched to automatic pilot; training took over. But still there was that utter aloneness. And you wonder why. It's against nature to be in a place like that."

The personal, private thoughts such as these rarely come up in reunion conversations. As if by tacit agreement, the men steer clear of them. Sometimes, though, in the late-night hours when it's one on one, men try to size up their own past and come to terms with it. It's not always easy: At a recent reunion, as two old noncoms got ready to call it a day, one broke down in tears. For forty years he'd felt he'd let his buddies down. After a stint of hard fighting he had collapsed; medics had sent him to an exhaustion center. Why, he'd kept wondering all these years, why hadn't he been able to make it then?

Those self-appraisals can also be complicated. Olson has puzzled a lot about it. "I think I was a good soldier," he says. "But I can look back and see things that bother me, make me wonder why I did that—we all can. You know one thing that bothers me? It was in Belgium in one of those small towns. I walked into this house and could hear wounded German soldiers in another room crying for water. But they didn't get water from me. I've often wondered why. Hell's fire, these Krauts had obviously been hit bad and had been left behind. That's bothered me, that I didn't make sure that they had water. But it's the circumstances, the times."

Looking at his own combat performance, he finds what he calls a contradiction. "While I wanted to serve, I also looked forward to the million-dollar wound. I believe most did," he says. "From time to time we talked about it—that's the way out. But *it* had to come to *me*—not the other way round. None of us were heroes. We were just there and trying to do the best we knew how under the circumstances. Maybe some days not doing a very good job of it. But as miserable an existence as it was, I felt very strong about it—goddammit, do the best I could."

Doing the best we could. We hope that was the case, and at reunions we look for reassurance. Gieszl sees that. "Men meet, there's a slap on the back. They are *individuals, seeking* and *gaining* the respect that is their due," he says. "I sensed this at the first reunion I attended; I felt it still more at Hot Springs, where for some of the men this would be of vital importance. But we all hunger for this self-respect."

Sabia sums it up in the Combat Infantry Badge, given to men on the line just for being there—and valued for that very reason: "There's not too many guys could put that blue Combat Infantry Badge on. You walk with it with a certain pride. I always put that blue badge number one. You could have your Medal of Honor and Legion of Merit, but there's nothing covers that blue badge, nothing tops it."

Wiley Herrell says more personally: "When I was in training a lieutenant told us, 'You ain't nothing but gun fodder, but you are essential and nobody can take your place.' I always felt more important than gun fodder. The foot soldier was just as important as any general back in Washington or as important as Eisenhower. That foot soldier, he's the last man out there, he's got to go in and claim the territory."

For K Company people there are "reunions" beyond the annual meetings of the Railsplitters Society. The Gieszls in Arizona and the Lances in Idaho travel the road that links their homes so often that they must own it by now. Don Stauffer, best man at the Sterners' wedding in 1944, invites Jim to Wilmington's University Club for drinks and dinner; the Sterners have the Stauffers out to their place on the Chesapeake for an outing on the Sterners' boat, the one with the registration number 333-K. The Dunns, Radoviches, and other Californians get together in Fresno. The Sabias and the Campbells meet in an old farmhouse in the Alleghenies, where before cooking the spaghetti Sabia opens a commemorative bottle of Johnny Walker Red Label.

For Mike DeBello, looking at the company's faded picture from Claiborne days provides a reunion of sorts. Mike studies the photograph and points out a face. "This guy here, he was a BAR man. I know all the faces—I just can't remember their names. Here's Pete Visconte, he's my best buddy. We were buddies all the way till he was killed. He used to write my letters for me—him and Captain Gieszl. Pete didn't have anybody but his little girl—his wife was dead. He worshiped this little girl. He used to talk about her all the time. But it's been so long ago."

Time has made it easier now for Mike to look back to those days. But for many years Mike couldn't talk about them. "I was terrible overseas, wanted to destroy everything, I was so mad. With all that excitement half the time I didn't know who was who, what was what. But I never got knocked out, even when I was hit. Maybe that's because I was a dago, who knows?" He recalls a proud moment. "I remember when we captured a hill. I was one, there was three other guys, and we put up this flag on a hill. We put it on the stem of a tree, all four of us. I don't know the name of the place, but it was a famous hill."

His journey back to that hill occurs only in DeBello's mind. For others, though, getting back to land once fought over has become the ultimate reunion. By now many K Company people have more time and resources for travel, and those who have returned to Geilenkirchen and beyond number in the dozens. They've gone back in twos and threes, with wives and families, in cars and by the busload. Exactly forty years after the fact one man, John Bratten, headed back to Belgium to experience again that December cold.

The need to recapture the past shows itself in different ways. We look for old foxholes and old gun emplacements, find their outlines, softened by time, undergrowth, and weathering, but still unmistakable. Bratten and the rest of us take snapshots and write on their backs: "our" château, "our" woods, "our" hill. Ed Stewart returns to Geilenkirchen and Lindern, and in his mind lays claim to "soil that I could never surrender."

Leinbaugh and Campbell are among those who have gone back. A high point on our return was the town of Verdenne, the town we'd hoped to capture, but had never reached on Christmas Eve. There on the first house as we entered the village we encountered a sign that might help explain why so many of us are drawn to the town. High on the house was one of the blue-and-white street markers commonplace throughout the region. But this was a marker fixed in the past, one that confirmed the personal importance, perhaps even the historical importance, of that place at that time: The street bears the name "Rue de Noel, 1944."

The most unexpected encounter of our visit to Verdenne began with a telephone call from Gerhard Tebbe. In December 1944, he had been a major, commanding all the tanks of the Panzerkampfgruppe that late on Christmas Eve stopped for a rest in the forest just beyond the village. For a year he had believed Germany could not win the war. "The losses were very big," he said. "It was simply a question of mathematics." As he examined his maps near midnight, over his radio came the sounds of bells, the cathedral in Cologne ringing in Christmas. And then K Company came up the road.

Now, over the telephone, he suggested that he drive from Bad Soden to Marche to meet us. Our prior meeting, he said, had been gun to gun. Now he would make our acquaintance face to face. He'd planned to spend three hours with us. He spent three days. Greetings were cautious, formal, but within an hour our initial reserve had passed. Soon we were poring over maps with this clear-eyed, firm-featured former Panzer officer who had been a veteran of over a hundred engagements on both the Eastern and the Western Front.

We both respected this man, indeed soon grew to like him. We talked with the former German major about the Christmas Eve encounter and others we'd had in the days that followed. We discussed troop strengths, weapons, and positions. But we didn't walk the ground with him. Why not isn't easy to explain. Old wounds had healed, but somehow it wasn't quite that simple. Perhaps it reflected the infantryman's tie with the land; soil once fought upon becomes transmuted by the alchemy of battle: It now "belongs" to the men who were there, and it is not that easily shared.

So we search out the places that have special meaning. Here the daisy chain got that tank; that's where we crossed the river; we must be somewhere near the cellar. We become tourists in our own past: We pause at the church in Geilenkirchen, climb on the Panther tank preserved at Houffalize, photograph the bronze plaque commemorating the division's role at Marche. There are special, poignant moments at Margraten, where K Company men are buried. Here Keith and Jeanette Lance bow their heads at the grave of Mutt Tomlinson, killed on February 28. He'd been her husband, his friend. For Keith and Jeanette it is a private moment. Yet it is a moment they share with others: A TV crew captures the scene. The past is now part of the public perspective; history has taken over.

UPDATE

The four hundred men who served with K company in Europe came from cities, towns, and farms scattered all over the country. We were hyphenated Americans, foreign-born, and Anglo-Saxon stock; Catholics, Protestants, and Jews; farmers, factory workers, students; men with college degrees and half a dozen who were illiterate. Our numbers are fewer now: thirty-six were killed in action in Europe, at least one lost his life in Korea. Sixty more men have died since the war. Another hundred are lost to the company. Among the two hundred remaining, the diversity still holds. There are about as many with doctoral degrees as there were illiterates then. A majority of the men are now retired, and a number receive disability payments. These exceed the company's 1945 payroll many times over. We've been lawyers and laborers, salesmen and storekeepers, ranchers and railroaders, merchants and ministers. Home may be in any of forty states or abroad. Many still live in the place they called home in 1944.

The old first sergeant, Dempsey Keller, keeps track of his men. Jim Grafmiller, Keith Lance, Riley Martin, and Dempsey provided much of the following information. We've striven for accuracy in this summary, but there may be errors or omissions.

LOUIS ALICANDRI works at Goodyear Tire in Pittsburgh, where he worked before he entered the service.

JUNIOR G. ALPERN was killed in action February 28. His wife lived in Detroit, Michigan.

GENE AMICI owns and operates Amici Tile and Floor Covering in Long Beach, California.

WALTER ANDERSON worked for the postal service for over thirty years. He and his wife, Mary Lee, live in Versailles, Kentucky. They have three daughters. Their only son was killed in Vietnam.

HARVEY AUGUSTIN, of Saint Thomas, North Dakota, is a rural mail carrier. He covers his 116-mile route six days a week.

CLETIS BAILEY has retired from the Air Force. He and Joyce live in McDonald, Tennessee.

WILLIAM BAIRD works for a railroad. He and his wife, Betty, live in Munhall, Pennsylvania.

BYRON BAKER has a fruit and vegetable business. The Bakers live in East Helena, Montana.

BRUCE BAPTIE returned to Yale. A chemical engineer, he is director of marketing for Upjohn's Fine Chemical Division. He and Betty live in North Haven, Connecticut.

LATHERIAL BARNES went back to farming near Temple, Oklahoma, and also worked in a gravel pit. He and his wife still live in Temple, but after two heart attacks he retired in the '70s.

JOSEPH BAUMANN is in insurance. He lives in Huntington, New York.

GLEN BEITEL and his wife, Virginia, live in Kingsford, Michigan.

FERDINAND C. BELL, JR., lives in Clearfield, Pennsylvania, where he is an attorney. Two of his three children are also attorneys.

R. J. BELL, from Coushatta, Louisiana, was killed in action January 10.

RAYMOND BOCARSKI completed college at Rutgers, with four years' physical-education credit for Army service. He has worked in insurance since then. He and Anne live in Caldwell, New Jersey.

GEORGE BOND, from Hobart, Indiana, was killed in action January 15. He was posthumously awarded the Bronze Star.

ELMER BOSWORTH recently retired from the ministry. He and his wife, Margaret, live in Atlanta, Indiana.

LEONARD BOWDITCH and his wife, Dot, live in Nanticoke, Pennsylvania. Now retired, Bowditch was an inspector and trainer at Owens-Illinois in Pittston. Watching war movies he finds "a hell of a lot of difference between doing it live and doing it in the movies. Doing it live, you don't have somebody to say, 'Cut, hold it, we'll start over.' Make a mistake, and you don't have a second time to make it."

JOHN A. BOWE, JR., from Worcester, Massachusetts, was killed in action February 28.

JAMES BRADFORD, from Baltimore, died some years after the end of the war.

JOHN BRATTEN graduated from Cornell in 1947. Retired from the electrical-supply business, he lives in Fort Worth, Texas. He and General von Manteuffel have written to one another since the war.

FRANKLIN BREWER settled in Carmel, California, dabbled in real estate, worked in a gourmet shop. Brewer, who crusaded to remove religion from his dog tags, wanted no burial services—just his ashes scattered in the Pacific. His ashes went to sea in 1973, but with them went a clergyman. "Brewer was the kind of guy you could talk your problems over with," remarked George Lucht. "Mother Brewer, they called him. Affectionately."

JOHN BRIEDEN, JR., is an oil-field worker. He and his wife, Jewell, live in Freer, Texas.

HOWARD BRODERICK earned a degree at Utah State; then as a soil scientist, he worked with the government's Soil Conservation Service and Forest Service. In retirement, he lives in Phoenix, Arizona, where he is with a real-estate company. He and Joyce have nine children and twenty-four grandchildren.

ROY BROUGHTON, from Chillicothe, Ohio, has an engine-repair business.

PAUL J. BROWNING, from Fouke, Arkansas, stayed in the service after our war. He was killed in action in Korea.

LEONARD BROYLES and Melvira, whom he married in 1940, live in Oklahoma. He worked as field man and ice-cream maker for an Oklahoma City dairy. Now retired, he raises cattle near Meeker.

FREDERICK I. BUTLER, Baltimore, Maryland, was killed in action, December 25, 1944. He left a wife and son.

WILLIAM BYFIELD has an appliance and furniture store in Muskogee, Oklahoma.

STEVE CALL, Lewiston, Utah, had further Army service. Promoted to first sergeant, he trained troops for Korea and became sergeant major at Camp Roberts, California. Returning to Utah, he worked for the railroads, then moved into health-care service as an administrator. He and Jeanne live in Ogden, Utah.

GEORGE F. CAMPBELL, of Lynchburg, Virginia, retired from his insurance business in 1984.

JOHN CAMPBELL earned a Ph.D. at Harvard, taught, and engaged in research at the National Institute of Mental Health. Retired, he and Nelle live in Rockville, Maryland.

GEORGE CAPPIELLO came back to his wife and children on Long Island. He worked for a trucking company there and was a terminal manager when he retired.

RAY CARLTON, a minister, lives in Monticello, Illinois.

LESLIE CARSON, married for nearly fifteen years when he joined K Company, has worked in a shoe factory and farmed. Retired, he and Myril live in Jonesboro, Arkansas.

HENRY CHAPMAN and his wife, Evelyn, live in LaFollette, Tennessee. They have six children, twenty grandchildren, and two great-grandchildren.

BERT CHRISTENSEN, from Fairview, Utah, died December 6, in the shelling of the cellar in Lindern.

LOUIS CICCOTELLO, mail clerk and barber, returned to barbering. Retired, he and Margaret live in Philadelphia.

DANIEL CIRILO worked for the state of Texas. He and his wife, Billie, now live in San Francisco.

RALPH CIULLO was the only GI from the company to get to Berlin. He ultimately became sergeant major with the Office of Military Government there. His 50 percent disability payment ($450 per month) supplements his income as a representative for John Hancock in East Northport, New York.

JAMES CLARK, from Passaic, New Jersey, a staff sergeant with the third platoon, was killed in action November 22.

ROYCE CLEMENTS was in the radio business. He and his wife, Nancy, live in Benton Harbor, Michigan.

MELVIN CLINE has worked for Sunbeam Corporation since 1947—from tool and die maker to division president. He and Marie live in Orange, California, and have two sons and two daughters.

JOHN B. COLE owns a neighborhood grocery in Wake Forest, North Carolina. After the war he married the widow of his brother, killed in the Battle of the Bulge. Semiretired, John B. remains active in the Baptist Church as a lay preacher.

JOE CONNER came home to his wife and daughter in Lima, Ohio. He helped build school buses. Retired, he puts in many hours with REACT, a citizens' radio emergency organization.

FATE COPELAND worked at a granite works in western Oklahoma. Now retired, he lives in Ravia, Oklahoma. He and his wife surely have K Company's largest family—eleven children.

OLEN COPELAND, from Cross Roads, Arkansas, was killed in action December 6.

JOHN (CORKY) CORKILL, from Mauch Chunk (now Jim Thorpe), Pennsylvania, was killed in action January 15. He was posthumously awarded the Bronze Star.

PAUL COSTE went back to Harvard, taught briefly, then studied at Saint Andrews, Scotland. He and his wife, Edna, have lived in Europe and Asia. He has been an educator and a UNESCO administrator, and a leading amateur among French golfers.

PAUL COTE, born in Montreal, with French as his first language, returned to Michigan. He is a salesman for the John Middleton Tobacco Company. He and Rose live in Harper Woods, Michigan.

J. A. CRAFT farmed in Mississippi before his lung collapsed. He and Doris now live in Huffman, Texas, and he repairs beds at the Houston Medical Center. "I've had a back pain ever since coming home," Craft says. "But as long as I'm able to work, I don't worry about it. I'm not looking for a handout. Men in worse shape than I am need it. I don't." With woodworking as a hobby, he is building a greenhouse. "I'll grow vegetables in it. I think about those sugar beets in Germany a lot."

LYLE CROOKSHANK and Mildred, whom he married in 1941, live in Altoona, Pennsylvania. A machinist, he later became a salesman for an auto-parts company. He is retired.

CLAUDIE DANIELL went back to Texas. He is employed by the town of McGregor, Texas, where he and his wife, Minnie, live.

CHALMERS DAVIS lives in Alabama, at Holly Pond, where he works as a carpenter and does a little farming. He claims he is "in as good shape now as I was then," and for anyone from the company he says, "Anytime I can help you, just holler."

MIKE DEBELLO left the hospital, married Rose, and went back to a California meat-packing plant. When it closed, Mike went to work at a produce firm. Rose continues at the smoked-fish plant. His right arm still bothers him. "It burns all the time. I quit going to the VA hospital—all they did was give me pills. I keep working keys in my hand to keep it going." At the packing house Mike worked as laundryman, sausage maker, and yard man. "Fact is, I did everything there but sign the checks." When the plant closed they gave him the .30-30 he'd used to shoot cattle.

ALEX DILLINGHAM became a radio announcer in his home state, Michigan. He died of cancer in the early '60s.

JOHN DOLAN, twice wounded, went home to Worcester, earned a degree at Bryant College, then went into the concrete business. He later worked for the post office, and in recent years has been a master technician in the audiovisual field. On February 28, 1985, John and his wife, Pat, attended a Fortieth Anniversary Mass for Jack Bowe at Christ the King Church in Worcester.

EDWARD DOWNES completed college and law school. He has been legal representative for a large insurance firm, and handled George Pope's legal matters. He and Marguerite live in Cheshire, Connecticut.

PAUL DULIN returned to North Carolina and finished college. He worked in the manufacture and sale of paperboard and paper boxes, and more recently, managed a real-estate brokerage. He and his wife live in Charlotte.

MORRIS AND DOROTHY DUNN live in Fresno, California. Until his retirement he worked in automotive parts and service.

JERRY DUNNE returned to Connecticut to Kay and their son. He continued working as a furniture salesman. He and Kay have one son and three daughters.

EARL EASTON is a salesman in Frederick, Maryland.

LESTER EDWARDS went home to Texas. He lives in Lufkin, where he is a self-employed carpenter.

EDWARD (LEN) ERICKSON worked with the Union Pacific Railroad. Beginning as a clerk, he worked his way up to traffic manager and director of regional sales in New York. Now retired, he and Helen have six children and live in Bellingham, Washington.

WESLEY FARRIS was a carpenter at Fort Hood, Texas. Retired, he and his wife, Almeta, live in Killeen, Texas.

FREDERICK FLANAGAN was an investment broker in Houston, Texas. He teaches courses for new brokers.

ERVIN FRANKENBERRY, father of year-old twins when he joined the company in Belgium, returned to Kansas and worked for an oil-field supply company as a store manager and purchasing agent. He and his family live in Wichita, and the "handle" for his CB radio is "Railsplitter."

JOHN FREEMAN returned to Porterville, California, where he and his wife, Joyce, live. He worked as assistant manager of an A&P. He later became office manager for a chemical company.

GEORGE GAEBLER, recalled to active duty in 1951, commanded a rifle company in Korea. His peacetime work has been with the Pacific Gas and Electric Company. He and Betty have six children and live in Berkeley, California.

GEORGE GEHRMAN, retired after nearly forty years with Western Electric, lives in Baltimore, Maryland.

GEORGE GIESZL graduated from Arizona State, then taught school, operated a farm, and worked for the Bureau of Reclamation. He later became principal of the Tuba City, Arizona, schools. He and Betty subsequently moved to Page, Arizona, where he was a school administrator and Betty a teacher. Both are now retired. George has had two heart operations in recent years, but he spends time boating and fishing on nearby Lake Powell. The Lances and Gieszls visit back and forth regularly.

JOHN GIMA, from Vermillion, Ohio, a replacement who came up a few days before the division's first action, served with the company ten days. He was killed in action November 24.

EDGAR GNUSE is a retired postal worker. He and his wife, Cynthia, live in Bridgeton, Missouri.

LEROY GOATS, from Harrison, Arkansas, was killed in action November 21.

J. T. GOFORTH is deceased. His wife lives in Altoona, Alabama.

LEWIS GOINS, from Brownwood, Texas, was killed in action November 22.

FRANK GONZALES came to the company from the family ranch near Hollister, California. He and Mary still live there. Frank is partially retired, so much of the ranch operation is handled by the next generation.

MELVIN GOODWIN came back to Crossett, Arkansas. In 1982, Goodwin, diagnosed as having leukemia, wrote a forty-eight-page letter looking back on his K Company experiences. Death came to him later in the year. His wife, Pat, lives in Edmond, Oklahoma.

HENRY GORDON is deceased. His wife, Opal, lives in Vardaman, Mississippi.

LORENZ GRAF, from Oconomowoc, Wisconsin, was killed in action February 28, a month after coming to the company.

JIM GRAFMILLER came back to Upper Sandusky, Ohio. He worked at a filling station and clerked in a sporting-goods store. He operates his own Sohio station there. On vacations, he and Donna carry their roster and try to track down the men from K-333.

HOWARD GREINER is a farmer. He and his wife, Viola, live near Claytonville, Illinois.

FAUSTINO GUERRA in the later 1970s was living in San Antonio, Texas.

RUFUS HADDOCK, from Cottondale, Florida, is a retired carpenter.

WILLIAM HADLEY, from Alton, Kansas, a staff sergeant with the third platoon, was killed in action November 22.

KERMIT HAGY, from Abingdon, Virginia, came up as a replacement late in January. On March 1, in the action at Dülken, Germany, he became the last K Company man to die in combat.

STANLEY HAIGHT, who lives in Bloomington, Minnesota, is a photographer.

FRANK (CHIEF) HAIR, from Salina, Oklahoma, served with the company throughout his Army career. Staff Sergeant Hair, killed in action February 28, was survived by his wife, Eliza.

JOHN HARGESHEIMER manages an 1,800-acre ranch and oil fields near Whitesboro, Texas.

DONALD HEATH is an architect. He and his wife, Margie, live in Uniontown, Pennsylvania.

ROBERT D. HENDERSON, from Minquadale, Delaware, was killed in action November 22. He was survived by his wife, Mary.

WILEY HERRELL lives in Kingston, Tennessee, where he was born. A widower, he has retired from a parts and maintenance job at Oak Ridge. War movies amuse him: "Those pictures give the impression you can stand up and the bullets will be bouncing all around you. They're good entertainment, I suppose, for somebody who's never been in combat."

RICHARD HEUER took electronics training after the war. He retired in 1981 after working for the federal government in quality control. He and Teresa live in St. Louis.

CARL (CURLY) HOFFMAN came home, then studied chemistry at the University of Illinois. In the floor and tile business for many years, Curly still lives in Chicago.

THOMAS J. HOGAN, from Rochester, New York, was killed in action November 21.

WILLIAM HOLLAND, who is a farmer, lives near Portland, Arkansas.

JAMES HUFFSTUTTER is retired. He and his wife, Marie, live in Trenton, Missouri.

ROBERT HURD is retired. He and Virginia, live in Newport, New Hampshire.

CLARENCE JARVIS, from Aurora, North Carolina, joined K Company on January 26. He was killed in action on February 28.

STEPHEN JEFFREY is deceased. His wife, Anna, lives in Mount Carmel, Pennsylvania.

NORMAN JEHLE, a retired postal worker, lives in Phoenix, Arizona.

JOHN M. JONES has an orchard near Greer, South Carolina.

DEMPSEY KELLER served as civilian deputy commander at Camp Atterbury and budget officer at the Army finance center at Ft. Benjamin Harrison and is now retired. Since 1968, the year he first attended a reunion, he and Susan have given much of their lives to the Railsplitters Society and K Company. Dempsey has served as executive secretary and as president of the Railsplitters. He and Susan mail out a company newsletter from the permanent K Company CP, their home in Nashville, Indiana. His sorties in search of missing company men have kept company ties strong and helped make this book possible.

HOWARD KENNEY, an Army retiree, lives near Wetumpka, Alabama.

DEAN KEYSER works for a firm that makes travel trailers. A widower, he lives in Elkhart, Indiana.

RAYMOND V. KLEBOFSKI, killed in action November 22, was posthumously awarded the Silver Star. His wife and children lived in Gary, Indiana.

ERVIN KOEHLER, from Gatesville, Texas, was killed in action December 6.

CARL LAFRENIERE, Johnson City, New York, is semiretired. He does repair work on radios and TVs.

MARIO LAGE lives in San Francisco. After the war he was a disc jockey in Alaska and later worked in radio in California. For a number of years he was in the furniture business in Southern California, but he is now retired.

KEITH AND JEANETTE LANCE live in Shelley, Idaho. In the '60s, Keith, who then operated a club and motel, began the Lance Agency to book entertainers throughout the Northwest. Keith and Jeanette are retired, and their son Kent, with some bookkeeping assistance from Jeanette, runs the firm.

MARCEL (FRENCHY) LARIVIERE returned to Massachusetts, where he operated a filling station and auto-repair business. Retired, he and his wife, Arlene, live in South Attleboro, and they are justifiably proud of their twelve granddaughters.

JOHN F. LAVELLE, from Fargo, North Dakota, was killed in action December 6.

PAUL AND KAY LEIMKUEHLER still live in Cleveland. He has played a significant part in the professionalization of a field: president of the American Orthotics and Prosthetics Association, president of the Board for Certification, member of the National Research Council's committee on prosthetics research. Paul, called the "father of amputee skiing" in the United States, became the first handicapped skier in the Ski Hall of Fame. He and Kay have sold Leimkuehler, Inc., to their three sons, university-trained, board-certified prosthetists.

HAROLD (BUD) LEINBAUGH became a special agent in the FBI and for most of his career was a supervisory official at the bureau's Washington headquarters. He ended his government service as deputy special assistant to the President in the White House communication office. He lives in Virginia.

FRED LONG has retired after building railroad cars for more than twenty-six years at the American Car Foundry. He lives in Apple Grove, West Virginia, and likes to hunt rabbits.

NORMAN AND MARY LONG, in Fort Smith, Arkansas, are "semiretired," though he still does some accounting and tax work. For a time they raised dachshunds, a hobby that began with Norman's dog Hexl, a trophy from Germany.

GEORGE LUCHT, with a doctorate from Indiana University, has taught and been an administrator at Kent State University for years. His secretary there interprets the "FYI" at the top of his memos as "four years in the infantry." He and Allee, whom he married when she was an Army dietician, have three children.

ARTHUR LYDIA is an auto mechanic. He lives near Spartansburg, South Carolina.

ORVILLE MCCLURE works in a sugar-beet refining plant and trains horses. He and his wife, Jackie, live near Kuna, Idaho.

BILL A. MCMILLAN, from Knoxville, Tennessee, was killed in action February 28.

GUY MCWREATH, JR., worked for an electric utility company. He lives in Midway, Pennsylvania.

HOWARD MADDRY, a boxer in college and a Golden Glove contender, spent time in a body cast after he was wounded and was given a disability discharge. Returning to college, he earned an engineering degree. He works for an electrical-engineering firm in Raleigh, North Carolina.

ED MAGEE, who left to attend OCS shortly before the company went overseas, later served in the South Pacific. Ed, an attorney, and his wife, Jane, live in New Hartford, New York. He is one of the regulars at division reunions.

LEONARD MAIURI, the company's supply sergeant, came back to New York City. He worked briefly for the VA, then worked as a bookkeeper, and then as a production man in a photoengraving firm. Survived by his wife, Marie, he died in April 1982.

JOHN MANESS is deceased. His wife, Ruth, lives in Liberty, North Carolina.

LUCIUS MARQUEZ is deceased. His wife, Isabella, lives in Denver, Colorado.

LOUIS MARTIN, JR., is deceased. His wife, Katherine, lives in Bowling Green, Kentucky.

RILEY MARTIN farmed, worked as a mechanic, and then served as postmaster at Peggs, Oklahoma. Married before he came to the company, he and his wife had six children. He died in 1985.

ROBERT D. MARTIN returned to Hope, Arkansas, where he and his wife, Mary, reside. For years he worked at Camp Chaffee, but his leg, badly damaged by a land mine, gradually worsened, severely restricting his mobility. He is now retired.

ROBERT J. MARTIN completed college at Stanford and then went into the insurance business. He is a regional manager for Fidelity Guarantee Insurance Company. He and Anne live in Fullerton, California.

ROBERT (MOOSE) MARUSICH, from Milwaukee, lost a leg during the Ardennes fighting. He returned to Wisconsin, where he died some years ago. His wife, Barbara, lives in Milwaukee.

BILL MASTERS returned to the University of Wyoming and later became a CPA. He and his wife, Emma Rose, live in Coolidge, Arizona. He is an active layman in the Episcopal Church.

RICHARD D. MEEK returned to Ohio State, taught ROTC, and earned his law degree. Back home in Connecticut, he spent more than thirty years with the state's Automotive Trade Association and became vice-president of that organization. He says his children have not been too interested in the war. "Maybe they think we made it up."

WILLIAM (DOC) MELLON worked as a civilian in Germany, married a German girl, was there for the Berlin airlift. Back home again, he became an office worker in a Birmingham, Alabama, steel firm. Severely injured in an automobile accident several years ago, Doc died in 1984.

CLARENCE MENKE returned to Nebraska and graduated from the university there in 1950. He has worked for the federal government in the Geological Survey, the Cape Kennedy space program, and the Department of Energy.

MAURICE MICHEL and his wife, Pat, live in Magnolia, Texas.

PHILLIP MICKEL runs a grocery store in Bluefield, West Virginia.

TOM MILLER, with an engineering degree from Marquette University, has worked in manufacturing, engineering, and sales supervision. He and Marylou live in Racine, Wisconsin.

JOHN S. MOORE, JR., from New Hope, Kentucky, came to the company from the ASTP. He earned a promotion to sergeant soon after combat began. Killed in action January 7, he was posthumously awarded the Silver Star.

BRUCE MORRELL graduated from MIT, worked in industry, entered the Air Force in 1951, and rose to the rank of colonel. He frequently used his K Company experiences in his lectures as a professor at the Air Force Academy. Retired from the Air Force, he is now a consulting engineer.

EVERETT (POP) MOTHERSHEAD was married and the father of two children when he came up to Company K. He has a third child, eight grandchildren, and two great-grandchildren, and brags that he is "still married to the same gal," Dorothy. He worked in security and as a printer and printing supervisor.

EDWARD MYRICK and his wife, Edith, now live in Artesia, California.

JOE NAMEY has sold his small chain of restaurants and is a real-estate broker specializing in commercial sales. He and his wife, Betty, live in Jacksonville, Florida. Joe calls his 10 percent disability payment his "cigarette money."

QUENTIN NELSON operates a large farm near Chappell, Nebraska, and his wife, Lois, teaches school.

FRED NEUHAUSSER returned to Plainville, Connecticut. Married, with one child, he has worked with GE throughout his career.

JAMES O'HARA has his own printing firm in Whitesboro, New York. Married in 1939, he has four children and sixteen grandchildren.

DONALD OKENFUSS was twenty years old when he came home to Sainte Genevieve, Missouri, and began to work in his father's grocery store. Some years after his father's death, the Okenfuss store merged with another grocery. Still living in Sainte Genevieve, Don is an assistant manager at a supermarket there.

FRED OLSON, nineteen when the war ended, came back to his parents' Iowa farm. After working there and in construction, he went to the University of Nebraska, then to Wyoming for an M.A. He taught briefly, then became a counselor working with the disabled. He is the assistant director for field operations in Iowa's Vocational Rehabilitation Agency. "I wouldn't have any other job," he says. "When I help someone who is disabled, I can see what I've done." He and his wife, Jackie, live in Des Moines.

ALFRED OYLER retired after thirty-five years as an executive with Sun Oil in accounting and administrative management. He and his wife, Billie, live in Tulsa, Oklahoma.

CALVIN PAHEL has been in the taxi and restaurant business and has worked as a heavy-equipment mechanic. He and his wife, Ardith, live in Gibraltar, Michigan.

RAYMOND PALUSZAK is deceased. His wife, Lottie, lives in Burnham, Illinois.

LEO PAQUETTE and his wife, Mary, live in Lancaster, Massachusetts.

COMER PARKER returned to Dade City, Florida, and worked in road construction. He has a few cows and a small garden. He and Lucille, married before the war, have two children.

JACK V. PARKER worked for an electrical firm in Appleton, Wisconsin. He has retired to Florida.

BILL PARSONS AND POLLY live in Dover, Massachusetts. His family may have more educational credentials than any other in the company: Bill's Ph.D. in chemistry is one of four degrees beyond his bachelor's. Polly and their two sons added six more to the total. Bill has had a full career teaching, most recently at the Massachusetts College of Pharmacy and Tufts School of Medicine.

JIM PATTERSON, an auto-body repairman before the service, returned to Texas and worked at the Red River Army Depot in Texarkana. Patterson hunts deer every year.

ROBERT PATTERSON and his wife, Catherine, live in Sharon Hill, Pennsylvania.

RAYFORD PETERS is retired and lives in Bristol, Tennessee.

JESSE PETRELLA returned to the Chicago area, where he and Josephine live. He works as a pipefitter.

DON PHELPS completed college at Cornell and joined the family florist firm in Rochester, New York. A widower, he is retired.

GEORGE POPE commanded a rifle company in Korea and had several service tours, both as officer and as noncom. A Regular Army man, he retired as a master sergeant, then went back to work in a silverware company in Connecticut. The 1983 reunion was his last. He died of cancer less than three months later. He is buried in Arlington National Cemetery.

FRANK PRICE, married before the war, went home to New Jersey and his wife, Betty, and saw his thirteen-month-old daughter for the first time. He is employed by Gulf Oil; his jobs have ranged from truck driver to controller of oil products.

JOHN RADOVICH worked as welder's helper, then maintenance man at a dehydrator plant. On their ranch near Fresno he and his wife, Angel, raise Thompson seedless grapes for raisins.

EDWARD REBBERT and his wife, Frances, live in Jersey City, New Jersey.

FLOYD REED, back in Franklin, Tennessee, worked as a grocery clerk, then as a refrigeration service man. He and Margaret still live in Franklin.

GEORGE REVOIR returned to Elkhart, Indiana, to his wife and children and went back to work driving a truck.

DALE ROBINSON and his wife, Arlene, live in Mayville, Michigan, where they have their own miniature golf course. Before their retirement the Robinsons kept dairy cattle.

WALTER ROMAN came back to New York. He was the proprietor of a tavern in Yonkers until his death a number of years ago.

JIM ROONEY farmed and drilled water wells back home in Arkansas. Now retired, he and Lola live in Guy, Arkansas.

JOSEPH ROYLE, now retired, lives in Gardena, California.

JOHN SABIA, discharged in 1945, came back to Pennsylvania, "stayed in Philly a couple of years and made Popsicles, then went upstate, bummed around about a year." Back in Philadelphia, he worked for a number of years as a brake operator at the Budd plant and later at GE's Trenton plant. Then he worked as a plumber and went on to U.S. Steel as a pipefitter. He retired in 1984. He and Anne live in Levittown, Pennsylvania. One of John's sons is also named John. "Not John junior," says Sabia. "He's named after Johnny Moore."

ROBERT SCHIEDEL came home to Silver Spring, Maryland, completed college, and worked for the Bureau of the Census in this country and overseas. Since retiring from the government he has spent time as a survey consultant in Egypt and other Mideast countries.

REX SCOTT spent ten months recuperating from his wounds. While in the hospital at Springfield, Missouri, he made up his mind that he wanted to be an architect. Finishing his education at Iowa State, he then worked for a time in Chicago, where he met his wife, Jean. For many years they have lived in the Denver area, where he has a thriving architectural practice.

CLAYTON SHEPHERD returned to Alexandria, Virginia. For more than thirty years he has been a welder with Joyce Iron Works.

RAYMOND C. SICKLER went back to White Bear Lake, Minnesota. For many years he worked as an electrician, but is now retired.

JAMES SLANGSTROM has been in the hardware business since leaving the Army. He lives in Colusa, California.

MILTON SLIMMER lives in Baltimore and works for a printing company.

GILBERT SMART of Oklahoma City, one of our indestructible sergeants, is now retired. For many years he was in charge of refueling operations at the Oklahoma City airport.

BRITT SMITH worked with a dairy in California. Now retired, he and Lula Jean are back home in Siloam Springs, Arkansas.

DURRELL SMITH is a self-employed contractor. A widower, he lives in Perkins, Oklahoma.

GARLAND SNOW and his wife, Geraldine, live in Wichita, Kansas. A technician at Boeing Aircraft, Snow recently went to Denmark as a member of a Boeing specialty team.

JOSEPH J. SOBCZYNSKI, from Chicago, came up as a replacement in late November. He was killed in action January 15.

MAX SOBEL completed a Ph.D. at Columbia and is professor of mathematics at Montclair State College in New Jersey. He is a past president of the National Council of Teachers of Mathematics. At last count he had written more than fifty math books. He and his wife, Manya, live in Fairlawn, New Jersey.

RICHARD STAGG, from DeWitt, Arkansas, was killed in action January 14. He was survived by his wife, Evelyn.

DONALD STAUFFER worked briefly for DuPont, completed college at Ohio State, and did graduate work at Princeton. He then worked for the Hercules Corporation in this country and abroad until his retirement. He and Muriel live near Wilmington, where he operates his own international consulting firm.

JIM STERNER came home to Wilmington and his wife, Sis, completed college at Rensselaer, and began working for DuPont. The Sterners have five daughters, and live at their retirement home in Chesapeake City, Maryland.

ED STEWART, born in Brazil, has lived all over the globe. After undergraduate work at Maryland, he earned a Ph.D. in psychology at Texas. His most recent teaching positions have been in Japan and Europe. He and his wife, Audrey, have four children.

CHARLES SULLIVAN lost an eye and received severe abdominal wounds on November 29. After his nine months in the hospital he was classed as 100 percent disabled and discharged. Several years before his retirement in 1982, Charlie, postmaster at Horse Cave, Kentucky, was chosen postmaster of the year.

LESLIE SVIHEL has retired from his hardware business. He and his wife, Lavina, live in New Prague, Minnesota.

JAMES SWATS, Swoope, Virginia, operated a gas station for twenty years prior to his death in 1976.

WILLIAM SWOREN and his wife, Ann, live in Washington, New Jersey.

RAYMOND TABOR and his wife, Mae, live in Rochester, New York.

OLIVER M. TANDY, from Anderson, Missouri, came up as a replacement on November 25. Killed December 6 during the shelling of Lindern, he was survived by his wife, Mary Margaret.

JAMES A. TEAGUE, from Bridgeport, Texas, was another late November replacement. Wounded on February 25, he was not hospitalized. Three days later he was killed in action. He was survived by his wife, Hattie.

WILLIAM T. TERMIN, from Moundsville, West Virginia, was killed in action January 15. He was survived by his wife, Ann.

GEORGE THOMPSON went back to Oak Grove, Virginia, and worked as a machinist and as a gauge inspector at the Dahlgren Naval Weapons Center. Weeks before his death in 1980 he marveled at his survival, said all the years since the war were "actually a bonus given us to live."

EMMETT (MUTT) TOMLINSON, from Twin Falls, Idaho, began with Company K when the division was activated in 1942. Killed in action February 28, he was survived by his wife, Jeanette, who later married Keith Lance.

LEO TOPEL came home to his wife and two children and went back to work for Firestone. He has been employed by the Air Force as a sheet-metal worker and supervisor. He and Althea live in Doylestown, Pennsylvania.

RAYMOND TRICE went back to his wife, young son, and his job on the police force in Vallejo, California. Later he was a farm foreman for a large land company. In the mid-fifties he began working with the California Packing Corporation and was a quality-control inspector when he retired. He and Verna live in Lucerne, California.

LEONARD VAN HOUTEN, who worked as head teller in a Michigan bank, died in 1983. He lived in Holland, Michigan.

JOSE VILLAGRAN, from Brawley, California, was killed in a truck accident after the war.

PETE VISCONTE, from Redding, California, was killed in action November 22. He was a sergeant at the time of his death.

BILLY WADDLE returned early to the States and became a tank commander. He was with an amphibious command by VJ Day. Later he farmed in Texas and worked in the postal service. Now retired, he and his wife, Billie Jean, live in Campbell, Texas.

WALTER WARNER, JR., from Albany, New York, was killed in action December 18.

ADRIAN AND LIB WHEELER live in Shirley, Indiana. Their son, Tommy, an optometrist, their daughter, Susan, and the grandchildren reside nearby. When Adrian retired, the Delco Remy plant where he worked gave him a special model of the light-dimming switch he'd assembled there. Much of his time goes into church work. He no longer teaches the adult class, but as chairman of the building committee, he coordinated the church's major renovations.

EARL WHITE is deceased. His wife, Marie, lives in Brinkley, Arkansas.

EARL K. WHITE is deceased. His wife, Chloe, lives in Arcadia, Louisiana.

LYLE A. WILLIAMS, from Dubuque, Iowa, was killed in action November 21.

MAURICE WOLFSON, for many years a traffic manager with a New Jersey firm, retired in 1982. He and his wife, Mildred, live in Iselin, New Jersey.

BRUNO YTUARTE, JR., came to K Company from Somerset, Texas. He was killed in action November 22.

MICHAEL YURCHAK is still in Nesquehoning, Pennsylvania. He worked in an iron foundry as a chipper, then as an inspector, and is retired.

RICHARD ZILLIOX worked in a steel mill and as a policeman in Grand Island, New York.

PAUL ZUPEN, from Grove City, Pennsylvania, came in as a replacement in November 1944. Killed in action December 6, he was survived by his wife, Hattie.

EDWARD R. ZURGA, from Coy, Alabama, went overseas with the company. He was killed in action February 28.

The following men were also with the company in Europe. Despite the best efforts of Keller and others, we have been unable to track down definitive information about them.

Hugh Aiken, Daniel Alexander, Jesse Anderson, Harold Ashby, Lee Aunkst (deceased), Carl Bauer, Robert Baxa, Hascal Bond, Donald Botz (deceased), Ernest Bowers, Walter Boyce, George Brantley, Sr., Edwin Breves (deceased), Clarence Brown, Donald Browne, C. W. Browning, Clifton Bruce (deceased), Harry Burch, Michael Burkett.

Jess Canchola, Joseph P. Carter, Jr., John Chlunsky, Arthur Clark, Charles Cohill, Jr., Gustine Constantino, Colon Cowart, Robert Coy (deceased), Crandler Crowson (deceased), Robert Dahlstrom, Louis Dill, John DiMaio (deceased), Francis V. Duncan, James Duncan, Abraham Epstein, Jack Esko, Charles Evans, Richard Fantin, Oliver Funk.

Santos Gaspar, Gifford Geronzin (deceased), William Gibbons, Charles A. Gibson (deceased), Jesse Gil, Sr., Alfred Gilbert, Jr. (deceased), John Gonzales, David Gordon, Newton Gorham, Richard Grabow, Alfred Granberg, Ernest Granger, Leroy Grant (deceased), David Guss, James Haley, Franklin Hazen, Lawrence Heffernan, Doyl Hill, Orville Hill (deceased), Arthur Hoffman (deceased), Morris Hoffman, Thomas Horton, John Howard, Wesley Howell, Claude Howerton, George Houghton (deceased).

George Icke, Howard James, Raymond S. Jarvis, Jr. (deceased), Hazel Johnson, Burrell Jones, Graham Jones, Claxton Jordan, Joseph Keenan, Frank Kelley, William Kiley, Edmond Konopcznski, Robert Krieger (deceased), Grady Lawson, Charley Leach, Pablo Luera (deceased), Daniel Lewis, Opel Littlefield (deceased), Glen Luckey, Sr., Jesus Lumbreras.

Floyd McCullough, Jr. (deceased), Hugh McDowell, Andrew McHenry, Paul McKerahan, Lawrence Maher, William Marple, Arthur Masker, Foster Mayes, George Metz (deceased), Tedd Meyer, Felix Miller, Augustine Moran, Jr. (deceased), Walter Morkal (deceased), William Morris, David Muniz (deceased), Hector Musgrave (deceased), Douglas Naehring, Willie Neisz (deceased), Max Ochroch (deceased), Leroy Oldham.

William Pallasch (deceased), Edward Pate, Clement Patten, John Patterson, Walter Patterson, Denzil Paugh, Charles Pfrang (deceased), Francis Phair, Arthur Phelan (deceased), John Pilgrim, Dennis Poling, Francis Power, Harris Pruss (deceased), John Puddington (deceased), Robert Rachlin, Jimmie Ray, Cornelius Reese, Richard Regar, William Reynolds, Simon Riesinger, John Rosinski, Gilbert Ross, Nick Ruiz.

William Sanders, Nicholas Scalzi, Edward Shaw, Eugene Shepard, James Shofner (deceased), Berlin Shortt, Stephen Siegel, Julion Skinner, John O. Smith (deceased), Alvin Solley, Merle Spaulding, Anthony Stelitano, James Suggs, Robert Summy (deceased), William C. Sullivan, Richard Sutton, Alfred Swanson, Ernest Swanson (deceased), William Swanston.

Wilfred Taylor, Willard Taylor, Elias (Pop) Teebagy (deceased), James Teets, Tommy Thompson, Richard Tice, Grady Tippit, Alexander Valdez, Peter Van Alstyne, Olen Varden, Charles Veneralle, Phillip Vertucci (deceased), Allen Ward, Charles Westbrook, David Whitley, Richard Whitson, Carlton Wilson, Shelton Wilson, William Winters, Donald Withers, Richard Woodworth.

John Yankovitch, James Yannett (deceased), David Ybarra, Joseph York (deceased), Joseph Young, Anton Zadnik (deceased), Leo Zelenke, Paul H. Zerbel (deceased), Richard Zermeno, Arthur Zimmerman, George Zimmerman (deceased).

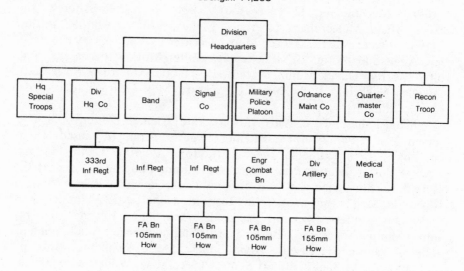

84th INFANTRY DIVISION
Strength: 14,253

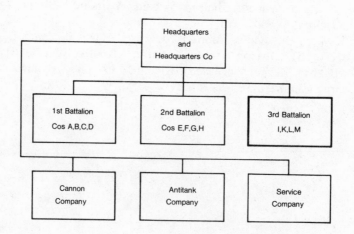

333rd INFANTRY REGIMENT
Strength: 3,257

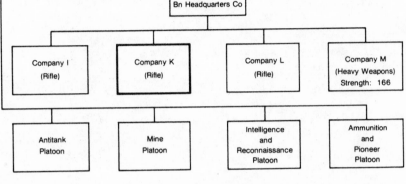

3rd BATTALION
Strength: 836

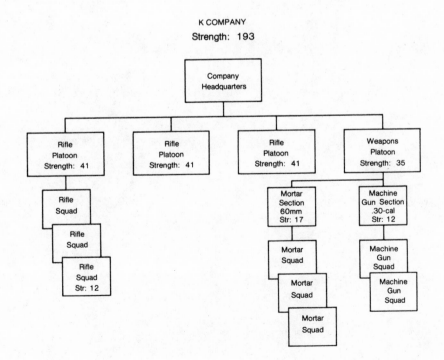

K COMPANY
Strength: 193

INDEX